THE GREEK MUSEUMS

PUBLISHERS
George A. Christopoulos
John C. Bastias

Translation:
Kay Cicellis, Harry Hionides,
Helen Zigada, Robert Lidell,
Brian de Jongh

Art Director: Chrysé Daskalopoulou

Special Photography: Spyros Tsavdaroglou
Makis Skiadaresis

Colour separation: Pietro Carlotti

THE GREEK MUSEUMS

MANOLIS ANDRONICOS
AND
MANOLIS CHATZIDAKIS
VASSOS KARAGEORGHIS

EKDOTIKE ATHENON S.A.
Athens

CARATZAS BROTHERS, Publishers
New Rochelle, New York

CONTENTS

Manolis Andronicos
INTRODUCTION
pp. 9-16

Manolis Andronicos
NATIONAL ARCHAEOLOGICAL MUSEUM
Text pp. 19-42
Illustrations (Nos. 1-120) pp. 43-106

Manolis Andronicos
PELLA MUSEUM
Text pp. 253-256
Illustrations (Nos. 1-8) pp. 257-264

Manolis Andronicos
ACROPOLIS MUSEUM
Text pp. 109-116
Illustrations (Nos. 1-40) pp. 117-148

Manolis Andronicos
THESSALONIKE MUSEUM
Text pp. 267-274
Illustrations (Nos. 1-32) pp. 275-290

Manolis Andronicos
DELPHI MUSEUM
Text pp. 151-158
Illustrations (Nos. 1-32) pp. 159-182

Vassos Karageorghis
CYPRUS MUSEUM
Text pp. 293-300
Illustrations (Nos. 1-42) pp. 301-324

Manolis Andronicos
OLYMPIA MUSEUM
Text pp. 185-192
Illustrations (Nos. 1-36) pp. 193-216

Manolis Chatzidakis
BYZANTINE MUSEUM
Text pp. 327-338
Illustrations (Nos. 1-39) pp. 339-362

Manolis Andronicos
HERAKLEION MUSEUM
Text pp. 219-226
Illustrations (Nos. 1-41) pp. 227-250

Manolis Chatzidakis
BENAKI MUSEUM
Text pp. 365-372
Illustrations (Nos. 1-51) pp. 373-404

PUBLISHER'S PREFACE

Greek art is distinguished by its long history. From its early beginnings in the Stone Age to the present day, the area and its inhabitants referred to as the "Greek world", created works of art which, in their magnitude, are a living testimony of man's highest aspirations and cultural achievements. Many of these works today grace with their presence the museums of Europe and America. These masterpieces, however, can be viewed nowhere with such comprehensiveness and visual immediacy as in the Greek museums where they gloriously reveal, to the art-lover as well as the serious historian, the entire evolution of Greek art.

It was during the first 150 years of Greece's history as a modern state, that most of these art-treasures were brought to light for the first time, mainly due to the dedication and unsparing efforts and energy of Greek and foreign archaeologists, as well as the active co-operation of the archaeological services and other agencies. These works of art, having been thoroughly studied, were then made available to the nation's leading museums where they now stand as imperishable examples of the Greek creative genius and the continuity of Greek culture.

These art-treasures cover a span of time that stretches from the early, highly expressive figurines of the Neolithic Age, and the frescoes of Thera, Knossos and Mycenae, to the exquisite embroideries of modern Greek folk art; and from the unsurpassed sculpture of the archaic and classical periods, to the intricate perfection of Byzantine iconography. As such, these masterworks offer us a magnificently variegated art collection, unique for its matchless quality and unsurpassed excellence.

We believe it is essential for the contemporary art-lover, as well as the dedicated scholar, to become familiar with the masterpieces of Greek art. Such a familiarity would provide not only the first necessary step towards a reawakening of aesthetic appreciation, but also towards a deeper understanding of whatever is of true and lasting significance in art.

It is this need that the "Ekdotike Athenon", with its new publishing venture, wishes to fulfill. It is a work that offers to discriminating readers and art-lovers the rare opportunity of making a first-hand acquaintance with the most prestigious of Greek museums —these veritable treasure- houses of Greece's artistic genius and rich cultural tradition.

In selecting what they considered to be the ten major art museums in the country, collectively representing every aspect, region and period of Greek art, the contributors to this volume have singled out from each museum those works specially marked for their artistic distinction and excellence. The works themselves are presented in colour reproductions of the highest quality, accompanied by full textual commentaries. Furthermore, in the scholarly and illuminating introductions, the authors have sought to provide the reader with an invaluable guide to the distinctive character of each individual collection, and to the historical and cultural environment that gave birth to these enduring works of art. As a result, the reader is enabled to understand and appreciate the magnitude of the Greek cultural heritage and the high place that it occupies in the history of civilization.

GEORGE A. CHRISTOPOULOS

INTRODUCTION

The Museums of Greece

Throughout the centuries the Greek earth has been the faithful repository of the relics of its ancient civilization. In every part of Greece today, the traveller may find some remains of ancient Greek art; a broken piece of marble, a truncated hand of stone, a slab engraved with a few words, a fragmented palmette — such things may still be found in remote Greek villages. It is not uncommon for the farmer's pickaxe to uncover the foundations of a temple or a mutilated statue, or for the fisherman's net to bring forth from the depths of the sea some masterpiece fashioned in bronze. The Greeks of today watch over these unearthed treasures with the greatest of care, not only for their own benefit, but for all those who travel from every country to contemplate the beauty of an art that once filled this small corner of the world with a unique radiance.

General Makriyannis, the illiterate soldier of the Greek War of Independence, the man with the noble spirit and humane heart which are the mark of the truly civilized, relates in his *Memoirs* an incident that illustrates in the most moving way the Greek people's deeply rooted faith in their artistic heritage. In 1831, in the town of Argos, Makriyannis happened to come upon a group of soldiers who were about to sell two ancient statues to some foreigners.

"I happened to be there," he writes, "I was just passing; I took the soldiers aside and spoke to them: even if they give you ten thousand coins for these things, do not deign to let them leave our country. This is what we fought for." This last brief phrase, so epigrammatic, coming from a Greek who could hardly write his own name, convinces us that it was not appreciation of art and history that evinced it, but a firm belief that these objects were sacred relics which had to be safeguarded at all cost.

This same belief helped to build the museums of Greece, most of which are archaeological. It also explains why the first Greek museum was founded immediately after Greece won her freedom, in March 1829, on the island of Aigina, which was the provisional capital of the new state; its founder was Greece's first Governor, John Kapodistrias. As soon as Athens became the capital city, it acquired its own museum, known as the Central Archaeological Museum. A royal decree, dated November 13, 1834, ordained that it should be housed in the "Theseum". In 1835 or thereabouts, the Bavarian architect Leo von Klenze prepared the plans for an impressive museum to be called the Pantechneion; this project, however, was never carried out. Interesting as the subject may be, it would be beyond the scope of this book to trace an outline of the history of Greek museums. Suffice it to say that during the 143 years of its existence, the Greek State has organized a complete archaeological service, and founded a considerable number of museums which shelter innumerable works of art. It would be quite impossible to include all these treasures in one or even several volumes. All we shall attempt here is to give a clear and concise picture of the ten most important museums of Greece, with particular emphasis on the essential artistic contribution of the treasures they contain. The texts in this volume will guide the reader, simply and accurately, to those realms where the works of art will speak to him in their own inimitable voice. The illustrations will be the next, important step: they will make the reader's preliminary acquaintance with each work of art. And so to the third and last step: the "voyage to Cythera", the pilgrimage to the museums themselves, which are situated, for the most part, either within or near the ancient sites, in the heart of Greek nature, the only place where masterpieces such as these can breathe freely.

The museums of Greece are scattered all over the country, from Crete to Thessalonike, from Samos to Corfu. Most of them shelter treasures found in their vicinity, with the exception of the National Archaeological Museum in Athens, which houses precious masterpieces assembled from various regions of Greece, and the Museum of Thessalonike, which contains antiquities from almost every part of Northern Greece. This means that nearly every Greek museum possesses works that range through the successive eras of ancient Greek history. However, each region had its particular character; though it was an integral part of the Greek world, it traced its own course and created its own cultural history. These numerous cultural currents often ran parallel to each other and were equal in importance, but during the long centuries of their existence, they each suffered a separate ebb and flow; some died away just as another began to gather impetus; their trajectories often shifted and at no point did their courses cover the same expanse. Thus each Greek museum presents the visitor with a section from the common artistic fund, while at the same time it brings together works that express either a particular historical period, or some specific aspect of Greek civilization.

It is necessary, therefore, that the visitor to the Greek museums should carry in his mind a rough outline of the history of this civilization, based on the monuments which archaeological research has brought to light throughout the entire Greek territory.

The Stone Age

The presence of Neanderthal man in Greece has been confirmed by the discovery of a skull at Petralona, in the Chalkidike peninsula (dating to between 75,000 and 50,000 years ago) and remnants of tools in Thrace, Epiros, Thessaly, the Ionian islands, the North Sporades and the Peloponnesos. In Boiotia and Thessaly, but above all in Epiros, archaeologists have discovered the oldest and most numerous examples of stone industry to come from the hands of Homo Sapiens, the human species who succeeded Neanderthal man some 40,000 years ago, living in caves and hunting for his sustenance until the 8th - 7th millennium B.C. At that time, the great revolution which took place in the Near East reached Greece: Neolithic man, settling down permanently to live on agriculture and cattle-raising, was no longer content with his elementary weapons and tools made of stone or bone, but began to create ceramic vessels and figurines with human or animal features; in other words, he began to produce works of art. This was when the Neolithic civilization (7000 - 2800 B.C.) spread to the whole of Greece, both the mainland and the islands. The agricultural and cattle-breeding economy on which this civilization was built gave Thessaly a natural advantage over the other regions; the dense and prosperous Thessalian settlements produced skilfully and colourfully ornamented ceramics of a high artistic quality, as shown by the exhibits of the special Neolithic Collection from Thessaly at the National Archaeological Museum in Athens.

The Bronze Age

At the beginning of the 3rd millennium B.C., a great new revolution took place in the East, with vast repercussions which can still be felt in our present age. It started in Mesopotamia and then spread to Egypt: man succeeded in smelting natural metallic ore containing copper; at the same time, the first large city-states were founded and writing was invented. The use of metal spread to the Aegean almost immediately, marking the beginning of the Bronze Age throughout Greece. The new conditions favoured the islands and the coastal areas, so that the civilization of the Neolithic period can be seen to branch off into three parallel, contemporary streams, each creating its own cultural elements, which lent the region where it flourished its distinctive character. In mainland Greece, the civilization known as Early Helladic was simply a continuation of Neolithic civilization. In the Cyclades, the Early Cycladic civilization burst forth with unexpected brilliance and artistic wealth; pottery and stoneware of exceptional quality and ornamental skill, but above all marble statuettes of unique plastic sensitivity, bear witness to the high level of civilization in those islands, which were destined to play an important role in the history of Greek art. The section devoted to this civilization at the National Archaeological Museum in Athens is of no less importance than other galleries which contain valuable treasures. However, the area that was to lead Prehistoric Greece to outstanding cultural achievements was the island of Crete. During the phase known as Early Minoan, and more recently as Pre-Palace period, Neolithic tradition underwent so great a transformation that in older times this was believed to be due to a "sudden miracle" brought about by new tribal elements. Nowadays, however, there can be no doubt that the change was neither sudden nor inexplicable. The new conditions created by the discovery of metal led this large island to a rapid and spectacular development. Towards the end of this period, *circa* 1900 B.C., when the historical and cultural aspect of the entire Aegean changed, the sudden forceful shift was accomplished in Crete as well, but in a manner so particular that Minoan civilization ceased at this point to move along with Helladic civilization and brought forth works and forms of art that were both unprecedented and unrepeated in the entire history of Greek civilization.

The first appearance of the Hellenes

In mainland Greece, the beginning of the 2nd millennium B.C. was marked by the appearance of the bulk of the Greek tribes that were to spread out across the Greek land, settling permanently to forge what was to prove a long, enduring political and cultural history. The most representative works of art produced by these new inhabitants were Minyan ware and matt-painted vases. During this phase, the civilization of mainland Greece, known as Middle Helladic (1900-1600 B.C.) went through a certain decline; the settlements of these early Greeks were scattered all over the southern part of the country, without any centre of importance emerging among them. However, during the last years of this period, a powerful dynasty managed to impose its rule in Mycenae, as shown by the tombs "rich in gold" found in the two grave circles dating from the late 17th to the early 16th century B.C.

Minoan civilization reaches its peak

But whereas on the mainland, the Greeks were laying no more than humble foundations for a civilization that was to bear fruit many centuries later, Crete became the scene of a unique achievement. In the central and eastern parts of the island, the first great palaces were being built; Knossos, Phaistos and Malia were to become the resplendant centres of Minoan civilization. During the period known as Old Palace or Middle Minoan (1950-1700 B.C.), this civilization proceeded with extraordinary speed to acquire the character which was to lend it such incomparable brilliance. In the cultural centres growing around the palaces, ceramic art reached an unprecedented peak, while seal-engraving and metal-work produced truly outstanding works of art.

In 1700 B.C., the old palaces were destroyed and were immediately replaced by new ones; thus began the New Palace period of Minoan civilization, which ended in two successive catastrophes caused by the tremendous eruptions of the volcano on the island of Thera (1500 and 1450 B.C.). Archaeologists have discovered the remains of a civilization that spread over nearly the whole of Crete with incredible splendour and vigour. A large palace was built at Zakros, while smaller palaces and splendid villas rose around the great centres; at the same time the existence of numerous prosperous settlements gives ample proof of the wealth and development of Crete. The remarkable architecture of the palaces, with their multi-coloured frescoes, the abundance and beauty of pottery, the marvellous products of stone-carving, miniature sculpture and metal-work all these testify to the growth of a robust and flowering culture that was clearly the result of an admirably organized society and state. Trade, well-protected by the powerful Minoan fleet, brought considerable wealth to the island. King Minos' sea-power became legendary; it was thanks to the Minoan ships that this civilization spread across the Aegean and sometimes beyond it. Recent excavations in Thera have revealed the power and wealth the Cretan metropolis must have possessed in order to have brought to this Cycladic island such brilliant cultural elements. The unique frescoes discovered on Thera, which now occupy a large room at the National Archaeological Museum in Athens, surpass in imaginative force and expressive power even the finest Minoan works produced by Knossos itself. It is enough to visit the Minoan palaces and then the Museum of Herakleion, where all the Cretan finds are exhibited, in order to form — without any other help — a clear and accurate image of that fascinating civilization.

Mycenaean civilization

The people living in other parts of Greece must also have felt this fascination. The Cretan influence on mainland Greece was profound and extensive. In the larger centres, where the powerful kingdoms of the first Greeks were being established, Cretan art and civilization were grafted on to the sturdy trunk of the world we have come to call Mycenaean — Mycenae being the glorious capital of that world and also the place where the impressive monuments that characterize it were first discovered. Thus the last phase of the Helladic civilization — known as Late Helladic (1600-1100 B.C.) — was marked by the emergence of a robust culture which broke through the narrow limits of the Prehistoric cultural context proper to small agricultural societies and drew its strength from mighty centres ruled by wealthy dynasties. These great centres were bound together by such close ties that one might well speak of a Mycenaean empire, stretching from one side of the Aegean to the other, and further east as well, to the island of Cyprus.

This distant island near the coast of Asia Minor had developed an important culture since Neolithic times, as confirmed by the archaeological finds exhibited in the Museum of Nicosia. The Bronze Age opened up new perspectives; rich deposits of copper were discovered on the island, attracting tradesmen from all over the Eastern Mediterranean. Minoan seamen made an early acquaintance with Cyprus and maintained this contact. During the Mycenaean period, the first Achaians landed on Cyprus, tradesmen to begin with, and colonists following soon afterwards. The permanent settlement of those early Greeks on the island gave Cyprus its definitive political and cultural character, as attested by the numerous archaeological finds which are indisputably products of the Mycenaean civilization. Since those times, Aphrodite's island, as Cyprus was known to the ancient Greeks, has followed a course strictly parallel to all the other Greek centres.

However, the nucleus of the Mycenaean world, the fountainhead of its power was in mainland Greece. In the great centres, such as Mycenae, Tiryns, Pylos, Thebes, etc., sumptuous palaces arose, decorated in the Minoan style, with multi-coloured and many-figured wall-paintings. Yet these palaces retained the austere aspect of the mainland *megaron* type of building and were protected by Cyclopean walls. The people who lived in these palaces were warriors, as shown by the weapons discovered in their tombs; their art, though considerably influenced by Cretan art, retained a structural austerity, an architectural solidity which was unknown in Crete. Ceramics, metal-work, and other minor arts, all produced objects bearing the distinctive features of Mycenaean society, which was totally different from the Minoan. Finally, there was another significant development: in the Mycenaean centres, the early Minoan script known as Linear A was transformed into Linear B, the Mycenaean script which was recorded on clay tablets and recognized as the earliest form of the Greek language, when Michael Ventris deciphered the tablets of the archives of the Palace at Pylos.

The Mycenaean room at the National Archaeological Museum in Athens is an eloquent testimony to the wealth, power and austerity of the Mycenaean world; its noble achievements were to provide the inspiration for the great Homeric poems.

The end of Mycenae and the emergence of Geometric art

Before the end of the 2nd millennium B.C., the Mycenaean kingdoms were destroyed and Mycenaean civilization came to an end. The invasion of the Dorians, who were once believed responsible for this catastrophe, cannot have been the real cause of the destruction and desertion of all those powerful centres, nor can it serve as a satisfactory explanation for the profound and widespread political and cultural changes that marked the early years of the last millennium B.C. How important these changes were can be clearly seen in the art produced during the first centuries of that millennium, especially in the field of ceramics. From about 1050 to 700 B.C., a new artistic concept became dominant, both in the modelling and the decoration of ceramic ware: the geometric concept. As opposed to the forms used in Mycenaean art, which were derived basically from the natural world, Geometric art produced forms with a strictly architectural structure and geometrical designs that obeyed rules of their own, thus fashioning a world disciplined to human reason. This new artistic style found its perfect expression in the Attic Geometric vases exhibited in the National Archaeological Museum in Athens.

Eastern influences

However, the Greek spirit, always respectful of tradition, yet never allowing tradition to restrict its freedom to seek out new modes of expression, now came into contact with the East. Around 800 B.C., the Greeks borrowed the new Eastern alphabet; they modified it ingeniously by introducing vowels, and thus handed over to the civilized world the first truly modern alphabet, in use to this very day in all Latin-derived and Slav languages.

A few decades later, in the 7th century B.C., Greek art put to fruitful use some of the main features of Eastern art and thus created a new style, known as Orientalizing. Rich, sensuous and flexible forms succeeded the severity of Geometric art; the plant and animal world erupted once again, full of vigour, into the repertory of artistic themes, but without quite shedding the discipline of the formal rules which had their roots in the preceding centuries.

Within the same century — the 7th B.C. — the Greeks modelled their first full-size statues and built their first great peripteral temples; for the first time they produced works of a monumental character. The basic forms of architecture and the main themes of the plastic arts were all to take shape within this extraordinarily fruitful century. In the field of pottery, Greek myths became the most widely used subject-matter, providing inexhaustible inspiration for artists of subsequent generations.

The Archaic period

The economic growth of a multitude of Greek city-states, the foundation of colonies in both East and West, North and South, the commercial activity of Greek seamen, were bound to spread Greek civilization to all the coastal areas of the Mediterranean and beyond — in fact, as far as the Northern coast of the Euxine. And so it was within the 6th century B.C., when the art style known as Archaic took shape, that the "Greek miracle" began to unfold. The cities of Ionia, the larger islands of the Eastern Aegean, the Cyclades, the Peloponnesos, Magna Graecia, and, above all, Athens, entered upon their first great artistic flowering. Temples began to punctuate every Greek landscape with their tall white columns: Ionic and colossal on the Asia Minor coast and the islands, Doric in mainland Greece and Magna Graecia. In the great pan-Hellenic sanctuaries, Doric and Ionic temples and treasuries were adorned with fine architectural sculpture, with pediments, friezes and metopes, upon which the chisels of craftsmen from all over Greece recounted the sacred and heroic myths of the Hellenes. In the museums erected next to sanctuaries such as the Athenian Acropolis, Delphi and Olympia, one can still see some of these sculptures, and next to them the votive offerings of the faithful: vases, figurines, bronze vessels and weapons; but most arresting of all, exquisite marble statues of towering youthfulness: the naked, vigorous bodies of the Kouroi, the slender, elegant bodies of the Korai in their stylish finery.

Classical art The Persian Wars (490-479 B.C.) marked the end of the Archaic period, without being the cause of it, for it was a gradual process and the result of important social and political upheavals. In Athens, where the change was more manifest in every domain, the new trends were embodied, politically, in the establishment of democracy, and artistically, in the birth of tragedy — the two major conquests which Greek civilization has bequeathed to the Western world. Art went through a phase of combined austerity and freedom, known as the "severe style" (480-450 B.C.). Nowhere has this style been expressed with such breath-taking majesty and vigorous plasticity as in the sculptures of the temple of Zeus at Olympia; from the museum on the sacred site, the visitor is transported with extraordinary immediacy to those deeply religious spheres sung by Aischylos and Pindar. But there remained one more difficult step which Greek art had to take before reaching that summit admired by the centuries to follow and known to us as Classical art, a term which became identified with the notion of perfection. The generation of 450-425 B.C., which found its political expression in the Athenian alliance of nearly all the Greek city-states under the leadership of Perikles, was to create in Athens works of art in such quantity and of such high quality as to enable the statesman who inspired them to proclaim proudly: "In a word then, I say that our city as a whole is the school of Hellas."

The masterpieces on the Athenian Acropolis alone are enough to make the spectator visualize the sheer spiritual quality, the artistic perfection of the Classical achievement. But though the admiration of many successive centuries may have glorified these works of art to excess, it has not been able to exhaust their inherent value or even to fully capture their inner dynamism. Indeed, our own age, strongly anti-classic as it is, cannot accept the fundamental message these works convey: the secret of balancing conflicting forces. The apparent serenity of Classical figures is not due to a lack of passion or internal strife; on the contrary, it is the happy conjuction, obtained after considerable perseverance and effort, of the strongest possible antitheses, the fusion of old, well-tried elements by new revolutionary methods, the creation of artistic forms fresh and glowing in their virginity, yet rich and mature with age - old experience. On the Acropolis, for instance, the architectural conceptions and the plastic compositions that adorn the edifices both represent unexpected and totally original artistic inventions. Never before and never in the centuries that followed did Greece produce such perfect structures. The Parthenon and the Propylaia are unique architectural creations of their kind, while the Erechtheion succeeds, with apparent simplicity, in providing a solution to a series of complex and almost insoluble problems set by the demands of a number of cults and the irregularity of the ground-level. As for the sculptures and carvings, it is enough to recall that the Parthenon frieze was the first to be placed on a Doric temple, and that its theme was not mythological, as was the custom at that time, but an innovation of the greatest audacity, to be encountered again only in the smaller frieze of the temple of Athena Nike. The sureness of touch, the incomparable mastery of this art cannot be fully enjoyed on the west side of the Parthenon frieze, because it is set very high; the finest section of all, possibly executed for the most part by Pheidias' own hand, can be better admired by the reader of this book than by the visitor to the temple itself. However, in the Acropolis Museum, one can see some of the most remarkable slabs of the frieze, that is, those which Lord Elgin failed to carry away. On the opposite wall of the museum the sculptures of the parapet from the temple of Athena Nike reflect the new trends that broke upon the scene towards the end of the 5th century B.C. and that were to lead Greek art in new directions.

One can see several fine examples of all the previous phases of Greek art in many Greek museums as well as the National Archaeological Museum in Athens. But from the Classical age onward there exists no other museum in the world with such a large number of representative works of art (especially the plastic arts) in an unbroken sequence from the 5th century B.C. to the end of the ancient Greek world in the early centuries of the Christian era. Here one can discern the new tendencies of the 4th century B.C., embodied in the elegant Aurai on horseback and the Nereids of the Epidauros sculptures; one may then admire the delicate, gracious figures of Praxiteles and the powerful, passionate figures of Skopas; one may feel the impact of the most important innovation of those times, the human portrait, which reproduced the distinctive features of the individual, who was henceforward to stand out decisively in Greek society and prove the most active factor, perhaps, in the dissolution of that society. And a great deal more — all those artistic elements, those incessant changes leading almost imperceptibly, yet inevitably, towards the breaking-up, and then the reforming of spiritual and artistic attitudes in the Hellenistic age — all this can be followed step by step on the series of funerary stelai (gravestones) dating from the years of the Parthenon to the end of the 4th century B.C., when the Macedonians appointed Demetrios Phalereus governor of Athens.

The Hellenistic period

At that time, the Greeks ceased to live and work and create exclusively in the ancient Helladic centres, abandoning a suffocating self-sufficiency. The Macedonians, after the amazing, meteor-like passage of Alexander the Great, the legendary commander who had led them to the vast expanses of Asia and Africa, began to lay the foundations of their large, wealthy, crowded kingdoms, introducing policies far more universal in outlook. This new world naturally created new centres; and art gave shape to the new visions it engendered. The Hellenistic creative spirit did not remain locked in a barren academicism, nor did it restrict itself to a tame, stifling aestheticism. By giving expression to the new forces of the last three pre-Christian centuries, it boldly shattered Classical canons and introduced innovations that were both revolutionary and fruitful, bequeathing to the modern world new themes in the plastic arts and new ways of expressing them which often seem more akin to us than the Classical ones. What we have named Hellenistic "baroque" is precisely the formalization of this new world. The Altar of Pergamon is a good example, both as an architectural and a plastic conception. In contrast to the Giants, modelled to human shape and proportion, of the earlier Greek Gigantomachies, the explosive, monster-shaped Giants of the Pergamon sculptures attempt to reconstruct the ancient myth in terms of a new demonology enriched by the pantheon of the Eastern religions. If the images of the ancient gods were drained of their vitality and became mere aesthetic elements in the service of an elaborate, highly decorative art, the images of human beings, in contrast, appear in a wealth of new forms, endowed with an unprecedented expressiveness, thus creating a new branch of the plastic arts: portraiture which has survived down to our own age.

If we turn to painting, we find there was more to it than just the conquests of perspective, or the fact that technical knowledge reached levels until then unknown to art; it was a whole new attitude, which found its visual expression in the representation of landscapes and still lives, introducing themes that were to affect European artists many centuries later, while portrait-painting was to offer Christian iconography great prototypes for the exquisite art of hagiography, particularly with respect to portable icons.

The National Archaeological Museum in Athens includes remarkable examples of Hellenistic art; it is an art that has much amplitude, loves realism, seeks the hidden world of the spirit behind external forms, dares to express unbridled passion, even ugliness. But other museums — e.g. of Thessalonike — also offer a representative image of Hellenistic art, and beyond that, of Greek art under the Romans, at which time entirely new elements and styles emerge, geared to a different society that grew out of a different constitution and hierarchy and was imbued with new religious ideas, new intellectual and spiritual orientations. Out of these forms the new universal religion, Christianity, was gradually to find expression. In the portraits of late antiquity exhibited at the National Archaeological Museum in Athens and the Museum of Thessalonike, the unworldly, introspective expression of the faces seems to have little relation with the human body, which has become almost non-existent; it is merely the necessary physical support of the spirit, which is now turning inwards in its struggle to know itself, obliterating the outer world. An attitude such as this negates the basic principles of Greek art, with its love of the human body and the visible world; because in these the Greeks perceived not only man and his world but, above all, his gods, "who had power, and reason, and beauty".

It was this godly beauty of man and his world that Greek art bequeathed to the subsequent generations, "their possession for evermore". The first to feel the attraction of Greek art were the Romans; the conquerors who had subjected the world by their military and political power, had to acknowledge their subjection to the Hellenic spirit; a subjection of which they were justly proud. But they were not alone in this respect; the entire Christian world drew inspiration and life from the old, pagan sources, adapting ancient forms to its own faith and needs.

Byzantine art

However, these needs had to find means of expression of their own, capable of accommodating the messages of the new, universal religion of love. When the Eastern Roman Empire came into being, its capital — New Rome — was only connected with the old capital by name; in reality, it was a Greek city of immense antiquity: Byzantium; and around Byzantium spread the Hellenic world and all the Hellenized people of the East. It was only natural that the Empire should be transformed, with amazing rapidity, into a Greek Christian state which came to be known as Byzantine. In the art of the new Empire, Hellenistic traditions merged with Christian needs; the result was an autonomous Byzantine art which was to produce magnificent creations. Sculpture had no place in this art; by contrast, painting gained a unique position, serving the Christian religion as adequately as sculpture had served the ancient Greek gods.

The exclusively religious character of Byzantine painting is the main feature distinguishing it from the art of latest antiquity which had been flooded by arrogant emperors and insolently wealthy men with portraits of themselves and with earthly, sensuous images of a world hastening to its end. The life of Jesus Christ and the Old Testament prophets, surrounded by the spiritualized figures of the saints, provided a new, inexhaustible source of subject-matter, which was to nourish and sustain the artists and craftsmen of the Byzantine world and later those of enslaved Hellenism. Within this framework, the pious painters were able to express, always anew, their religious faith, but also the innermost yearnings and hopes of mankind. From the tender message of hope contained in the Saviour's Nativity to the unbearable poignancy of the Crucifixion, and beyond that, the triumph of the Resurrection, there were innumerable scenes from the earthly life of Jesus that offered artists the opportunity to seek and communicate the most profoundly human messages. Although Byzantine art was always fettered by austere and strictly determined dogmaticism, it found a way of overcoming its own restrictions and producing works of the highest quality, equal in importance to the finest creations of ancient Greek art. The miraculous architectural achievement of Hagia Sophia, for instance, can only be paralleled with that of the Parthenon. The most important examples of Byzantine painting are to be found, in various parts of Greece, within the surviving monuments of which they were part. A large number of Byzantine icons, however, have been collected in the Byzantine and the Benaki Museums in Athens, together with all kinds of works of the minor arts and portable objects produced by Byzantine artists over a span of a thousand years.

The survival of Greek civilization

During the Middle Ages, it almost looked as if the ancient Greek world had been extinguished from human memory forever. Yet, some centuries later, when the Europeans began to seek new forces to lead them where they might freely conquer beauty and truth, they came upon the Classical prototypes of art and literature, and it was upon those foundations that they built the intellectual and artistic world of modern Europe. Greek statues and their Roman copies, Greek vases and *objets d'art* began to appear in stately palaces and collections, forming the nuclei of the great European museums. At the same time, the architectural styles of Greek temples were imitated to such an extent and with such passion as to bring on a feeling of satiety. Once again, after many centuries, Greek myths illustrated books, decorated buildings, and enriched modern European literature. The figures of Athena and Hermes, Herakles and Oedipus, have grown as familiar to us as they were to the Greeks of Classical times. A visit to the Greek museums has thus come to mean for all of us today a direct and long-desired meeting with the archetypes of our civilization, an intimate conversation with the great minds that bred us, a touch from the land of our spiritual birth, in which our roots plunge deep, still drawing vital sustenance.

> "Because we have known this fate of ours so well
> wandering among broken stones
> for the last three or six thousand years."

NATIONAL ARCHAEOLOGICAL MUSEUM

NATIONAL ARCHAEOLOGICAL MUSEUM

History of the Museum

The National Archaeological Museum celebrates its first centenary in the course of this year (1974). As a result of a generous donation made by Demetrios Bernardakis the construction of the building was begun in 1866 on a plot of land presented by Helen Tositsa. The plans were drawn up by the architect Ludwig Lange. In 1874 the Greek state provided financial aid for the completion of the west wing to which the exhibits, until then housed in the Theseum, the Varvakeion and the Stoa of Hadrian, were removed. All the various collections belonged officially to the Central Archaeological Museum, which was founded by a royal decree of 13th November 1834 and whose headquarters were situated in the Theseum. The original name was officially preserved until 1888, when, by a royal decree of 19th April, it was changed to the National Archaeological Museum. Construction work continued and was finally completed in 1889. Lange's original design for the main façade, east wing and central hall was modified by the well-known architect, Ernst Ziller. The capital was thus embellished by another fine neo-Classical building and the country acquired its first large imposing museum. Various antiquities scattered about in different buildings in Athens were removed to the museum in 1891. Panayiotis Kavvadias, then general superintendent of Antiquities, placed the sculptures in the new halls and drafted the first catalogue. Christos Tsountas, the eminent Greek archaeologist, assembled the magnificent Mycenaean collection consisting of Schliemann's finds from the acropolis of Mycenae which he had recently excavated, and compiled the valuable index. The need to expand became imperative by 1925, and the construction of a new wing was begun. The new halls were completed in 1939. At the beginning of the Second World War, however, it was found necessary to close the museum, and bury the antiquities under ground in order to protect them from possible damage or destruction.

As soon as the war was over the prolonged and laborious task of uncovering the buried objects began. It was not only a case of cleaning and restoring them. The halls in which they were to be displayed were themselves in need of restoration. The fact that an initial temporary exhibition should have been organised in three halls of the Museum as early as 1946 was a remarkable achievement. More and more halls were opened at an ever-increasing speed, and both scholarly erudition and impeccable good taste were shown in the arrangement of the various collections. Many men and women made invaluable contributions, but it was Christos Karouzos' enlightened personality and indefatigable patience that constituted the driving force in initiating, supervising and accomplishing the laborious task. No marble memorial has yet been raised to his memory in the entrance way to the museum, but his spirit still roams the halls which he restored to life, rejoicing at the sight of the most beautiful sculptures.

The number of sculptures is staggering. Every site in the ancient Greek world, every period of ancient history, is represented. The epithet "National", as applied to the Museum, could not be more apt. It epitomizes the true character of its contents. For this is the only archaeological museum in the world in which so many masterpieces of ancient art have been assembled, in which it is possible for the visitor to follow the history of Greek art in all its manifestations, in an unbroken sequence from its genesis in the Neolithic age to its final swan song in the Roman period. In spite of the enormous quantity of exhibits it is not difficult to distinguish the basically most important collections. Scholarly specialists and lovers of art alike will be able to form a lucid and coherent picture of Greek art and its originality of form. The manner in which the exhibits have been arranged was not fortuitously arrived at; it was actually conceived with a view to facilitating the visitor's progress through the various halls. The first distinction to be made is between the four Prehistoric collections: those of Thessaly, the Cyclades, Thera and Mycenae. These serve as an excellent introduction to the principal works in the museum: the works of art of the historical era, which are represented in the two main branches of sculpture and vase-painting. The various categories of the minor arts, ranging from coins and bronze idols to the products of the goldsmith's craft, are similarly dealt with. But among all these collections, it is one and one only that gives the National Archaeological Museum its special character: namely, the collection of incomparable monumental sculptures. For it was in the art of sculpture that the ancient Greeks excelled themselves more than any other people, either before or after them.

The Neolithic and Helladic civilizations

The first civilization to grow in Greece was the Neolithic; and the most important Neolithic sites have been identified in Thessaly. When Christos Tsountas, a pioneer in Prehistoric archaeology, started to excavate the two settlements of Dimeni and Sesklo near Volos, he opened the first chapter in the history of Greek civilization. The unexpectedly rich finds he brought to light in the course of these excavations were only a forecast of the undreamed of harvest of future archaeological research. At the beginning of the present century, there were no museums in those then remote parts of the country fit to house the important objects discovered in those exploratory excavations of Prehistoric sites. That is why Tsountas had them removed to the National Archaeological Museum, where they still remain, truncated, as it were, from the main body of finds, subsequently discovered, which now enrich the museum at Volos. Visitors to the National Archaeological Museum will consequently obtain their first glimpse of the dawn of Greek civilization in the clay idols and pottery of Neolithic Thessaly. And although idols may be no more than sculptural objects of the most primitive character, their robust composition, which is strikingly expressionistic, and the rough quality of their execution does not mean that they are devoid of any artistic or spiritual content. In their sharp clear-cut forms, their full sometimes outsize volumes and the abundance of their motifs, they not only possess a deep and many-faceted religious symbolism; they also reflect the basic social and economic differentiations which existed in the first permanent agricultural societies of the Neolithic settlements. The *kourotrophos,* the woman holding a child, found at Sesklo, is depicted enthroned; she is relatively richly adorned; and she has obviously climbed higher up the social ladder than those wide-hipped female figures of the earlier Neolithic age which are found in Thessaly and other parts of Greece (fig. 5). The intricate plasticity and architectural quality of a large idol (50 cm. in height) representing a seated male figure (fig. 2) completes the picture, in so far as it illustrates the fact that religious and social requirements reflected in these works derive their source from relatively fairly developed levels of human existence.

Conclusive evidence is found in the Neolithic vases. The clean outlines and flowing curves of the earlier examples (fig. 4) are superceded by the more elaborate forms of the vases of the Middle Neolithic period with their simple though accurately conceived and carefully elaborated decoration. In the Late Neolithic period these are replaced by volumes and decorative work of an unexpected dynamic quality (fig. 3), with complicated designs and colours and an intricacy of composition which raises the question whether aesthetic feeling has mastered the calculated disposition of forms or whether the potter, in his wisdom, has succeeded, within the limits of the geometric motifs at his disposal, to harp back to some rich and ancestral world and thus transcend his purely instinctive sensibility as an artist.

In this hall the visitor may cast a brief glance at the elegant Early Helladic "sauce-boats" with their delicately curved spouts before proceeding to look at the austere Minyan vases with their resemblance to metal vessels and the opaque decoration of the matt-painted vases which archaeologists ascribe to the Middle Helladic period and which are probably the artistic creations of the first Hellenic tribes.

Cycladic civilization

If variety is the hallmark of Greek civilization, the different currents discernible in its earliest stages may be likened to rivulets gushing out of innumerable springs flowing in different directions, converging and diverging, until they finally unite into the larger stream in order to pour into and swell the waters of the main river. While continental Greece continued to follow its own course, renovating the road initially opened by its Neolithic inhabitants, the Cyclades, scattered all over the Central Aegean, rendered prosperous by their trade in a recently discovered metal (namely, copper), entered the scene with a flourish in the 3rd millennium B.C. Once again we must recall the achievement of Christos Tsountas, who was the first archaeologist to uncover and present in the late 19th century the remarkable remains of the Cycladic civilization. The atmosphere of the Cyclades is distinguished by the refractory light that emanates from the marble strata of the soil. This white stone, which is one of the chief glories of Greece, was extensively quarried in the Cycladic archipelago. Crystalline in texture, lacking the hard quality of the stone which craftsmen elsewhere found so difficult to work, marble enabled Cycladic artists to exploit the possibilities of the material at hand with excellent results. Marble vases with daring and elegant forms reveal the artists' skill and the high standard of civilization reached by the people who made use of them. But the sphere in which Cycladic artists excelled themselves was in that of sculptured idols. Innumerable marble idols depict the figure of a nude woman with her hands placed across her stomach. Only the breasts and nose are plastically rendered; other features, such as the mouth and eyes, were most probably painted. The little idols must have been immensely popular, for great quantities have been found, not only in the Cyclades themselves, but in the more remote parts of continental and insular Greece. The significance of the idols in the context of the history of art might have been a limited one had the artists simply confined themselves to rendering this enigmatic female figure (Mother Earth?) in the form of a small-scale object. But the more talented and inspired artists seem, on occasion, to have had the opportunity to create much larger idols, distinguished for their admirable sculptural finish. The large almost life-size idol from Amorgos (fig. 8) is a masterpiece of large sculpture. The sculptor seems to have been particularly daring in rendering the general form and, more important, in providing the plastic levels of the human body with animation. The clarity of the figure and the vibratory quality of the marble surfaces are likely to draw the attention of experts in modern abstract art. Henry Moore, greatest of living sculptors, was intensely moved when he first saw it, lying, as it then was, in a case in the museum. Besides possessing both skill and sensitivity, Cycladic artists had acquired an intelligent conception of volumes. The remarkable idol of a harpist is an outstanding example (fig. 6). Notice the rhythmical intricacy of the modelling and the special function of the curve followed in the movement of the members of the body and of the harp itself. The architectural modelling vies with the delicate finish applied to the marble surface. It also confirms the fact that the simpler but no less charming and intelligent rendering of a flute-player depicted in another idol (fig. 7), was not purely fortuitous, but a happy combination of artistic sensibility, long experience and patient labour. A similar painstaking feeling for decoration is observed in the strange clay utensils shaped like frying-pans (fig. 9) whose function remains an enigma and which were found lying in tombs beside the idols. The clay surface is incised with tangent spirals, star-shaped decorative designs, and even representations of ships, all of which are executed with the accuracy and sensitivity associated with a true feeling for aesthetic expression and the existence of an evolved social structure.

The Thera frescoes

At one time a number of archaeologists believed that the decline of Cycladic civilization had set in by the end of the 3rd millennium B.C. More recent archaeological excavations, however, have brought to light important remains which indicate that the end of the millennium was not characterized so much by decline as by a complete transformation wrought by the expansion of the Minoan maritime empire of the New Palace period (c. 1600 B.C.). Fragments of frescoes and vase-paintings excavated at Phylakopi on the island of Melos do not merely stress the fact that the influence exercised by Minoan civilization undoubtedly prevailed throughout the Eastern Mediterranean; they go much farther, enabling us to envisage a Cretan colonization and domination of the Aegean islands, especially of the most southerly ones. This argument could not have been so effectively supported but for the recent excavations at Kea and, above all, the astonishing discoveries made by Professor Marinatos at Thera. The Thera exhibits, now displayed in the halls of the National Archaeological Museum, consist, among other objects, of frescoes which are among the most striking in the whole of Minoan painting. The circumstances in which Thera was destroyed by a tremendous volcanic eruption account for the fact that large sections of the frescoes have survived in such a good state of preservation. A systematic method of excavation has also contributed greatly to their undamaged condition and to the possibility of their admirable restoration.

The first frescoes to be uncovered and restored revealed an art, at once so lavish and so full of charm, that they clearly seemed to be the works of the most skilled and inspired painters of Minoan Crete. They also supplied evidence of the existence on the island of a city, whose economic, social and cultural evolution bore comparison with those of the most important centres of Minoan civilization. Among the most remarkable features of the fresco of the Spring (fig. 15) are the harmonious deep-toned colours of the rocks, and the delicacy of the slender leaf-stalks of lilies which terminate in innumerable purple-petalled flowers, like little tongues of flame of the utmost elegance and fragility of form. Swallows flutter among the flowers in a state of celestial intoxication: sometimes in couples, their bills half-open, as they pursue their erotic games in the perfumed air. It is like a paean to nature, a hymn of joy and hope. A fresco of this kind could only have been conceived in a society which, knowing the meaning of true felicity, dwelt, under an azure sky, on the wave-lashed island of Santorine, "queen of the earth's vibrations and of the flutter of Aegean wings", as the poet O. Elytis says.

The lyrical quality of this fresco borders on the unique. But for sheer sensibility, gaiety and lightness of touch, reflecting a love and knowledge of everyday life, the fresco of the Boxing Children is even more impressive (fig. 11). It portrays two children with exquisite eyes and long wavy locks. Their expressions possess a disarming seriousness. Wearing nothing but a loin-cloth, their limbs burned by the sun, they stand erect, with clenched fists and an air of anticipation that suggests they are about to deal the first blows of a harsh sport which is transformed here into the noblest and most innocent of games. Beside the fresco of the Boxing Children is that of a nude fisherman (fig. 12), which provides further proof of the high standard of artistic ability of the Minoan painters of Thera. A typical Aegean figure, at once familiar, lively and warm-hearted, he holds his catch of fish in both hands in a relaxed yet purposeful attitude.

There are also depictions of nimble antelopes (fig. 13) rendered with well-judged simplicity and accurately calculated contours, and fragments of other figures, such as those of the Blue Monkeys. It would appear that we now have a fairly complete picture of Minoan painting in Thera. But no. The picture would not be absolutely complete. It would not do full justice to the accomplishments and capabilities of these painters had not the fresco of the Ships been uncovered and restored (figs. 16-17). This astonishing work was discovered in the West House, one of whose walls was decorated with the fresco of the Fisherman. It consists of an oblong frieze (six metres are preserved lengthwise) in which a series of crowded "historical" events are depicted in miniature painting. The archaeologist who uncovered it believes that the scene represents the events of a naval campaign rendered in a sequence not unlike that of a film unfolding on a cinema screen. A fleet of seven warships, accompanied by smaller vessels, approaches a well-built maritime city crowded with human figures. Two more cities are represented in other parts of the fresco; in yet another a naval battle is depicted (the figures of the drowning soldiers are masterpieces of draghtsmanship and invention). This fresco cannot be considered as just another masterpiece of Minoan painting; it carries a more important message, revealing a new aspect of Minoan art which permits us to form a true picture, both in the artistic and historical contexts, of the actual width of range of Minoan art.

Mycenaean civilization

At approximately the same period, that is to say, in the 16th century B.C., the first powerful dynasties were establishing their authority over the great citadels of mainland Greece. First, and most important of all, was Mycenae, which acquired an even greater glory in the ancient world than Athens itself. The opening Mycenaean chapter begins with a flourish, for its kings founded a dynasty whose legendary celebrity not only outlived antiquity but remains alive to this day. When Agamemnon, the most famous descendant of these kings, decided to wage a campaign against Troy, he united the whole Greek world: a world known as Mycenaean because of the fame of Agamemnon's capital. It remained for Homer to immortalize this war in world literature as none other ever has been, either before or after. The memory of the legendary city, Homer's "rich-in-gold Mycenae", remained alive in the imagination of the ancient Greeks just as the memory of Constantinople survived in the dreams of later generations of Greeks. In 1876, when Heinrich Schliemann excavated the royal shaft graves of Mycenae and found them filled with priceless treasures, he laid the foundations of Mycenaean archaeology. The introductory chapter in the history of the first Greeks who came here in the beginning of the 2nd millennium B.C. was thus opened. The precious objects discovered in the graves were removed to the National Archaeological Museum to form the first Mycenaean collection, which is being constantly enriched by new finds.

The large well-lit hall facing the monumental entrance contains crowded groups of objects characteristic of a civilization which possessed an almost embarrassingly exaggerated feeling for power and wealth. The show-cases are filled with objects wrought in gold and ivory. The clay vases, large and of infinite variety, do not detract from the prevailing sense of unity. Both the materials employed and the forms given to these works of art would appear strange to a Greek of the Classical age. From the outset it is clear that all these valuable objects — vases, weapons, architectural fragments and works of the minor arts — are the expression of an attitude towards life that differs wholly from that of the Greeks of the historical era. Their chief characteristic, one might say, is *élan vital*. The vegetation is pliant; flowing lines characterize the plants; nature is wild and untamed, populated by felines; the forces of nature are presented in their most elemental ungovernable form. The bull, the octopus, the lion and its hunters, the trees thick with leafy branches and the slender plants with flowers, all combine to present an image of an elegiac existence in which man, rejoicing in his freedom moves impulsively and embraces the world with uncontrollable vitality. There can be no doubt that the art of Minoan Crete exercised an enormous influence on the creative forms of expression of the Mycenaeans. But the inner core of the Mycenaean world is a wholly indigenous one. Compared with the Minoans, the Mycenaeans emerge as a more robust people, possessed of a more dynamic vision. They delight in the creation of more vigorous sturdier forms. It is the harsh reality of ceaseless struggle, not the joys of pleasurable dalliance that motivate the impulsive actions of these figures. Among all these forceful shifting shapes it is not impossible to discern a firmer structure destined to develop and, with the passage of time, lead to the more rational rhythm and architectural composition of Greek form.

The treasures of the royal shaft graves

Schliemann, who possessed a boundless imagination, was always an inveterate enthusiast. He believed the gold mask found in the fifth grave of the inner Grave Circle of the Mycenaean acropolis to have been that of Agamemnon, and to have somehow reproduced the actual facial features of the mythical king (fig. 20). But neither this mask, nor the other four that have survived, are likely to be faithful reproductions of the actual faces they once covered. It is even less likely that they can be identified with specific individuals. But the pale sheen of gold and the different features rendered on each of the masks conjures up a vision of the chill hand of death that has lain so long on the faces of the ancient rulers of Mycenae. "Emptiness... below the buried gold mask," as G. Seferis says. All around the masks lay the gold chest ornaments, the gold diadems, (fig. 18), the heavy costly swords and finely wrought daggers with inlaid decoration and lavish handles (figs. 24-31), as well as all kinds of vases executed in gold and silver. Although this impressive, but never barbaric, display of wealth, these costly raw materials moulded into forms and shapes with matchless technical skill and genuine artistic inspiration combine to provide a picture of a strong thoroughly disciplined military organization, the feeling for cultural development, the love of art and beauty for its own sake is never absent. Every object may be worthy of note, but particular attention should be paid to certain works of the minor arts of the early Mycenaean period. First, the rhyton, (libation vessel), in the shape of a bull's head (fig. 23), fashioned out of silver, with horns of gold and a gold rosette on the forehead. An impression of the awesome but sacred animal's nature is successfully conveyed by the carefully calculated volumes. Another rhyton, in the shape of a lion's head (fig. 32), made of gold, forms a striking counterpart to the bull's head. But the disposition of the volumes in this example is more austere and geometrical; there is a different feeling — more tectonic, one might almost say, more native, more Greek — which is particularly evident in the sharply defined edge of the surfaces and in the rendering of details.

The Vapheio cups

The finest works of Mycenaean art wrought in embossed gold were not found in the royal shaft graves of Mycenae, but in a tholos tomb near ancient Amyklai. These superb objects are the two so-called Vapheio Cups dated to the late 16th or early 15th century B.C. (figs. 21-22). A turbulent scene of the capture of a bull in a net is depicted on one cup; on the other we have a serene picture of shepherds accompanied by their cattle. These two works are unique, not only because of their creator's technical skill; the sensitivity of his approach to his theme, combined with the admirable composition, the power of expression and well-calculated filling up of the spaces raise his work to the highest level of artistic achievement. It is not hyperbole to say that the impression made by the Vapheio cups is indeed an indelible one.

Gravestones

Among the wealth of objects discovered in the royal shaft graves the funerary stelai occupy a special place because they are the earliest specimens of large-scale Greek sculpture in relief. They consequently play an extremely important role in the history not only of Mycenaean but of the whole of Greek art. The representations of chariots and beasts are well judged, but the execution is inferior to that of contemporary works of the minor arts. The geometric decoration, which consists of spirals, however, is composed and incised with such an assurance and feeling for decorative embellishment that the stelai may unreservedly be classed as works of high quality. More important, they are creations of manifestly Mycenaean origin, firmly rooted in indigenous elements, which survived in the midst of an attractive world of Minoan influences, only to blosson forth in their pure form in the historical era, well after the final dissolution of the Mycenaean world.

Frescoes

Works of art wholly representative of that Mycenaean world which dominated Greece for more than four hundred years are not only found in the astonishing yield of the royal shaft graves. Specimens of frescoes with strong Minoan influences have been uncovered in a very fragmentary condition in the Mycenaean palaces of the last phase of the period. In 1970 Professor G. Mylonas discovered and restored part of a fresco showing a female figure which he called the Mycenaean Woman (fig. 41). The facial features, together with the artistic expression, with its strong Mycenaean character, its bold and revolutionary originality, distinguish this attractive lady from the numerous female figures of the Minoan frescoes. Unlike the Minoan figures, the Mycenaean Woman is no longer depicted in profile. The figure stands frontally, in an attitude of exquisite nobility. Only the head is turned sideways, enabling the onlooker to obtain a view of the delicate profile. The arms are animated by harmonious movements. A third dimension is thus created for the first time in Greek art, and the feeling for space is admirably rendered.

Vase-painting and sculpture

The ivory objects of the minor arts (fig. 37) discovered both at Mycenae and in other parts of the country should also be ascribed to the last phase of Mycenaean civilization. Among these a group depicting a small childlike figure between two larger female ones is worth noting (fig. 38). It has been suggested that it may be a representation of Demeter, Persephone and Iakchos. The idea is certainly an attractive one. But can it be proved? The religious faith of the Minoans and Mycenaeans is shrouded in obscurity. Not a single record has yet shed any light worthy of serious attention. We can only guess at the contents — not interpret them.

It is equally impossible to interpret the mysterious sculptured limestone head with deep blue eyes, eyebrows and hair, red lips and three dots on the cheeks and chin (fig. 39). Is it a depiction of a sphinx? Or the representation of some great goddess sculptured for the first time on such a large scale in the Hellenic world? Identity apart, the head may nevertheless be considered to be the distant precursor of the Greek sculptures of the historical period.

Particular attention should be paid to the unique Warrior Vase (fig. 40), which is also a forerunner of things to come. Entirely foreign to the Minoan vase-painting tradition, which was assimilated into Mycenaean art, this superb krater has the quality of a symbolic representation of all the various elements of which the Mycenaean empire was composed. Heavily armed hoplites, complete with cuirasses, greaves, helmets, shields and spears march solemnly in single file. At the end of the procession a woman raises her hand in a gesture of farewell. It is as though the artist had caught the very essence of the moment when the "bronze-clad Achaians" set out from home to engage the enemy in one of their famous campaigns. Only after many centuries shall we again see such a well-knit composition, such well-designed, well-set up figures in Greek vase-painting. The vision of this procession of marching men, contemporaries of the first great catastrophe that befell the Mycenaean world in *c*. 1200 B.C., haunts the imagination. The warriors themselves were destined to perish in the ruins of Mycenae. It remained only for the great rhapsodist of the Geometric period — for Homer himself — to restore them to life in his immortal epic.

The end of the Mycenaean era

The end of the Mycenaean world left a deep mark on Greek history. Although we do not know what actually happened in the 12th century B.C. nor what was the cause of the destruction of the Mycenaean cities in *c*. 1200 B.C., followed by the end of Mycenaean civilization in *c*. 1100 B.C., we may be absolutely certain that a profound and radical historical change took place — but that it took place without completely sapping the roots of the old civilization. A study of the art of the centuries following the Mycenaean period, synoptically referred to as the Geometric age, leads to two important conclusions: (1) that the earlier forces were exhausted and replaced by new ones inspired by a primitive impetus and fresh dynamic quality; (2) that this new world was nevertheless no more than a continuity of the old one and its roots sprang from the same soil. The finest and most lavish creations of Geometric art, which originated in Attica, were ceramic products. During four centuries — from the 11th to the 8th — the potters' workshops in Athens evolved an unparalleled tradition in the art of ceramics and vase-painting that suffered no break in continuity and laid the firm foundations of all the admirable creations of succeeding centuries. A fundamental change had already occurred in vase decoration during the earliest phase of that period, the so-called Protogeometric phase (1050-900 B.C.). Pure geometric patterns, characterized by rythm, symmetry and precision, gave new vigour to art and offered artists new means of expression. This style displayed a novel structure and crystalline purity, features that were unknown, or rather lost, in the prolific diversity of the natural forms of Creto-Mycenaean art. An even more radical change than the one observed in decorative work occurred in the architectural solidity acquired by the vases. The flexibility and extreme tension of the Minoan forms had, in the course of the development of Mycenaean pottery, lost the vital force of the initial creation and gave the impression of a certain lack of firmness. The forms, now purged of these earlier elements, acquired a new plastic purity which proved a determining factor in the genesis of genuine Greek art. It is as though the Greek races, freed themselves of the spell of the Minoan world, and returned once more to the sobriety of the Middle Helladic age.

Geometric art

Nowhere can the progressive development of the early stages in the art of ceramics be more usefully examined than in the National Archaeological Museum. The first Protogeometric specimens consist of relatively small vases. There is little variety in shape, and they are very simply and soberly decorated with concentric circles and plain meander patterns. Development in the sphere of geometric abstract forms may be slow, but it is organic. In time the simple rhythmical lines are transformed into lavish and varied decorative motifs. The forms of the vases acquire a greater sensitivity and the contours become increasingly calculated and opulent; the inherent simplicity of a vase does not handicap the potter's imagination; he creates new forms, new variations on old themes. In the field of decorative work, the artist's imagination vies with his skill, his sensitivity with his long-acquired knowledge. The lavish decoration created by means of the repetition and elaboration of straight lines in a series of impressive compositions is astonishing. At first the artist reserves two or three unpainted bands on the dark surface of the vase: on the belly, neck and base. On these he then adds a motif which is developed by means of repetition all round the vase. Gradually, the bands increase in number, covering the vessel's entire surface which is thus rendered increasingly brighter. At the beginning of the 8th century B.C. the surface is covered with bands of unequal height decorated with geometric motifs. A special role is reserved for the meander pattern, both in its simplest and most intricate forms. This motif, which is full of momentum and possesses an incalculable dynamic quality and capacity for infinite development, both as regards height and width, acquired numerous variations in Greek — particularly Attic — art and was transformed from a formal ornament into a flexible dynamic feature.

In the process of evolving geometric decoration Attic artists laid down the first principles of representational painting which were inherited and fully developed by future generations. Limited representations of animals and scenes of everyday life were initially painted in a confined space within the area reserved for abstract designs. These representations quickly increased in number and during the last phase of the Geometric period (750-700 B.C.) they tempered the severity of the decorative system, thus opening the way for the radical changes effected in the early 7th century B.C. Furthermore, an exceptional opportunity to carry out these changes lay in the fact that the Athenians were in the habit of placing vases on tombs. The bottom of the vase was drilled in order that libations for the dead might be poured into the vessel. At first small and insignificant, they gradually acquired monumental size, up to a height of one or even one and a half metres. These large vases, amphoras and kraters (figs. 42-43), no longer executed in order to serve a purely functional purpose, were thus raised to an altogether higher level of art. The larger dimensions, the structure and organization combined to produce not only an outstanding creation of the potter's art but also an architectural and sculptural form. On these vases artists of the Geometric period depicted funerary scenes, such as the lying-in-state of the dead, the funeral procession, chariot processions and representations of ships. Some of the representations are perhaps related to mythical events. It was at this point that vase-painters certainly began to draw inspiration from mythology. Another precious contribution was thus made to Greek art. As one follows the course of Geometric pottery in the objects displayed in the show-cases of the National Museum and is finally confronted with the imposing funerary vases which rise up like genuine statues, one cannot fail to be moved by an art capable of creating masterpieces out of such a common material as clay.

Assimilation of Oriental influences

Towards the end of the 8th century B.C. another profound change took place in the Greek world, and the new currents were strongly reflected in the sphere of art. During the first half of the 7th century B.C. Oriental influences affected artistic forms to the extent that the period came to be known as the "Orientalizing" one. Ceramics too were not unaffected by the new ideas. An unusual situation, which will continue to be discerned throughout the history of Greek art, arose; and we are thus able to distinguish two contradictory elements: on the one hand, a tendency for innovation; on the other, a tenacious attachment to tradition. Greek artists were always open-minded, always ready to exploit anything gained from their contacts with foreign or associated civilizations. At the same time they preserved and developed all the finest elements they had inherited from their own art and civilization. Old forms were thus fertilised by new ideas, and rejuvenated by foreign formal features. It is consequently more accurate to speak of Hellenization of Oriental influences than of an "Orientalizing" Greek art.

The best example is found in the Protoattic vases, as those produced in Attica at the time (700-630 B.C.) were called. The exotic plants and animals of the Orient were now included in the decoration of the large Protoattic vases — but their role was a subordinate one. Human figures, horses and processions of chariots — subjects established by Geometric tradition — still occupy the chief place in vase decoration. Their forms, however, acquire a new substance and therefore a new content, because the changes wrought by Oriental influences on Attic art had the effect of rejuvenating the essential nature of the form rather than of enriching it with borrowed foreign themes. This rejuvenated form reflected the essence of the Greek world in its most profound sense, expressing it in terms of mythology. The number of painted themes derived from mythology expanded at an ever-increasing rate. Mythology became a limitless source from which artists drew their inspiration, and for the first time the myths themselves were provided with eloquent and tangible forms. The fact cannot be sufficiently stressed that contemporary artists were now emboldened to provide the shapeless visages of the gods and heroes of whom the poets had sung with positive forms.

The fragile shapes of Cycladic vases, notable for their pronounced Oriental influences, their less austere structure and their creators' greater love of picturesque and pictorial detail, which now stand beside the Protoattic examples in the halls of the National Archaeological Museum, are like an echo from an early Archaic island world. Two large amphorae, (both about one metre high) from Delos, are outstanding examples of the standard of workmanship attained by a Cycladic workshop after 650 B.C. These vases used to be called "Melian": an epithet now considered to be certainly incorrect. It is more commonly believed that the vases were products of some other island, possibly Paros. One of the vases is decorated with a magnificent representation of Apollo riding a chariot drawn by winged horses, followed by the two Hyperborean virgins and led by Artemis (fig. 44). On the other, Herakles is depicted bidding farewell to the parents of his bride who is already mounted on his chariot.

Black-figure vases

The life span of the other potters' workshops, each of which possessed its own individuality, its own list of achievements, was of shorter duration. One might almost say that they served as a complement to the great Attic workshops whose productivity was seemingly inexhaustible. The creative range and rejuvenating force of the Attic potter remain unique. The act of creation was accompanied by the acquisition of experience and the assimilation of the technical accomplishments of other schools. During the 7th century B.C. Corinth was the greatest centre of productivity and Corinthian workshops had soon captured all the markets in the East and West. Corinthian potters seem to have specialized in small-scale vases, the decoration of which possessed a singular precision and crystalline clarity, as well as sensitivity of feeling. These miniature Corinthian compositions are a unique achievement in Greek art. And it was precisely because of the small dimensions of their vases that the Corinthians were obliged to develop faultless technical methods in order to achieve in miniature what other craftsmen were accomplishing in the field of large-scale pottery. The technique of the black-figure vase was a Corinthian achievement. A superb technique designed to reflect the atmosphere of the early Archaic world was achieved by means of filling in the figures with black paint, of registering details with precision and extremely carefully executed incisions, and using a deep reddish-violet paint which provided richness of colour without harming the unit of the decoration.

Attic artists were quick to learn the lesson from their Corinthian colleagues. Cautiously, somewhat hesitantly at first, then more boldly, they sought to adapt the perfection of the black-figure technique to their own more inspired vision. By the end of the 7th century B.C. Attic artists were thus producing their own black-figure vases. If the Piraeus amphora, on which a magnificent cock is depicted on the neck and a procession of chariots on the body, is the earliest example of this style, the first great vase-painter must be the one known as the "Nessos painter", because he executed the amphora in the National Archaeological Museum in which Herakles and the centaur Nessos are depicted on the neck and the legend of Perseus and Medusa on the belly (fig. 45). A new world is now reflected in the forms and paintings of the vases. A new structure, severe and solid, yet opulent and dynamic, shapes the body of the vase and its various parts. In the sphere of vase-painting a new world, at once vigorous and majestic, is peopled by mighty heroes and "terrible monsters". The lions and wild beasts of the east have acquired a Greek sturdiness as well as a different content. Almost the entire work of the great Attic artist who painted this new vision of the world may be seen in the National Archaeological Museum, because Attica had not yet captured the foreign markets, and most of the Attic products thus remained at home, where they were eventually found centuries later.

By the beginning of the 6th century B.C., the charm of the black-figure vases had begun to make its impact abroad and the finest products were exported to wealthy foreign commercial centres, chiefly in Italy. The Tyrrhenians, as well as the Greeks of Magna Graecia, collected Attic masterpieces in the 6th and 5th centuries B.C. and placed them on well constructed tombs as offerings to the dead. It was therefore from these tombs that Europe subsequently acquired its knowledge of Greek vases. Priceless collections were assembled from the treasure-house of antiquity and eventually found their way to the Vatican, the Louvre, the British Museum and other great museums of the world. Consequently, the National Archaeological Museum's collection of 6th and 5th century B.C. pottery cannot compare with some of those now in foreign museums. The National Archaeological Museum has, nevertheless, quite a great deal to offer, both to the scholar and the enthusiastic amateur, in the way of ceramics which were produced in such abundance during the 6th and 5th centuries B.C. All the vases are characterized by perfection of form and an infinite variety of decorative themes drawn from Greek mythology. Some of the show-cases contain fragments of vases that littered the Athenian

Acropolis: all that survived the Persian holocaust. These may not attract much attention; nor are any of the compositions intact. But the excellence of design, the elegant incisions and the technical experience of the artists are clearly apparent. Among these are the sherds with the inscription "Sophilos painted me". For the first time, we thus learn the name of an Athenian vase-painter (c. 580 B.C.). It is only on the sherds too that we read the inscription "Lydos painted me", and learn the name of one of the greatest artists of the 6th century B.C. The name of another equally gifted contemporary artist, who executed the magnificent *dinos*, which was found on the Acropolis and established him as the "painter of the Acropolis 606", is unfortunately nowhere to be found. The cauldron-shaped vase is covered with decorative representations. A mythical combat, in which a fine array of chariots take part, is depicted on the main band. Sir John Beazley, an outstanding expert on Greek vase-painting, says: "This is at last a picture that for size, grandeur and vehemence may rank with the masterpieces of the 'Nessos painter' and his colleagues". "Its merits", he adds, "make this one of the best battle-pieces in Archaic art". Magnificent examples of black-figure painting are to be found in some of the flat rectangular plaques on which funerary scenes were depicted. These would appear to have constituted the decoration reserved for sepulchral memorials raised above ground. Evidence of the importance attached by the family of the deceased to this form of decoration lies in the fact that the plaques in the National Archaeological Museum are the works of Lydos, whom we have already mentioned, and of Exekias, the great black-figure vase-painter — perhaps the greatest of all Attic vase-painters — who executed a whole series of master-pieces over a period of three decades (550-520 B.C.).

A special category of black-figure vases is to be found in the so-called "Panathenaic amphoras" (fig. 53). These vessels, filled with oil from Athena's sacred olive trees, were presented as awards to victors in the Panathenaic games. They were first produced in 566 B.C. with the institution of the Panathenaic games and their production continued until the Roman period in the twilight years of antiquity. Evidence of the particular function for which they were destined is also found in their decoration: a depiction of Athena Promachos on one side, scenes of contests on the other. It was because of this function, which aimed at preserving the tradition of awarding first prizes, that vase-painters retained the Archaic technique of the black-figure style until the very end. The innovations so effectively introduced by the red-figure style were thus ignored by the painters of the "Panathenaic amphoras".

Red-figure vases

The workshop of Exekias was one of the busiest in Athens. There Exekias, both potter and vase-painter, fashioned vases of new attractive shapes and painted them in his own incomparable manner. The artist known as the "Andokides painter", who had the brilliant inspiration to reverse the chromatic relation between the figures and the surface of the vase and thus create the red-figure style, seems to have served his apprenticeship in Exekias' work-shop. The figures in this new style no longer resemble black sketches on a red ground; in fact the ground acquires a black metallic glaze and the figures, which remain red and luminous, are thus provided with an unexpected corporality. New horizons were now opened up to Athenian vase-painters. Beyond them extended untrodden and alluring paths. No longer inhibited by the severe and limited capacities of the black-figure technique, draughtsmen were able to put their abilities to the test, enchanted by the infinite variety of theme execution at their disposal. The National Archaeological Museum does not possess fine works of such great craftsmen and innovators as Euthymides and Euphronios, the "Kleophrades painter" and the "Berlin painter", but it has a large number of less important works, which nevertheless illustrate the extent to which the art of the Classical period encompassed the entire range of human existence. Even the most modest works — seldom beyond the means of the humblest Athenian citizen — displayed a freshness of outlook and the achievements of art in that age.

Among the vases of this common category which were, for the most part, found in Attic tombs, where they had been placed as offerings to the dead, a fair number may be distinguished for their size and artistic merit. On them the name of some eminent artist is sometimes inscribed; on other occasions we may discern the seal of the artist's personality, the originality of whose design we have learnt to recognise from the audacious and unparalleled studies of the great expert, sir John Beazley. In a broken *kylix* of the late 6th century B.C. decorated with the subject of the wedding of Peleus and Thetis, always a great favourite with Attic vase-painters, we have the signature of the potter and painter, Euphronios. In another piece, which is intact, decorated with the representation of a kneeling warrior, we read the inscription "Phintias made me", which means that it was a work by the contemporary of Euphronios. In a third *kylix,* which is of a later date than the other two, a young man is depicted holding a *kylix* in his left hand, an *oinochoe* in his right, advancing towards an altar inscribed with the words "Oh, Douris!". Douris is known to have been one of the most able and prolific vase-painters of the early 5th century B.C. A superb *pelike* (a kind of amphora) is the work of a vase-painter, known as the "Pan painter", which he decorated with a representation of the combat between Herakles and Bousiris, a mythical king of Egypt (fig. 50). The dramatic force of this tumultuous composition, combined with its effortless humour and felicitous conception, is so judiciously adapted to the form of the vase as to fully justify the feeling of veneration that often overwhelms the visitor when contemplating the masterpieces of Attic vase-painting.

During the Classical period, Attic vase-painters, whose works were advancing on lines parallel to those of monumental sculpture, executed a series of masterpieces which are wholly remarkable for the elegance of draughtsmanship, the fullness of form and the sense of balance. The "Achilles painter", a contemporary of Pheidias, painted figures comparable to the noble youths of Pheidias' frieze and provided his entire composition with an architectural firmness that recalls the Parthenon sculptures. But dangers lay ahead. The works of large painting, now lost to us, exercised so great a fascination on vase-painters that, in so far as decoration was concerned, they inevitably went too far. The result was the execution of Attic works that went beyond the limits of Classical balance and, more important, exceeded the potential capacity of expression inherent in a vase-painting. The style known as the Beautiful Style soon became the Rich Style, which was characterized by extreme emphasis on draughtsmanship and compositional skill, together with an excessive exploitation of painting impressions spread carelessly over the surface of the vase, thus breaking up its aesthetic unity. Although the calligraphic and extremely fine treatment of old themes in the works of such notable artists as Polygnotos and the "Eretria painter", who executed the elegant Eretria *epinetron* (fig. 54) deserve respect, the dynamic force and expressive quality of the design of the earlier craftsmen are absent. Moreover, as the representations became increasingly covered with gaudy colours and designs which possessed no interior vitality and, more important, were devoid of any aesthetic justification, the fate of red-figure vase-painting was sealed. The end came in the 4th century B.C.

White-ground vases White-ground lekythoi

In Athens of the 5th century B.C., the art of the vase-painter found, as the 19th century poet, Dionysios Solomos says, "its good and sweet hour". For some time artists were to experiment with yet another technique destined to produce a series of matchless masterpieces. The projection of light-coloured figures of the red-figure style on a black ground created a strong contrast with the introduction of sharp outlines and the isolation of the figures from their surroundings. By means of this new method, the entire surface of the vase, covered with a very fine white glaze, acquired cohesion. The figures were painted on the glaze, the hair — sometimes, but more rarely, the garments and other minor details — being rendered in dark colours. The monotonous black colour too was replaced by a variety of lighter shades. The composition thus acquired a more pictorial character and created a gentler and uniform atmosphere. Above all, the merits of the representation rested on perfection of design, quality of line and the painter's ability to render the plasticity and volumes of the figure solely by means of outlines. Among the earliest and finest examples of white-ground vases is the *kylix,* on which the murder of Orpheus by the Thracian women is depicted, by the so-called "Pistoxenos painter" (*c.* 470 B.C.). The few surviving fragments (the head of Orpheus, part of his lyre and a woman holding a double axe) are sufficient to enable us to observe the excellence of the work. The savage theme is rendered in the grand manner; the beautiful faces possess a deep spiritual quality and the "character" of the protagonists is expressed through the quality and purity of the design.

This technique was particularly well suited to a type of vase known as the white *lekythos* which was intended to accompany the dead on their journey into eternity. The National Archaeological Museum possesses the largest collection of white-ground *lekythoi* which are displayed in a hall almost entirely reserved for them. The subject-matter of the representations is invariably associated with the deceased. If one may borrow a musical metaphor, one might describe them as "variations on a theme". The *lekythoi* require the closest possible attention if one is to appreciate their poetical quality and infinite variety both as regards composition and elaboration of the subject. In front of the tomb, which is indicated by a tall funerary stele, the dead man sits (or stands) (fig. 55). His relatives, generally women, approach the tomb. They come to adorn it with ribbons, to place *lekythoi* on the steps, to crown it with garlands of flowers and anoint it with myrrh. Generally speaking, the scene cannot be interpreted in terms of actual events. It is an artistic creation which combines various elements of inner spiritual meaning: the dead man, his tomb, his relatives, the attention paid to the maintenance of the sepulchre. The perfect cohesion of these various elements creates an inspiring image filled with emotional content and profound grief. Over it all reigns a kind of occult silence. In front of the mourning relations rises the image of the young man taken in his prime, a handsome virile youth, carrying long spears and a round shield, his broad-brimmed felt hat thrown back over his shoulder. He rejoices in his sadness as he watches them tending his tomb; for he is aware that their mission is a token of the fact that he will always remain alive in their memory. Sometimes, exhausted by the long journey through the land of shadows, he rests on the steps of his own funerary stele. In one of the later *lekythoi* the youth's intense weariness and grief, if not despair, seems to have broken his spirit. In this *lekythos,* the work of the "Reed painter", as well as in those belonging to the same group (fig. 56), the form of the human figure has lost its solid substance. But the new sense of awareness in which the figure seems to have been immersed, provides it with an unquestionably enchanting quality. The youth is "so saturated in light that his heart itself is visible". He cries out for the world he has lost. But as we too mourn beside him, we too may experience the "extraordinary passion" that fills the spirit with a strange elation as it soars into the rarefied and ethereal atmosphere of pure art. "From afar, bells of crystal can be heard ringing", as the poet O. Elytis says.

The different kinds of Greek sculpture

The National Archaeological Museum, which possesses the greatest masterpieces of ancient sculpture, is the only museum in the world to cover the whole range of ancient Greek sculpture without a single break in historical continuity.

In order that the reader may follow the detailed descriptions of the sculptures both in the National Archaeological Museum and other Greek museums with greater facility he may, at this point, find a few introductory remarks of some use.

The first monumental sculptures were executed in Greece in about the mid-7th century B.C. From then on, until the last days of antiquity, innumerable sculptured works were executed in stone and metal. Soon marble, which is both abundant and of the highest quality in Greece, became the favourite material of sculptors. In about the mid-6th century B.C. two Samian artists, Roikos and Theodoros, invented the technique of executing hollow bronze works. Statues of bronze began to vie with those of marble, and, with the passage of time, marble and bronze took precedence over all other materials in the Greek sculptor's workshop. In Greece marble statues were painted all over: not with the natural flesh tints of the human body, but with deep bright colours — red, blue, yellow, etc. A vivid chromatic harmony reflecting the rays of the Mediterranean sun was thus created.

Sculpture in Greece was dedicated to the service of religion and the state, and it was only after the 4th century B.C. that sculptured works devorced from the affairs of the social community as a whole made their appearance. Free-standing statues and reliefs, which may be classified in two main categories — votive and funerary — had been executed by the earliest Greek sculptors. Votive sculptures depicted gods or men, and were presented as offerings in holy sanctuaries. The cult statues of gods and goddesses, which were placed within the temple, belong to this category. The funerary sculptures, which were raised on tombs, depicted the image of the dead, whose memory was thus enshrined in the minds of the living, and assumed the function of memorials. A separate group consists of the architectural sculptures which decorated the pediments, friezes and metopes of temples, as well as the *akroteria* placed on the apices of the pediments.

In the Introduction to this book we have already referred to the successive periods of Greek art and to the main characteristics of each period. A more detailed examination of the particular character of the 'sculpture of each period in the course of an imaginary tour of the museums may enable the reader to form a more complete picture of Greek art as a whole, and of Greek sculpture in particular, and to acquire a more intimate knowledge of the most important creations of each category and each period. It will then be found that the National Archaeological Museum provides an excellent framework within which one may examine the whole of Greek sculpture because its contents range over the entire sculptural spectrum, covering every period and including every category.

The fact that the so-called Daidalic style reached its zenith in the mid-7th century B.C., i.e. the age in which Greek sculpture was born, cannot be a mere coincidence. The existence of large sculptures executed in solid materials and of the emergence of the firm tectonic Daidalic style must be considered as the consequence, if not the expression, of a general and profound social and cultural differentiation. After the introduction of Oriental influences at the beginning of the century and the consequent enrichment of Greek art, it seemed dialectically imperative to follow some new direction, whereby it would be possible to synthesize the old with the new, to submit the vague and undisciplined trends of post-Geometric and "anti-Geometric" art to the laws of symmetry and balance of form. "The Daidalic style carried with it a conscious arrangement of nature, a subjection to a norm inherent in its very self". The Daidalic prelude in Greek sculpture produced a longing for grandeur and sobriety; it provided evidence of a sense of pride in the projection of conscious self-abnegation. The Daidalic sculptor certainly admired the imposing dimensions of his works, but he also knew how to subject these dimensions to a new geometric arrangement invigorated by the vital force with which forms were imbued in the ferment of the first half of the 7th century.

The first important example of this sculpture is the statue presented as a votive offering by the Naxian Nikandra at Delos in *c.* 660 B.C.: a work that contained the seeds that would eventually produce the beautiful korai, executed both in Athens and the islands, during the period of full maturity of Archaic art; ultimately, it would also lead, through a long process of development, to the creation of the supreme masterpieces of the Classical period. The Naxian work possessed all the internal still unhibited energy that was capable of fertilizing the achievements of later years. In the context of the 7th century B.C., it was enough that it should possess a firm structure, that it should be disciplined to the closed geometric form, that there should be no breaking up of the surface of the volumes, and that there should be a total absence of any picturesque details and disruptive elements in the overall image.

The Mycenae relief, the work of an artist of a later generation, represents a figure tugging at an *epiblema* (a kind of shawl) with the right hand. No previous work possesses such complete geometric clarity or conveys such a powerful sense of interior life as that reflected in the taut stretched quality of the flesh of the head. The same feeling of tension is also apparent in the rendering of the eyes, nostrils, mouth and chin. It is the moment when the bow is drawn back to the farthest possible point, ready to hurl the arrow at the target.

Archaic Kouroi

The Cycladic statue and the Peloponnesian relief, exhibited in the first hall of sculptures, serve as curtain-raisers to the statuary's art of the Archaic period when the Greeks reserved their most maturely evolved and thoroughly integrated conception of sculpture for the creation of the figure of the kouros, the nude "man-boy". The image of the young man was placed in sanctuaries; it was an *agalma,* dedicated to the god for his own delight, a depiction either of the god himself or of the donor who presented the statue as a votive offering. Similar figures were raised on tombs not as an ephemeral reflection of a particular incident, of a passing moment in the life of the dead youth, but as a memorial to his strength and beauty. The famous series of kouroi in the National Museum begins in 620 B.C. with the Dipylon head (fig. 58), so-called because of the locality in which it was found. From it stems the long line of Attic kouroi which came to an end a hundred years later in the statue of the youth Aristodikos. In the Dipylon head the pure and severe oval of the face is dominated by two large almond-shaped eyes below the arched eyebrows; the broad smooth surfaces of the cheeks terminate in the helices of the beautifully stylized ears; the locks of hair in the form of countless strings of beads are ranged above and below the ears.

The colossal Sounion kouros is of a slightly later date. It is the best preserved of the four kouroi raised as votive offerings in the temple of Poseidon on the southernmost headland of Attica. As the entire body has been preserved one is able to appreciate the firm architectural quality of the execution. While the statue retains the clear geometrical form, the sculptural volumes of the body have acquired a more pronounced differentiation, which provides both the outlines and details with greater animation. The "dormant motion" as it was first described and called by the Greek art historian, Constantine A. Romaios, is clearly discernible in this kouros. Although all Archaic figures stand frontally, presenting the clearest and most developed image of the human body, they all seem to possess an invisible, a "dormant" though conscious sense of movement. As a result of this inner mobility the body, no longer subject to the severe axial line, acquires numerous small asymmetrical features, all of which derive from the same source and all ultimately lead, one way or another, to the same goal: the actual and positive animation of the figure. This observation and its theoretical development has provided the study of Archaic art with the means of interpreting it in terms of the most profound aesthetic appreciation and of penetrating its secrets in the most objective manner.

We are now confronted with two kouroi, representative of the mature period of Archaic art and executed some fifty years after the Sounion kouros, in the mid-6th century B.C. The kouros of Volomandra (fig. 59), an outstanding work executed by an Attic sculptor, has acquired an air of spirituality and incomparable nobility. The oblong head — notice the oblique eyes, the flame-shaped locks of hair harmoniously yet loosely arranged across the forehead, the fine nose and the smiling lips — rests on a neck whose curves incline gently towards the shoulders. Animated by the reflection of a deep interior life, the Volomandra kouros is indeed a unique work of art, a uniform as well as manifold composition. The kouros of Melos continues the old tradition of the Naxian workshop. The soft slender body is sensitively modelled and the dignity of the hair style almost exaggerated, while the fluently traced contours follow one another in continuous curves. The youth seems to dwell in a world contemporary to but different from his Attic counterpart.

The series of Archaic kouroi is completed by two Attic masterpieces, both funerary monuments, found at Anavyssos. The first (fig. 60) should be dated to *c*. 525 B.C. The following epigram is inscribed on the base:

"Stand and mourn by the tomb of dead Kroisos,
whom furious Ares snatched from among the warriors
of the front rank."

There is a new strength in the kouros' attitude. All the members of the body have gained in fulness and vigour. Kroisos is no longer a "man-boy"; he is a man. An unprecedented interior dynamic force gives the surface of the flesh a closely-knit aspect vibrating with vitality. The face with the tense and at the same time balanced sinuosities, the broad build of the body, the stricter arrangement of the volumes and structural forces, combine to create an image of a young man of the late Archaic period who possesses a more mature conscience, a richer experience of life, the self-confidence of a virile man in his own strength, a pride born of reasoned judgement, and a sense of humble submission to human fate.

The second Anavyssos kouros (fig. 61), whose name, we learn from the inscription on the base, is Aristodikos, represents the last stage in the development of Archaic sculpture in Attica. The statue is also the last chapter in the history of Archaic art and of the 6th century B.C. But while closing one door, it opens another in order to usher in the art of the next century. Ernst Buschor, the German art historian, describes it as "the termination and culmination of all the kouroi". The youth's attitude, characterized by extreme tension and the constriction of all the forces at his command, is that of someone standing on the "razor's edge". He is like a chord stretched to breaking-point; and when the chord breaks we know that its echo will resound for a long time to come. Never before has there been such a striking demonstration of the co-existence of the three successive stages in the representation of the human attitude. It is not only the tension of the youth's body which is so characteristic of the composition. The freedom and ease with which the taut attitude is reproduced are even more striking. The spirit has tamed matter and completely transformed the substance of the marble into a submissive form with ontological depth and weight. Aristodikos possesses the nobility of a man who is no longer the victim of fate; he stands fearlessly in the full light of the sun, with the dignity of a thinking man conscious of the tragic responsibilities of freedom. He is the personification of the responsible citizen of the newly-born democracy. All these diverse elements combine to find their most mature expression in this last representation of an Attic kouros.

The Piraeus Apollo

The bronze statue of Apollo, discovered at Piraeus in 1959, is unique in many respects (fig. 65). The oldest of bronze statues, it is the only Archaic one to have survived. It is also the oldest image of the god in monumental sculpture and the only outstanding Archaic work which clearly distinguishes the divine nature of a god from that of a mortal. The differentiation is achieved by means of the attitude of the figure and the attributes held in both hands: a *phiale* in the right, a *bow* in the left. Similarities between the Apollo and the kouroi are of a purely superficial nature. The initiated scholar and attentive onlooker will observe that the figure is endowed with a new structural and architectural concept of the body which in itself is an expression of a completely different spiritual world. The bent elbows and the different position of the forearms (the palm of the right hand open, the fingers of the left clenched) are not mere inconsistencies, superficial variations of the established form of the rigid vertical line of the arms, but they are organically linked to the modelling and attitude of the whole body. It is easier to realise the underlying significance of the particular attitude of the figure if one bears in mind that the god, in all hieratic dignity, the weight of his body resting on both feet, is extending his right hand, in which he holds the *phiale* for the libation, inclining and slightly turning his head, in order that his gaze, filled with an expression of intense spirituality, should remain fixed on the focal point. The fact that the right leg is only very slightly advanced forward is in complete accord with the artist's conception of the figure and has no connection with the projection of the left leg forward common to the kouroi. Modelled with unusual sobriety, the god, in full control of all his spiritual, intellectual and physical powers, turns inward on himself; his introspection exceeds the bounds of all terrestrial and corporeal existence. Without discarding his divine nature, he appears before mortals in a splendid Olympian epiphany. That such a vision of god-like grandeur and Apollonian radiance could only have been conceived and executed with such penetrating wisdom by an Athenian artist does not seem, in my opinion, to be beyond the bounds of probability. It would be also difficult to deny that this god basically expresses the genuine religious faith associated with the mature Archaic period in the course of which the magnificent pediment of the Peisistratidai was raised on the Athenian Acropolis (525 B.C.).

During the early Classical period, which, in terms of art history, is known as the period of the Severe Style (480-450 B.C), the Greeks piously sought to conceive and then express the essence of divinity. Aischylos and Pindar tried to penetrate the subject in depth, to reveal to mankind the forces underlying the application of the laws of God in the world of men. A similar attempt was made in the visual arts: namely in sculpture and painting.

The Poseidon of Artemission

A striking contrast to the radiant young Apollo will be found in the formidable figure of the Poseidon of Artemision (460 B.C.) (figs. 1, 68). There is little in common between him and the youthful god, who, with all the penitence of a libation-bearer, consorts with mortals in a mood of serene introspection. The epiphany of the mature deity is rendered with tremendous power. In his right hand, the god holds the trident, chief attribute of the mighty lord of the earth and sea, who "watches over earth and makes her shake". The trident is indeed just about to be cast. It is precisely this movement which gives the statue its main structural basis and, as it were, epitomizes the fundamental nature of the god. The modelling of the entire statue, together with all the forces that derive from it, depend on this movement of the right arm. The elevation of the arm has the effect of organically shifting the whole force of the body backwards (this explains why the toes of the left foot are raised), and of transmitting and concentrating all the tension on the right foot, the toes of which support the whole body; the constriction of the right shoulder-blade pulls back the muscles of the right side and chest which, together with the stomach muscles, are thus fully stretched. At the same time the pronounced emphasis on the great horizontal axis of the two arms counterbalances effectively all the vertical and oblique axial lines. The broad-chested body is crowned by a magnificent head; and the face, with its wide hairless surfaces, the harmoniously arranged locks of the wavy hair and beard, has an expression of supremely self-assured composure. The indomitable strength of the figure reflects the serene effortlessness and awesome grandeur of the god's inner being.

In the early Classical period repeated attempts were made to capture the essence of god-head and render it in terms of sculpture. The sculptor of the Poseidon is also believed to have executed a statue of Apollo in bronze soon after completing his magnificent depiction of the "Earth-shaker". The statue no longer survives, but an excellent Roman copy of the 2nd century A.D., known as the "Apollo of the Omphalos" (it was found along with a marble navel-stone), has been preserved. The statue, executed in deliberate *contraposto,* was notable for its free austerity and the firm yet sensitive modelling of the volumes. It was a representation of that kind of introspective god which was so much admired in an age when men's attitude to life was above all a spiritual and intellectual one. Archaeologists ascribe the original work to Kalamis, a celebrated sculptor of the mid-5th century B.C.

We would have been fortunate indeed, if any of Pheidias' statues depicting deities had survived. It appears that this greatest of Athenian sculptors had succeeded in endowing his divine figures with incomparable grandeur and profound spirituality. Advancing beyond the Aischylean conception of divinity, he reached a concept of Olympian beauty and immortality, equal to the enlightened vision of Sophokles, the poet who became the first priest of Asklepios in Athens and was heroized after his death under the characteristic name of Dexion. The diminutive marble Varvakeion Athena is but a poor reproduction of Pheidias' magnificent statue of Athena Parthenos in the Parthenon. Possibly useful for archaeological observation, it cannot attract the visitor's attention, any more than the various copies after Pheidias' works (assembled in one of the Museum halls) can replace the masterpieces now lost to us.

4th century B.C. bronze statues

The depiction of the nude male figure favoured by Greek sculptors from the earliest times reached its apogee in the Classical works of Pheidias and Polykleitos. The subject continued to be a great favourite with the sculptors of the 4th century B.C. who laid the foundations of Hellenistic art. Praxiteles, Skopas, Lysippos, each in his own way, presented an image of men and gods in conformity with the transformation of Greek society and the new ideas current at the time. In addition to these masters, many other artists, less famous perhaps, but no less worthy of note, created a number of attractive works which have been preserved.

The attitude of the human body established by Polykleitos in his superb Doryphoros (the Spear-bearer), which came to be known as "the canon" (= Norm) had been a landmark in the history of art. By placing the weight of the body on one leg, Polykleitos stressed the flex of the other at the knee and then pulled it back. The carefully calculated rhythmical turning movements and *contraposto* provided by this form of support for the body brought new life into the depiction of the human form. All the representations of the human figure which followed Polykleitos' creations derived from this established norm. It was certainly varied and enriched, the roles of the relaxed and standing legs reversed, and one leg placed either more or less to the side; but sculptors never deviated from the basic principles of a "canon" which possessed so many potentialities. Fortunately two bronze statues have survived intact; we are thus in a position to appreciate the sculptural achievements of a century as advanced as the 4th B.C. and to distinguish the profound differences that exist between the new creations and the archetypes of Polykleitos. One of the statues, which was found in the sea near Antikythera, belonged to a consignment of works that suffered shipwreck in ancient times. The Ephebe of Antikythera (fig. 78), as the statue is now known, depicts an alert, agile and athletic young man. The well-built body is lithe and fully developed, the face expressive. The right arm is thrust forward, thus placing movement in a third dimension and cautiously opening up new horizons for some of the more daring sculptors of the Hellenistic period. Archaeologists believe an apple may originally have been held in the bent fingers of the extended right hand and that the figure might

therefore have been a representation of Paris in the famous judgement scene with the three goddesses. In these circumstances, the work could be identified as the Paris of Euphranor, a renowned
Corinthian sculptor of the second half of the 4th century B.C. Whether he is Paris or just some
ordinary athlete, it is nevertheless interesting to note that the youth's expression and facial features,
which possess a far more human and personal quality, seem to reflect a world devoid of the solid
structure and inner cohesion of his 5th century B.C. antecedents.

The child-like, gentle and fragile figure of a boy, found in the sea in the bay of Marathon (figs.
81-82), is a more attractive work. The delicate modelling, the fluidity of the contours, the S-shaped
movement of the spine, by means of which the figure acquires an unusual suppleness and a kind of
undulating effect, possess an almost Praxitelean quality. But the new proportions in relation to head
and body, which may be discerned in the boy's intelligent face with the deeply concentrated expression, deprive the figure of stability, while increasing its agility. The boy's right arm is somewhat
shyly raised and his left forearm is thrust forward as though it were shearing lightly through space.

Sculptured female figures

Even the earliest Greek sculptors had not confined themselves exclusively to carving figures of
nude men. But the women represented in their statues were always fully and elegantly clothed in
peplos, chiton and *himation*. The lavish drapery remained an inexhaustible source of inspiration and
plastic invention, which was not only intended to represent feminine stylishness and coquetry but to
reflect the nature and interior world of womanhood. In one single identifiable volume with its undulating facial surfaces, a woman' s head crowned by a skilful arrangement of the hair or some form
of head-gear, would reflect all the radiance of feminine beauty, whether it were that of an innocent
virgin or a mature woman. The National Archaeological Museum does not possess a great number of
large free-standing females. That is why the recent acquisition of a superb Archaic kore, found
together with a kouros at Merenda in Attica, is such a fortunate event. A fine inscription with the
girl's name, Phrasikleia, is preserved on the base. In addition to Phrasikleia we have a small kore
from Piraeus (height: 0,77 m.), possibly a representation of Persephone, which is an original example
of Attic sculpture of the Classical period (420 B.C.). The severe well-balanced attitude and freshness
apparent in the elaboration of the extremely delicate folds of the *chiton* and more ponderous *himation*
recall the work of Agorakritos, Pheidias' favourite pupil, who executed a large number of sculptures
in Attica after his master's death.

Unfortunately only the head of a statue of a woman, which must have been an admirable example
of sculpture in about the mid-4th century B.C., is preserved. In this highly praised work, known as
the head of Hygeia (fig. 77), we find a remarkable synthesis of all the sculptural trends and achievements observed in statues of women executed in the mature period of the 4th century B.C. The
sculptor's technical skill in the execution of the facial details is beyond praise; and his inspired
conception is fully matched by the structure of the head and the rendering of the most delicate
inflections and movements. Complete agreement does not exist among archaeologists whether the
head does in fact represent Hygeia. Nor are they in accord as to the identity of the sculptor. Some
discern the technique of Praxiteles in the limpid extremely sensitive modelling; others detect the fire
and interior passion of his Parian contemporary, Skopas. It is worth noting, however, that art in the
age when the work was produced had assimilated the achievements of both these masters.

Two bronze statues of female deities, which were found together with the Piraeus Apollo, are of
considerable value — like all rare originals of Greek antiquity. The goddesses represented are
Athena (fig. 79) and Artemis (fig. 80). Almost contemporary with two other bronze statues in the
National Archaeological Museum, the Ephebe of Antikythera and the Boy of Marathon, the representations of the two female deities provide us with a very clear picture of the creativity of original
Greek art and of the wide experience acquired by the sculptor in bronze. At the same time, both
statues also reveal a flaccidity which is evident in both the structure and the treatment of plastic
surfaces. It is as though the statues themselves mirrored the instability of the world in which their
creators dwelt. Even more strikingly than their male counterparts, the figures of the two goddesses
betray signs of the deterioration suffered in terms of form, of the attempt to replace inner dynamic
force and genuine inspiration by a kind of external aestheticism coupled with an air of fictitious
god-like serenity. We consequently find it somewhat difficult to agree with that expert on Classical
art, K. Schefold, who suggests that the Athena may be the work of Kephisodotos, Praxiteles' father,
executed at an advanced stage in his career.

During the early years of the 3rd century B.C. all the progressive trends which owed so much to
the great forerunners, of whom Skopas was one, and to the more daring innovators, such as Lysippos
and Leochares, came to a temporary halt. An attempt was made to revive the now vanished austerity
of the old Classical tradition and to contain the figure within a severe and noble framework; the result
was merely the execution of a number of well-set up but coldly decorous figures incapable of transmitting the message of the times. The statue of Themis, in the temple of Rhamnous in Attica, for

instance, depicted by Chairestratos in a high-waisted garment and executed in such a way that the emphasis was strongly laid on the relaxed leg (fig. 86), may have been a perfectly agreeable work but it possessed little genuine artistic merit. The *Herakleotis* (Woman of Herculaneum) type, dated to the transitional period between the 4th and 3rd centuries B.C. is, thanks to the feeling of complete abandonment to nostalgia for the past, more attractive and elegant. The ·type proved to be very popular during succeeding centuries and was repeated with almost wearisome monotony throughout the Hellenistic era and, to an even greater extent during the Roman period.

Reliefs

Before examining the various sculptural forms and trends peculiar to Hellenistic art, we must once more span the whole range of Greek art in the context of the second great category of sculptures; namely, the reliefs. Although equal in quality to the free-standing statues, they greatly exceed them in quantity. If the Greeks succeeded in rendering the form of god and man in their ontological completeness by free-standing sculptures, the technique of sculpture in relief provided them with an opportunity to represent their presence in the world.

In the statues the various elements that contribute to the representation of the divine or the human essence are concentrated and self-sufficient; in the reliefs man's or god's existence unfolds in every moment of action or is depicted during a specific and variable moment of "becoming". From the beginning, the Greeks were aware of this profoundly important difference. They were thus able to endow the sculptural relief with the special character to which it was obviously most effectively suited and, at the same time, to reveal another aspect of man and the world he lives in. That is why it would be a mistake to conclude that the reliefs are a mere technical variation of the same theme.

Pedimental sculptures

There are two categories of sculptural relief: architectural groups and single pieces. Of the second category there are again two subdivisions: funerary and votive reliefs. The architectural sculptures which embellished the buildings of ancient Greece with matchless works of art were executed by outstanding artists who did not hesitate to try out the most daring innovations. Among the architectural sculptures, those adorning the pediments of temples occupy an important place in the history of art. Set at the highest point of the temple, and usually possessing considerable depth, pedimental sculptures were executed in very high relief in order that they might be properly viewed and appreciated by the onlooker below. Sculptors consequently resorted to the use of increasingly higher relief. Finally the reliefs themselves were replaced by statues sculptured in the round, although they were never seen as such. The sculptor, like the onlooker, invariably saw the figures on the pediment, with backs attached —at least, optically— to the tympanum of the pediment which possessed the same function as that of the flat surface of the plaque on which the other type of reliefs were carved. Pedimental sculptures do not therefore consist of groups or assemblies of statues carved in the round and placed at the highest point of the temple, but of compositions conceived and executed in obedience to the fundamental principles of sculpture in relief. Free-standing ornamental sculptures placed as *akroteria* on the three apices of the pediment were executed, as a rule, on the same principles.

Remains of the pedimental compositions and *akroteria* from two important 4th century B.C. temples, now in the National Archaeological Museum, give us a good idea of the artistic trends prevailing at the time no longer in isolated (and not necessarily representational) works, but boldly inspired sculptural groups which effectively breathed new life into old themes and whose creators resorted to the most daring innovations. An entire hall is filled with the pedimental sculptures and some *akroteria* from the temple of Asklepios at Epidauros. We know that they are the work of four sculptors, two of whom were Timotheos and Hectoridas. We also know that Timotheos was an Athenian, probably an apprentice in the work-shop of Agorakritos. The *Amazonomachia* (battle of the Amazons) of the west pediment is outstanding for the dramatic quality of its composition, for its striking groupings of figures, its astonishing innovations in relation to modes of expression, and its echoes of remote mythological events. It is yet another contribution made by the Attic workshop whose creative influence extended beyond the boundaries of Athens itself. Beside the fragmentary figures of the pedimental sculptures are the charming equestrian Nereids, Aurai and Nikai (from the *akroteria)* with their light, dignified and elegant movements (fig. 75.) These works seem to advance the achievements of 5th century B.C. sculpture another step forward, without in any way effecting the precise decorative function they were originally intended to fulfil.

From Epidauros Timotheos went to Halikarnassos, where he worked on the Mausoleum, the greatest monument of the century. There he must have met Skopas, one of the most inspired sculptors of the age, who is generally believed to have been responsible for some of the sculptural reliefs carved on the Mausoleum. The only sculptures which can be ascribed with any degree of certainty to

Skopas, however, are those of the pediments of the temple of Athena Alea at Tegea, where he worked on his return from Halikarnassos, decorating the west pediment with a representation of the battle between Telephos and Achilles and the east with that of the Hunt of the Kalydonian Boar. The only surviving fragments of the pedimental figures now displayed in the National Archaeological Museum are the boar itself and a few heads which are animated by a feeling of deep passion and interior strength. In the following words, Sir John Beazley has not only given these sculptures the importance due to them as works of art, but also appreciated their historical significance. "The massive heads with their thickish features and the fury in their deepset eyes are the opposite of everything Praxitelean, and remind us that there was another kind of Greek left besides the cultivated Athenian —especially in Arkadia. Such were not all but most of the men who fought against the Macedonian and for him, who swarmed over the east and north, and who brought not only Greek culture, but Greek valour and resolution, wherever they went."

Attic gravestones of the Archaic period

The funerary monuments executed in relief play a very important role in the history of Greek art. Closely linked with the life of the ancient Greeks, they clearly reflect the changes which occurred in the social structure and intellectual and spiritual attitudes of the people. The National Archaeological Museum possesses a prolific collection of funerary reliefs ranging from the early Archaic age to the end of the Hellenistic period, and beyond, to the late Roman times. The collection consists of reliefs from almost every part of Greece, and in particular from Attica, where the tradition continued almost unbroken. It was the Attic model of funerary relief, too, that was finally adopted throughout the rest of the Hellenic world.

The history of the gravestones is a long one, and its origins lie in the Prehistoric period. The function of a simple stone plaque raised on a tomb was to serve as a "sign" or mark — in modern parlance, one might almost say to serve as a "signpost". Evidence of this function rests in the Greek word "σῆμα" (a sign, marker). Plaques of this kind have been found in tombs of the Middle Helladic period. The gravestones raised on the royal shaft graves at Mycenae possessed a more striking character. They had in fact acquired a monumental aspect. After the end of the Mycenaean age and the subsequent period of decline we find small undecorated plaques set up on tombs, whose position they served to indicate. But in the 7th century B.C. two very important features were added to the gravestones: an inscription with the name of the deceased and a representation of his figure. Although they first appeared separately, both features served the same end. Originally there would be a simple inscription with the name of the deceased. This simple plaque thus became the bearer of a more concrete message. It indicated not only the position of the tomb, but also who was buried in it. The representation of the figure of the deceased transformed the "sign" into a "memorial". Henceforward the funerary monument was to acquire a special character of its own both in the history of art and the social history of ancient Greece.

In the early Archaic period the gravestone consisted of a tall oblong fairly thick stele terminating in a capital, surmounted by a sphinx, the daemon guardian of both the tomb and the deceased. On the face of the stele, the deceased, generally a youth, would be depicted in low relief striking a characteristically manly pose as an athlete or hoplite. He was generally naked and often held a weapon identifying him as an hoplite. As a rule he was depicted advancing to the right. An image of aristocratic sobriety, he stood alone on his memorial, "ideal in his grief" as the poet Cavafy says. His youthful vigour and beauty were invariably idealised. Sometimes a brief epigram described his origins and the cause of his death. Not a few of these stelai were genuine sculptural masterpieces executed by the most able sculptors. A precious fragment of one of these stelai, the incomparable head of the Discophoros (the discus-bearer) (fig. 62), dated to c. 550 B.C., was no doubt the work of the sculptor who executed the "Peplos Kore" and the Rampin Horseman of the Athenian acropolis. The stele of Aristion (fig. 64), in which the figure of a hoplite is carved with a remarkable feeling for plasticity, is the work of Aristokles, a sculptor whose name is known from other works executed by him in the one but last decade of the 6th century B.C. The stele of the "Running Hoplite" (fig. 63), unique in both its shape and representation, is a work of such delicate modelling, such elegant conception, that if it was not executed by Antenor himself, the outstanding sculptor of the late Archaic period, it must surely be attributed to some member of his work-shop.

Gravestones from other parts of Greece

During the first half of the 5th century B.C. no further stelai were raised in Attica: probably as a result of some proscriptive law passed by Kleisthenes. But the tradition was preserved in other parts of Greece, and the works executed by non-Attic sculptors were not without artistic merit. The shape of the stelai remained basically the same, but there was a decisive change in the representation of the figure carved in relief. The stele no longer showed a young athlete or hoplite —lone, dignified and invariably handsome. Men of mature age, leaning on a staff as they turned to play with their faithful dog at their feet, are represented in a whole series of stelai executed in the islands. The stele of Alxenor is a good example of this category, and the inscription eloquently describes its significance and the pride the sculptor felt in his work, when we read, "Alxenor the Naxian made me. Admire me". The subject of another stele of a very slightly later date is unique. A provincial work, of Akarnanian provenance, devoid of the finished workmanship associated with other Greek sculptures, it nevertheless indicates the extent to which the influence exercised by the great art centres had spread. Again the deceased is represented as a man of mature years; a *himation* thrown over his shoulder, his head raised, he plays on a lyre which he holds in his left hand. The young man represented in a later stele, found at Larisa, has a less sophisticated air; he is more rooted to his fertile Thessalian soil. The drapery of a woollen garment falls in heavy folds and a *petasos* covers his head. In his right hand he holds a hare, in his left a fruit. Nothing could be more striking than the difference between this peasant of a remote province and the elegant citizens of Athens or the active landowners of Attica who breathed the stimulating air of the great capital. The same difference is observed in the buxom women of the countryside, clad in austere dowdy garments, like the figure represented on the stele of Polyxenaia and the slightly more elegant figure on the stele of Amphotto which came respectively from Larisa and Boiotia. Recalling the supremely distinguished maidens of the Cyclades, immortalised in the gravestones displayed in other museums, one realises the extent to which their grace and beauty must have been inspired by their environment, by the cool breezes and foam-crested waves of the Aegean. Any kind of comparison between them and their cumbersome graceless sisters of the mainland would indeed be a cruel one.

Attic funerary reliefs of the Classical period

Gravestones began to be raised again in Attica in the mid-5th century B.C. — or, possibly, a little later. But they now seem to belong to another world. Both the form of the stele and the subject matter of the relief have undergone a radical change. The stele is no longer a tall oblong plaque with the representation of the single figure of the deceased, but has lost height, while gaining in width. As a logical sequence of this transformation its finial has assumed the shape of a pediment instead of a palmette. Figures of women now appear beside those of men, and the deceased is no longer always depicted standing: he is sometimes seated. The deceased is accompanied by a second person, standing opposite him. This person frequently extends his hand towards the deceased in a gesture of greeting — *dexiosis* the ancient Greeks called it. The gesture most probably expresses the feeling that the living are still attached to the dead person and that this attachment has not been wholly severed by the reality of death. With the passage of time, more figures are represented on the stele; an entire family may even be seen accompanying the dead person. There is more variety in the representation of the deceased. Not only age but also social and professional status, even the actual cause of death, may be indicated or hinted at. But the deceased always preserves an air of other-worldly dignity, and his (or her) serenity is not devoid of a trace of regret for the lost world of the living.

From the purely plastic point of view, it is possible to follow the gradual process through which the figures became almost detached from the plaque. At the time of the construction of the Parthenon (430 B.C.) figures carved in relief were attached to the plaque, as the figure's thickness was minimal. Gradually, however, figures acquired an entity of their own as they were carved in increasingly high relief, until before the mid-4th century B.C. the plaque had assumed the aspect of a separate body against which the volumes of the figure, now carved almost in the round, were projected.

While this decisive change in the sculptural form of the stelai was taking place, the representation of the deceased was also being transformed into that of an "individual character". At first it was a kind of distant faraway expression, or even the actual attitude of the figure, that indicated the person to be the deceased. Later the face acquired an other-worldly air; the eyes no longer met those of the other persons; the gaze went far beyond, as though fixed on some remote and infinite void. In about the middle of the 4th century B.C. the figure appears to become increasingly isolated; sometimes it acquires a special glow and on occasion, it reaches the point of a "heroic" isolation.

Wandering through the hall of the Classical gravestones one is soon conscious of the fact that these curiously withdrawn figures emanate an atmosphere of strange beauty — the kind of beauty which is difficult to disassociate from the grief caused by death — and of a feeling of serenity akin to the attainment of eternity. In the Salamis stele (fig. 71), the young man who holds a bird in one hand seems to belong to the rarefied atmosphere of the Parthenon sculptures. He is a blood-brother of the handsome young riders of Pheidias' frieze. Some sculptor who worked on the frieze, probably a Parian, must surely have carved the face of the Salamis youth on the marble plaque. The body, though liberated and independent, gives the impression of being subject to an interior spiritual discipline.

It would not be an exaggeration to say that no gravestones achieved such classical balance and "celestial beauty" as that of the Salamis youth, had not the stele of Hegeso, which is of slightly later date, survived intact (fig. 72). "In the lines of the design, in the feeling of animation produced by the sculptured surface and in the attitudes of the two figures..." writes Christos Karouzos, "one finds a rare distinction and evident nobility. The longer one looks at this work, the more one inclines to the belief that not a single line in the design, not a single detail of the attitude of the body and arms can be changed, even to the most infinitesimal degree, without effecting a radical alteration of the whole work. One might go so far as to say that the spirit of human nobility had achieved its final and definitive form in this work."

The fact that these two works may be set apart as supreme masterpieces of Attic art does not mean that other stelai are not of the highest quality. They are all evidence that Classical art in Athens not only attained supreme heights but also expanded and embraced the whole of the social community. The spiritual wealth of the Athenians and the remarkable sensitivity of Athenian artists (both as regards conception and execution) are clearly reflected in the variety of representations carved on the stelai. At random, let us take those of Ktesileos and Theano, or the one from Piraeus in which the deceased and her servant girl are depicted, or again those of Mnesarete, of Prokles and Prokleides, and of Polyxene. They all present a different picture of the same disturbing theme, a new interpretation of the eternal tragedy of death. The series which began with two supreme masterpieces (the Salamis youth and Hegeso) may be said to come to an end with two equally fine works of the last decades of the 4th century B.C., the stelai of Ilissos (fig. 73) and of Aristonautes (fig. 74). Many archaelogists detect the hand of Scopas in the former. We have now come, as we have already observed, to the highest spiritual level, and the young in the stele of Ilissos has reached complete isolation, while his aged father gazes at him with an expression of profound sorrow, his little serving boy crouches at his feet and his dog sniffs at the ground. The young man's state of complete nudity, which permits the sculptor to give a perfect finish to his body, together with the youth's expression and attitude, combine to raise the figure to "heroized" stature. In the stele of Aristonautes the deceased hoplite, depicted all alone against the deep background of a temple-shaped edifice, advances impetuously across the uneven ground. Sorrowfully he seems to watch some passer by — or perhaps only gazing into infinity, "beyond this earth and men" (G. Seferis). With the close of the 4th century B.C. the history of Attic gravestones comes to an end. Once again a law, this time passed by Demetrios Phalereus (317-307 B.C.), proscribed the raising funerary monuments. Assuming different forms, they were now confined to modest little columns, insignificant stelai or works remarkable only for their ostentation and pomposity.

Votive reliefs

The second category of single pieces of relief sculpture consists of the votive ones; and there is a large collection of these ranging from the early Classical to the late Hellenistic periods in the National Archaeological Museum. The upper part of a stele found at Sounion shows a young athlete crowning himself (fig. 70). The stele, which depicted a nude youth, is a striking example of Attic scuplture of the Severe Style, and it foreshadows the figures of the Parthenon frieze. The "Melos discus" on which the head of Aphrodite is depicted in profile is absolutely unique. The admirable profile of the goddess is the work (dated to 460 B.C.) of a great Parian sculptor who, combining an extraordinarily sensitive execution of the curves with a delicately carved relief, succeded in conveying the essence of exquisite feminity.

But the most impressive of all the votive sculptures of the Classical period is the large Eleusinian relief in which Demeter is depicted presenting Triptolemos with the precious ears of corn, while Persephone crowns him (fig. 69). The majesty of the figures, their god-like austerity and the profound religious quality of the scene are superbly rendered. The conception underlying the composition of the relief, the nobility and fullness of the lines and volumes, the perfect harmony of the folds of drapery are a revelation of what Attic artists were capable of accomplishing in Classical times, in the age of the Parthenon.

A votive offering sculptured on both sides dedicated to Hermes and the Nymphs, which was found at Neon Phaleron, once the deme of Echelidai, where the hippodrome of ancient Athens lay, is dated to the late 5th century B.C. On one side it shows the pair of heroes, Echelos and Basile, riding a chariot, in front of which stands Hermes himself (fig. 76). On the other side are representations of Artemis, Kephisos, horned in the manner of river gods, and three Nymphs. The work is notable for the liveliness and grace of the figures and its superb sculptural finish.

The curtain comes down on the 5th century B.C. with the Peloponnesian War. Disease, destruction and slaughter were now the lot of the Greeks. The great gods of antiquity no longer possessed the attributes required to offer solace to a people faced with so many problems. Men's hearts began to warm increasingly to Asklepios, a forgotten provincial deity, a simple healer and philanthropist.

First at Epidauros, then in Athens and other parts of the Hellenic world, the sanctuaries of Asklepios were crowded with worshippers in search of medical treatment. The fame of Asklepios' miraculous "healing remedies", soon spread throughout the country and his faithful worshippers presented him with countless votive offerings. A hall in the National Archaeological Museum is entirely filled with reliefs from the Athenian Asklepieion which was situated on the southern slope of the Acropolis. The god is generally depicted leaning on a stick, accompanied by two of his daughters, Hygeia and Iaso, and sometimes also by others like Akeso and Panakeia, whose names have a clearly therapeutic connotation. The worshippers, bearing offerings of animals or fruits, include men and women of every social class. In one of the votive offerings a cart-driver is represented; from the inscription we learn that he was saved by the god.

Similar reliefs from the great sanctuary of Asklepios at Epidauros, displayed in another hall, provide further evidence of the power exercised in the 4th century B.C. over men's minds by the figure of this benign god and of the faith he must have inspired in all those pilgrims who flocked to his sanctuaries laden with rather costly votive offerings. The offerings of the poorer people consisted of clay objects or wooden tablets which were hung on the walls of the sanctuary buildings. Such tablets were found in the cave of Pitsa near Corinth (fig. 49) and constitute unique and consequently precious specimens of Archaic painting. An idea of what one of these sanctuaries may have looked like can be obtained in a hall in the National Archaeological Museum. In the centre stands an altar dedicated by the Athenian Boule in c. 210 B.C. to Aphrodite Hegemone and the Charites. Statuettes and reliefs of every kind and every period are placed around it. Among these are two reliefs: one of Hermes and the Nymphs dated to 460 B.C. discovered in a cave on Mt. Pentelikon; another of the late 4th century B.C. in which Hermes and the Nymphs are again depicted, accompanied this time by Pan playing on his *syrinx*. There is also a Roman relief of allegorical figures depicted in a garden which was discovered on the site of Herodes Atticus' villa at Loukou in Kynouria. The hall is furthermore filled, just like the great or small sanctuaries once were, with an enormous and confused collection of statuettes and reliefs of Pan, of Herakles, Zeus and Aphrodite.

Portraiture

All the works so far examined, including certain specific depictions of figures in the funerary sculptures, clearly reveal the artist's idealistic conception of his subject, which prevented him from rendering personal facial traits: in other words, from creating a genuine portrait. In the course of the 4th century B.C., however, one finds that certain figures go beyond the established "type" and may be considered to be representations of specific persons. The National Archaeological Museum possesses an outstanding example: the bronze boxer from Olympia (fig. 83). Without departing from the established "type", the sculptor succeeded in rendering the individual features of an actual person; more important, he managed to model the boxer's features, which possess all the coarse characteristics associated with a man of his profession, amid a mass of thick hair, beard and moustaches.

Another bronze head, known as the Philosopher of Antikythera, is an example of the outcome of this trend in the Hellenistic era (fig. 84). In this work every trace of the old idealism has vanished; the man's personal features are revealed in his face, and the modelling is executed in such a way that the flabby flesh, untidy hair and wrinkled face are all very carefully rendered. The eyes seem to reflect the man's profound and restless contemplation of the world; his lips appear to be ready to speak. The last stage of Hellenistic portraiture is represented by a remarkable bronze head of a man found at Delos (fig. 85). The longer one looks at it the better one is able to distinguish all the adventures through which Greek art had gone. The expression of the man's face epitomizes his anxieties: the uncertainty, the sense of emptiness and anguish caused by something he has lost, by something he seeks beyond this world.

Henceforward sculptured portaits become increasingly popular and during the Roman period countless portraits of emperors and high-ranking officers were executed not only in Rome itself but in every part of the far-flung empire. The National Archaeological Museum possesses an important collection of these sculptured portraits which are of considerable interest both to scholars of the Roman period and to amateurs anxious to cover the entire span of ancient sculpture.

Hellenistic sculpture

In this introductory review of the sculptural works in the National Archaeological Museum the examination of Hellenistic sculptures has been left to the end. The reason for their apparent disassociation from the rest of Greek sculpture lies in the fact that the products of the Hellenistic period cannot be included in any of the established categories and that in their great variety, which lacks definition, they reflect the countless trends, demands and requirements of the people who created them. Besides the portraits of ordinary mortals, statues of gods, now depicted on a colossal dimensional scale, continued to be executed. Among the most impressive works are the heads and other fragments of the cult statues of Despoine, Demeter, Artemis and the giant Anytos from Lykosoura in Arkadia, executed by Damophon, a famous 2nd century B.C. sculptor, as well as the head of Zeus from Aigeira in Achaia, an admirable example of the period. Other figures of gods, such as the Poseidon of Melos (fig. 87) and the Aphrodite with Pan of Delos (fig. 88) illustrate how remote is the age when faith filled men's hearts. The pompous attitude of Poseidon and the sugary feminity of Aphrodite seem to have less in common with the deities themselves than with actors impersonating them. And just as the hearts of men are now devoid of faith so are the structure and modelling of the figures drained of their former divine force.

Hellenistic artists were not incapable, however, of creating some powerful and attractive works. The statuette depicting the figure of a little boy holding a goose (3rd century B.C.), found on the northern foothills of Mt. Parnassos in ancient Lilaia, possesses a freshness which strikes a very different note from anything seen in earlier Greek art. The boy has a charming smile, the flesh of the body is soft and tender and the air of seriousness which distinguishes the attitude of the figure is not without an attractive quality. The so-called "little refugee" which reached the National Archaeological Museum from Gerondiko near Nyssa in Asia Minor after the exodus of the Greeks in 1922 possesses the same kind of unusual charm and reflects the eternal freshness of Ionian art. Barely able to stand on its tiny feet, the child, clad in a heavy hood, clasps a dog tightly in its arms. It is not only charm, however, that characterizes Hellenistic art. The sense of power and *élan* that overwhelmed the world following the conquests of Alexander the Great is admirably reflected in the art of the period. The long voyage through Greek sculptural masterpieces is brought to a fitting conclusion by two important works: a large funerary relief and the 'jockey boy" of Artemision. A horse, an animal always popular with Greek sculptors of all ages, is depicted in both sculptures. In the relief the stubborn untamable beast, which may be favourably compared with any of the noble horses depicted on the Parthenon frieze, raises its head proudly, while a young negro groom, standing in front of it, frantically tries to control it (fig. 89). We should certainly have possessed a more flattering and accurate picture of Hellenistic art had more masterpieces of this kind survived. In the circumstances let us be thankful that the relief has been preserved, together with its bronze counterpart: the bronze horse on which the jockey boy is mounted (fig. 90) and which we are at last able to appreciate in its original completeness, as a result of the prolonged efforts made by skilful craftsmen of the National Archaeological Museum to piece it together. The youthful rider seems to be of diminutive size in relation to the enormous animal which gallops along frenziedly. The boy's face, constricted with tension, is a supreme example of realism in Hellenistic art, comparable only to the striking modelling of the horse's body and head. The unique skill displayed in the modelling of the head actually induced Ernst Buschor, a very highly esteemed scholar in Greek sculpture, to suggest that the work was one of the 5th century B.C. and place it next to the archetypal figures of the Pheidian horses. In actual fact, however, it has been established beyond doubt that the whole composition, including horse and boy, which were recovered from the sea off Cape Artemision together with the great bronze Poseidon, is a work of the Hellenistic "baroque" period of the 2nd century B.C.

Metal works
The minor arts

The National Archaeological Museum possesses a very fine collection of small-scale works in bronze. The most important is the Karapanos collection which consisted basically of bronze objects of the minor arts from the area of Dodone, although it also included works of exceptional craftsmanship from other parts of Greece. It is not easy for the modern observer to assess the true significance of the bronze works of art executed in ancient Greece owing to the fact that the greater part of the large bronzes have not been preserved and those that have indeed survived were discovered quite fortuitously, as in the case of the Piraeus statue; others, it will be remembered, were hauled up in fishermen's nets from ancient shipwrecks. The bronze objects of the minor arts thus help us to fill in the picture we have formed from an examination of the monumental sculptures. They furthermore enable us to realise that the high quality of both technique and artistic expression was not limited solely to monumental sculpture but extended to all levels of creative art throughout the Hellenic world. Many of these bronze objects, such as the rider from Dodone (fig. 94), were presented as votive offerings in sanctuaries by pious worshippers who did not possess the financial means to commission lavish statues, Some of these works, such as the weapons, cuirasses, helmets, tripods, mirrors, etc. possess a functional purpose; others formed part of the decoration of the above objects, as, for instance, the small Geometric horses, griffins and numerous small idols. The production of these objects during all periods ranging from Geometric times to late antiquity provides evidence of the sculptural skill of the Greeks even in those early times when large sculpture was as yet unknown. At the same time, the artistic form of these objects, which kept strictly in step with the continuous transformations of large sculpture, enables us assuredly to consider them as a part of the whole artistic spectrum and, consequently, to appreciate them as such.

The head of Zeus from Olympia (fig. 96), which must have formed part of some small statue of the god, is representative of the most mature achievements of Archaic art in the beginning of the 5th century B.C. A small head of a youth from the Athenian Acropolis (fig. 97), which is of a slightly later date and perhaps came from a Peloponnesian workshop, reflects the profound spiritual quality of the art of the Severe Style. The Geometric horses, which either adorned the rim or handle of cauldrons or stood alone on a separate base constitute the earliest examples of Greek sculpture (fig. 91). Their clear form and firm structure foreshadow the basic princples on which Hellenic sculpture was to develop. The Oriental origin of the griffins' heads, which adorned the rims of cauldrons (fig. 92), indicates the foreign influences to which Greek art was subject in the early 7th century B.C. The awe with which the greatest of the Olympian deities must have filled the hearts of pious worshippers is revealed in the numerous bronze idols of Zeus represented in the act of preparing to cast his thunderbolt (fig. 93). These idols were the first attempts made by craftsmen to depict the figure of the god at the moment of his mighty sypremacy. The idols of Athena Promachos (fig. 95) provide a parallel image of a deity depicted in all her martial spirit, a spear held in her raised right hand, a shield in her left, always ready to champion the cause of her beloved Athens.

There are also numerous figures of women clad in a *peplos,* supporting in their raised arms circular bronze mirrors. Aphrodite too, surrounded by her beloved doves, is represented supporting a mirror. The elegance and nobility of these idols, combined with the firm architectural solidity of their structure provide them with a unique charm; despite their small size, they attain the level of the most noteworthy sculptural achievements of the Severe Style.

Jewellery

The gold objects in the Mycenaean collection provide sufficient evidence of the fact that the goldsmith's craft was practised in Greece from the earliest times. The execution of superb ornaments wrought in metals (particularly gold) and precious stones, continued in the historical era. The National Archaeological Museum always possessed some exquisite specimens of this craft ranging over all the periods; but a recent donation made by Helen Stathatos has further enriched it with a collection of the most rare and remarkable objects. The show-cases contain every kind of precious ornament: necklaces, bracelets, earrings, pins, diadems, funerary crowns and a quantity of other objects which reveal the unique skill and sensitivity of the Greek goldsmiths. Among the most rare and unusual objects is the remarkable medallion with a female bust carved in relief, framed by a fine and delicately worked chain, which is a genuine masterpiece of the minor arts (fig. 106). Then there is a magnificent relief carved in gold in the shape of a little temple (fig. 99), in which the figure of a drunken Dionysos is represented supported by a Satyr. The base and pediment, studded with small polychrome stones, is superbly executed. The object's function remains a mystery. But whether it was costly votive gift offered to the deity of some sanctuary or a mere ornament in the house of some wealthy Greek family, it provides us with another reminder — as indeed all the other objects in the collection also do — of the wealth owned by the citizens of Greece and of their impeccable taste and refined way of life (figs. 100-107).

The Numismatic collection

The point may now have been reached when the visitor to the National Archaeological Museum, having examined such a vast variety of collections, feels a sense of surfeit. Nevertheless, it would be a mistake to omit one last collection from our review of the museum's priceless treasures: namely, the numismatic (figs. 108-120). The first Greek coins appear to have been struck in the 7th century B.C. From the outset coinage played a special role — different from that of any other object in the minor arts — for the very reason that some characteristic symbolical representations were stamped on the circular surface of the coins of each different city. We thus have representations of deities or figures with daemon-like natures, of local fruits and animals, of symbolic depictions of place names, such as a rose *(ϱόδο)* for Rhodes, an Apple *(μῆλο)* for Melos, etc. Finally, after the Classical period, we get portraits of kings. As Charles Seltman, the numismatist, has said, the Greeks possessed an irrepressible impulse to decorate every object of common use with the utmost good taste. They thus created the finest coins in the world, executed by famous craftsmen who had acquired all the experience required for working on precious metals and stones. And as the Greek city states were in the habit of frequently changing their coinage — with the notable exception of Athens — we are able to follow the stylistic development of forms — frequently in all its unbroken continuity — in a whole series of coins. An examination of the numismatic collection thus completes the picture of Greek art, as we originally conceived it, in the form of a journey, taken step by step, in all its various stages and all its different manifestations, from the dawn of prehistory to the twilight years of the ancient world.

2   3

4

2. Large clay idol. The firmly modelled male figure with its sturdy plastic volumes is an excellent example of a Thessalian idol of the early Bronze Age.

3. Vase from Dimeni. Admirable works, in which the elegant shape of the vase vies with the well-conceived intricate decoration, were produced by Thessalian potters in the last phase of the Neolithic Age.

4. Vase from Lianokladi. The skill of the potters of the earlier Neolithic Age is evident in this spherical vase with its remarkable outlines and simple yet striking decoration.

5. Stone idol from the area of Sparta. The corpulent female figure, with prominent buttocks, breasts and stomach, is a typical example of a work of the very earliest phase of the Neolithic Age (6000-5000 B.C.).

6. *Marble idol of a harpist from Keros. The firmness of the architectural structure of the figure and the intricate harmony of the curves of the volumes developed within the space in which the work is confined combine to create a unique sculptural entity. 2800-2200 B.C.*

7. *Marble idol of a flute-player from Keros. Contemporary to the idol of the harpist and of equally high quality, the work provides evidence of the skill of Cycladic artists in rendering the human figure in different and unusual attitudes. 2800-2200 B.C.*

8. *Large marble statue of a female figure from Amorgos. The primitive creator of this masterpiece of Cycladic sculpture (2800-2200 B.C.) achieves a plastic rendering of the female form by means of delicate undulating lines. The sculptural work was complemented by paint applied to the mouth, eyes and other facial features.*

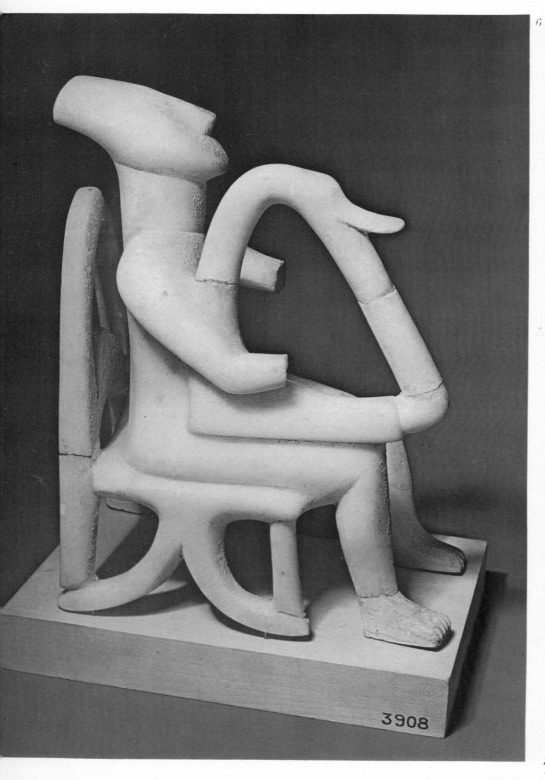

9. *Clay object in the shape of a frying-pan from Syros, with incised decoration of tangent spirals among which a ship is depicted. A very characteristic example of a large group of similar objects whose function remains unknown. 2800-2200 B.C.*

10. *Stone utensil with lid from Naxos. The artist's skill in working on stone contributes to the creation of a genuine minor work of art of great elegance. 2800-2200 B.C.*

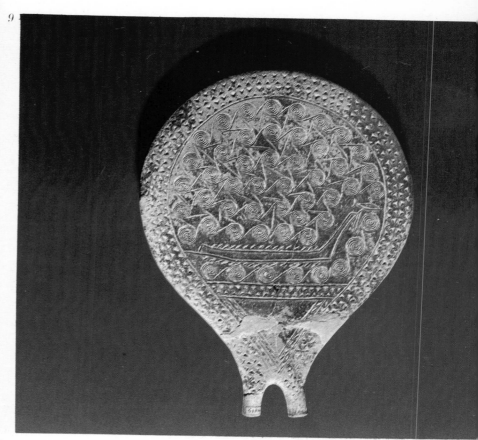

11. *The fresco of the Boxing Children from a house at Thera. Two children engage in a boxing game with an air of disarming seriousness. They wear boxing gloves (this is the earliest known representation of boxing gloves). The faultless rendering of the bodies and their movements reveal a very considerable knowledge of a child's anatomy. c. 1550 B.C.*

12. *The fresco of the Fisherman. One of the best preserved frescoes from the so-called West House at Thera depicted two fishermen, one of whom (height: slightly more than one metre) is almost wholly undamaged. Unique in Minoan art, the fisherman is represented nude. In both hands he holds his catch of fish (mackerel), the mouths of which are hooked to a piece of string.*

13. *Fresco of the Antelopes, two of which are depicted here. The composition consisted of six similar animals. The originality shown in the sketching of the animal's outlines by means of alternately wide and narrow brush strokes, the sinuous curve of the contours and the rendering of the heads and legs of the animals reveal the high artistic level attained by the artist and his thorough knowledge of his subject-matter. Provenance: Thera.*

14. *The fresco from the House of the Ladies, in which a representation of a group of three women was found, gives us an idea of the elegance and intricacy of the clothes worn by Minoan women. The 'lady' in this fresco is depicted advancing to the left; her movements are lively, and she extends her arms forward. She may have been making an offering to a female deity. Provenance: Thera.*

15. *The fresco of the Spring. Fragment of an enchanting fresco depicting a rocky site overgrown with bright red lilies. Pairs of swallows fly overhead in pursuit of their erotic games, as though intoxicated by the air of spring and the flower-scented earth. The composition is most probably associated with the performance of some spring rite. Provenance: Thera.*

15

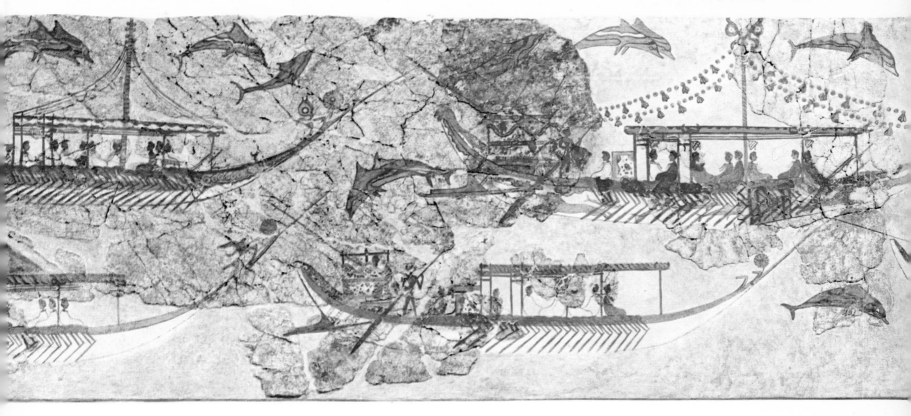

16-17. The fresco of the Naval Campaign. The most recent and astonishing discovery made in the course of the Thera excavations is a painted frieze depicting a naval expedition in room 5 of the West House (where the fresco of the Fisherman was also found). Unlike the other frescoes, in which large imposing figures are represented, this composition is executed in 'miniature style' familiar from the fresco work of the palace at Knossos. The artist's intention to create a crowded representation in the form of a continuous frieze obliged him to condense his figures in order to achieve the necessary unity and cohesion. Six metres are preserved of the entire frieze. In these we see seven warships, many smaller vessels, three cities, about eighty human figures and a number of tame and wild animals. In the sections illustrated here, we see (above) a city against the background of a hill on which a lion chases a herd of deer. The hill ends in a headland along the shore of which the ships sail in two parallel lines. Only one of the ships (below) has its sails unfurled; the others are propelled by oarsmen. In the next section (below) the ships approach another city; the buildings near the sea are discernible. This immense fresco is unique. With great sensitivity, exceptional skill in composition and the lavish use of colour, the artist (or artists) succeeded in rendering a pictorial description so effortlessly and professionally that it may have been intended to represent some specific historical event.

18

19

20

18. *Rhomboidal gold sheet with seven lance-shaped laminae found in Grave III of Grave Circle A at the acropolis of Mycenae. It must have crowned the head of the young woman buried in the grave. 16th century B.C.*

19. *Hexagonal wooden pyxis covered with plates of gold with embossed decoration. A mesh-work of spirals alternates with scenes of lions chasing deer in a boscage. Found in Grave V of Grave Circle A at the acropolis of Mycenae. 16th century B.C.*

20. *Gold funerary mask which Schlieman believed to be that of Agamemnon. It is the most characteristic of the masks found at Mycenae, and the facial features of the Achaian king buried in Grave V of Grave Circle A are rendered very realistically. 16th century B.C.*

21

22

21, 22. The two gold cups with decoration in embossed relief, found in a tholos tomb at Vapheio in Lakonia, are masterpieces of Mycenaean goldwork. The capture of a bull in a net, which has been spread between two trees, is depicted on one cup, an idyllic scene with cattle on the other. 15th century B.C.

23. Silver rhyton in the shape of a bull's head. The horns and rosette on the forehead are of gold. This magnificent example of the Mycenaean goldsmith's art is comparable to the rhyta, also in the shape of bull's heads, of Minoan Crete. Found in Grave IV of Grave Circle A at the acropolis of Mycenae. 16th century B.C.

23

24. *Gold sword-handle (length: 0.24 m.). The fact that this is the largest of all preserved Mycenaean sword-handles indicates that the blade must also have been of unusual length. Found in a Mycenaean grave (1500 B.C.) at the site Staphylos on the island of Scopelos. According to an ancient legend, the island was colonized by Staphylos, an associate of Rhadamanthys, brother of Minos.*

25. *Bronze dagger with elaborate gold handle inlaid with cyanus and rock-crystal in a combination of the cloisonné and à jour techniques. The covering of the handle is in the form of two snake-dragons whose heads face each other on the shoulder of the blade. Found in Grave IV of Grave Circle A at the acropolis of Mycenae. 16th century B.C.*

26-31. *Small bronze daggers with inlaid gold, silver and niello decoration. The daggers Nos. 26, 27, 30, 31 were found in graves of Grave Circle A at Mycenae and are dated to the 16th century B.C. Nos. 28 and 29 come from the tholos tomb at Myrsinochorion, Pylos, dated to c. 1500 B.C. The technical skill and sensitivity shown in the rendering of violent hunting scenes, the sinuous decorative spirals and depictions of marine creatures unquestionably place these objects in the class of genuine masterpieces of the minor arts.*

24

25

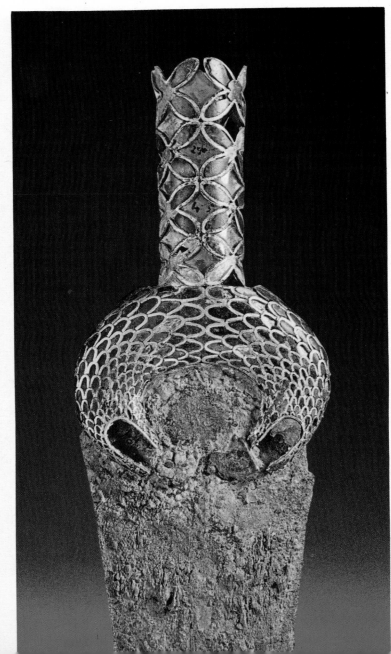

26

27

28

29

30

31

32. *Gold rhyton in the shape of a lion's head. It comes from Grave IV of Grave Circle A at the acropolis of Mycenae (16th century B.C.). This work, unlike others in which Minoan influences are strikingly evident, is rendered unique by the austere geometric modelling of the head, the stylization of the eyes and muzzle and the cleanly-cut surfaces.*

33. *Gold signet-ring from the 'Tiryns treasure'. Lion-headed daemons are represented advancing towards the goddess, bearing ewers for the libation. The goddess raises a calyx-shaped vessel which is commonly encountered in ritual scenes. The rite is associated with an invocation for fertility. 15th century B.C.*

34. *Gold seal-stone. A male figure is depicted in combat with a lion. From Grave Circle A, at the acropolis of Mycenae. 16th century B.C.*

35. *Gold head of a silver pin. The figure of a woman is represented holding a foliate symbol. Found in Grave III of Grave Circle A at the acropolis of Mycenae. 16th century B.C.*

36. *Vessel of rock-crystal in the shape of a duck. The finish given to the work is of outstanding quality. The rendering of the bird's neck and head and the exceptional delicacy of the carving of the curved line raise the object to the level of a masterpiece of sculpture in stone. Found in Grave O of Grave Circle B at Mycenae. 16th century B.C.*

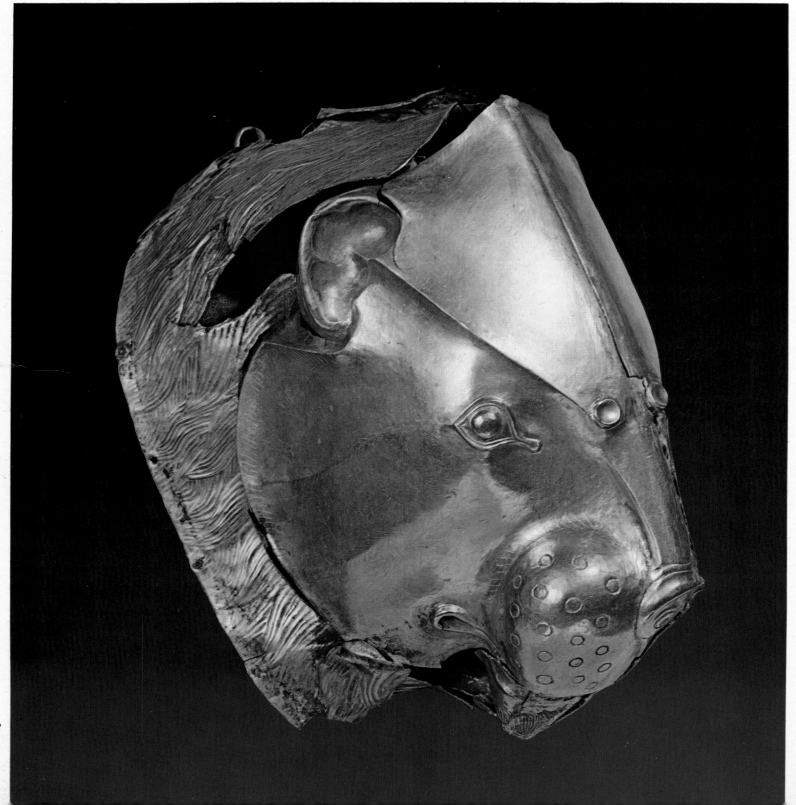

33

34

35

36

37. *Ivory head of a warrior carved in relief. The warrior wears the usual Mycenaean helmet, the exterior of which was reinforced with boar's tusks. There was a rivet hole for the attachment of a crest at the top of the helmet. It comes from a chamber tomb of the lower city of Mycenae. 13th century B.C.*

38. *Masterpiece of Mycenaean minor sculpture in ivory. Two women are depicted embracing each other. One of them holds an· infant in her arms. The identity of the persons depicted in the group remains an enigma. It has been suggested—somewhat rashly, perhaps— that the group is a very early representation of Demeter, Persephone and the young god, Iakchos. Other scholars associate the group with the myth of the orphan child nursed by two female deities. The belief that it was a representation with a religious significance is supported by the fact that it was found in the area of the repository of the sanctuary of Mycenae. 13th century B.C.*

39. *Rare specimen of Mycenaean sculpture. Limestone head of a woman whose features are not only rendered plastically, but also painted with bright colours. Some archaeologists believe it to be the head of a sphinx. It was found in a house south of Grave Circle A at the acropolis of Mycenae. 13th century B.C.*

40

40. *The famous Warrior Vase, in the shape of a krater, is unique in Mycenaean vase-painting. Mycenaean hoplites are depicted marching in phalanx (probably on their way to battle). Behind them a female figure raises one hand in a gesture of farewell. The subject-matter and character of the figures are wholly Mycenaean, devoid of any Minoan influences. One might say that the work is a remote ancestor of 7th century B.C. Greek vase-painting. The krater was found in a house south of Grave Circle A at the acropolis of Mycenae. c. 1200 B.C.*

41. *Fragment of a fresco, labelled the Mycenaean Woman, found in 1970 by Professor G. Mylonas in a house built within the west wall of the Mycenaean acropolis. It is the finest example of Mycenaean painting known to us. The firm design, the lavish colours and, above all, the originality shown in the rendering of the dignified figure are unique in Creto-Mycenaean painting. Dated to the last years of the 13th century B.C.*

41

42. *Monumental Geometric amphora from the Dipylon Gate of the Kerameikos. The architecture and general organisation of the parts are faultlessly executed. The decoration, based on variations of the meander pattern, is both lavish and a perfect expression of Geometric art. The prothesis (lying-in-state of the dead) is depicted in a band between the handles. The vase was placed on a tomb as a funerary monument. 760-750 B.C.*

43. *Monumental krater from the Dipylon Gate of the Kerameikos. Like the amphora reproduced in fig. 42, it was placed on a tomb as a funerary monument. Geometric decoration is strictly restricted. The carrying out of the corpse to burial on a carriage, followed by the deceased's friends and relations, is depicted on the main band, a procession of chariots on the lower one. 740 B.C.*

44. *Amphora from Melos. The representation on the neck shows two warriors in combat. A suit of armour is depicted between them. On either side stand two female figures, possibly the mothers of the combatants. Apollo is represented mounted on a chariot drawn by winged horses on the body of the vase. He holds the kithara with seven strings in his left hand and the plektron in his right. Behind him are two female figures, probably the Hyperborean virgins. He is greeted by Artemis, who stands in front of the chariot, leading a stag by her right hand and holding a bow in her left hand. 625-620 B.C.*

42

43

44

45

45. *The Nessos amphora, found at the Dipylon Gate of the Kerameikos, is one of the earliest black-figure vases. The combat between Herakles and the Centaur Nessos is depicted on the neck. The body is decorated with a representation of the legend of Medusa's decapitation by Perseus and the pursuit of the latter by her sisters, Euryale and Stheno, flying over Ocean. 620 B.C.*

46,47,48. *Sculptured vases in which human faces are depicted. The fact that Athenian vase-painters created a large number of similar works in the late 6th and early 5th centuries B.C. provides indisputable evidence of the great influence exercised by large sculpture over the artists who worked at the Kerameikos.*

49. *Wooden votive tablet found, together with other similar ones, in the cave of Pitsa, near Corinth. A rare specimen of Greek painting in the Archaic period (540 B.C.), it represents a sacrificial scene. To the right is the altar which the worshippers approach with their offerings. A small boy leads the sacrificial animal (a lamb). All the participants are crowned with garlands in accordance with ritual ceremony. The two youthful figures immediately behind the boy play on a kithara and a flute; the others hold branches.*

46, 47, 48.   49

69

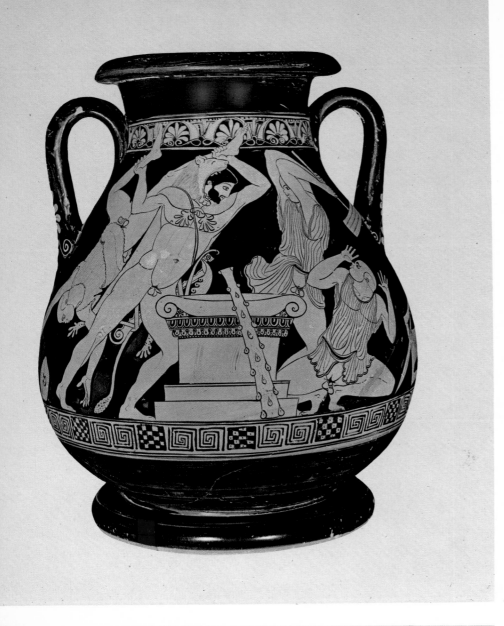

50

51

50. *Red-figure pelike, the work of the so-called 'Pan painter', decorated with a depiction of the tragic-comic episode in which Herakles slays Bousiris and his panic-stricken attendants in Egypt. Superb specimen of the period of the severe style. 470 B.C.*

51. *Red-figure calyx krater, the work of the so-called 'Syriskos painter'. On one side Theseus is represented with the Minotaur in the Labyrinth; on the other, the sons of Pandion, king of Attica, Pallas, Nisos and Lykos (brothers of Aegeus) and the son of Erechtheus, Orneus, all holding royal sceptres. 470 B.C.*

52. *Red-figure stamnos, the work of the vase-painter Polygnotos, whose creations are assigned to around 425 B.C. A young man, holding two javelins, pursues a female figure (Theseus and Helen?). A charioteer is depicted about to mount a chariot.*

53. *Panathenaic amphora. On the front side an inscription records the name of the archon Kallimedes (360/59 B.C.). A wrestling match is depicted.*

54. *The epinetron of Eretria. This curious product of the potter's craft was worn by women on their thigh (the fore part was adjusted to the knee) for spinning wool. The epinetron shown here is ascribed to the so-called 'Eretria painter' (c. 425 B.C.). Alkestis is depicted in her bridal chamber, while her sister-in-law, Hippolyte, accompanied by her sister, Asterope, plays with a bird. Behind them other women place flowers in nuptial vases. The work is one of the most elegant examples of red-figure vase-painting of the late 5th century B.C.*

55. *White-ground lekythos. In front of the funerary stele, the tall base of which consists of six steps, stands a young spearman wearing a chlamys. Lekythoi and garlands are placed on the steps. The mound itself is visible behind the stele. The young man is dead. Time and space have no reality in the white-ground lekythoi; all is confused in a kind of other-wordly unity. The work is by the so-called 'Bosanquet painter'. c. 440 B.C.*

56. *White-ground lekythos found at Eretria. The dead man, depicted as a warrior, wearing a chlamys, sits wearily on the base of the stele, using the two upright spears beside him as support. A woman and a young man flank the central figure of the deceased who dominates the scene. The freely and easily drawn line of the design succeeds in conveying the sense of weariness felt by the dead warrior who finds himself alone and abandoned in a realm beyond the terrestrial world he knows. The work is one of the last in the series of white-ground lekythoi of the late 5th century B.C. and is ascribed to the 'R' group associated with a masterly vase-painter, the so-called 'Reed painter'.*

57. *White-ground lekythos bearing the representation of a female figure (not apparent in the plate), Charon and Hermes. The work is by the so-called 'Sabouroff painter', one of the outstanding vase-painters of white-ground lekythoi, and a contemporary of Pheidias.*

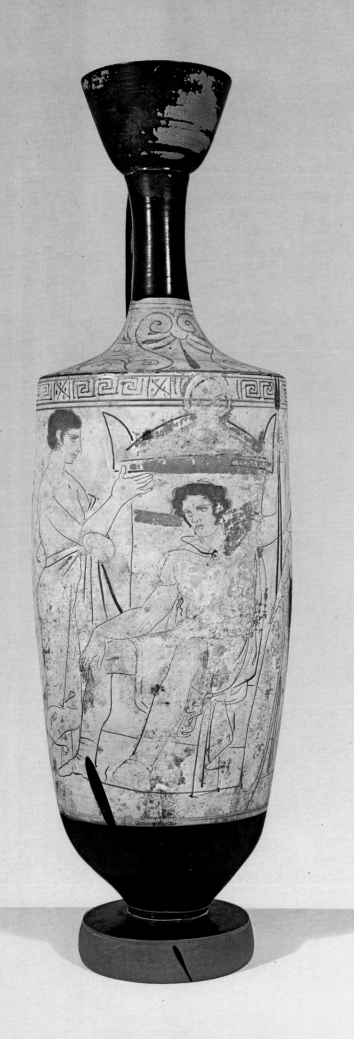

58. *The Dipylon Head, which formed part of a statue of the earliest Attic Kouros (620-610 B.C.). The severe geometric shape, the wide forehead and bead-shaped locks of hair provide the work with an austere charm.*

59. *Funerary Kouros, known as the Kouros of Volomandra (after the site in Attica where the statue was found). The work is representative of the mature phase of 6th century B.C. Attic sculpture.*

60. *Funerary Kouros, whose name we learn from the inscription on the base was Kroisos. The statue was found at Anavyssos in Attica. 525 B.C.*

61. *Funerary Kouros, whose name, as recorded by the inscription on the base, was Aristodikos; also found at Anavyssos. The work is the last in the series of great Attic Kouroi and the terminal point reached by Archaic sculptors. 500 B.C.*

58

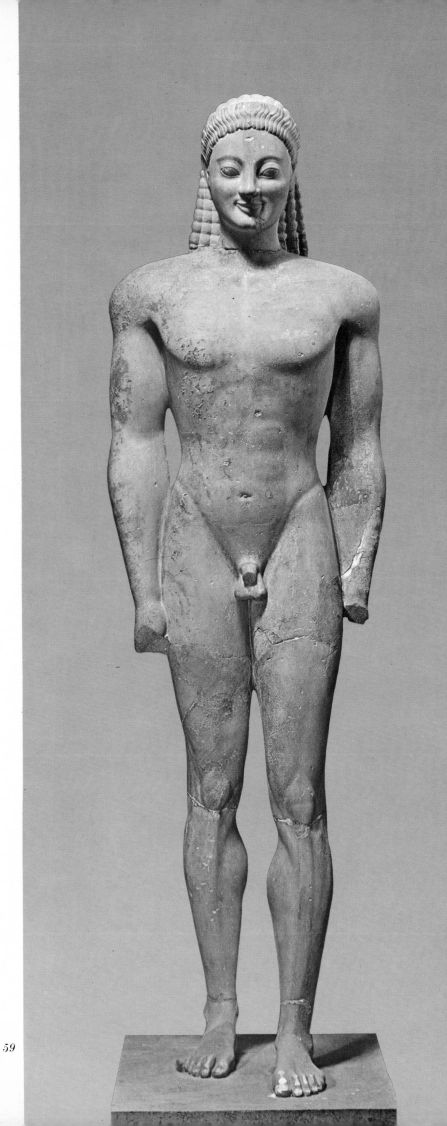

59

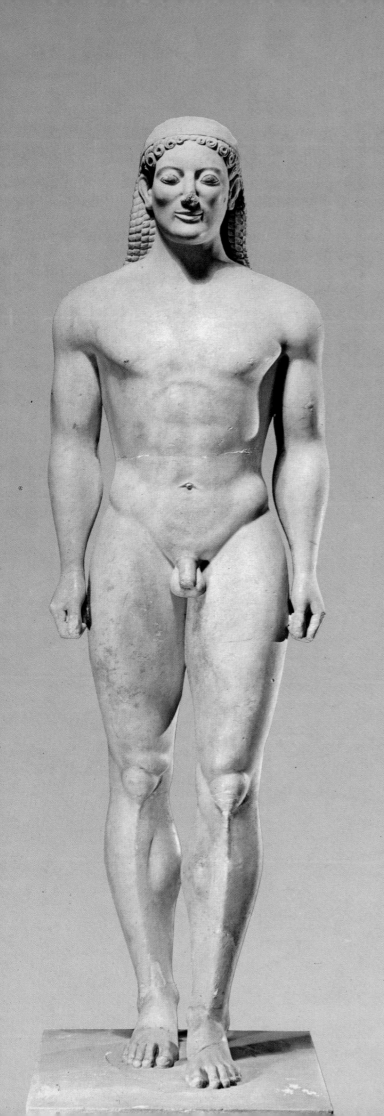
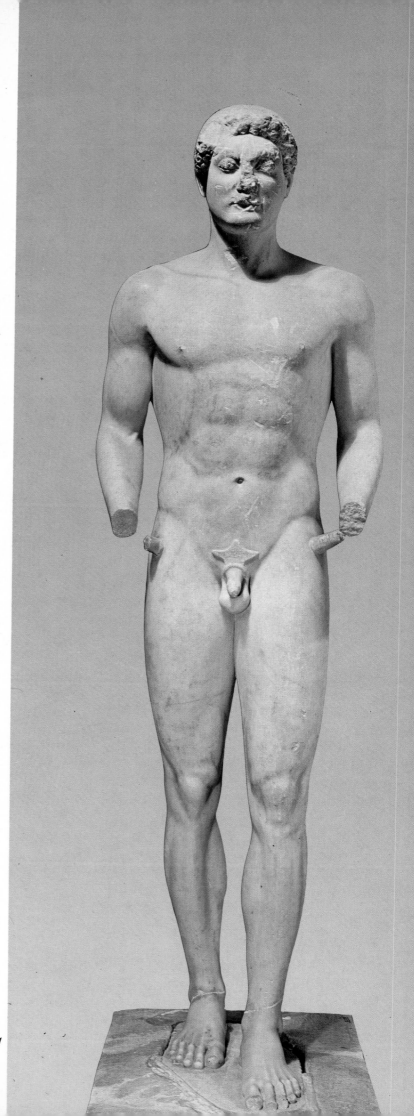

61

62

63

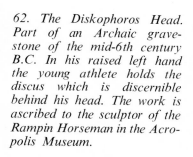

62. *The Diskophoros Head. Part of an Archaic grave-stone of the mid-6th century B.C. In his raised left hand the young athlete holds the discus which is discernible behind his head. The work is ascribed to the sculptor of the Rampin Horseman in the Acropolis Museum.*

63. *The stele of the Running Hoplite. An unusual work depicting a nude helmeted young man in the act of running. The work must have formed part of a funerary monument and was probably surmounted by a palmette. 510 B.C.*

64. *The stele of Ariston, 'the work of Aristokles' as recorded by the inscription on the base; one of the best preserved Attic stelai of the Archaic period. It must have been crowned by a palmette. The dead man is depicted as a warrior. 510 B.C.*

65. *The Piraeus Apollo, the earliest bronze statue in Greek sculpture. In his left hand the god held a bow; in his right a phiale (a vessel like a bowl) for the libation he was about to offer. A superb example of mature Archaic art. 525 B.C.*

66. *Base of an Archaic statue of a Kouros, found built into the Themistoklean wall (478 B.C.). Representations of young athletes are carved in relief on three sides. On the side reproduced in fig. 66 six athletes are depicted playing a ball game in teams of three each. The figure on the left-hand edge of the relief holds the ball which he is about to throw. The low relief carving set against a painted red ground gives the work a charming pictorial quality. 500 B.C.*

67. *Base of a statue found, like the one reproduced in fig. 66, built into the Themistoklean wall. Again the base is carved with representations in relief on three sides. On the middle side young men play a game which looks like hockey. On the two other sides are depictions of a procession of chariots and hoplites (reproduced in fig. 67). This work, too, was executed in low relief and the ground was painted red. 490 B.C.*

68. *The Poseidon of Artemision. This magnificent bronze statue was found at the bottom of the sea-bed near Cape Artemision, Northern Euboia. The arm was first discovered in 1926, and the rest of the statue, together with the jockey boy of the Hellenistic period (see fig. 90), in 1928. The god is represented at the moment when he raises his right arm with tremendous force in order to hurl the trident against an adversary, while the left arm and hand are stretched out straight to direct the throw (some archaeologists believe the representation to be one of Zeus about to cast a thunderbolt). The plastic rendering of the god's body, depicted in an attitude of extreme tension, and the forceful expression of the face, which possesses a genuine spiritual quality, combine to create a matchless masterpiece, executed by some very great sculptor in bronze of the last years of the severe style (460-450 B.C.). Art historians believe the sculptor to have been Kalamis.*

66

67

126

69. *The great Eleusinian votive relief offered by some wealthy initiate in the Mysteries. To the left, Demeter holds her divine sceptre in her raised left hand; in her right hand she holds the ears of corn which she is about to present to Triptolemos, the young king of Eleusis. The nude youth strikes a heroic attitude as he stands in front of the goddess and respectfully raises his right hand to receive the precious gift. Behind him, to the right, stands Kore (Persephone), holding her divine attribute, a tall taper, and raises her right hand to crown the young hero, fully conscious that he is worthy of the great mission entrusted to him. The work is a masterpiece of Attic sculpture of the Classical period. 430-420 B.C.*

70. *Votive stele found near the temple of Athena at Sounion. A nude ephebe raises his right hand to crown himself after winning a victory in an athletic contest. A particularly fine example of Attic sculpture of the early Classical period. 460-450 B.C.*

71. *Upper part of an Attic gravestone. A young man, his well-built chest bare, a himation thrown over his left shoulder, holds a bird in his left hand and raises his right arm towards a cage. A cat sits on the summit of a stele below the cage. In front of the stele stands a nude serving boy gazing mournfully before him. The spirit of great artistic creation which distinguished the supreme moment in Attic sculpture, as witnessed in the Parthenon sculptures, is reflected in this sepulchral memorial. All art historians agree that the stele must have been executed by a great artist who worked on the Parthenon sculptures.*

70

71

72. *The epistyle of the pedimental finial of this much-admired gravestone bears the inscription* Ἡγησὼ Προξένου *(Hegeso, wife or daughter, of Proxenos). The young and dignified Hegeso is seated on a beautifully-wrought chair with back, her feet resting on a footstool. In front of her stands her maid-servant, holding a pyxis filled with jewels, one of which Hegeso singles out. The empty space between the two figures, which one can imagine to have been painted blue, conveys an impression of celestial isolation, of an immortality akin to eternity. 410 B.C.*

73. *The stele of Ilisos. To the left a young man, almost entirely nude, leans against a stele with a two-tiered base, holding a lagobolon (club for flinging at hares), and gazes into space. To the right stands an elderly man, clad in a himation, supported by a stick, resting his chin on the palm of his right hand and staring at the young man, surely his son, with an expression of indescribable grief. At the young hunter's feet, his dog snuffs the ground, while his little serving boy crouches on the base of the stele, his head resting on his knees. The work is an outstanding example of the last phase of Attic gravestones. The melancholy isolation of the young man who seems to gaze beyond space itself cannot be anything less than an expression of the creative genius of a great sculptor of the 4th ecntury B.C.—possibly, in the opinion of some scholars, Skopas. 340 B.C.*

74. *A funerary temple-shaped little edifice, the memorial of Aristonautes. The inscription on the epistyle of the pedimental finial reads:* Ἀριστοναύτης Ἀρχεναύτου Ἁλαιεύς. *The unknown sculptor, inspired by his dramatic subject-matter, has succeeded, by means of creating new plastic forms, in achieving a total expression of the pain of death and of the complete isolation of the deceased. The figure's violent movement beyond the confines of the temple-shaped edifice seems to surpass the limits of space as conceived by Classical artists. 320-310 B.C.*

72

73

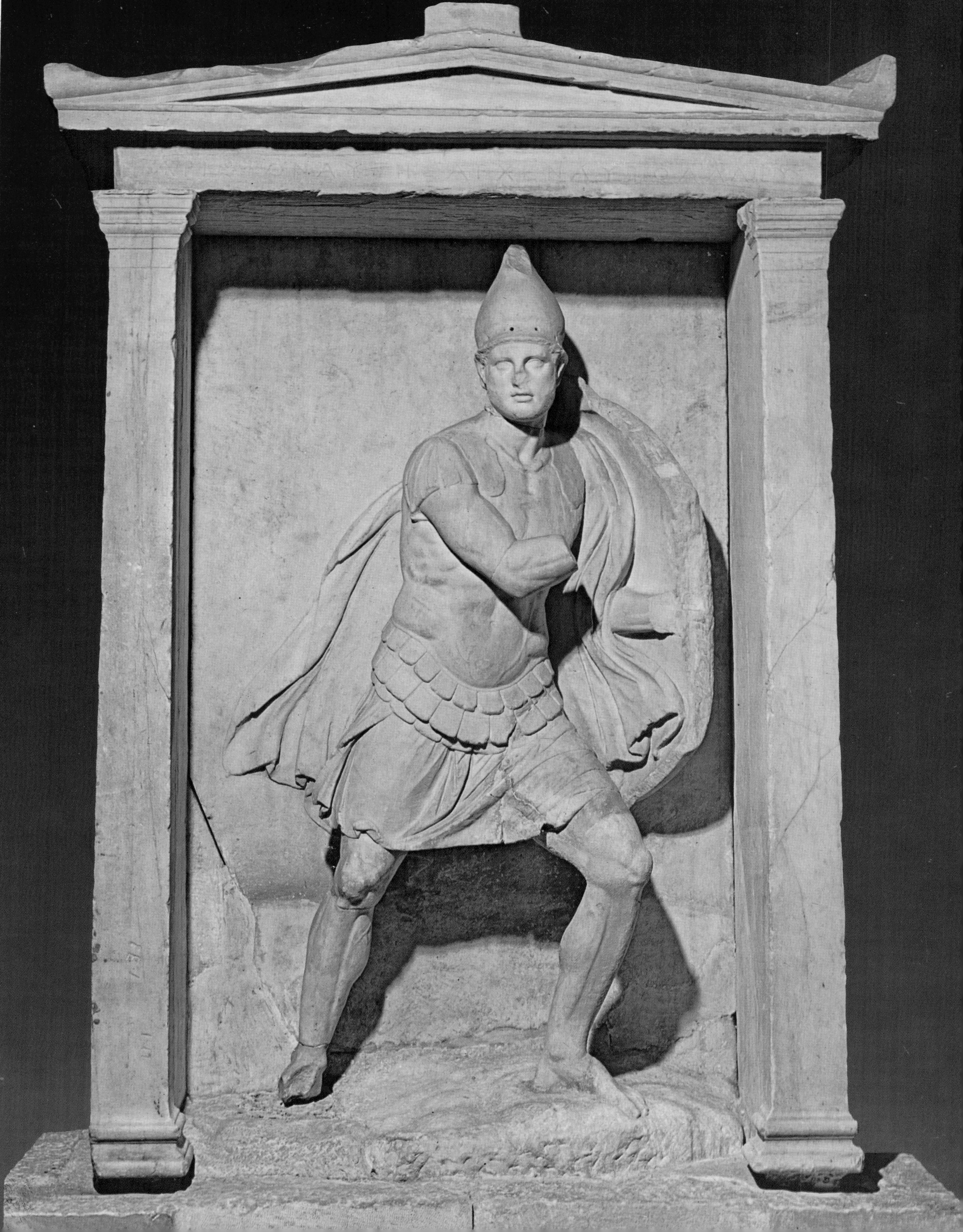

75. *Akroterion from the temple of Asklepios at Epidauros. A female figure—a Nereid or Aura—is seated on a horse which is probably in the act of emerging from the sea. The horse has raised its front legs slightly, thus obliging the Nereid to incline her head forward towards the animal's neck. Her garment, as witnessed in the finely carved folds of drapery, clings to her body as it is blown in the wind. 380 B.C.*

76. *Votive relief carved on both sides. On the side reproduced here the hero Echelos is depicted in the act of abducting the heroine Basile (their names are inscribed above their heads). On the uneven ground in front of the four-horse chariot stands Hermes, holding his wand in his right hand. On the other side of the plaque are depicted a horned river god with three Nymphs and (to the left of them) a goddess and a bearded god. On the epistyle of the pedimental finial runs the inscription Ἑρμῆ καὶ Νύμφαις (to Hermes and the Nymphs). The plaque was found at Neon Phaleron near the deme of Echelidai where the hippodrome of ancient Athens lay. c. 400 B.C.*

77. *The head of Hygeia, generally considered to be one of the finest in the whole of Greek sculpture. The deep 'interior life', which seems to emanate through this work, has led some art historians to conclude that the head is a creation of Skopas who executed the magnificent pediments of the temple of Athena Alea at Tegea. On the other hand, the flowing and exquisite modelling of the flesh surfaces has led others to classify it among the early works of Praxiteles. 350-340 B.C.*

77

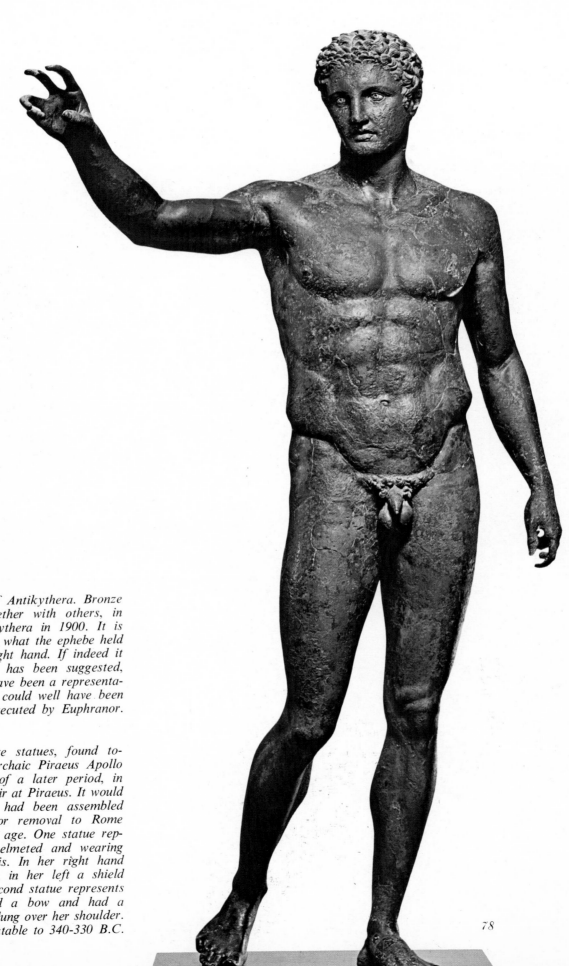

78. *The Ephebe of Antikythera. Bronze statue found, together with others, in the sea off Antikythera in 1900. It is not known exactly what the ephebe held in his extended right hand. If indeed it was an apple, as has been suggested, the ephebe must have been a representation of Paris and could well have been a famous work executed by Euphranor. 340 B.C.*

79,80. *Two bronze statues, found together with the Archaic Piraeus Apollo and other works of a later period, in a street under repair at Piraeus. It would appear that they had been assembled at this locality for removal to Rome during the Roman age. One statue represents Athena, helmeted and wearing a peplos and aegis. In her right hand she held a phiale, in her left a shield and spear. The second statue represents Artemis who held a bow and had a sheath of arrows slung over her shoulder. Both works are datable to 340-330 B.C.*

78

81-82. The Boy of Marathon. Bronze statue found in the sea in the bay of Marathon. In the middle of the concave open palm of the left hand is a pin which indicates that something was attached to it; and it is on this point, moreover, that the boy's gaze is fixed. The right arm is raised and the attitude of the fingers suggests that the boy was either holding some small object or simply expressing pleasurable astonishment. None of the interpretations suggested so far seems satisfactory. K.A. Romaios suggests that the statue represents Hermes holding the tortoise from whose shell he made the sounding-plate of the first lyre. Another unexplained feature of the statue is the horn-like protuberance among the curly locks of hair in the front part of the head. The identity of the boy apart, the figure's lithe and elegant attitude, the smooth and sensitive modelling of the body place it within the cycle of Praxitelean works. 330 B.C.

82

83. Bronze head of a boxer. Part of a statue of a victor in a boxing contest, a votive offering from the sanctuary of Zeus at Olympia. The work is a portrait in the modern sense of the word. While remaining faithful to the tradition of rendering the 'type' of his model, the artist ventures to go one step further and endeavours to depict the personal characteristics of a specific person. This work stands on the threshold of the long history of portraiture. The boxer in question is probably the famous athlete Satyros, and the portrait may have been executed by the well known Athenian sculptor, Silanion. 330 B.C.

84. Bronze head of a philosopher. Found in the sea, together with the bronze ephebe, at Antikythera. The rendering of the individual features of a specific person is self-evident. The pensive pene-trating expression, the wrinkled forehead, the thick nose, the seamed flesh around the nostrils, the flabby face, the untidy hair

and beard give the portrait a strikingly realistic air. Comparing this work with the head reproduced in fig. 83, we may observe the extent to which the 'type' has been replaced by a more direct and personal form of actual characterization. 240 B.C.

85. Bronze head of a man found in the palaistra at Delos. It prob-ably formed part of a statue of a standing male figure, wearing a himation. The head is turned to the left, but the man's glance, directed slightly upwards, as though he were gazing into a void, reflects an interior world full of anxiety and uncertainty. The work is a superb rendering of a man of the early 1st century B.C. who is perhaps meditating nostalgically on the turbulent years of the Hellenistic era, yet without faith or hope in a world filled with doubts. The work is one of the finest sculptured portraits of the late Hellenistic period. Early 1st century B.C.

83

84

85

86. *Statue of the goddess Themis, found in the temple at Rhamnous. In her extended right hand the goddess must have held a phiale (a kind of bowl) and in her left a pair of scales. She is clad in a chiton, high-waisted immediately below the breasts (in accordance with post-classical custom) and a himation. From the inscription on the base we learn that the work, executed by Chairestratos, was presented as a votive offering by Megakles of Rhamnous. 280 B.C.*

87. *The Poseidon of Melos, found at Melos together with other marble statues, in 1877. The lower part of the god's body, which rests on the right foot, is covered by a himation. In his raised right hand he holds the trident which serves as a support. The god's attitude has a somewhat pompous and theatrical air, an interior emptiness and ostentation which has lost the strength and warmth of feeling of authentic Hellenistic art. End of 2nd century B.C.*

88. *Group including Aphrodite and Pan, found at Delos. Pan, goat-footed, is trying to embrace the nude goddess who has removed her left sandal with which she teasingly threatens to strike him. A little Eros flies above the goddess' shoulder and seizes hold of one of Pan's horns. A show of more warmth of feeling would have provided charm to a work which is, in reality, little more than a purely pictorial representation devoid of inspiration. c. 100 B.C.*

86

87

ΔΙΟΝΥΣΙΟΣ ΖΗΝΩΝΟΣ ΤΟΥ ΘΕΟΔ...ΟΥ
...Ρ..ΤΙΟΣ...ΕΡΓΕΤΗΣ ΥΠΕΡΕΑΥΤΟΣ
...ΑΙΠΩΝΤΕΚΝΩΝΘΕΟΙΣΠ..ΤΡΙΟΙΣ

89

89. *Fine relief from a funerary monument. A fiery horse, whose body is covered with an animal-skin, raises its head violently, while a little black groom tries to control it. One of the most powerful works of the early Hellenistic period.*

90. *Horse and jockey boy of Artemision. The problem whether the horse and rider actually belong to the same composition remains unsolved. Only painstaking research on the part of art historians is likely to produce conclusive evidence. The horse is rendered in an attitude of extreme tension, both as regards the modelling of the head and the forward projection of both head and forelegs. The tremendous speed at which the horse is galloping causes the little chiton with numerous narrow folds worn by the jockey boy to be blown back. The boy's little face is constricted to the point of ugliness and his small lithe body contorted by the effort he is obliged to make. The work is a fascinating example of the human passion which artists of the peak period of the Hellenistic era succeeded to infuse into their most inspired works. Dated to about the mid-2nd century B.C.*

90

91. *Geometric bronze horse on a perforated base. The neck and legs are composed of laminae. Only the head and body are rendered in terms of volumes. c. 750 B.C.*

92. *Bronze bust of a griffin from Olympia. Like other similar figures, it formed part of the decoration attached to the rim of a cauldron. The work is an admirable geometric composition of harmonious curves. c. 750 B.C.*

93. *Bronze statuette of Zeus found in the course of excavations at Dodone. The 'plinth' on which the figure stands must have been attached to a special base. In his raised right hand, the god holds a thunderbolt which he is about to cast. c. 460 B.C.*

94. *Bronze rider from Dodone. The rider was part of the Karapanos Collection, whereas the horse was found in 1956, during excavations at Dodone. There is a similar horse, also from Dodone, in the Louvre. The rider in the Athens piece may have been mounted on the Louvre horse. The two pieces may have formed a single votive offering representing the Dioskouroi. The rider, it seems, wore a 'petasos' and held a spear in the right hand. c. 560 B.C.*

95. *Bronze idol of Athena with helmet and aegis, from the Acropolis of Athens. The goddess is represented in the Promachos type, extending her left hand in which she carried a shield and raising a spear with her right hand. On the base runs the inscription: Μελισὸ ἀνέθεκεν δεκάτεν τ᾽ Ἀθεναίαι (offered by Melisso as a tithe to Athena). c. 450 B.C.*

95

96. Bronze head of Zeus from Olympia. Part of a votive statuette of the father of the gods. The eyes, which were executed in a different material and inlaid, slant obliquely below the curved eyebrows which form two perfect arches starting from the nose, thus giving the face an air of spiritual austerity. A very fine piece of work of the late Archaic period.

97. Bronze head of a young man from the Athenian Acropolis. Part of a statuette dedicated to Athena. The eyes were inlaid. The structure of the head is firm, the plastic modelling of the cheeks and chin severe and heavy; the eyelids, eyebrows and lips are thick. The man's expression possesses the austerity of a work associated with a Peloponnesian workshop of the period of the severe style. c. 470 B.C.

98. Cheek-piece of bronze helmet from Dodone. Karapanos Collection. Two warriors are represented; the one standing, wearing a chlamys and helmet (or pilos) and holding a shield, gazes at his opponent whom he has overthrown. The defeated warrior is depicted kneeling on the ground. Last quarter of the 5th century B.C.

96

97

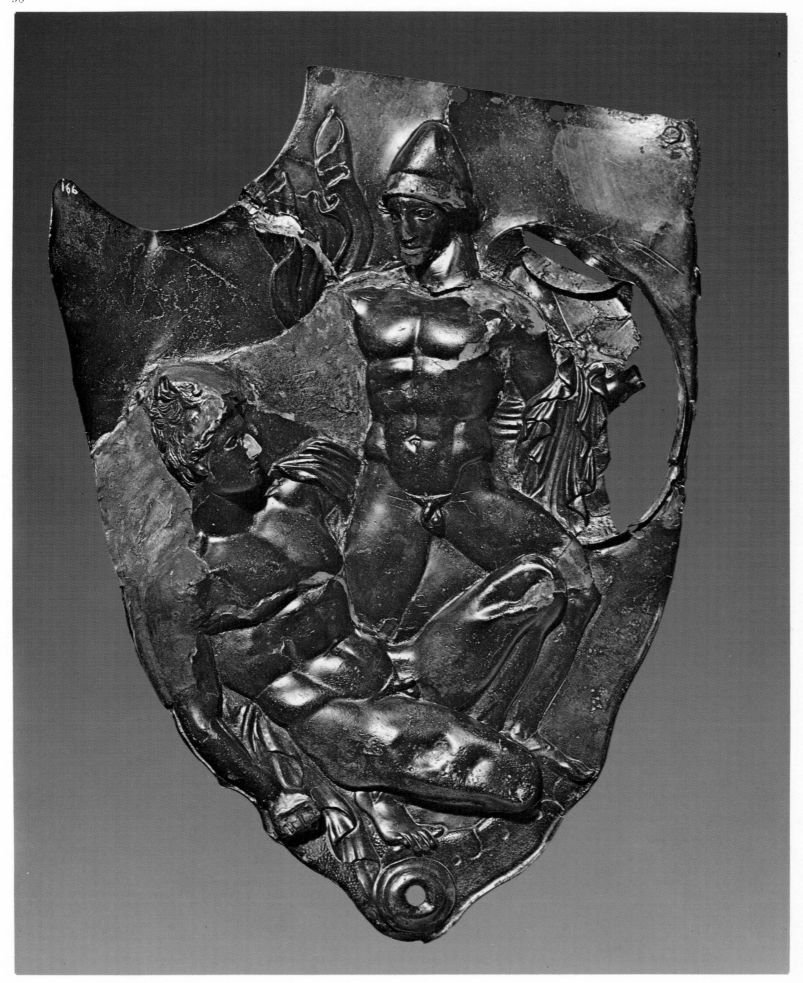

99. *Gold object in the form of a little temple. Dionysos is depicted in very high relief, flanked by a panther (left), and a Satyr (right). The god, behind whom a thyrsos is placed obliquely, wears a wide garment held by a clasp round the neck, leaving the upper part of the body bare. Dionysos, who appears to be in ecstasy, leans and supports himself on the young Satyr. Provenance: Thessaly. Dated to the late Hellenistic period. H. Stathatos Collection.*

100. *Gold bracelet, composed of two thin tubular sections covered with filigree, terminating at the upper end in bulls' heads. Possibly dated to the 3rd century B.C. Provenance: Thessaly. H. Stathatos Collection.*

101. *Two gold bracelets with double spirals, the upper parts of which terminate in snakes' heads, the lower in the reptiles' tails. Precious stones are placed in the spaces between the coils of the snake's body in one of the bracelets, which bears on the inner side the inscription ZΩIΛAC. Hellenistic period. Provenance: Thessaly. H. Stathatos Collection.*

101

102. *Gold earrings with precious stones. Hellenistic period. H. Stathatos Collection.*

103. *Gold earring with precious stones. 5th century A.D. H. Stathatos Collection.*

104. *Two small gold clasps. Classical period. H. Stathatos Collection.*

105. *Gold diadem. Hellenistic period. Provenance: Thessaly. H. Stathatos Collection.*

106. *Gold medallion with bust of Artemis. Provenance: Thessaly. Hellenistic period. H. Stathatos Collection.*

107. *Gold necklace. Provenance: possibly the Troad. 3rd century B.C. H. Stathatos Collection.*

105

108

109

110

111

112

113

114

115

116

117

108. *Tetradrachm. Athens. 5th century B.C.*

109. *Tetradrachm. Mende. c. 425 B.C.*

110. *Tetradrachm. Rhodes. 4th century B.C.*

111. *Gold stater. Pantikapaion. c. 350 B.C.*

112. *Tetradrachm of Philip II. Mid-4th century B.C.*

113. *Stater of Amphiktyonic Council. 336 B.C.*

114. *Tetradrachm of Lysimachos. Early 3rd century B.C.*

115. *Gold stater with representation of head of Titus Quinctus Flamininus. c. 196 B.C.*

116. *Tetradrachm of Perseus. First half of 2nd century B.C.*

117. *Tetradrachm. Smyrna. 190-175 B.C.*

118-119. *Gold octadrachm of Ptolemy V. Early 2nd century B.C.*

118,119

120. Cameo of sardonyx. The head may be that of Alexander the Great. Hellenistic or early Roman period.

ACROPOLIS MUSEUM

ACROPOLIS MUSEUM

**History.
The Prehistoric
Age**

The sun-bathed plain of Athens extends in a semicircular sweep from Phaleron Bay to the foothills of the mountains in the hinterland of Attica. In its centre rises an imposing rock 156.2 metres above sea level, measuring 330 metres in length at the base, 270 metres at the summit, and slightly over 156 metres in width.

This is the much-sung and much-praised Acropolis of Athens. The early inhabitants of the Neolithic Age built their crude dwellings in the confined space since it offered complete security and a safe refuge from enemies. All sides of the hill are precipitous and the only feasible approach is from the West. Moreover, a stream of clear sparkling water — a blessing to the early settlers — gushed from a crevice in the northwestern corner of the rock. This was to feed in later years the famous Klepsydra spring. In all probability the inhabitants of the Acropolis worshipped their benevolent god of water and the magnanimous deity who had blessèd them with the olive-clad plain and the security of the natural citadel, the name of which signifies peak or crest. No one possibly could have dreamt that the roughly hewn stones supporting the masonry of their crude dwellings would some day become the foundation stones of an architecture second to none and of a story unique in the annals of history.

When the visitor ascends the hill and looks upon the rock beneath the dazzling light of the Grecian sun, he is overawed by the grandeur of the monuments and the richness of its history. Well might he exclaim in astonishment that he has never set eyes on a more glorious stony vision. One can still touch stones whose age goes back to remotest times, those huge boulders of the Cyclopean walls which protected the royal palaces in the Mycenaean period when kings and retainers had their residences built in a fortified acropolis for security from their foes. The Athenian Acropolis was one of the numerous Mycenaean citadels, though not among the foremost. With the end of the Mycenaean world it would appear that the royal palace was replaced by a structure that was to be known to the Athenians as the "Old Temple" dedicated to Poseidon, god of the spring, and to Athena, goddess of the olive-tree. In addition to these patron deities the Athenians honoured and worshipped other gods, and demi-gods, heroes and benevolent spirits, and "guardians of the city".

Archaic period

In the early Archaic period, at the close of the 7th and the beginning of the 6th century B. C., in addition to the large "Old Temple" which had been rebuilt, there were erected other temples and sacred buildings. In the age of Peisistratos, when the first Panathenaic festival was celebrated (566 B. C.), the Mycenaean gate in the western entrance and the Mycenaean tower were demolished to be replaced by the first monumental Propylaia and an altar to Athena Nike. During the rule of the Peisistratidai (529-520 B.C.) the "Old Temple" was again reconstructed more sumptuously and adorned with remarkable marble sculptures in the pediments. This was the period when Athens and its art flourished. The worshipper who visited the sacred rock could rightfully gaze with pride on both the Archaic structures with their multi-coloured pediments and the numerous statues, delightful maidens and graceful horsemen set on elegant pedestals in the open air, pious offerings of the faithful and the grateful to the patron goddess who watched over the city, its citizens and its artists.

Towards the end of the Archaic period the Athenians began to build to the south of the "Old Temple" another large temple of Athena, probably on the site of an older edifice. But calamitous events occurred soon after the foundations had been laid and the first columns raised. In 480 B. C., after crossing the pass of Thermopylai, the Persian host invaded Athens and put the city and its altars to flames. The Acropolis was not spared. Then followed the naval battle and momentous victory of the Greek fleet at Salamis and the final annihilation of the Persian invaders at Plataiai. The Athenians, who had wisely followed the counsel of Themistokles to adandon the city before the advancing Persians, returned to find nothing but ruins and ashes. The sacred buildings and temples on the Acropolis had been consumed by fire, and the broken statuary lay scattered on the sacred rock. There was neither time, nor the means available to restore immediately the shattered shrines. An ancient tradition has it that following their victory at Plataiai the Greeks had taken a vow to their gods to the effect that they would not touch the destroyed temples but preserve them as eternal reminders of the barbarian invasion. Nevertheless, they gathered with great care and piety all the fragments of despoiled statues and architectural sculptures and buried them on the Acropolis in pits which they covered with soil. Known to the archaeologists as the "Persian deposit" or "layer of Persian destruction", these fragments were found *in situ* by Greek archaeologists when they undertook excavations from 1885-1891 to explore and clear the Acropolis of its debris. This most remarkable and totally unexpected discovery shed a unique light on the Archaic period of Attic art and revealed to the world for the first time artistic creations that existed long before the years of the Parthenon. These finds, now on display in the first rooms of the Acropolis Museum, enriched the then newly founded Museum, which had been built unobtrusively in the southeast corner of the rock in order not to interfere with the ancient monuments.

The Periklean plan

The new generation of Athenians after the Persian Wars built the famous long walls, organized the first Athenian League as a defence against the Persian menace, and laid the foundations of the economic and social structure which was to lead to the city's political and cultural renaissance. Those who had fought in the battles of Marathon and Salamis lived with memories of heroic deeds when their sons assumed the reins of government. Born in the year of the battle of Marathon (490 B. C.), Perikles, who led the democratic faction and was a friend of Sophokles and Anaxagoras, had grandiose plans for the city. He dreamt of Athens as the leader of a panhellenic confederacy, as an ideal democracy, and above all as a city with magnificent edifices, temples and public buildings, theatres and odeia. Never before or since have so many architectural and artistic works been planned for such a short period of time. Certainly the most significant and ambitious project of Perikles involved the reconstruction of the Acropolis. With Pheidias as adviser, the plans were soon laid. First and foremost would be a new large temple to Athena Parthenos, the Parthenon, then would follow the monumental entrance to the sacred rock, the Propylaia. Third in order would be the small temple of Athena Nike, the plans of which had already been prepared before the Periklean works. And finally would come the temple to Athena Polias, the Erechtheion. This would replace the "Old Temple", burned down by the Persians, of which only a part of the western section had been subsequently repaired, in order to house the divine wooden image of the goddess, — the *xoanon* "fallen from Zeus" (i.e. from heaven) — which the Athenians had so reverently carried when deserting the city to escape the Persians.

The Parthenon

The execution of the plan began in 447 B.C. Under the general supervision of Pheidias and the architect Iktinos the marbles of the Parthenon began to fall into shape, and there was created the finest Doric peripteral temple in the entire Greek world (fig. 2). Pheidias had revolutionary ideas and Perikles gave him the means to apply them. Pheidias decided to adorn all 92 metopes of the temple with reliefs, something no Greek city had hitherto dared to attempt, for the cost of such a project would have been prohibitive. The themes selected were derived from the mythical and legendary struggles of Athena and the Athenians: the Gigantomachy – the battle of the Gods against the Giants in which martial Athena fought bravely – was depicted on the eastern side; the Amazonomachy – the fight of the Athenians led by Theseus against the Amazons who had reached the very hill of the Areopagos – was represented on the western side. The southern side told the story of the Centauromachy — the battle of the Lapiths and their king Peirithos who with his friend Theseus overcame the terrifying Centaurs.

The northern side contained scenes from the Trojan War related to Attic heroes, including the sons of Theseus, Demophon and Akamas, who had joined Agamemnon in the great expedition. The metopes adorned the exterior of the temple and suffered severe damage with the passing of centuries. Most of those that have survived (largely from the southern side) are now exhibited in the British Museum.

The metopes provided Pheidias with ample space to record the age-old myths of Attica and that legendary story of the Gigantomachy showing the triumph of the Olympian gods who first destroyed the primordial Titans, then crushed the Giants, the younger offspring of Ouranos and Ge, to establish themselves as the almighty deities of the new divine rule and order. This was a grand theme giving any master scope enough to display his talents. Yet it was not enough for Pheidias. With Perikles and other inspired poets and philosophers of their intimate circle, spurred on by the vision of an Athenian democracy at its most creative moment, Pheidias conceived a daring and unique plan: he would immortalize Athens in marble, her people, the youths, the maidens, the men, and their gods, all in a single composition, on the happiest and most celebrated day in their lives when the joyous Athenians, with their hearts beating as one, climbed in procession up the Acropolis to worship their beloved goddess Athena Parthenos amidst all the gods who joined them in the celebration. Pheidias had often seen the splendid procession on the occasion of the Great Panathenaia in the heart of summer towards the end of July (the 28th day of Hekatombaion), beneath the brilliant sun of Attica, moving in wave after wave of people behing the sacred vessel upon whose mast hung the *peplos* of Athena, woven by the maidens of Athens to be handed to the priests of the goddess. This vibrant vision, a living image of Athenian democracy, inspired the hearts of her leading men. Perikles praised the glory of Athens in his *Funeral Speech* when he called upon the citizens to be "lovers" of such a unique city whose power and glory were reflected in her remarkable works. (And it is certain that Perikles must have glanced with pride at the Parthenon, which had only then been completed, when he delivered his speech.) Sophokles, too, then an old man of 90 years, sung the praises of the great city with incomparable lyricism in the chorus of the tragedy *Oedipus at Colonos*.

But Pheidias was a sculptor; and a hymn is not easily rendered in stone. One had to combine the mind of a genius, the experience of a craftsman and the daring of a pioneer to achieve this feat. To express his vision in marble the space available in the metopes or the pediments of the Doric temple was far too limited. And so he introduced a new element to the Doric edifice by adding a feature that traditionally was part of the Ionic order: a frieze, an uninterrupted zone of marble slabs on which he could carve his vision in relief. A suitable architectural space was needed for this additional feature and the inspired artist unhesitatingly placed the frieze above the temple proper, that is above the architrave of the *pronaos* and the *opisthodomos* and over the side walls of the *sekos*. He thus had at his disposal an area measuring 160 metres in length and 1.06 metres in height. In this space he unfolded the picture of a Panathenaic procession in truly remarkable fashion. Starting out from the southwestern corner the procession moves in two directions: from the end of the western side the horsemen move towards the north, and from the northwestern edge the procession continues along the north side towards the northeastern end. The other wing of the procession advances along the southern flank from the southwestern to the northeastern end. The two gracefully moving streams of people, the northern and southern, converge at the centre of the eastern side where the gods are seated in divine majesty (for more details see captions to figs. 4-12 and 36-39). The sections of the frieze running along the eastern and western sides of the temple are the most remarkable both in conception and execution. Of these only the western section has survived *in situ*. But its location makes it difficult for the observer to see it at close enough range and appreciate the incomparable perfection of the sculptures. To make up for this and enable the reader to enjoy the Pheidian masterpiece, special emphasis has been given to the subject in this book. Of the rest of the frieze, several slabs, in fact some of the very best, are now housed in the Museum. But by far the greatest number along with what has survived of the pediments are today the pride of the British Museum, which purchased them from Lord Elgin in 1816.

The temple was finally completed in 438 B. C., when the famous gold and ivory statue of Pheidias' Athena was set up in the *sekos*. The only portions of the temple not then completed were the sculptures of the pediments. These two vast compositions were the high points in Pheidian art, for they could be more easily enjoyed than any other sculptural work by all the citizens of Athens. Pheidias himself and his most talented assistants Alkamenes and Agorakritos worked on the figures of the gods and heroes who were represented in the two pediments. On the eastern pediment Pheidias related the birth of Athena who sprang in full armour from the head of Zeus. Zeus was seated in the centre, while on either side the gods were arranged in a happy and harmonious assembly. In the two corners were the chariots of Helios, the sun god, and of Selene, the moon goddess, the former mounting from the ocean, the latter descending into the ocean. The western pediment depicted the dispute between Athena and Poseidon for the possession of their beloved city. Poseidon produced water by striking the rock with his trident and Athena made an olive-tree grow. Athena was judged the winner of this divine contest. The two deities occupied the centre of the pediment. To the right and left were their chariots and the mythical ancestors of the Athenians, the families of Kekrops and of Erechtheus. What had been spared in the passage of countless centuries, by weathering and destruction at the hands of man, was removed by Lord Elgin. These pieces, the priceless survivals of the finest creations of Classical sculpture, are now displayed in special rooms of the British Museum. On the temple itself, the mutilated figures of Kekrops and one of his daughters are all that has remained of the household gods and patrons of Attica.

The Propylaia

With the completion of the Parthenon, artists and labourers began in 437 B. C. to work on the other monumental structure of the Periklean programme, namely the Propylaia. It was the custom of the ancient Greeks to separate the sacred precincts from the worldly. The entrance to the sanctuaries was usually through a gate or *propylon,* an imposing entrance that prepared the worshipper for entry into the area sacred to the deities before which he would shed all profane thoughts and mundane feelings. We have seen that in the age of Peisistratos a Propylaion had been built in precisely the same spot where its successor was to stand later. But now Perikles wished to provide the new sanctuaries of the Acropolis with a monumental entrance which would be worthy of the newly built Parthenon and the other temples included in the programme, particularly the building intended to replace the ruined "Old Temple". Iktinos was unavailable for this structure since Perikles had assigned to him the plan for another magnificent temple, the Telesterion at Eleusis, where the very ancient and mystic cult of the venerated deities Demeter and Kore was conducted. The Propylaia project was therefore assigned to Mnesikles. Even if nothing else were known about Mnesikles, the Propylaia is sufficient proof that he was a peer of Iktinos in the architectural arts. Never before or since has such a monumental entrance been built, in which grandeur and magnificence were so harmoniously united in the most daring and imaginative architectural fashion to resolve the nearly insurmountable problems arising from the narrowness of space and the irregularity of the terrain. When in 432 B. C. Pheidias was putting the finishing touches to the sculptural ornamentation of the Parthenon, Mnesikles was completing his equally imposing Propylaia.

The Temple of Athena Nike

The worship of Athena Nike on the Acropolis was very ancient. To the south of the Propylaia, on the right as one ascends the sacred rock, there existed an ancient bastion, where an altar was set up in 566 B.C., the year in which the Great Panathenaic festival was instituted, and a small poros temple was built in the period of the Persian Wars (490-480 B.C.) In 448 B. C. the Athenians decided to erect a new temple to their goddess of victory, designed by Kallikrates. But the execution of the Periklean programme left little room for implementation of the plan until 427 B. C., during the Peloponnesian War, when Kallikrates was finally able to begin the structure which he completed in two or three years, in all probability in 425/4 B. C.. It is the small amphiprostyle Ionic temple (fig. 3) which rises gracefully on the edge of the rock, where the Athenians worshipped the goddess of victory expressing their hopes for a new triumph in the war of those years when they were fighting desperately for victory on land and sea against the Spartans and their allies. Following the example of Pheidias' frieze of the Parthenon, the representations on the frieze of the temple of Athena Nike recalled not a traditional legend of Athens but the historical battle of Plataiai where the Greeks decisively defeated the Persians. When the temple was completed in the turmoil of the Peloponnesian War the Athenians added a protective rampart. The parapet was composed of marble slabs decorated on the outside with fine reliefs depicting winged victories with folded or extended wings setting up trophies or leading sacrificial animals to honour the great goddess who was seated proudly on the rock. It was but an expression of the Athenians' determination and hope for final victory. Those of the slabs that have survived are now in the Acropolis Museum (fig. 40).

The Erechtheion

There can be no doubt that the Periklean programme included plans for the temple which was to shelter the ancient cult statue. The western portion of the "Old Temple" destroyed in the Persian invasion was in all probability restored in order to house the *xoanon* of the goddess and other cult relics. Yet no one, least of all Perikles, could possibly have accepted the sheltering of the most sacred image of the goddess in a temporary and incomplete structure, particularly since she was worshipped there under the name of Athena Polias, patroness of Athens. Another good reason for believing that the sanctuary had been included in the original plan of Perikles is the fact that on the site at which it was eventually built there existed other very ancient relics of the Attic cult, the "divine marks", which would have been probably enclosed during the Archaic period in a *peribolos* north of the "Old Temple". But the Peloponnesian War erupted as soon as the Parthenon and the Propylaia were completed. Not long after this, Perikles died in the epidemic which had raged in Athens. Yet the Athenians did not abandon his plans. With the temporary cessation of hostilities brought about by the peace of Nikias in 421 B. C., work began on the temple of Athena Polias, subsequently known as the Erechtheion. The architect who designed the building is unknown, but one finds it difficult not to recall Mnesikles when gazing upon this remarkably graceful Ionic structure, unique in Greek architecture for its originality of conception and its functional adaptation to accommodate the needs of so many cults. Who but Mnesikles could have given such a daring and original solution to the most difficult problems of an irregular terrain and especially the multiple religious needs of the numerous cults. For the structure would primarily provide for the worship of Athena Polias and at the same time that of Poseidon. Moreover, the sanctuary would hold the graves of Erechtheus with the sacred snake, and of Kekrops, the ancestors of the Athenians, as well as the signs from Poseidon's trident which produced water, the "Erechtheis Sea", a well that contained salt water, and the marks from the thunderbolt of Zeus. The altars of Zeus Hypatos, of Poseidon and Erechtheus, of Hephaistos, of the hero Boutes, of the Thyechoos, and the very ancient *xoanon* of Hermes, all had to be accommodated harmoniously. Lastly room would have to be found for the sacred olive and the sanctuary of Pandrosos which included the altar of Zeus Herkeios. The architect succeded by subtle and ingenious use of the differences in level to produce an astonishing temple which satisfied the requirements of all these cults. He respected the traditions and at the same time introduced striking innovations. One has only to look at the much-admired "Porch of the Maidens", (fig. 1), the superb and refined southern extension to the temple where the "Karyatids" act as supports for the entablature without losing any of their feminine grace and delightful nobility. These six maidens are fine examples of Attic statuary further specimens of which are included in the collection of the Acropolis Museum. Work on the Erechtheion proceeded with brief interruptions throughout the Peloponnesian War until the temple was finally completed in 406 B. C.

The Museum

Built as inconspicuously as possible in the southeastern corner of the sacred rock, the Acropolis Museum contains in its few rooms the sculptures found on the Acropolis, votive offerings to Athena or adornments from her temples. When the last Turks left the Acropolis on the 1st of April 1833, the site was full of numerous constructions of all kinds. In 1834 began the task of removing all these subsequent additions which had no connection with the antiquities. At the same time the ancient marbles were carefully collected and efforts were made to preserve and in some instances to restore the much damaged monuments. Work continued slowly over many years but the results were most rewarding. Discoveries were at times surprising. In the ruins and accumulated debris many of the slabs from the frieze were uncovered. These had mercifully escaped the eye of Lord Elgin to remain in their place of origin and find a permanent home in the Museum. The construction of the Museum, begun in 1864, was temporarily halted when further antiquities were unearthed in the foundations, to be resumed on altered plans in the following year and reach completion in 1874. The Museum in fact was ready when the excavations of 1885-1891 conducted by Panayiotis Kavvadias uncovered the pits in which the mutilated remains of the Persian destruction had been buried by the reverent Athenians. These Archaic fragments together with the remains of the sculptures from the Parthenon provide a brilliant display of Attic masterpieces created during the peak centuries of artistic production, namely the 6th and the 5th centuries B. C. The Museum thus has the finest collection of sculptures and reliefs dating from the culminating period of Greek art. The creations of the Archaic art of the 6th century B. C., collected and displayed in the first rooms of the Museum, and those of the flowering of Classical art which attained its most perfect expression during the thirty or forty years of the second half of the 5th century B. C. in the shape of the sculptures of the Parthenon and the parapet of the temple of Athena Nike, offer the visitor a unique vision of beauty. The purity and intensity of these artistic creations are much enhanced by the manner in which they are presented. Their display to best advantage is due to the painstaking efforts of a scholar of great experience and rare sensitivity — Yannis Meliadis, the Museum Curator in the post-war period. When the Museum was reconstructed, he and his able assistants undertook with great devotion and patience to dismantle nearly all the sculptural pieces, to remove the harmful iron links that held them and to reassemble them as they are seen at present. In certain instances the work involved a major rearrangement of the fragments and Meliadis succeeded in giving us practically new masterpieces, such as the superb Athena from the pediment of the temple of the Peisistratidai.

Archaic pedimental sculptures

The first collection of Archaic sculptures holds one's undivided attention for here are seen the remarkable pedimental sculptures of the early 6th century B. C. The "frightening monsters" with their superhuman strength and daemonic power, and the poros lions tearing at the flesh of frail calves are the first striking sculptural works to meet the eye. One should visualize them in their deep blue and flaming red colours set in the pediments of a temple bathed by the bright sunlight of Athens. They now rest in a very confined space with their frightening countenances suggestive of power as it had been skilfully and boldly expressed by the Archaic artists. Their purpose is not to relate a story, but merely to remind one of the existence in the world of terrible powers that are overawing and overwhelming. Such are the "frightening monsters". Yet there is no one more powerful than man. The renowned Herakles fights and overcomes one such terrible monster, Triton, and the "old man of the sea" with his three-bodied dragon-like figure and the three human heads awaits at the other end of the pediment holding in his human hands a bird — symbol of the air —, water and fire (fig. 14). In this characteristic pedimental composition which preserves the colours remarkably well, especially in the faces and the torso of the "three-bodied monster", Attic sculpture displays the terrible power of supernatural beings but at the same time projects the human being, both heroic and mythical, who succeeds in harnessing this power. And it is certainly not a coincidence that among these sculptures in poros stone dating to the early third of the 6th century B.C., in addition to the above-mentioned fight scene between Herakles and Triton, there is a second pedimental group depicting the same theme, and yet a third representing the theme of the Lernaian Hydra (fig. 13), where the artist succeeded for the first time to convey a unity of plasticity, and narrative power. Finally there is a fourth scene depicting the introduction of the hero to Olympos. It should be remembered that the son of Zeus and Alkmene did not use his divine powers merely to make a show of his strength. Nearly all his famous labours had a single purpose which one could perhaps describe as philanthropic and cultural. Man's presence and triumph are the subject of the pedimental compositions just described, which date from the early period when Solon first established his constitution and new order of society in Athens.

From the pedimental sculptures, which had belonged to the earlier Archaic temples of the Acropolis until their ruin by the Persians, the visitor moves on to the precious votive offerings that adorned the rock before its desecration.

Early Archaic votive offerings

Sphinxes set on columns, four-horse chariots boldly carved in relief on marble slabs, modest Korai and other such dedications were the usual themes in this early period. Yet among these works there were certain masterpieces which now hold a prominent place in the Museum. "Rhombos son of Palos dedicated this", reads the inscription carved in Archaic fashion from right to left on the base of the "Calf-Bearer" (fig. 17). One cannot but admire the Athenian artists who in so early a period of their history were able to attain such a flowering of expression. For this superb group of man and animal, dated to *circa* 570 B. C., is an outstanding work of art. The solid sculpture, the well-balanced figures, and the distribution of weight with the fine positioning of the arms of the man and the legs of the animal in crosswise fashion, are convincing evidence that the anonymous artist must have been an innovator with much experience, unusual sensitivity and rare skill. This work marks the beginning of a remarkably productive period of sculptural art, the likes of which would only be found in the great eras of art history.

A few steps farther, one comes to a second incomparable artistic creation. The name of the artist is unknown, hopefully not forever, for he is represented in this beautiful corner of the Museum in a succession of works. The National Archaeological Museum houses the fine relief of the "Discus-Thrower" which could well be his work. And the Louvre contains another of his works, a head from the Rampin Collection, that has given the artist the name by which he is now known: "sculptor of the Rampin head". In 1935 a torso was identified as belonging to the head and is displayed at present in the Acropolis Museum. The identification owes much to the scholarly and artistic acumen of the well-known British archaeologist Humfry Payne. Thus one of the finest works of Attic art dating to the mid-6th century B.C. has survived. The work in question is none other than the horseman one can see in the Acropolis Museum (fig. 18) — the head of the statue is a cast made from the original in the Louvre (a cast of his torso has been made for the Louvre head). Next to the horseman is the famous "Peplos Kore" and beyond that the hunting dog and the lion's head, all evidence of what this great artist was able to create in the twenty or thirty years of his career.

The Archaic Korai

The statue of the "Peplos Kore" is remarkable for its structure: the firmly shaped lower part of the body, the sensitively modelled breast, covered by a double fold of the dress (the curve of the fold, which follows the movement of the figure, is exquisite) and discreetly framed by the fine locks of her hair. The attractive young head has features that are vivid and at the same time soft and gentle. (fig. 22). It is extraordinary how the artist has succeeded in conveying so much humanity, nobility and feminine grace in so delicate a figure of a young maiden and at the same time to make her so intimately familiar, yet unearthly and divine. She regards one with complacency and dignity, with an imposing air, as she becomes the symbol of a fully developed artistic and spiritual expression. The next exhibit, the hound with its tensed muscles ready to pounce forward (fig. 19), holds the eye and compels the visitor to linger a while longer in this magnificent corner of the Museum. But so many other korai await, so many graceful maidens dressed in fine Ionic *chitons* and rich *himatia*, decked with earrings, their hair adorned with diadems, a smile on their lips, standing in a circle as though ready to begin a dance.

Broad-chested, robust, and imposing, the firm figure of the representative Athenian maiden stands before the visitor (fig. 20). This is a dedication by Nearchos Kerameus to the patron goddess of the city. The donor must have been both a wealthy and a pious man to commission Antenor to carve this statue. Antenor was the artist whom the Athenians would ask a few years later to make the splendid group of the Tyrannicides. The dignity of the kore is more impressive than her grace, since the sculptor emphasized the severe vertical and horizontal lines, diminishing the oblique and diagonal movements characteristic of the korai of that period (525-500 B. C.).

The height of the small head (Mus. Inv. No. 643) seen nearby measures a mere 14 centimetres.

(fig. 25). It should date a few years later than her bigger sister, the kore of Antenor, yet how remarkably different is her attitude and expression. It is doubtful whether in the entire production of Archaic art — or for that matter of any art — there is another figure so attractive, so refined and so spiritualized. The dominance of the flowing curve, of eternal movement, conveys an almost ethereal impression. The young flower that has just blossomed and is vibrant with life may be likened to this exquisite face glowing under an imperceptible vibration of the soft skin.

Perhaps for the first time in the history of sculpture the female body had found its fullest expression in the kore with the "almond eyes" (Mus. Inv. No. 674) (figs. 27 and 30). She is no longer the young maiden with the broad and raised shoulders, the robust woman of Antenor. Here the shoulders, narrow and gently curving, support a long fine neck, sensitively modelled. Without being a frail creature, she is nonetheless so refined, fragile and delicate, that the visitor is immediately drawn to her with a feeling of tenderness. Her face, reflective, reserved, and at the same time full of radiant confidence, rouses both respect and admiration, in addition to a subtle attraction. The visitor gazes at a maiden of unique personality and perhaps it would not be exaggerated to regard this statue as a brilliant Archaic portrait.

The last kore on display stands as a landmark dividing the receding Archaic age from the emerging Pre- Classical period. She had been dedicated by Euthydikos (fig. 28). For the first time one sees in this maiden a perfected carving of the body. The artist reveals even the finer details beneath the dress. This is very evident especially in the back where one can distinguish the furrow of the vertebral column beneath the abundant hair falling over the shoulders. The head with the simple hair-do is a distinctly new element. The delightful expression with the happy interplay of the facial features has been now replaced by an unusual severity that almost suggests melancholy. It reflects the spirit of the early years of the 5th century B. C., of the generation of the warriors of Marathon and the tragic events of the Persian Wars.

The horsemen, brothers of the korai, accompanied the maidens in the sacred Panathenaic procession. Descendants of the "Rampin Horseman", and forerunners of the riders in the frieze of the Parthenon, the devout Athenians dedicated their images in marble to their beloved goddess. A quick glance at the few superb horses that survive from the final Archaic period reveals the Athenians' fondness of this noble animal, but even more so, the unsurpassed talent of Athenian sculptors in creating its likeness in such memorable marble masterpieces (fig. 31).

The pediment of the temple of the Peisistratidai

All this statuary was created to please Athena, daughter of Zeus, the great goddess, who had joined her father in the forefront of the terrible war between the Gods and the Giants. In about 525 B.C., the Athenians rebuilt the "Old Temple", predecessor of the Erechtheion. For the first time, during the rule of the Peisistratidai, the entablature and pediments were made of marble. And for the first time on the Acropolis the eastern pediment related the battle with the Giants. There is no doubt that the entire work was put in the hands of a master sculptor. The fragments which have survived from the pediment show that this was the most striking composition of the Archaic period. The Athena and the Giants preserved, particularly the two figures from the extremities of the pediment, reflect the fullest and highest flowering of Attic sculpture. The goddess, who has been restored, has acquired a superd firmness and forcefulness (fig. 21). The sharp lines of the shoulder and legs, the vigorous thrust by the left arm of the shield with the serpents, and the tension in her right arm as she grasps the spear, express in the most effective manner both the divine rage and self-assurance of the martial goddess. These fragments give one a clear idea of how the Athenian sculptors could conceive and transfer into marble the vigorous movements and feelings in the closing years of the Archaic period, and permit one to visualize Antenor's group of the Tyrannicides, which was carried off as a war trophy by the Persian invaders when they left Athens. It would not be strange to presume that the master sculptor who gave Athenian democracy its first official monument was the same person who a few years earlier had carved the splendid pediment which holds one's attention in the last room of the Archaic section of the Museum.

From Archaic to Classical art

Now the visitor moves beyond the limits of Archaic art and stands before the first outstanding specimen of the sculpture of the severe style. The National Archaeological Museum houses the last kouros of Attica, the statue of Aristodikos, wherein had been exhausted all features of the Archaic modelling of the male figure. We have strong reason to believe that the youthful figure seen here is a creation of the great Attic artist Kritios. The sculptor has freed himself from the confines of the Archaic past and has created a new balance in the stance of the body (fig. 34). The weight is no longer distributed evenly between the two legs. One is bent slightly at the knee, leaving the support fall fully on the other limb. The poised leg transforms entirely the overall image and the structure of the body, gracing it with a contraposto movement. One cannot exaggerate the significance of this striking breakthrough in Greek art, which was to become the heritage of European art. For it is not an external technical solution to the problem of posture. It is in fact a deeper inner refinement and transformation conveying to the figures a new rhythm, replete with spiritual depth. This same style would have been applied to the "Blond Youth" of which only the head survives (fig. 32-33). Divine and attractive in its severe expression, it is simple and firm in conception and reflects an inner vision.

The Parthenon sculptures

The "Kritios Boy" and the "Blond Youth" lie between Archaic strength and Classical balance preparing the visitor for the next rooms which contain the sculptures of the Parthenon. Few in number and badly mutilated are the figures that have survived from the pedimental compositions. Most of them had been removed by Lord Elgin to London together with the largest part of the frieze and numerous metopes. No matter how sufficient they are, even in their present state of preservation, to convey some idea of the magnificence of the original composition, they do not hold the visitor's attention long. It is preferable to move on to the fragments of the frieze that have survived in their place of origin.

In this inspiring creation of Classical sculpture, which reveals an unparallelled vision of Athenian glory, divinities and humans acquire a familiarity yet retain a superhuman form. The uniformity of the figures represented subjects them to the polyphonic harmony of the whole without in any way depriving them of their self-sufficiency as individual entities. This creation can and should be enjoyed only as a unified and indivisible whole. Within this unity the horseman is still as noble as is his steed — the presence of man and the animals led to sacrifice cannot be evaluated by different standards. The young and the old, maidens and youths, deities and humans, are all carefully balanced and placed so effectively that they become irreplaceable. Each part fulfils a particular function in the artistic whole so that it becomes impossible to separate and speak of one specific part only. For not only the figures of humans and beasts but also the garments (indeed with what power!), the flying mantles and flowing robes, and even the empty spaces within the reliefs, have their particular reason for being where they are and contribute their share to the aesthetic whole.

Bearing this in mind, we shall pause for a moment before the three figures of Poseidon, Apollo and Artemis, from the eastern section of the frieze (fig. 38). The figures of the deities are carved on the same slabs and with the same dimensions as the remaining figures of the frieze. Yet even though limited by the height of the frieze measuring but one metre, these figures manage to assume such an imposing grandeur and stature as to reflect unmistakeably their divine nature. The relaxed posture on the throne, the measured but free movement, the firm bodies of the male divinities, the folds of the *himatia* with their marked regality, next to Artemis' many-pleated *chiton* with its delicate harmony, all set in the ample unencumbered space carrying a striking perception of depth, transport the observer to the serene and lofty abode of Olympos.

Among the outstanding sections of the remaining frieze are the marble slabs carved in relief with the figures of youthful horsemen who convey lively movement to the great Panathenaic procession. Pheidias, creator of the Parthenon, friend and adviser to Perikles, drew from the noisy and tumultous picture of reality the splendid figures that one now sees in a vivid yet disciplined style, rich but concise, both festive and sober. These figures of youths and horses so full of life, with their robust and vibrating strength, have harnessed in artistic manner the movement and the power of the natural being and have attained the highest point of the art of sculpture as they stand forever on "the razor's edge". Along the path to art and artistic expression they reached that height which lasted but a few brief years when the struggle between the spirit and matter was finally resolved by the unique blending never again to be repeated, between the two components of life, alloting to each its rightful and equal share. This brilliant moment found in 5th century B. C. Athens the man who created artistic perfection in the harmonious features of the Parthenon.

The sculptures from the parapet of the Temple of Athena Nike

In the next moment art began to be transformed. Those who had worked with Pheidias – and perhaps one can distinguish their individual work in certain figures of the Parthenon – charted a new path. They became intrigued by one or another discovery which they now wished to apply in their works. The slabs from the rampart surrounding the bastion where the elegant temple of Athena Nike stands, are displayed opposite the marble slabs of the frieze in the same room of the Museum. They date a few decades later, yet one observes that the Classic moment is beginning to give way to a new vision. The exquisite female figures open or fold their wings surrendering to their rich wavy draperies and to the vigour of their varied movements with multiple artistic results. They rejoice in their suppleness (as when Nike unlaces her sandal, fig. 40) or twist gracefully to create a flying movement of their robes (as when they strive to tame their rebellious victim). Here one still breathes the air of the Parthenon. But the new currents are now considerably stronger and one can foresee fresh forces that will develop to lead to a new era of Greek art.

A few other beautiful examples of Greek art may be seen before departing from the Museum. The Prokne of Alkamenes, one of the marble tiles of the Parthenon, a fragmented relief, an excellent portrait of later antiquity. Yet it would be perhaps wiser if the visitor were to leave this sacred site with the image of the sculptures of the unique Classical moment.

2

1. Erechtheion. The porch of the Karyatids. 421-406 B.C.

2. The Parthenon. 447-432 B.C.

3. The temple of Athena Nike. c. 425 B.C.

6

123

7

4-12. The frieze of the Parthenon is the most striking innovation in the temple. Although the artist was bound by tradition, his genius introduced a daringly new element to temple construction: to the Doric edifice he added a sculptured frieze, i.e. an Ionic element, without in any way destroying the basic Doric structure. The frieze rested on the side walls of the sekos and above the pronaos and the opisthodomos. Henceforward this innovation was to become a traditional feature. But the fruitful imagination of Pheidias did not restrict itself to this novelty alone. The theme he selected for the frieze was indeed a radical one. He would not, as tradition required, relate the standard myths normally seen in sacred edifices. Next to the age-old myths venerated by the Athenians, Pheidias —a friend of Perikles and Anaxagoras— believed that the legend of the new Athenian democracy should and could be recorded on marble. The city's crowning achievement in peace, an achievement of no less importance than glorious military feats in war, was carved in relief in the grandiose composition of the Panathenaic procession. The Panathenaia was the greatest festival celebrated by the Athenians in honour of Athena, their patron goddess. The festival was held annually, but every four years it assumed a special magnificence, and was hence known as the Great Panathenaia. The wooden xoanon of the goddess, the one believed to have fallen from heaven, was removed from the 'Old Temple' (the Erechtheion) and dressed with a new peplos woven in a traditional design. The peplos, spread as the sail of a trireme, was carried from the Kerameikos to the Acropolis in a grand procession. It was this most sacred and splendid procession that Pheidias aspired to immortalize on the frieze of the Parthenon. The frieze itself is a poetic composition in marble which illustrates and glorifies the holy procession through the art of sculpture. The elements of time and space disappear and all the figures move within an artistic dimension where both mortals and gods coexist harmoniously. The whole composition of the frieze conveys to us the festive spirit of the procession and at the same time transports us ecstatically into the realms of great art. To bring this vision to life the great sculptor resorted to methods that were simple and persuasive. Only a genius could possibly have found the solution to the many problems, the most critical of which was to find suitable points for the beginning and the end of the procession. Moreover he had to select the most

124

8

characteristic elements that would lend themselves to plastic rendering and to the rhythmic arrangement of the seemingly endless flow of figures. The final solution adopted by Pheidias breathed life into the procession and transformed it into a symphonic unity, in the musical sense, in which were orchestrated all the available elements of reality, art and religion. Thus the entire composition culminates on the façade of the temple at the eastern side where the procession terminates. In the very centre of the eastern side, a male figure (possibly a priest) is depicted receiving the sacred peplos, while two maidens carrying seats are facing a priestess. To either side of this central scene the Olympian deities are seated in relaxed positions, in groups: Zeus, Hera and Iris (?) to the left, Athena and Hephaistos to the right. Next to Hera are Ares, Demeter, Dionysos, and Hermes. Next to Hephaistos is the slab containing the figures of Poseidon, Apollo, and Artemis (fig. 38). The brilliantly calculated placement of this sculptured group above the entrance to the temple in the middle of the eastern side determines the basic arrangement of the remainder of the frieze. For the procession to terminate at this point, two separate streams of figures were

required on the two long sides of the temple moving toward and culminating in the eastern façade. In fact, this was Pheidias' own plan; but had the double procession been divided into two equal parts, the starting point would have to be in the centre of the western side, and at that point there would have been two groups, moving in opposite directions, the one towards the left and the other towards the right. Such a solution was unacceptable to Pheidias. Hence with great ingenuity he selected as starting point the southwest corner, the only point at which the continuity of the moving procession would not be broken. Thus the procession begins at the south end of the western side and moves to the north. In the first slabs, the youths have not as yet mounted their horses, but are preparing to do so. In this way Pheidias appears to be following the ceremony from its very beginning, both in place and time, but in fact he is making good use of this element to open his symphony on a plain low-key (pianissimo). In the sixth slab (fig. 4) the first two riders appear and the rhythm becomes more dynamic, yet always retains a subdued tone, as the figures move along at comfortable distances from each other, with two figures at the most in each slab (figs. 7-9). At about

13

15

14

16

13. *Poros pediment from an uniden-tified small building of the early 6th century B.C. Herakles is depicted over-coming the Lernaian Hydra. To the left on the chariot is Herakles' friend Iolaos and in the corner is the Hydra's ally, the 'crab'.*

14. *Large poros pediment of the Ar-chaic temple of Athena. On the left Herakles fights against Triton. To the right the 'Three-headed Daemon'. c. 570 B.C. .*

15. *The four horses come from a marble votive relief. The slab probably carried the representation of a four-horse char-iot and the charioteer. c. 570 B.C.*

16. *Archaic marble Sphinx. It was set up on a tall column. c. 560-550 B.C.*

17. The 'Calf-Bearer' was one of the earliest compositions of large sculpture in the Archaic period. Rhombos, the man who dedicated this offering, carries on his shoulders the calf he intends to sacrifice to Athena Pallas. His offer is not only the animal sacrificed to the altar of the goddess but the fine statue itself which commemorates the sacrifice and also pleases the great goddess with its own beauty. An excellent Attic work dating in c. 570 B.C.

18. Shortly before the middle of the 6th century B.C. a splendid monument was erected on the Acropolis, depicting two young horsemen crowned with oak leaves, a symbol of victory possibly in the Pythian Games. One of the horsemen has survived in a fairly good state of preservation (the head in the Acropolis Museum is a cast of the original head now displayed in the Louvre). It is the oldest statue of a mounted rider in Greek art and the work of a great sculptor of the Archaic period whose name is unknown.

19. It is quite possible that the same artist produced this remarkable hound with its highly tensed body, its sharp planes and the crystal-clear outline capturing in exquisite artistic fashion the spirit of the noble beast. c. 530 B.C.

18

19

20. The 'Kore of Antenor'. From an inscription on a base on which this statue probably stood, we learn that it was dedicated to Athena by the potter Nearchos and was executed by the celebrated Athenian sculptor Antenor who made the first group of the Tyrannicides. The 'Kore of Antenor' possesses the dignity and maturity of monumental art. Fashioned with perfect architectural balance, she raises her imposing figure, supported on strictly vertical axes. In contrast with her graceful sisters, she presents a severe structure that was to influence Athenian sculpture in subsequent years. c. 525 B.C.

21. The figure of Athena from the Gigantomachy depicted on the pediment of the temple of the Peisistratidai (c. 525 B.C.). One of the most daring works, it stands as a forerunner of the Attic sculpture of the later Archaic period, and opens new ways to architectural sculptures. It is certainly the work of a great artist' of that age—the suggestion that it may well be a work of Antenor seems quite plausible.

22. The 'Peplos Kore' is a work of the artist who created the 'Rampin Horseman'. c. 530 B.C.

23. A later Kore of great artistic sensitivity. She is the only maiden not lifting her himation. c. 500 B.C.

24. One of the most charming of Korai is the so-called 'Maiden of Chios', presumably made in a workshop of that island. It retains in excellent condition the colouring of the garments. c. 510 B.C.

25. This small head of a Kore is a real masterpiece of Greek sculpture. The uninterrupted flow of planes gives it a unique attraction. c. 510 B.C.

24   25

26., This delightful Kore wears only a chiton (the others wear also a himation). The statue is wholly preserved and presents an unusual variation of the Kore type. c. 510 B.C.

27. The most attractive Kore of the Athenian Acropolis. In no other statue has the essence of youthful feminine grace been conveyed with such expressive force. The imperceptible curves in the folds of her himation, the refined locks of hair and the superb partition of the hair over the forehead, the full lips, and the enigmatic expression of the eyes, make up an incomparable composition that must have been a harmony in colour in its original state. c. 500 B.C.

28. The 'Kore of Euthydikos'. The inscription on the base records that the statue was 'Dedicated by Euthydikos son of Thaliarchos'. In contrast to the previous Korai with the Archaic smile, she possesses a severity of expression. The facial features are more simple and austere, the body fuller and riper. These elements suggest a new attitude to life and art that foreshadows the works of the severe style. c. 490 B.C.

28

29. *Votive relief. Three female figures with fine chitons hold hands and dance, while Hermes plays a double-flute before them. The last female figure holds by the hand a child that has lost the step in its endeavour to follow the dance. Some archaeologists believe this to be a representation of the Aglaurides with Erichthonios as a child. The background of the relief was painted blue. A charming work probably of some island school. c. 500 B.C.*

30. *The attractive head of the Kore no. 674. Archaeologists have named her 'the Kore with the pensive face', or 'the Kore with the almond eyes'. The vibrating surface of the flesh, the triangular forehead framed with the fine arrangement of wavy and flowing hair, the varied colours of the chiton and the harmonious folds of the himation are indeed remarkable.*

29

31

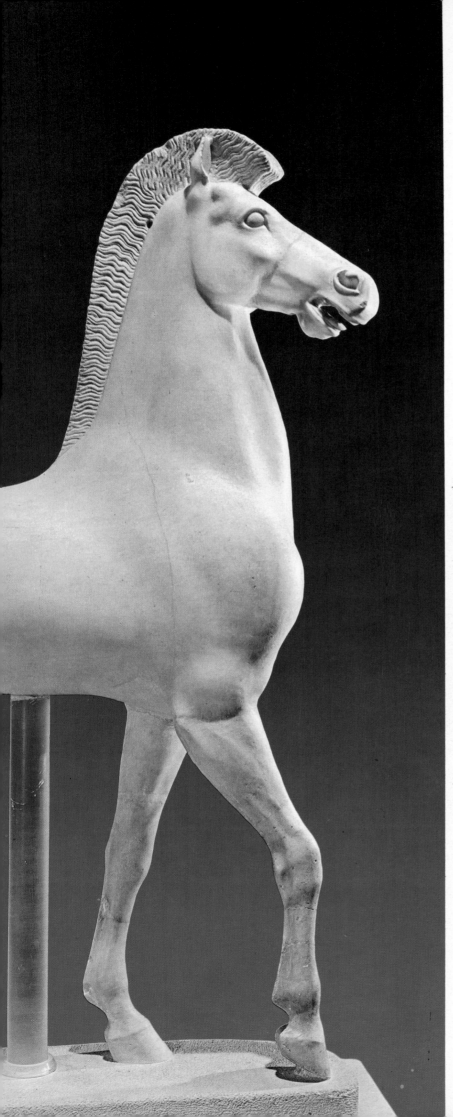

31. The fore part of a superb horse. The artist conveys with ingenuity and fondness the pride and nobility of the animal that was so admired by the Greeks. There existed on the Acropolis many dedications of horsemen, offered by members of the noble families of Attica. c. 490-480 B.C.

32-33. Head of a boy known as 'the Blond Youth' because when first found a deep yellow tint was still discernible in the hair. The severe expression of his face and the fullness of his flesh are reminiscent of the 'Kore of Euthydikos' and indicate the new tendencies in the sculpture of the early 5th century B.C. Judging by the inclination of the head towards the right shoulder, we may conclude that his posture was similar to that of the youth pictured next to him. Shortly before 480 B.C.

34. The well-known 'Kritios Boy', so called because many archaeologists believe it to be a work of the sculptor Kritios. This work marks a decisive break from the Kouros tradition and opens the way to Classical art through the slight bend in the right knee. This apparently minor innovation had incalculable results. The human body was liberated creating successive movement and counter-movement which enabled the artist to use hitherto unknown techniques of expression and stance. c. 485 B.C.

32

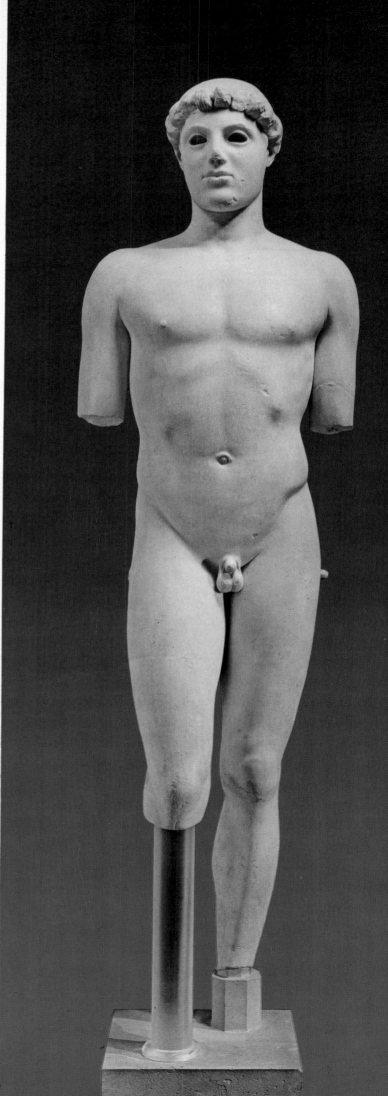

35. The so-called 'Mourning Athena'. The goddess wears a helmet and a folded peplos, girded at the waist. Leaning on her spear with the left hand, her body slightly inclined forward, she bends her head and contemplates the stele standing before her. This latter may have been a stele marking out the boundaries of the sacred precinct of the goddess. A superb example of the severe style. c. 460 B.C.

36. Slab from the north side of the Parthenon frieze representing three youths leading two oxen. The rhythmic alternation between the upright youthful figures, dressed in long himatia appropriate to the religious occasion, and the horizontal bodies of the animals results in a composition of counterpoints of a hitherto unmatched harmony and architectural solidity. The superior artistic quality of this relief has led some archaeologists to the belief that it was executed by Pheidias himself.

37. Slab from the north side of the Parthenon frieze representing six thalophoroi (men carrying olive-branches, which were painted on the slab). They all wear long himatia falling over the left shoulder, exposing their chests.

36

37

38

146

38. *One of the finest slabs of the eastern side, in all probability executed by Alkamenes, pupil and collaborator of Pheidias. It represents Poseidon, Apollo and Artemis. Seated in dignity in a relaxed posture they manage to assume greater stature in contrast with the mortals in the procession. Their divinity and majesty are enhanced by the wide space that separates them and the spaces beneath the thrones, conveying at once the feeling that we are now in a different realm from that of the earthly procession in the remainder of the frieze. The relief is of outstanding workmanship.*

39. *Relief with three 'hydria-bearers': a fourth at the right end has bent over to lift his pitcher. The triple repetition of similar forms with only a very slight variation between them and the equal spaces separating the figures, the contrasting folds of their himatia that acquire an even greater intensity as they are accompanied by the plain surfaces of the hydriai, make up a unique ensemble that is but another harmonic theme blending in with the entire composition of the Parthenon.*

40. ´Nike unlacing her sandal´. This exquisite figure from the parapet of the Temple of Nike expresses the new trends of Attic sculpture at the close of the 5th century B.C. The graceful movement of Nike produces the rich and refined draperies of her chiton and himation.

DELPHI MUSEUM

DELPHI MUSEUM

Delphic myths

The first diviner to occupy the Delphic oracle was the mother of the gods, Gaia. She was succeeded by her daughter, Themis. The third occupant was another daughter of Gàia, the Titaness Phoibe, who gave Apollo the surname of Phoibos as a birthday present. We have this information from the Pythia's own mouth, in the opening lines of Aischylos' tragedy *Eumenides*. As regards the rest of the story: how Apollo founded his first temple at Delphi, and how he slew the fearful dragon (a female serpent) near a spring, this is recounted in the ancient Homeric hymn to Apollo. In later times, men believed this serpent to have been male and even more redoubtable, none other than the famous Python, guardian of Gaia's oracle; the battle that the young god who had come from the north — from the valley of Tempe — fought against the serpent was indeed a great and terrible one. They also believed that although a god, Apollo complied to the divine rule which he himself had set: that whoever defiled his hands with the blood of murder should be sent into exile. Thus the god departed for eight years and worked in the service of Admetos, King of Pherai, in order to cleanse himself of the pestilent blood of murder; then he returned, purified and clean at last, sole master of the Delphic oracle.

This is what the ancients had to say about the beginnings of the legendary oracle. But concerning the site itself, that unique site which overwhelms whoever visits it for the first time, they had another story to tell. Zeus, wishing to find the centre of the earth, let loose two eagles from the two ends of the world; the sacred birds met at Delphi, which meant that there was the "navel" of the earth. Hence, Apollo's sanctuary contained, since remotest times, an *omphalos* (navel-stone), and votive offerings in the shape of the *omphalos* were presented to the god by pious pilgrims from all over the world (fig. 1). The Apollonian oracle was indeed celebrated and venerated throughout the inhabited world. Not only Greeks, but barbarian monarchs as well sent envoys to consult the oracle and expressed their gratitude by dedicating sumptuous gifts and votive offerings to the god.

The site

Such are the myths of the ancients concerning Apollo, Delphi and the celebrated oracle.

Anybody coming upon the holy site for the first time is struck with awe. "It is as if the earth had been cleft asunder by some cosmogonic spasm; the valley is a vast and profound chasm... And as soon as we reach the foot of the Phaidriades, at the exact spot of the Kastalian Spring, we are faced with something that appears like the chasm of chasms: the two rocks are separated by a tremendous gorge, narrow and impassable — the Arkoudorema (the Bear's Gully) as it is known today — which continues all the way down the slope, deep into the thicket" (Ch. Karouzos). And there, at the point where the two rocks meet, in the deepest recess of the gorge and at the foot of the east rock (known anciently as Hyampeia and presently as Flempoukos), the most limpid water gushes forth: it is the water of the celebrated Kastalian Fountain where both priests and pilgrims cleansed themselves before entering the temple. On the western side, at the foot of the rock named Rodini, Apollo's sanctuary, the most famous in ancient Greece, extends across the opening on the rising ground. And down below, the deep valley of the Pleistos river spreads out, green and silver with olive-groves, and merges with the plain of Itea stretching all the way down to the sea-coast.

The history of Delphi

The history of Delphi is inextricably bound with the history of the sanctuary and the oracle; to be more precise, Delphi only existed as a township under the shadow of the sanctuary. Archaeological excavations have revealed the existence of an insignificant settlement on the site of the sanctuary and further east, dating back to *c*. 1400 B.C. This settlement was destroyed at the end of the Mycenaean period, but came back to life in Geometric times, when Apollo's cult began to take root in that region. Hence-forward, Delphi acquired world fame and power of a kind unparallelled in Greece, although it remained a small town, sparsely populated. Over the course of 250 years, four sacred wars were waged for this small town, and at the end it caused the annihilation of the Phokians.

It is no easy task to embrace the whole history of Delphi in a few lines, or to interpret the significance of the Delphic oracle since the earliest times of antiquity. Nevertheless, one should point out the fact that the Delphic oracle was by no means neutral to the historic destiny of Hellenism, nor did it restrict itself to the passive role of handing out prophetic advice. In a way that was unique and very nearly inexplicable to people of our times, the Delphic contribution to wartime and peacetime enterprises, to political and civil controversies, to intellectual and religious pursuits, was always highly relevant and decisive in the context of the Greek world.

During the peak period of Greek colonization, (late 8th-7th century B.C.), Greek cities that had resolved to establish a colony to some distant land first consulted the oracle as to where they should go and who should become the *oikistes,* the leader and founder of the future colony. Thus the prestige and fame of the god and his oracle spread East and West, far beyond the bounds of metropolitan Greece. As early as the 7th century B.C., Midas, the legendary king of Phrygia, sent his own royal throne to the Pythian Apollo as a token of his veneration. At about the same time, another legendary king, Gyges (675 B.C.), founder of the Mermnad dynasty and ancestor of Croesus, dedicated magnificent votive offerings of pure gold to the Delphic god. Kypselos, the renowned wealthy tyrant of Corinth, built in the Delphic sanctuary the first "treasury", i.e. a small building in the shape of a temple, which had the double function of serving as a votive offering and sheltering the smaller, precious offerings dedicated by each city to the sanctuary.

The glory, power and wealth of the Delphic oracle grew steadily. However, it appears that the Phokians of Krisa decided to exploit their position as neighbours to Delphi, and levied heavy dues on the faithful who disembarked at the port of Kirrha, in Phokian territory, on their way to the oracle. Delphi then appealed to the Amphiktyony for help and the First Sacred War was declared. It was to last ten years, ending in 591 B.C. with the annihilation of the Krisaians. Kirrha and Krisa were destroyed and their territory was dedicated to the Delphic deities. The Amphiktyons then proceeded to reorganize the Pythian festival, which took place every 8 years to commemorate Apollo's return from his voluntary exile after the slaying of Python. From 582 B.C. this festival was celebrated every four years; gymnastic and equestrian contests were added to the earlier musical competition.

About the middle of the 5th century B.C., the Phokians once again gained political power over Delphi; this led to the declaration of the Second Sacred War (447 B.C.), to restore the sanctuary's independance. In 373 B.C., a terrible earthquake uprooted huge pieces of rock and flung them on the temple of Apollo. Reconstruction started immediately, thanks to pan-Hellenic contributions, but it was interrupted in 356 B.C. by a Third Sacred War. The Phokians occupied the sanctuary for a period of ten years and confiscated not only sanctuary funds, but also a large number of valuable votive offerings. The Greeks felt highly indignant at this sacrilege. Following the intervention of Philip, king of Macedonia, the Phokians were routed, excluded from the Amphiktyony and obliged to pay a colossal indemnity (420 talents). Finally, the Fourth Sacred War broke out in 339 B.C., against the Lokrians this time. Once again, Philip assumed leadership; after defeating the Lokrians, he proceeded to Chaironeia, where he fought the famous battle (338 B.C.), which made him master of Greece.

The Hellenistic period

During the Hellenistic period, the Greek world underwent a radical transformation. The old faith was shaken; the cities gradually lost their independance and merged within the larger context of great kingdoms. The powerful kings began to rely on their own armies rather than on divine assistance. They still consulted the oracle and sent rich gifts, but this was done in a wish to display their own wealth rather than honour the god. In 279 B.C. once again with the miraculous assistance of Apollo, Delphi was saved from the brutal invasion of the Galatians. To commemorate this event, the Aitolians — who now ruled the area — instituted a new annual festival, the *Soteria* (Salvation festival). This invasion is mentioned in one of the two Delphic hymns engraved on the walls of the Treasury of the Athenians; these hymns have become famous because the musical notation that accompanied them has survived in the intervals between the lines. The kings of Pergamon, well-known for their generosity and love of the arts, built stoas, restored the old wall-paintings by Polygnotos, sent numerous offerings, but also made sure that their statues occupied a prominent position in the sanctuary.

In 168 B.C. the Roman Aemilius Paulus defeated the Macedonians at Pydna; and at Delphi, upon the pedestal which Perseus, the Macedonian king, had prepared for his statue, the Roman set up his own equestrian figure. The hour of Rome had come. In 86 B.C., Sulla removed all the valuable offerings that had survived the Fourth Sacred War; and in 83 B.C., barbarians from Thrace plundered the sanctuary and set fire to the temple; this was the first time, according to tradition, when the flame burning since time immemorial was extinguished, depriving both Greeks and barbarians of its beneficent radiance. Nevertheless, the Delphic sanctuary still prospered; Nero removed no less than 500 statues from Delphi; and yet when Pausanias visited it in the 2nd century A.D., he still found it full of masterpieces. However, when the Roman emperors were converted to Christianity, the ancient religion no longer had any place in the new State. And when Julian, that most romantic of emperors, sent Oreibasios to consult the Pythia at Delphi, the prophetess uttered her last oracle, as a kind of epitaph for the ancient sanctuary:

The growing fame of the Delphic Oracle

"Tell ye the King: the carven hall is fallen in decay;
Apollo hath no chapel left, no prophesying bay,
No talking spring. The stream is dry that had so much to say."

The fame and power of Delphi was based on its oracle, which was one of the oldest in Greece. Nearly all ancient authors mention it at some point, or record some story or incident relating to it. Nevertheless, it would be a mistake to believe that we possess all the information we would wish to have, or all the details we consider necessary, concerning the procedure of divination at Delphi. A great many problems remain unsolved and numerous questions have not yet found an answer. We shall try, therefore, to set down as briefly as possible the results of recent research into the methods of divination at the Delphic oracle.

The Delphic myths mention the existence of nymphs known as Thriai — in ancient Greek this word denotes the pebbles used in divination; one can therefore assume that these nymphs were simply the personification of divination by lot. The Delphic myths provide clear enough evidence that every known method of divination was practised at Delphi. But Delphi owed its fame to the oracles delivered by the Pythia, who received direct inspiration from Apollo and spoke in his name; in other words, the god of divination himself delivered the oracle, using the Pythia as a medium.

The Pythia was a woman over 50 years old. She was not necessarily a virgin, but from the moment she undertook this highest of duties — serving the god — she was under the obligation to abandon her husband and children, to move into a house destined for her alone, within the sacred precinct, to be chaste and irreproachable, and to observe certain religious rules. In spite of her age, she wore the garments of a young girl, as a mark of the virginal purity of her life. In the beginning there was only one Pythia; but when the requirements of the oracle grew more numerous, two more Pythias were added.

Until the Classical period, nobody had ever thought of questioning the Pythia's sudden transformation and the fact that Phoibos spoke through her. All that has been written about the natural vapours emanating from the chasm in the sanctuary, or about the laurel leaves the Pythia munched and the water she drank is but an attempt to find answers to the mystery, at a time when the faithful began to lose their faith, thinking they could explain the divine miracle with the cold instrument of reason and encompass the supernatural within a recognizable human measure. However, the ancient Greeks were certain of one thing alone: the importance of Apollo's sacred tripod, in other words, his throne, which had once been equipped with wings and carried him across land and sea. It was upon this throne that the Pythia sat in order to become the god's instrument. It was enough for her to take Apollo's place, to shed her ordinary identity, fall into a trance and deliver the divine messages in a series of mysterious, inarticulate cries.

In early antiquity, before the 6th century B.C., divination took place only once a year, on the seventh day of the month Bysios (February-March), on Apollo's birthday. Later on it took place every month, again on the seventh day of the month, except for the three winter months, because during that time the god left the Delphic sanctuary in order to travel far away to the land of the Hyperboreans, conceding his place to Dionysos, who was worshipped next to Apollo in his own temple. On the sacred day appointed for divination, the Pythia was the first to visit at dawn the Kastalian Spring to cleanse herself. Then she burnt laurel leaves on the sacred hearth and immersed herself in smoke. Meanwhile the priests prepared the sacrificial goat; if the god gave his consent, the animal was sacrificed on the great altar — a dedication of the Chians — in front of the temple, and thus all the pilgrims knew an oracle would be delivered that day at Delphi. In the meantime, the *Prophetai* and the *Hosioi* (priests of both Apollo and Dionysos) and certain delegates from the township of Delphi also cleansed themselves in the sacred waters of Kastalia. Finally, all the pilgrims who wished to consult the oracle similarly purified themselves at the spring.

When everyone was ready, they advanced in a festive procession towards the temple, filled with awe and anticipation. Delegates from the cities (*theopropoi*) and private individuals stood outside the temple and offered the *pelanos* at the altar — a kind of consecrated bread sold on the spot at a high price, the pilgrims' first contribution to the sanctuary.

The Pythia was already seated on the tripod in the *adyton* or inner shrine. The *Prophetai* stood nearby, and the pilgrim — it could only be a man — sat in a corner at some distance from her, having already posed his question to one of the *Prophetai,* either in writing or orally. The Pythia, hidden by some kind of partition, was not visible to anyone. The *Prophetes* put the question to her and she would give the god's response, deep in her trance. This was apparently unintelligible to others, but the *Prophetes* was able to comprehend it and write it down in hexameter verse; it was this written reply that was handed over to the pilgrim. The equivocal replies of the Delphic oracle have become famous in history; they were so obscure, so incomprehensible that additional divinatory gifts were required to interpret them correctly and avoid unfortunate mistakes. The case of Croesus is a good example: in answer to his question, the god said that if he waged war on the Persians, he would destroy a great power; he never suspected that *Loxias* (a surname of Apollo, meaning the Oblique One, because of the ambiguous replies he was giving) meant to convey that he would destroy his own kingdom if he fought the Persians.

Those nine days of the year when the Pythia spoke with the voice of the god must have had a tremendous impact on the pilgrims fortunate enough to be present in the Delphic sanctuary. Only a very small percentage of those who wished to consult the divine oracle had the privilege of receiving an answer within those nine days in the year when divination was performed. For this reason, since the Archaic age, most of the pilgrims' questions were answered in a different manner: by drawing lots. This kind of divination took place every day of the year, not in the *adyton,* but in public view; it was the most common method of divination as regards simple and concrete questions, that is to say questions that could be answered by a simple affirmative or negative.

The sanctuary of Athena Pronaia

Before reaching the Delphic sanctuary proper, we come upon the sanctuary of Athena Pronaia (now called Marmaria), situated on a narrow terrace on the left-hand side of the road looking down the valley of the Pleistos river. In remote antiquity, this must have been a place where some goddess was worshipped, as attested by the discovery of numerous Mycenaean figurines representing a goddess with outstretched arms. This sanctuary was later dedicated to Athena: it was she, together with Phylakos, a local hero, who guarded the sanctuary and temple of Apollo; hence she was given the name of *Pronaia,* i.e. the goddess who stood before the temple.

The remains of only a few buildings have survived within the enclosure of the sanctuary; but they are among the finest examples of ancient Greek architecture. They include the Archaic temple of Athena (built around 650 B.C.), which is one of the oldest monumental temples known to us. On the same site, but larger, was the second Archaic temple (built around 500 B.C.). Then there are two small treasuries, one of them Ionic and the other Doric; they are made of Parian marble, fashioned with sensitive, masterly skill, and their glowing beauty is a fitting preparation for that other "precious ornament" of the sanctuary of Athena, indeed, of the whole group of Delphic monuments: the celebrated *Tholos.* Finally, at the western end of the sanctuary, there is the third temple of Athena (370-360 B.C.), also in the Doric style, but built with "the most beautiful and most difficult stone to have been used in Delphi", the hard, grey limestone of Mount Parnassos.

The sanctuary of Apollo

Leaving the sanctuary of Athena Pronaia behind us, and before reaching the cleft of the Phaidriades, we see on our left the *Gymnasion* as it was modelled in the 4th century B.C. We continue on our way westwards. To the right is the awe-inspiring gorge, from which emerges the limpid sound of the sacred Kastalian Spring; Apollo's waters flow down generously into the rich green valley. The two great rocks of the Paidriades, Flempoukos to the east and Rhodini to the west, tower above us forbiddingly, and seem to touch the sky. And opposite, at the foot of Rhodini, extends the great Delphic sanctuary, the *temenos* of Apollo. Surrounded by a built enclosure, it clings to the slope, occupying an almost rectangular space with a particularly narrow and irregular south side. The main entrance, used by the pilgrims of antiquity, and the visitors of today, is on the southeast corner of the site. In the days of its glory, the holy site must have been the most impressive museum in the world. Elegant edifices, porticoes, official buildings, scattered in a disorderly pattern over the uneven mountain slope, huddling as best as they could to the right and left of the Sacred Way, some of them in a privileged position right by the road-side, others crowding behind, half-hidden, but all of them without exception fashioned with absolute faith in the master of the sanctuary, Apollo Phoibos. And among these buildings, thousands of statues and votive offerings, apart from the more precious ones which were kept in safety within the small, temple-shaped treasuries, as they were called. These treasuries, which were themselves votive offerings to the god, sheltered the other sumptuous offerings presented by the cities which had built them. The ruins of several treasuries have survived, an eloquent reminder of the sanctuary's worldwide fame. There are the ruins of the treasuries of the

Knidians, the Kyrenaians, the Thebans, the Potidaians, the Akanthians (from the Chalkidike peninsula) and the Corinthians. Other treasuries, like those of the Siphnians and the Athenians, have been less ravaged by time and have preserved their admirable sculptures, which are now exhibited in the Museum of Delphi.

But it is the god's temple that has pride of place in the great sanctuary. Half-way up the slope, there is a large terrace, supported on the south side by a fine polygonal wall which was intended to provide a firm base for the temple's foundations. On the north side, there is a retaining wall whose purpose was to protect the temple from falling rocks. The temple we see at present, erected in the 4th century B.C., is the third to have been built on that site (not including of course the three mythical temples of which the first was said to have been made entirely of laurel leaves, the second of feathers and wax, and the third of bronze). The first temple of Apollo was built in the 7th century B.C. and was destroyed by fire in 548 B.C. It was replaced by the Archaic temple of the Alcmeonidai, which was built with contributions by both Greeks and non-Greeks; it is the temple that displayed on its eastern pediment (made of marble) the god's Epiphany to mankind, when he arrived at Delphi on a chariot with his mother, Leto, and his sister, Artemis. This temple, too, was destroyed, in 373 B.C., and was rebuilt between 369 B.C. and 330 B.C. It is in this temple that the Pythia probably uttered her last oracle, addressed to Emperor Julian, and it was on the walls of the temple's *pronaos* that the visitor read those famous engraved proverbs "nothing in excess" and "know thyself", and the mysterious Delphic letter E, the secret significance of which neither the ancient Greeks nor modern scholars have been able to discover.

To the north of the temple, on the northwest corner of the sanctuary, lies the theatre, and east of that the famous *Lesche* (club) of the Knidians, where the great artist Polygnotos painted the sack of Troy and Odysseus' descent into Hades.

The excavations

In the centuries that followed the closing-down of the oracle, the site was stripped of all the invaluable works of art which had survived the repeated plunder of the emperors. As time went by, the buildings gradually fell into ruin and were covered with a thick layer of soil, which only just allowed some piece of marble, some faint inscription to appear here and there. Then there came a time when a tiny village, Kastri, was built on the site where the old sanctuary had once stood. In 1892, when the French Archaeological School began excavating the site, the entire village was expropriated by the Greek government and removed to its present position. The French archaeologists uncovered the whole sacred site; their excavations brought to light Apollo's sanctuary and revealed to our bedazzled eyes, the most sacred monuments of the ancient Greek world. The works of art that had escaped destruction, however few, suddenly spoke to us in their own divine fashion about their lost gods.

The Museum of Delphi, built in 1902, rebuilt in 1937-1938 and repaired after the war, shelters masterpieces of an artistic Amphiktyony, as it were, that had sent its representative works from every corner of the Greek land and from every period of Greek history.

The Museum
Kleobis and Biton

First among the cities represented here is Argos. In the dawn of the Archaic age, Argos sent its offering to the god; it is the first exhibit to be seen in the Museum of Delphi. The dedication consisted of the statues of two Argive youths, Kleobis and Biton, who harnessed themselves to their mother's chariot and drove her from the city of Argos to the sanctuary of Hera, i.e. a distance of no less than 45 stadia (8 klm.). Everybody marvelled at her good fortune in having two such sons; and the proud mother prayed to the goddess and begged her to bestow upon her sons the greatest blessing men dare hope for. Then all three offered sacrifice, ate their supper and went to sleep in the sanctuary. But Kleobis and Biton never woke again. The goddess had granted their mother's wish. It was the statues of these two youths that the Argives set up in the sanctuary of Delphi, as Herodotos recounts. Their physical vigour enabled them to gain immortality. In these two Archaic Kouroi Polymedes has admirably rendered the sense of physical strength, of athletic fitness; there is the sturdy modelling of the bodies, the broad chests and narrow waists, the powerful muscles, the square heads, the sharp emphasis on the articulations which both join and separate the various parts of the anatomy (fig. 2).

A few years later (560 B.C.), Naxos, a prosperous Cycladic island, also sent a votive offering to the Delphic god; it is the famous Naxian Sphinx, whose exquisite figure towers above a tall column 9.32 metres high (fig. 6). This daemonic creature, with its powerful form fascinated Greek artists, especially in the Archaic age. The Naxians' offering presents us with one of the earliest examples of this mythical figure. However, the craftsmen of Archaic Greece had already covered much ground by the time they reached this level of artistic achievement. The rhythmical juxtaposition of curves betrays a wealth of experience and a highly cultivated sensitivity; the large wide-open eyes, the tight lips convey a fascinating unwordly expression; the brilliant side-view reveals the artist's skill and audacity. The whole work testifies to the piety and wealth of the Naxians in the early Archaic period.

The metopes of the Treasury of the Sikyonians

Other even wealthier cities raised whole edifices — the famous "treasuries" — to honour the god and display their own power and piety. In these buildings, sculptural decoration competed with, and sometimes surpassed, architectural beauty. The city of Sikyon, rich and powerful in Archaic times, raised its treasury at the beginning of the Sacred Way, around 560 B.C. It seems that this edifice presented many unusual features (it was later replaced by another building). One of its singularities was that the metopes did not have the customary square shape, but were rectangular, as we can see in the surviving pieces exhibited in the Museum of Delphi. One of the metopes (fig. 3) represents the Dioskouroi, Kastor and Polydeukes, and the Apharidai, Idas and Lyngeus, following each other in an impressive formation; in between, we can see the heads of the oxen which they had stolen in the course of some joint raid — probably the one that ended with the murder of Kastor and the Apharidai. The artist illustrates the myth with remarkable order and clarity; he has even added the characters' names next to their figures, so that the spectator shall be in no doubt about their identity. Another metope, much more audacius both in conception and execution, represents the mythical ship, Argo, beaching upon the distant shores of Kolchis. In both these metopes, the dominant intention is to depict clear, solid figures in the plenitude of their motionless presence. A third metope, representing the rape of Europe by Zeus who had assumed the form of a bull, and a fourth, representing the wild boar in the celebrated Kalydonian hunt, convey impetuous movement in the most convincing manner.

The Siphnian Treasury

Next to the treasury of Sikyon, the Siphnians erected their own treasury in the year 525 B.C. The small Cycladic island of Siphnos, lived in great prosperity in those distant times, drawing immeasurable wealth from its gold and silver mines. Herodotos considered Siphnos as "one of the richest islands". Its inhabitants, therefore, aspired to dedicate to Apollo a votive offering that would be unique both in beauty and opulence. The Siphnian treasury was not very large (8.55×6.12 metres), but it was built entirely of glowing Parian marble: the first edifice in mainland Greece to be built wholly in marble. However, it was not the building itself that acquired fame in ancient Greece or that moves us most today, but its magnificent ornamentation. The predominance of sculpture over architecture reaches its highest peak in the Treasury of the Siphnians; statues were even used in place of main architectural parts. For instance, between the two antae, instead of Ionic columns there were two Korai supporting the architrave (fig. 5), a solution that was later to be put to brilliant use in the Erechtheion. The Korai stand upon high pedestals and are shown in sumptuous Ionic attire and jewellery. The artist has managed to maintain the self-sufficiency of these auxiliary figures without neglecting their fundamentally architectural function. Perhaps no other work of art can help us appreciate so clearly the ability of the Archaic sculptors, the sureness and confidence with which they fashioned any form they wished, always remaining keenly aware of both the requirements of their art and the functional demands of their work.

Pedimental sculptures

Above the architrave, the building is adorned on all four sides by a splendid frieze, the most exquisite in the Archaic period, a remote forerunner of the Classical frieze of the Parthenon. The east pediment at the back of the treasury has retained its sculptures, depicting a charming and typical myth related to Delphi, a favourite theme to both sculptors and vase-painters in the late Archaic period. Herakles, frantic with remorse for having murdered Iphitos, consulted the Delphic oracle about how he should cleanse himself. The Pythia would not answer him, because he was still defiled with the blood he had shed: upon which the son of Zeus snatched away the oracular tripod and prepared to leave. But Apollo also a son a Zeus and master of the oracle, could not remain indifferent to Herakles' action; he tried to take the tripod back. The carving on the pediment depicts the very moment when Athena intervenes and takes the two opponents by the hand in order to stop them from fighting each other (fig. 7).

The frieze

The most exquisite feature of the edifice, though, is the frieze. On the west side, it depicts the judgement of Paris, on the south the rape of the Leukippidai by the Dioskouroi, on the east an assembly of gods (fig. 8), who watch a battle of the Trojan War (fig. 9), and on the north which is the finest and best preserved section of the entire frieze, the Gigantomachy (figs. 10-12). Here we see the gods fighting hard to defeat the Giants, who are attacking from the right, wearing heavy armoury: helmets and shields, and in some cases breastplates and greaves; their weapons are spears, swords and stones. The left section of the frieze is taken up by the gods. On the extreme left, Hephaistos, wearing the short *chiton* of a craftsman, is shown standing in front of his fellows and preparing his redhot bolts. Next come two goddesses, Demeter and Kore; then Dionysos, wearing a panther skin, and Kybele riding a chariot drawn by lions (figs. 11 and 13). Then come Leto's beloved children, Apollo and Artemis, shooting arrows at their opponents; they are facing a warrior with a *kantharos* on his helmet: he is the Giant Kantharos (figs. 12 and 15). The next section of the frieze which has been damaged, showed Zeus riding his chariot. Hera (fig. 14) and Athena have survived, in a good state of preservation; next to them Ares is wearing a helmet and holding a shield; Hermes follows, wearing the conical cap of Arkadian shepherds (fig. 10); finally, come Poseidon and Amphitrite, but only fragments of the lower part of their bodies have survived.

The sculptor who produced the Gigantomachy and the battle between the Greeks and the Trojans must have been one of the great artists of his age, endoed with a powerful and daring imagination, unique technical skill and a deep awareness of the difficulties of relief sculpture. It is enough to notice the extraordinary rendering of the successive surfaces of the figures, which though frequently intertwined, always remain clearly distinct from each other. The impetus of the conflict and the mingling of the adversaries is reproduced with great power and intensity, without however damaging the clarity of form and the easy, flowing rhythm which carries us from left to right and back again, with admirable skill, in a movement not unlike the ebb and flow of a wave. But apart from its power and robust expressiveness, the frieze retains its decorative character; it is a sensitive arrangement and exploitation of a surface demanding to be filled, an impressive, but also festive development of the theme, with all the spiritual exaltation appropriate to the sacred site of Delphi.

The Treasury of the Athenians

There is a third treasury, which has survived in a fairly good condition and has been restored *in situ* with very few additions: it is the treasury which the Athenians dedicated to the sanctuary during the last years of the 6th century B.C., soon after the establishment of democracy in their city (508 B.C.). Only a few fragments remain from the pediments; but of the metopes there are enough left to enable us to reconstruct their themes almost in their entirety (figs. 17-19). On the main sections — i.e., the façade and the south side, which was more exposed to public view, there are representations of the exploits of Theseus, whom the Athenians regarded as the legendary founder of democracy; at the back of the treasury amd on the north side we see the labours of Herakles. These reliefs are a good example of Attic sculpture during the last phase of the Archaic period, and they bring to the spectator's mind the early, red-figured vase-paintings of that time, with their elegant figures, lightly-balanced proportions, firm and spirited movement, daring postures, flexible contours, careful and thoroughly studied rendering of muscles and draperies.

The Charioteer

The tyrants of Syracuse, the famous sons of Deinomenes, were wealthy, ambitious and much interested in the arts. They set up golden tripods at Delphi after the battle of Imera (479 B.C.); they also sent their chariots to win laurel crowns at the great pan-Hellenic games, and commissioned great poets like Pindar or Bakchylides to sing their victories. One of them, Polyzalos, "king of Gela", won the chariot-race at the Pythian Games of 478 B.C. He then sent a magnificent votive offering to the sanctuary of the Pythian Apollo: a bronze chariot drawn by four horses and driven by a charioteer. The earthquake of 373 B.C. dislodged huge rocks from the mountain-side, destroying the temple and several other edifices and votive offerings, among which Polyzalos' splendid gift. However, fortune proved relatively kind. the Charioteer was saved, practically intact, and Delphi reverently buried him when the site was levelled down for the construction of the new temple. That is how the magnificent Charioteer has reached us and taken its place as the most prized exhibit in the Museum of Delphi (figs. 20-21).

The young man, whom we call the Charioteer, stands upright, his two bare feet well planted on the chariot, proudly carrying his tall frame (1.80 metres), his hands (only the right one has been preserved) loosely holding the reins. He is wearing the long robe of a charioteer, secured tightly under the armpits by the *analabos,* to stop it from fluttering in the strong wind as he races along on his chariot; the victor's band (made of silver and inlaid) is tied on his brow; his gaze is fixed ahead, luminous but betraying a slight fatigue due to the excitement of the race. His stature, the structure of his tall and slender body, the arrangement of the folds in his robe, the firm position of his bare feet, the sense of strength combined with ease conveyed by his right hand holding the reins, the tiny, imperceptible movements, the subtle divergences from a strictly frontal position, the secret signs of a pulsating inner life — all this, acomplished with the help of innumerable details and in a manner that has remained quite unique, give the Charioteer of Delphi a monumental impressiveness and at the same time the glow of a living creature. The firm structure of the body is crowned by that unique head, with its extraordinary clarity of form, with the exquisite tracery of the hair, the intelligent gaze, the fleshy lips and cheeks, all powerfully framing the inner bone structure. The strength and fascination conveyed by every great work of art are successfully combined in this masterpiece with a noble gracefulness and a style that is both severe and joyful, so that the spectator is carried back in time to that triumphant moment when the victorious charioteer, proud and self-controlled at the same time, receives the crowd's applause as if it were an additional laurel wreath.

The votive offering of Daochos

All this is now lost forever. But in the Museum of Delphi, we can still see whatever remains from another offering of the late 4th century B.C. Although it cannot be compared to the splendid monuments presented by the proud Greek cities, the votive offering of the Thessalian Daochos, who represented his country at the Delphic Amphiktyony from 338 to 334 B.C., gives an unmistakable impression of opulence. It consisted of a large pedestal (which has survived) upon which stood Daochos himself with his son and his forefathers, five generations in all, facing Apollo's statue. Enough remains of these men's bodies to gain a fairly accurate estimate of this work's value. One of the best preserved figures among them is Agias, Daochos' great-grandfather, an athlete who had won considerable fame in the middle of the 5th century B.C. He won an Olympic victory in the *pankration* contest and was five times victor of the Nemean Games, three times of the Pythian Games and five times of the Isthmian Games. This is then the legendary figure represented by the young athlete standing today in the Museum of Delphi, with his sinewy body, his bent elbows and weary head (fig. 23). The structure of the naked body, made up of a multitude of expressive, counter-balancing movements, the modelling of masses, the powerful proportions, these all embody the artistic *credo* prevailing in the late 4th century B.C. There can be no doubt that this is the work of a major artist. We also know that a bronze statue of this athlete was set up at Pharsalos, with the inscription: "this is the work of Lysippos of Sikyon". It is highly probable, therefore, that the marble statue at Delphi was a contemporary copy of the Pharsalos statue, and that it was made with his approval.

The "dancers"

The dedicant of the elaborate and unusual offering known as the "column with the dancers" (fig. 22) has remained unknown to this day. A tall, slender column ll metres high is entwined at the base with acanthus leaves; other leaves seem to grow out of the column's trunk at intervals. Three maidens, their backs leaning against the top of the column, lead a light and graceful dance all around it, like flowers growing among the thick foliage of this strange plant. It is impossible for us to say who were these exotic figures with their short tunics and high headdresses. They have been called Graces, then thought to be Thyadai, i.e. Maenads (dancers of Dionysos); they have even been described as Karyatids, i.e. Lakonian girls dancing. Whatever they may be, their dance is undoubtedly sacred, dedicated to the god for his own enjoyment together with the votive offering set up in the Delphic *temenos*.

Hellenistic and Roman votive offerings

From the remaining exhibits at the Museum of Delphi, the visitor will surely single out a remarkable early Hellenistic statue representing a philosopher (fig. 24). There is also a portrait head, the beard beautifully and precisely rendered, the features sharp and alien-looking (fig. 25). Whether it portrays some Macedonian prince or some Hellenized personage from the East, or whether it is, as some archaeologists suggest, a portrait of the Roman Flamininus, this fine head certainly gives an idea of how much Hellenistic art had to offer at its peak years in the field of portraiture.

Finally we come to the statue of Antinoos (fig. 26). When Apollo's priest, Aristotimos, set it up in the sanctuary, the radiant god of Delphi may have considered it a provocation or he may have delighted in the presence of this beautiful boy. It is rather improbable that the priest of the Pythian Apollo should have thought it irreverent to present this enchanting youth to his god. For all we know, the priest may well have believed in Emperor Hadrian's command, proclaiming his beloved youth a god after his death. All we can say at present is that the gentle figure, meditating nostalgically upon a glorious past, closes the long series of votive offerings on a note of tenderness and serenity. It is obvious that by that time the last spark of inner energy and ardour has died away, that the oil in the lamp of the ancient world is running low, and that men sadly contemplate the abandonment of their old ideals. Antinoos is a noble, though languid and lifeless figure, which eloquently shows what remains of plastic form when it lacks inner force, the vigorous manly spirit which gave life to the glorious athletic youths of Greek sculpture.

1. *Hellenistic or Roman copy of the Archaic omphalos (navel-stone). It is covered by the agrenon, a kind of thick net, and was surmounted by the two golden eagles of Zeus that flew from the two ends of the world to meet at its centre, at Delphi.*

1

2. *Kleobis and Biton. This group of the two Kouroi was dedicated to the Delphic sanctuary by the Argives in the early 6th century B.C. It is the work of the Argive sculptor (Poly)medes and a good example of the style of this Peloponnesian workshop. The inscription at the base records their achievement and preserves part of the artist's name. c. 590 B.C.*

3. *One of the metopes of the Treasury of the Sikyonians. It represents Kastor, Polydeukes and Idas (followed by Lyngeus on the section now missing). The names of the figures represented are designated by inscriptions, barely legible at present, painted in colour. Armed with spears, they are shown leading away the oxen they had stolen in a joint raid. c. 560 B.C.*

3

4. *Flying Nike (Victory); corner akroterion on the façade of the Archaic temple of Apollo. c. 510 B.C.*

5. *Torso of one of the two Korai supporting the entablature of the Siphnian Treasury. These female figures were used instead of columns and became known later as Karyatids. c. 525 B.C.*

4

5

6. The Sphinx of the Naxians. This demonic Sphinx, offered to the sanctuary by the wealthy Naxians, crouched upon a tall Ionic column that stood south of the temple of Apollo, near the Sibyl's rock. The Cycladic island of Naxos possessed considerable riches and power in the Archaic period, and the Naxian workshop of sculpture produced a number of important works of art. c. 560 B.C.

7

8

7. *The east pediment of the Siphnian Treasury. It illustrates the myth of the dispute between Herakles and Apollo over the Delphic tripod. In the middle we see Athena intervening between Herakles (on the right) and Apollo (on the left), as they each tug away at the tripod. Artemis is shown behind Apollo, trying to support her brother by the arms. c. 525 B.C.*

8. *Left section of the east frieze of the Siphnian Treasury. The subject here is the assembly of the gods who watch a battle of the Trojan War. The gods shown on this section championed the Trojan camp: Ares, Aphrodite, Artemis, Apollo and Zeus (whose head is missing). c. 525 B.C.*

9. *Right section of the east frieze of the Siphnian Treasury. A battle between Greeks and Trojans.*

10. *Right section of the north frieze. From left to right: a Giant, Ares stooping over a dead Giant, two Giants, Hermes wearing his conical cap and two more Giants.*

11, 12. *Left section of the north frieze of the Siphnian Treasury, representing the Gigantomachy. The gods are fighting the Giants, who are shown as hoplites. From left to right: two Giants, Dionysos, Kybele riding a chariot drawn by lions. Fig. 12: Apollo and Artemis, the Giant Kantharos, a dead Giant and three other Giants.*

10

12

13

13. Detail from the north frieze of the Siphnian Treasury. One of the lions drawing Kybele's chariot is shown tearing a Giant to pieces with its claws and teeth.

14. Detail from the north frieze of the Siphnian Treasury. Hera is shown kneeling over a fallen warrior.

15. *Detail from the north frieze of the Siphnian Treasury. Apollo and Artemis are shooting arrows at the Giants; one of the Giants is trying to escape, looking backwards. The inscription next to him informs us that his name is Kantharos; that is why the artist has put a vase known as kantharos as a crest on the Giant's helmet.*

16. *Four-horse chariot, from the south frieze of the Siphnian Treasury. This side of the frieze, like the west side, is probably the work of an artist of Ionian origin; both sides are not as well preserved as the rest. A number of horses have survived, either ridden by horsemen or harnessed to chariots. If we compare this artist to the creator of the east and north sections, the artistic excellence of the latter becomes obvious.*

16

20

20 - 21. *The Charioteer is one of the finest products of the 'severe style'. He was found practically intact; the composition included a bronze chariot drawn by four horses. It was dedicated to the sanctuary by Polyzalos, tyrant of Gela, around 475 B.C., following his victory at the Pythian Games.*

22

22. *One of the most attractive and enigmatic monuments found at Delphi is this column with the three female dancers. The entire monument must have been about 13 m. high; it consisted of a column encircled with acanthus leaves; at the top, three maidens, wearing the sacred headgear, are engaged in what is obviously a ritual dance. The column was surmounted by a tripod. The dedicant of this offering is unknown. All we can say is that this is a work by an Ionian artist of the early 4th century B.C.*

23. *The statue of Agias was one of a group of nine dedicated by the Thessalian Daochos; it comes from the workshop of Lysippos, the great Sikyonian sculptor of the second half of the 4th century B.C.*

24. *Statue of a philosopher. It is a remarkable work, typical of the early Hellenistic period and possibly a product of the Attic workshop. c. 250 B.C.*

23

24

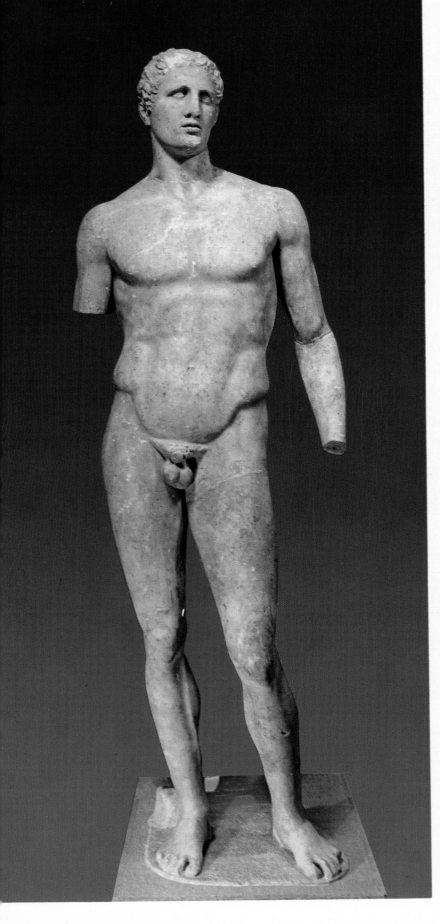

25

25. This fine portrait occupies pride of place in the art of portraiture of the mature Hellenistic period (first half of the 2nd century B.C.). The forceful plastic modelling, the expressive intensity of the face combine to produce a composition which represents Hellenistic art at its best. Some archaeologists regard it as a portrait of Flamininus, the Roman general who defeated Philip V in 197 B.C. at Kynos Kephalai.

26. The statue of Antinoos at Delphi is one of the finest portraits of this lovely youth. After his death, Emperor Hadrian, who loved him passionately, proclaimed him a god and ordered his statue to be set up in innumerable cities throughout the Roman empire. This graceful, melancholy figure, which reflects the world of the Imperial age, embodying the external strength and aesthetic passion that tempted to conceal the decay and decline of the ancient world, was encountered in the remotest regions of the Mediterranean, from Africa to Greece, from Syria to Western Europe. A.D. 130 - 138.

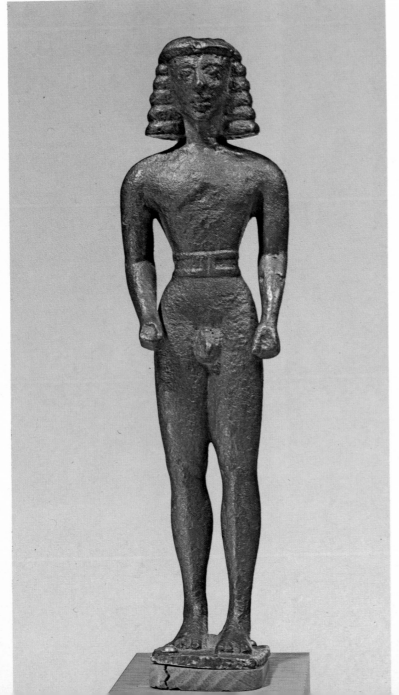

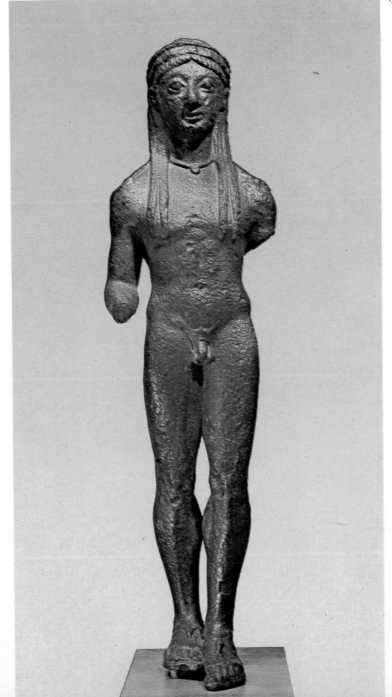

27. *Head of a griffin adorning a bronze tripod. 7th century B.C.*

28. *Composition representing Odysseus (or one of his companions) clinging to the belly of a ram in order to escape unnoticed from the cave of the Cyclop Polyphemos. This was part of the ornamentation on an early Archaic bronze tripod.*

29. *This very early bronze Kouros from Delphi is an exceptionally fine example of 'Daidalic art'; it transcends the limitations of its small size and produces a monumental effect. Mid-7th century B.C.*

30. *Bronze figurine probably representing Apollo. c. 525 B.C.*

31. *Bronze censer; the peplos-clad female figure holds a semi-spherical vessel in her raised hands. c. 450 B.C.*

31

32. *Apollo pouring libations . Interior of a white kylix found at Delphi. Apollo is seated, with great poise and majesty, upon a folding diphros (stool). His garment is unusual for a male figure: he is wearing a peplos and a himation. In his left hand he holds his lyre, and with his right he pours the libation from a phiale. On the left-hand side of the composition a bird is perched on a wooden bar; this may be Apollo's sacred bird, the raven, or (more likely) a wild dove, like those that come to roost in his temple. There is a divine nobility and a profound spirituality about this beautiful, laurel-crowned head with its finely dressed hair. The precision and flowing ease of the design, the colour harmony and the architectural solidity of the whole composition indicate that this vase must have been painted by one of the finest artists in the early years of the 'severe style'. c. 470 B.C.*

32

OLYMPIA MUSEUM

OLYMPIA MUSEUM

The ancient cult and myths of Olympia

Places, like men, have their destinies. On the remote slopes of Mount Parnassos, Apollo brought together the Hellenes under the Delphic Amphiktyony, and delivered oracles to both Greeks and "barbarians". There was, however, another remote corner of Greece, in the western Peloponnesos, which became the first home of athletics and whose name, as a result, spread throughout the world: Olympia.

The green landscape of Olympia, peaceful and serene, unfolds between two rivers, the Alpheios and the Kladeos. In ancient times, it was full of plane-trees and wild olives; in the dialect of the local inhabitants, the beautiful grove was known as the *Altis*. Whereas the god Apollo had found it necessary to lead men himself to the awe-inspiring rock of Delphi, the rich plain of Olympia was easily accessible and hospitable, as if asking to be chosen for habitation. It was only natural that men should decide to build their houses there at the beginning of the 2nd millennium B. C., or perhaps a little earlier. The apsidal dwellings discovered in the deeper layers of soil on the site of the sanctuary belong to the Middle Helladic period (1900-1600 B.C.). The first settlers knew nothing of Zeus and the Olympian gods. Tradition has it that the earliest cult was that of Kronos. This ancient god, father of Zeus, was worshipped on the imposing hill that dominates and bounds the northern side of the sanctuary. The hill was dedicated to him, as its name – Kronion – implies. At the foot of the hill stood other sanctuaries dedicated to female deities: Aphrodite Ourania, Eileithya (and the dragon-shaped daemon Sosipolis), the Nymphs; finally there was the "Gaion", one of the earliest sanctuaries and oracles, belonging to the very first diviner, the goddess Gaia (Earth), and to her daughter Themis. We have no way of knowing when and how the cult of Pelops — the mysterious hero who gave his name to the Peloponnesos — reached Olympia, or why he became associated with the sacred Altis as the local "daemon", holy and venerable, worshipped next to Zeus. It is quite probable that his cult is older than that of Zeus, and that his *temenos* — the Pelopion — within the sanctuary, is the oldest known monument of the cult, dating back to the same period as the Hippodameion — Hippodameia's sanctuary — whose position is unknown to us. The ancient Greeks knew that this region, named Pisatis, from its capital, Pisa, was ruled by king Oinomaos, who had a daughter called Hippodameia. Before giving away his daughter in marriage, Oinomaos demanded that her suitor should defeat him in a chariot-race. If, however, the suitor lost the race, Oinomaos would kill him. The king had killed thirteen such suitors when Pelops came to Pisa. He was the son of Tantalos, from distant Lydia, and his purpose was to take Hippodameia as his wife. During the crucial chariot-race, he defeated the cruel king and married Hippodameia. This was how Pelops became associated with Olympia and was henceforth worshipped in the sacred Altis.

There exists another myth, however, which supplies us with clearly historical information. The myth says that when the time came for the Herakleidai to return to their fatherland, the Peloponnesos, they went through a series of mishaps and calamities. Finally, the Delphic god advised them to find a "three-eyed" guide and go through "the narrow pass". On their way they encountered the one-eyed

Oxylos, a descendant of Aitolos, who had been king of Elis before going into exile to the land that later took his name Aitolia. Oxylos was riding a horse, and therefore was "three-eyed". The Herakleidai asked him to guide them across to the Peloponnesos. Oxylos took them to Arkadia, while he turned west with the Aitolians and travelled to Elis, which was then inhabited by the Epeians. A battle ensued between the Aitolians and the Epeians and culminated in a heroic duel between the Aitolian Pyraichmes and the Epeian Degmenos; Pyraichmes emerged the victor. Thus Oxylos became once again King of Elis and the Aitolians lived peacefully side by side with the former inhabitants of the region.

The myth of Oxylos is a good illustration of what recent historical research refers to as the descent of the western Greek tribes into the Peloponnesos at the end of the Mycenaean era. It appears that the cult of Zeus dates from that time, and that he was worshipped as a warrior god, as shown by the early figurines representing him with a helmet. This warlike attribute is still manifest in the archaic cult statue of Zeus (circa 600 B.C.) which was housed in the Heraion, next to the seated Hera.

The Olympic games

It was only natural that the new cult of the "father of men and gods" should acquire a predominant place in the sacred grove and that the shrine should end by belonging mainly to him. But apart from the great altar, where the richest sacrifices were offered there were several other altars in the Altis. Pausanias mentions 69, and we know he has not included all of them in his account. This means that Olympia was a sacred site where the ancient cults of the indigenous people continued to be practised next to the Olympian religion introduced by the settlers from western Greece. But this was not the factor that consecrated Olympia as the greatest Panhellenic sanctuary and determined its character and significance. Olympia owes its very special place among the other Greek sanctuaries to the games performed there every four years. The ancient Greeks ascribed the beginning of the Olympic games to mythical times. This implies that the Olympic games were believed by the Greeks to be of a most ancient and sacred origin and that they formed an integral part of the ancestral cult.

Modern research is far from unanimous in interpreting the institution of the games. Some scholars believe that man's natural disposition to train himself and compete with others was the main motive that led the Greeks to introduce athletic games. But most scholars associate the introduction of the games with burial rites, because we know that in Homeric times games were held in honour of the dead.

However may one interpret the birth of the Olympic games, their importance exceeds the limitations of both the time and the place where they wery originally instituted. It is no exaggeration to say that those games gave birth to yet another Greek idea, a whole attitude to life — the attitude of a free man competing with his peers, naked, unfettered by any element foreign to his own body, conforming only to the rules of the game, with the sole aim of winning for himself an olive crown — in other words a purely moral victory – and the praise of his fellow-men.

The significance of the games in Greek history

The Olympic games proved to be historical landmarks for the ancient Greek world. The year 776 B.C., which was the date of the first Olympiad, is also the first certain and accurate chronology in Greek history, because henceforth the names of victors in every Olympiad were officially recorded. The first victor was Koroibos of Elis, who won the one-stade race. But there is a second, far more important historical conclusion to be drawn from the Olympic games: the Greeks, though divided into numerous tribal groups, though scattered over a vast area from Asia Minor to Italy and from Africa to Macedonia, though organized into hundreds of small states often at war with each other, had a deep awareness of their ethnic unity, which set them apart from the other inhabitants of the world. Only free Greeks were allowed to participate in the Olympic games; that is why the highest officials and judges of the games were named *Hellanodikai,* an ancient title that shows the supreme significance of the Olympic games in the life of the Greeks. Their celebration demanded that all Greeks be present in peaceful assembly in the sacred grove. For this purpose the *spondophoroi,* noblemen of Elis followed by an official retinue acted as heralds travelling to all the Greek cities well ahead of the games, in order to proclaim the "ekecheiria", i.e., a truce, a suspension of hostilities that would last up to three months. Thus all the Greeks could proceed without fear to Olympia and attend the most splendid Panhellenic assembly, where they could not only admire youths excelling in athletic games, but also single out famous noblemen and illustrious sages, listen to poets and musicians, and above all mingle among themselves: the Dorians of Sicily with the Ionians of the east, the Greeks of Kyrene with their distant brothers from Macedonia.

All this took place under the gaze and protection of the great Zeus, a warrior himself, who always stood by the Hellenes, whether in the struggles of war or in the peaceful contests of athleticism. In return, the Greeks, being a deeply religious people, offered him the arms which had brought them victory and the spoils of war which the god had helped them appropriate. The victors set up their own statues in the shrine of Zeus, not out of arrogance, but with the piety of those who can accept a god's gift in perfect humility. As the years went by, the votive offerings in the sacred grove grew more and more numerous, till they could be numbered by the thousands; they included precious and famed weapons which eventually made Olympia the most complete museum of the war history of Greece.

Architectural arrangement of the sanctuary

In Olympia as in Delphi, many Greek cities raised "treasuries" in which to shelter their votive offerings. The Treasuries here were not scattered within the *temenos*, as they were in the Delphic sanctuary, but were built in a row at the foot of Mount Kronion during the Archaic period (with a few exceptions). Apart from two of them, they were all offerings from Greek colonies overseas. However, it is noteworthy that until the early 5th century B.C., there was only one monumental edifice near the Treasuries in the sacred grove; this was the very early temple of Hera (600 B.C.), in which Zeus was also woshipped. Two other buildings, the Prytaneion and the Bouleuterion — the former west of the Heraion and the latter at some distance to the south, beyond the sanctuary enclosure — did not singificantly alter the image of the shrine, which always consisted of the sacred grove, the altar of Zeus, the tomb of Pelops, the Hippodameion and of cource the vast *stadion* and the *hippodromos*. Zeus, himself, the god of the sanctuary, did not possess a temple of his own. But in 472 B.C., when the state of Elis underwent a radical reorganization along the lines of the Athenian democracy, and when, a year later, the new capital, Elis, was founded as a result of a synoecism, it appears that the inhabitants decided to erect a temple to Zeus in the Altis. We know that the architect who built this temple was the Eleian Libon and that it was completed in 457 B.C., because that was the year when the Lakedaimonians dedicated to the temple a solid gold shield, which they set up on the akroterion, in commemoration of their victory over the Athenians at Tanagra. The dimensions of the temple were 27. 68m × 64.12m, which made it the largest in mainland Greece at the time. It was decorated with two admirable pediments and twelve metopes in relief, which are the most mature and powerful works produced by the severe style. A few years later, when Pheidias had completed his great works for the Athenian Acropolis, he came to Olympia and set to work on the gold and ivory statue of Zeus (12m. high) seated majestically upon his throne.

Excavations and research

It is from then onwards that the site began to be organized architecturally; numerous buildings appeared in rapid succession: porticoes, a *gymnasion*, a *palaistra*, a *katagogion* (guest-house), public baths, etc; a multitude of votive offerings filled the empty intervals between the buildings, particularly in the area east of the temple. The fame of the sanctuary and of the games persisted throughout the following centuries; the Romans added their own buildings and offerings to the already crowded site. The 293rd Olympiad was held in A.D. 393, i.e. 1169 years after the first. It was to be the last; the following year, emperor Theodosios issued the well-known decree prohibiting the practice of the ancient cult and the performance of the games. A few years later, an early Christian basilica took the place of Pheidias' workshop. In the 6th century A.D., a tremendous earthquake, such as often befalls the region, toppled to the ground all that had remained standing of the great temple. The two rivers, the Alpheios and the Kladeos, gradually covered up the ruins, protecting them under layers of silt till the day when the French archaeological mission of General Maison started digging up the site in April 1829. But systematic excavations began much later, on September 22, 1875, and have continued to this day, under the auspices of the German Archaeological Institute. These excavations were conducted with exemplary order and brilliant results, as was only to be expected if one recalls that among the first to participate in them were scholars like E. Curtius, and later on, eminent archaeologists such as Dörpfeld, Furtwängler, and more recently, E. Kunze. The first finds were numerous and important enough to warrant the creation of a museum. With funds supplied by Andreas Syngros and on plans designed by the German architects Adler and Dörpfeld, the Museum of Olympia was built in 1886; and it is this museum that still shelters part of the finds, all those that have not yet been transferred to the new museum which was recently opened and which allows a better display of the sculptures and the innumerable bronze votive offerings that represent one of the most valuable and rare collections in the whole world.

The Museum The pediments of the Temple of Zeus

We can fully appreciate the sculpture of the severe style (480-450 B.C.), when contemplating the Poseidon of Artemision, at the National Archaeological Museum in Athens, or the Gharioteer at the Museum of Delphi. Works of this class are landmarks of the age in which they were produced, and they enable us to comprehend certain aspects of the severe style; but they do not provide an overall picture of the spiritual foundations and artistic conquests of this style. Fortune, however, has saved, for our delight, the most impressive group of sculptures embodying the claims and achievements of the severe style in a supreme and unparalleled creation: the pediments and metopes of the temple of Zeus at Olympia.

On the east pediment (fig. 5) the composition draws its inspiration from the myth of the chariot-race between Pelops and Oinomaos. We see all the characters of the drama just before the beginning of the race; the two teams, Oinomaos and Sterope on the one side, Pelops and Hippodameia on the other, and next to them, the chariots and charioteers. Between the two teams, the imposing figure of Zeus forms the axis of the pediment. The "severe harmony" has never found a more appropriate aesthetic form: the vertical lines of the characters and the spears create a ponderous, hieratic atmosphere of tragedy in the centre of the composition, while on either side the chariots and the kneeling or reclining figures, act as a frame, thus strikingly combining two elements that not only function differently, but antithetically; there is the same antithesis between the broad, clear surfaces of the central figures, which are conceived idealistically, as superhuman beings, and the realistic gestures and postures of the secondary figures (fig. 7-8).

The west pediment (fig. 6) depicts a Centauromachy during which the Centaurs,. invited to the wedding of Peirithoos, a Lapith hero, get drunk and try to abduct the bride, Deidameia, and the other women present. This composition differs totally from the one on the east pediment. The incomparable figure of Apollo in the centre is the only one to maintain the vertical majesty of divine quietude; on his left and right, we see Theseus and Peirithoos, and then groups of Lapith men and women grappling with Centaurs, in a rhythmical and impetuous alternating movement, literally caused by opposite tensions, as it fluctuates incessantly from the centre to the two ends and back again, like the ebb and flow of the sea. The scenes depicted here are unequivocally violent, and the antithesis between the smooth virginal beauty of the girls and the bestial deformity of the Centaurs remains unbridgeable (fig. 9-12).

The contrast between the pediments is quite obvious to the spectator. On the east pediment, everything has come to a standstill, as if with suspended breath; forces are poised in expectation of the tragic conflict. On the west pediment, the conflicting forces have come to grips and are now locked in deadly combat. And yet both pediments are but a supreme expression, in plastic terms, of the tragic element. The power of tragedy is equally perturbing in both; it is only the expression that differs, in its selection of a different phase in the drama. On the east pediment, everything forebodes the coming catastrophe; the bride, who has broken away from her father's group to take up her position at her husband's side, already announces its outcome. On the west pediment, the imposing figures of the two heroes standing on either side of the great god of light, assure us that they will victoriously oppose the criminal violence of the Centaurs, with the help of the blessing expressed by the god's outstreched hand.

The metopes of the Temple of Zeus

The twelve metopes which were placed over the *pronaos* and the *opisthodomos* — divided into sets of six — represent the twelve labours of Herakles; for the first time in Greek art the *dodecathlon* becomes codified, so to speak. Some of the metopes have suffered severe damage, and three of them were removed to the Louvre by the first French excavators. However, thanks to intensive efforts, the archaeologists have succeded in reconstituting several missing sections, so that we can now form a fairly accurate picture of the compositions and their plastic skill, which is indeed remarkable. The artist's imagination, wisdom and audacity, his flexibility, his wealth of expression have enabled him to obtain truly unique results, unsurpassed even, in several respects, by the metopes of the Parthenon itself. From the deeply exciting metope of the Knossian bull, with its conflict of forces, to the idyllic scene with the Stymphalian birds (fig. 15), from the unexpected version of the myth of the Nemean lion, lying dead at the feet of the exhausted Herakles, or the impressive and imaginative solution given to the story of the golden apples of the Hesperides (fig. 13), to the truly unique representation of the Augean stables (fig. 14), the conception, composition and execution in all these scenes convince us that we are in the presence of a genius, a creator of the highest order.

It goes without saying that a large number of craftsmen must have had a hand in producing this magnificent collection of sculptures; archaeologists have been able to pinpoint their various contributions in the figures of the metopes. However, as in the Parthenon later, towering above all these assistants and disciples, there existed a great artist who conceived, designed and supervised the execution of the three compositions. The highly original and noble conception of the whole work was the first, vital achievement; it took form in unusually bold and vigorous figures and their architecturally dynamic synthesis. We do not know who this great artist was; art historians, filled with admiration and awe at his achievement, admit their inability to determine even his artistic affinities; some believe that he belonged to the indigenous Peloponnesian tradition, while others suggest an island origin. However, as Sir John Beazley, the greatest historian of ancient art, only recently lost to us, might have said, the name of the artist is of little importance, since we are privileged to have before us his own work, which conveys the highest artistic messages, as well as the spiritual and religious exaltation of those distant times; one may safely assert that it shares the same degree of eminence as the poetry of Aischylos and Pindar.

Archaic sculptures

These unique sculptures dominate the Museum of Olympia and make such a tremendous impact on the visitor that he finds himself unable to turn his eyes (or his mind, for that matter) to anything else. However, there exist in the museum a number of marvellous creations which mark the history of Greek sculpture in its most significant phases. For instance, the poros lion once serving as a spout, is one of the earliest – if not *the* earliest – works of Greek large sculpture, dating, as it does, from the period prior to the mid-7th century B.C.

The colossal head of Hera wearing a sacred headdress (*polos*) (fig. 2) takes first place in the history of Peloponnesian art, which was to produce in subsequent years a number of fine works. This head probably belonged to the very early cult statue of Hera which was set up in the Archaic Heraion, and which represented the goddess seated upon a throne, next to the standing Zeus. It is a creation of the early years of the 6th century B.C., practically contemporary with the Kouros of Sounion at the National Museum in Athens, of Kleobis and Biton at Delphi and of the sculptures of the temple of Korkyra. It shows us that from that early Archaic period, Greek sculpture succeeded not only in producing figures of a remarkable plastic plenitude and sensitivity, but also in representing the divine form with a combination of audacity and piety.

Clay sculpture in the severe style

The centuries gone by have stripped the sanctuary of Olympia, like many others, of innumerable statues, that would have enabled us to follow step by step the transformation of form and content in successive representations of the god. However, we find some compensation for this great loss in the small bronze statuettes of various periods, which have fortunately survived in large numbers. By another stroke of good fortune, a few examples of clay sculpture have reached us; this kind of sculpture must have been fairly common in ancient Greece, but most of it has perished. Only a few such works were found in Olympia, but they are comparable to the best marble and bronze sculptures, for their size distinguishes them from miniature art and places them in the class of large sculpture. It is enough to stand before the clay head of Athena (fig. 3) to sense the power concealed in this work; the face has been incomparably rendered; the flesh seems to pulsate with some inner tension; the sensitive, yet tightly drawn curves of the lips, and the flexible, watchful arches of the eye-lids and eye-brows framing the extraordinary inward-looking gaze — all this, crowned by the double row of curls in the archaic style, testifies in the most brilliant way how much Corinthian art had achieved in the later Archaic period, a few years before the battle of Salamis.

The finest of these clay statues in Olympia probably dates a few years later than the head of Athena (*circa* 470 B.C.) This admirable composition barely exceeds one metre in height; it probably stood on top of some pediment as an attractive akroterion. It represents the abduction of the beautiful Ganymedes by Zeus (fig. 4). The yellowish Corinthian clay of which it is made acquires incomparable warmth with its deep colouring. It is a daring and original work, which gives the great god a more familiar expression, less unwordly and awe-inspiring, without however detracting anything from his superhuman and divine character.

After the austere postures of Archaic sculpture, the statues fashioned in the severe style seem to be trying to exhaust all the possibilities afforded by the motion of the human body in its most vigorous and triumphant moments, thus obtaining an effect of unprecedented dynamism.

The Nike of Paionios

Next to the unique examples of the severe style in the Museum of Olympia, the works representing the Classical age occupy only a limited space; they do not enable the visitor to form as complete a picture of Greek sculpture as one might expect from a site which was once overflowing with such works, as we are told by Pausanias and as we can ascertain for ourselves from the surviving pedestals, now deprived of the statues they once supported. Only two statues of the Classical period have escaped plundering; but they are so important and so representative that they compensate to a certain extent for the loss of all the others.

The first of these statues is a Nike (Victory) offered by the Messenians and Naupaktians in gratitude for their victory over the Lakedaimonians in 424 B.C.; it is known by the name of the artist who made it: the Nike of Paionios (fig. 16). It stood upon a tall triangular pedestal (about 9 m. high) in front of the east side of the temple of Zeus, and gave the spectator the impression that Victory, descending from her heavenly abode, was about to land on that very spot. This work is an exceptionally audacious achievement. It is the first time in the history of Greek sculpture that the flight of the winged goddess is rendered with such a keen feeling for the subject, without sacrificing either the plastic values or the structure of the work. The exquisite draping of the lower part of the *himation*, which counterbalances the two enormous wings, spread out wide open from the shoulder-blades, the marked inclination forward, impetuous, yet at the same time skillfully balanced, the suspended projection of the left limb, the slight bending of the head – all this is welded together into a composition that is full of vitality and majesty, not devoid, however, of grace and feminine refinement.

The Hermes of Praxiteles

A little further away stands the second Classical statue, perhaps the most renowned work of ancient Greek sculpture: the Hermes of Praxiteles (fig 17). His fame is so great that he hardly needs our introduction. Though a few archaeologists doubt his authenticity insisting that it is but an admirable Roman copy of the Praxitelian masterpiece, most scholars believe it to be the original, with a few interferences on the back part of the body which are due to a number of causes. The ravages of time have fortunately spared not only the slender body of the god, but also his face, with its pensive, humid gaze, the opulent, finely chiselled hair, the gentle curves of the brow and cheeks. However, if one is coming from the hall where the austere pedimental sculptures are exhibited and pauses before this lithe, rather soft body, produced in the late 4th century B.C., that is to say in an age of greater experience, yet weary from the long progress through the years, one inevitably finds it difficult to pass judgement and to adapt oneself to this new artistic climate. But whoever has resolved to travel through the immense scenery of the history of art must know that he is bound to encounter all kinds of flower and fruit, all equally important and valuable, and that he must not be taken aback by the unexpected shifts and changes he will find. This is precisely what makes for the inexhaustible wealth of art.

The bronze statuettes

We have already said that the statuettes compensate to some extent for the loss of the major sculptural works dedicated to Zeus, because their size does not in any way detract from their quality, which in some cases is remarkably high. For instance, the small figure of a bearded warrior, with a large sword on his left side, is an exquisite product of the Lakonian workshop in the mid-6th century B.C. (fig. 19). This figure, together with another surviving figure of a bald old man and several others, adorned the rim of a huge bronze vessel, most probably a krater, presented as a votive offering to the sacred grove. We know that the Lakonian bronze workshop was famous for its high skill in the Archaic period, and that it was particularly renowned for its kraters.

The Argive workshop was equally famous during that period; it maintained its reputation and high quality well into the Classical age, when it won an eminent position thanks to its outstanding artist Polykleitos and his descendants. One has only to look at the tiny statuette of a runner, arms outstretched and left knee slightly bent forward in preparation for the race, to understand how the Argive craftsmen succeeded in rendering, economically and effectively, both the athletic body and the elusive moment of self-propulsion (fig. 20). The inscription on the runner's right thigh "I belong to Zeus" suggests that the statuette was presented as an offering to the patron of the Olympic games by some athlete in the years 480-470 B.C.

The small figure of a horse (fig. 21) – once part of a composition representing a four-horse chariot – also seems to have originated from the Argive workshop. Like the runner, it was dedicated, a few years later (470-460 B.C.), to the sanctuary of Zeus. The austere posture of the horse's body, the simple yet skillful workmanship, the precision and sureness of touch in rendering the details of the head, place this work in the very first rank of creations in the severe style and enable us to visualize all those impressive bronze four-horse chariots dedicated by the rich archons of Sicily to the Panhellenic sanctuaries, such as the one from which the Delphi Charioteer originates.

Bronze sheets

Pausanias, the traveller of the 2nd century A.D. whose writings have proved so invaluable to us, describes in great detail, among the many things he saw at Olympia, a sarcophagus made of cedarwood. It was placed in the temple of Hera, a votive offering from the Kypselidai, the famous tyrants of Corinth in the early 6th century B.C., and it bore some representations in ivory and gold, and others engraved on the wood itself. Pausanias then goes on to describe the numerous Greek myths that were illustrated on it. The sarcophagus itself has not survived; but the sanctuary of Olympia yielded hundreds of bronze sheets with relief representations of great variety, which are not only admirable examples of Greek bronzework, but also offer a very early and lavish illustration of Greek myths. Many of these sheets are probably remnants from wooden sarcophagi like the one described by Pausanias or from wooden tablets, while some of the others were used as decorations for tripod legs or shield handles. On a bronze sheet belonging to a tripod of the 8th century B.C., we can see the earliest representation of the myth of the Delphic tripod, which Herakles attempted to take away in order to found an oracle of his own. However, the most interesting bronze sheets date from the 7th and 6th century B.C.; in many of these, archaeologists believe they can discern the technique of Ionian art as practised in the Cyclades, or of the eastern workshops of Samos, Chios, etc. This does not necessarily imply that they came to Olympia from those particular regions, because we are well aware that in the early Archaic period, several Ionian craftsmen worked in the Peloponnesos; it is not improbable that some of them even founded workshops in Olympia itself, where their work must have been in great demand.

Be that as it may, the works themselves are what matters most, the sensitiveness of the reliefs, the enchanting way they tell their stories. In one of the earliest bronze sheets (*circa* 630 B.C.), we see two Centaurs holding fir branches, and between them an armed warrior, whose feet seem to disappear into the ground from the middle of the calves down (fig. 22). An ancient spectator would immediately recognize here the myth of Kaineus, the hero who had been made immortal and whom the Centaurs wished to exterminate by nailing him into the ground with the help of fir-trunks. The representation of a warrior departing for the battlefield which we see on another bronze plate must also be mythological; before mounting his chariot, where the charioteer is already holding the reins, the warrior turns his head to throw a last glance at his wife, who is carrying a child in her arms and bidding him farewell (fig. 23). It is not easy to say which of the innumerable heroes who departed again and again on military expeditions the artist had in mind in those early decades of the 6th century B.C. What is certain, however, is that he succeeded in rendering the emotional atmosphere of such a moment simply and effectively, with restrained yet highly expressive gestures and attitudes. The two scenes that are depicted, one above the other, on a third bronze sheet, of a later date than the two previous ones (*circa* 570 B.C.), are even more concentrated and dramatic. In the scene at the bottom, Theseus is shown abducting Antiope, while in the upper scene, Orestes is seen killing his mother, Klytaimnestra (fig. 24). The characters' gestures have now grown intense and passionate as befits the themes represented; the compositions have a thematic and artistic self-sufficiency such as we can only encounter later in the relief metopes of Greek temples.

Bronze weapons

All the objects we have just mentioned were votive offerings to the god, or *agalmata* as the Greeks of the Archaic period used to call them, for they were intended to make the god rejoice. But nothing could cause a warrior-god, such as Zeus of Olympia, to rejoice more than a gift of splendid weapons. Therefore mortal warriors who also loved weapons, and wished them to be not only strong and enduring for the battle, but also beautiful to look at, so that they could take pride and pleasure in wearing them, offered their arms to the god unsparingly, in their wish to thank him for the victory he had granted them or the victory they hoped to win. Thus the *chalkotheke* (bronze-store) of Olympia possesses the richest and finest collection of ancient Greek weapons of every kind. It contains real masterpieces which astound the modern, practically-minded visitor with their unbelievably ingenious and inspired ornamentation.

Breast-plates

One of the most outstanding pieces, from every point of view, is the bronze breast-plate which came to light in the last century in the bed of the river Alpheios, became part of a private collection in Zakynthos and finally disappeared. Some archaeologists made drawings of it in 1883 in order to study the admirable representations engraved on it. Quite unexpectedly, it made its appearance again in 1969, at an auction of antiquities in Switzerland. Thanks to private contributions, it was purchased and brought back to the place where it had first been dedicated, in the middle of the 7th century B.C., by some rich sovereign, perhaps one of the famous "tyrants" that ruled a number of Greek cities throughout the 7th century B.C. Six figures are drawn on the lower part of the breast-plate; on the right, Apollo with his lyre, and behind him two girls, possibly the Hyperborean maidens; on the left, Zeus, with two young men standing behind him. In the upper part of the breast-plate, there are lions, bulls and sphinxes (fig. 31). The clear, sensitive design, the rich attire of the figures, the love of ornamental detail betray the Ionian origin of the artist.

There is another magnificent breast-plate, which archaeologists ascribe to a Cretan workshop. It is of a slightly earlier date than the first one and was discovered at Olympia not very long ago; it represents Helen among her two brothers, the Dioskouroi.

Such superior pieces were naturally not the usual equipment of warriors, even the wealthier ones. However, the simplest and most inexpensive of breast-plates testify to the exceptional skill and artistic sensitivity of Greek bronze workers. This is evidenced by a breast-plate of the first half of the 6th century B.C., which is relatively unadorned, but beautifully made and shaped (fig. 30).

Greaves and helmets

Greaves were a necessary complement to an ancient warrior's armour. This simple protective covering for the legs was given such striking artistic form that it became an incomparable work of art, instructing us about the ways in which an artist's feeling for form can give life to the lines and volumes of an object (fig. 29). The same creative force is present in the innumerable helmets found on the site of Olympia. If one compares them to the hopelessly uniform and expressionless helmets of our modern soldiers, one cannot help being amazed to see that hardly any two of them are alike. Each helmet is a unique creation, and its decoration, always strictly conforming to the dictates of its form and functional requirements, converts it into a delightful work of art (figs. 26-28).

But beyond their artistic and technical interest, some helmets and other weapons have a unique historical significance, for they evoke in the most tangible way dramatic moments in ancient Greek history. For instance, oxidation has destroyed the upper part of a helmet of the common Corinthian type; it is simple and unadorned, so that one might easily walk past it without giving it much attention, unless one happens to read the inscription engraved on the edge of the cheek-piece "Miltiades presented this to Zeus" (fig. 28). A simple name, all by itself, without a patronym or place of origin, as was the custom among the ancient Greeks. But who needed this additional information in order to recognize the helmet of Miltiades, the glorious Athenian general, the victor of Marathon, known to all the Greeks? This must have been the helmet he wore when he fought his great battle. He then offered it, humbly and reverently, to the god at Olympia. Next to it, we see another helmet, a foreign-looking one this time, standing out among the numerous Greek helmets of various types. Here too, there is an inscription on the cheek-piece, which proudly answers our question: "To Zeus from the Athenians, who took it from the Medes" (fig. 27). The helmet of the victorious general and the spoil of a vanquished enemy were thus preserved by the soil of Olympia, and now provide us with this unexpected contact with the first legendary victory of the Greeks at Marathon.

Shield devices

Ornamentation on helmets and greaves was necessarily limited and of secondary importance; but with shields it was a different matter; artists had plenty of scope to display all their skill and imagination. The circular surface of the shield could be decorated with a central ornamental design known as *episema* (device or insignia). A large number of such devices have been found at Olympia, giving us an idea of the wealth of decorative themes devised by the artists of that time. One of the most adaptable, and therefore popular, motifs was Gorgo and the Gorgoneia; for the ancient Greeks, these creatures possessed a hideous power, which was supposed to enhance the defensive properties of the shield. A Gorgoneion device of this kind, surrounded by three revolving wings, is all that remains of a shield from the first half of the 6th century B.C. (fig. 25). Another shield device, however, far more elaborate and fearful, unique of its kind, has reached us in excellent condition. It consists of a monstrous figure, the like of which is not to be found in the whole of Greek art. The upper part of the composition represents Gorgo holding in her hands two snakes that are coiled around her waist. Her wings grow out of her chest instead of her back. The lower part of her body turns into a sea-dragon at the back, while in front she displays powerful lion's limbs (fig. 32). Could this possibly be a version of *Phobos* (fear) and *Deimos* (terror) which according to Homer, decorated Agamemnon's shield, coupled with Gorgo? Was this strange work fashioned in some workshop of Magna Graecia, as suggested by E. Kunze, the archaeologist who discovered it? Both these suppositions concerning this amazing creation of the mid-6th century B.C. may well be true.

Architectural bronzes

The imagination of the artists of the Archaic age was inexhaustible, giving a new life to familiar themes, at times in the most unexpected way. The griffin was one of the most popular motifs in early Greek art; Greek artists borrowed it from the East, but transformed it and endowed it with the nobility and dynamism of the Greek form. But the griffin produced by the creator of an early Archaic bronze plate (630-620 B.C.) which perhaps served as a covering for a wooden metope — as its size seems to indicate — is both unique and charming: we are shown a female griffin suckling her young. It is a representation which ennobles the fearful creature by unexpectedly transforming it into an affectionate mother! (fig. 36).

Tripods

The tripods, the most common votive offerings at Olympia and all the other Greek sanctuaries, are the last to be mentioned here. From early Geometric times onward, the tripod was the votive offering *par excellence*. At first, it was adorned with two large, upright, circular handles (fig. 33), surmounted by small bronze figurines, usually miniature horses with or without a male figure holding them in rein. Later on, the rim of tripods was decorated with busts of griffins, their menacing beaks turned outwards (fig. 35). Finally, the rim came to be adorned with all kinds of other figures, human or animal, such as lions, sphinxes, etc. It is under this highly ornamental and splendid aspect that we must visualise the innumerable bronze tripods of that time, only few of which have reached us intact. However, what has survived are the bronze sheets that decorated the legs of the tripods and the numerous griffin's heads; these enable us to trace with great certainty the constant change and growth of Greek form as it proceeded, with crystalline limpidity, to express the spiritual message of each successive era.

1. *Figure of Apollo from the west pediment of the temple of Zeus.*

2. *Colossal head of Hera from the cult statue of the goddess that was set up in the Archaic Heraion. Hera was represented seated on her throne and wearing a polos , the sacred headdress worn by numerous female deities. c. 600 B.C.*

3. *Clay head of Athena. A number of fragments found along with this head suggest that it was part of a votive offering consisting of several figures. The goddess is wearing a diadem decorated with flowers over her finely modelled locks. An outstanding work of the late Archaic period. 490 B.C.*

4. *Zeus and Ganymedes. The god, carrying off the beautiful boy, proceeds briskly towards Mount Olympos, to grant him immortality and keep him forever at his side as his personal oinochoos (cup-bearer). This clay group of the severe style (470 B.C.) is probably the work of a Corinthian artist, as evidenced by the fine-grained, pale-coloured clay.*

2

3

5

Alpheioses or Kladeos   *Diviner*   *Charioteer*   *Horse from Oinomaos'*   *Kneeling*   *Sterope*   *Pelops*
or Pelops' chariot   *youth*   *or*
(Myrtilos?)   *Hippodameia*

6

Lapith woman   *Old Lapith woman*   *Lapith*   *Centaur*   *Lapith*   *Centaur*   *Theseus*   *Centaur*   *Lapith*
woman   *and Lapith*   *woman*

Oinomaos   Hippodameia   Kneeling   Horses from Oinomaos'   Old diviner   Crouching youth   Kladeos
         or   girl   or Pelops' chariot   (Iamos?)   (possibly Arkas)   or
       Sterope   Alpheios

Deidameia and   Peirithoos   Lapith and   Lapith woman   Lapith   Old Lapith woman   Lapith woman
Centaur Eurytion   Centaur   and Centaur

5-6. *The pedimental sculptures of the temple of Zeus are the most impressive group of sculptures in the severe style. The east pediment (fig. 5) illustrates the myth of the chariot-race between Oinomaos and Pelops. The artist has depicted the heroes a few moments before the start of the race. In the centre stood the majestic figure of Zeus; to his left and right were the two opposed couples: Oinomaos with his wife Sterope, and Pelops with Oinomaos' daughter, Hippodameia. (Archaeologists are in disagreement as to which couple was on the left of Zeus and which on the right.) Next to these central figures are depicted the chariots and several auxiliary figures; at the two corners of the pediment, we see the personifications of the two rivers of Olympia, the Alpheios and the Kladeos. The west pediment (fig. 6) represents a Centauromachy. Apollo stands in the centre; to his left and right there are groups of Centaurs and Lapiths, engaged in a fierce fight over the abducted women. Archaeologists agree that the three figures on the left of Apollo should be transposed and substituted for the three figures on his right, so that the two heroes, Theseus and Peirithoos, would stand next to the god. The figures at the two ends of the pediment, of a later date, replaced the original ones, which had been destroyed by some unknown cause. c. 460 B.C.*

7. *The male figure is Oinomaos; as for the female figure, most archaeologists believe her to be his wife Sterope, although a few insist that she is Hippodameia, and should be placed next to Pelops. Oinomaos had a himation thrown over his shoulders, leaving his body naked; in his left hand he held his spear, and there was a helmet on his head. Sterope is wearing the Doric peplos girded at the waist, and raises her left hand to her left shoulder in a slightly perplexed manner.*

8. *This figure of the old diviner with his intensely realistic features, dramatic facial expression and eloquent gesture, is one of the finest works among the pedimental sculptures of Olympia and of Greek art in general.*

8

9. *Deidameia and the Centaur Eurytion, from the west pediment. This composition was completed by the figure of Peirithoos, his armed right hand raised as he prepares to strike the Centaur who has abducted his young bride during the wedding feast. The young woman struggles to save herself from the grasp of the inebriated Eurytion; in her effort to free herself, she throws her body forcefully backwards, causing her dress to slip off her shoulder and bare her left breast.*

10. *The figure of Apollo on the west pediment of the temple of Zeus. The god has thrown back his himation over his right shoulder, leaving uncovered his divine body with its sturdy, austere structure and firm flesh. His head is turned to the left, offering the spectator a profile of exceptional sensitivity, in which the compact flesh of the face stands out even more strikingly in contrast with the fluid, well-combed hair. Apollo's right arm is extended towards the group consisting of Peirithoos, Deidameia and Eurytion (not the group shown in the picture), in a gesture of blessing, indicating the restoration of Apollonian order and the condemnation of the lawless violence of the Centaurs.*

9

11. *One of the most powerful compositions of the west pediment of the temple of Zeus; a young Lapith is holding a Centaur by the neck in the crook of his right arm; the Centaur has got hold of the youth's arm with both hands and bites into his flesh forcefully. There is an expression of pain on the youth's face, rendered by the parted lips, the contraction of the eyes and the wrinkling of the forehead. But the Centaur's rage and pain, as he is caught in the Lapith's strangulating grip, are registered on his brutish face in an equally masterly manner. However, these intensely realistic elements do not deform the two figures or deprive them of their particular characteristics: the nobility and beauty of the young Lapith, the violent bestiality of the mature Centaur.*

12. *A Lapith woman attempts to break away from the violent grip of a Centaur. In her effort, her peplos comes loose over her left shoulder, leaving her youthful breast uncovered. The young woman's posture is quite remarkable, in the way her whole body and the peplos undulate with a rhythm that is both impetuous and disciplined, giving an impression of fluidity, like a sea-wave.*

12

13

14

13. *Metope from the east side of the temple of Zeus. It depicts one of the twelve labours of Herakles, the Golden Apples of the Hesperides. The hero has placed a pad on his shoulders; his arms are raised and slightly bent as he carries the tremendous burden of the sky, in the place of Atlas who has gone to fetch the apples for him. Athena stands behind him, lending her support; Atlas has just returned and holds out the palms of his hands, laden with the mythical fruit.*

14. *Metope from the east side of the temple of Zeus. It represents one of Herakles' labours, the cleansing of the Augean stables. Herakles strikes at the bottom of the stable walls with a large lever to make an opening that will let in the waters of the river. Athena stretches out her right hand, pointing at the spot where he must strike.*

15. *Metope from the west side of the temple of Zeus. It records another labour of Herakles, the extermination of the Stymphalian Birds. The hero has slain the dreadful creatures and has come to show his spoils to his patroness, Athena. The goddess, wearing a peplos but not her helmet, the aigis visible on her breast, is seated barefoot upon a rock. This scene has no parallel in the whole of Greek art. (Athena and Herakles' head and right hand are in the Louvre; in the Museum of Olympia these missing pieces have been replaced on the metope by plaster casts.)*

15

16. The Nike (Victory) of Paionios. The statue with its tall triangular pedestal had a total height of 11.90 metres. Her wings extended, her himation spread out and held with her left hand as it billowed out by the wind in her rapid downward flight from the sky to the earth, she was shown standing on an eagle. An inscription on the pedestal records that this was a votive offering of the Messenians and the Naupaktians and the work of Paionios of Mende in the Chalkidike peninsula. c. 420 B.C.

17. The Hermes of Praxiteles. This famous statue, found in the temple of Hera, shows Hermes holding in his left arm the infant Dionysos, while in his raised right hand he holds a bunch of grapes, dangling it before the child-god, who stretches out his small hand to grasp the sacred fruit. Hermes has draped his himation over a nearby tree-trunk, revealing his beautiful, youthful body in all its nudity. c. 340 B.C.

17

18. *A one-winged figure of hammered bronze. A rare example of the hammered bronze technique used by the Greeks in the Archaic period for the production of large bronze statues, prior to the invention of the 'cire-perdue' (melted wax) technique which enabled them to cast statues that were hollow. c. 590-580 B.C.*

lost-wax

19. *Bronze statuette of a warrior carrying a sword. The base supporting the figure leads to the conclusion that together with another figure—that of an old man, also discovered at Olympia—it decorated the rim of a large bronze vessel. It was made in the Lakonian workshop in the mid-6th century B.C.*

20. *Bronze statuette of a young runner at the aphesis, i.e. at the point of starting a race. The inscription on his right thigh reads: TO ΔIFOΣ IMI (I belong to Zeus). It was made in the Argive workshop in the early years of the severe style. 480 B.C.*

21. *This bronze horse was part of a votive offering representing a four-horse chariot, probably dedicated by a charioteer who had won a race. It is possibly also a product of the Argive workshop. c. 470-460 B.C.*

18

19

20

21

22. Bronze sheet with an embossed representation of two Centaurs hitting a hoplite with fir-trunks. The victim is the mythical hero Kaineas, who was immortal and could be exterminated only if nailed to the ground. c. 630 B.C.

23. Bronze sheet with embossed representation of a warrior about to mount his chariot. His charioteer has already mounted and stands waiting for him; but before leaving for the battle, the warrior turns his head to look at his wife, who is carrying their child on her shoulders. c. 590 B.C.

24. Bronze sheet with embossed representations in two registers. The lower one shows Theseus abducting Antiope; the upper one Orestes killing his mother. Klytaimnestra. c. 570 B.C.

25. Shield device. A gorgoneion encircled by three revolving wings First half of the 6th century B.C.

26. Bronze helmet of the Illyrian type. The frontal section is decorated with applied silver animals (two lions on either side of a boar). The cheek-piece is decorated with the applied silver figure of a horseman. 530 B.C.

27. Persian helmet; there is an inscription round the lower edge: ΔΙΙ ΑΘΕΝΑΙΟΙ ΜΕΔΟΝ ΛΑΒΟΝΤΕΣ (To Zeus from the Athenians, who took it from the Medes), which indicates that it was part of the spoils from the battle of Marathon. 490 B.C.

28. Miltiades' helmet. After the battle of Marathon, the victorious general dedicated it to Zeus, as recorded by the inscription: ΜΙΛΤΙΑΔΕΣ ΑΝΕΘΕΚΕΝ ΤΟΙ ΔΙΙ. 490 B.C.

29. Bronze greaves; one of these was dedicated to Zeus by the Kleonaians. Second half of the 6th century B.C.

30. Bronze breastplate from a hoplite's armour (early 6th century B.C.). Its simple ornamentation, subordinated to the main formal elements and functional requirements of the object, raise it to the level of a work of art.

31. A fine bronze breastplate with engraved representations. The lower part shows Apollo with his lyre and two Hyperborean maidens, then Zeus with two youths; the upper part depicts lions, bulls, sphinxes and leopards. A little later than the mid-7th century B.C.

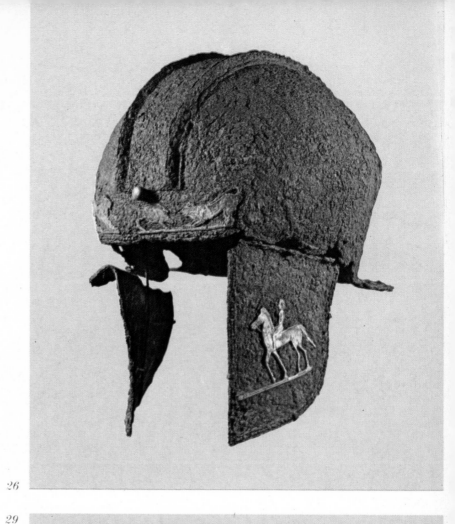

26

29

25

28

30

31

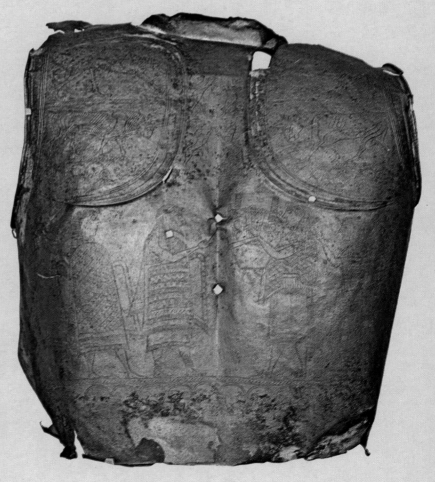

32. *A shield device unique in its theme and in the quality of its workmanship: Gorgo with wings growing out of her breast, girded with serpents, the lower part of her body ending in a dragon's tail and lion's legs. Mid-6th century B.C.*

33. *Bronze tripod of the 9th century B.C. Innumerable tripods of this kind were dedicated to the Altis, the sacred grove at Olympia.*

34. *Two heraldic sphinxes. They were attached to the rim of a large bronze vessel. 600-550 B.C.*

35. *Head of a griffin; together with other similar figures, it was attached to the rim of a votive tripod. 7th century B.C.*

32

33

35

34

36. *Bronze sheet; it probably covered a wooden metope. Its subject is unusual and unexpected: a female griffin nursing her young. The fruitful imagination, the profoundly human sensitiveness of the Greek artist thus transformed the ferocious imaginary bird, borrowed from Oriental art, into a peaceful and loving creature. c. 630-620 B.C.*

36

HERAKLEION MUSEUM

HERAKLEION MUSEUM

A brief history of the Museum

The Museum of Herakleion contains a unique collection of Cretan antiquities. The very ancient civilization of Crete had remained practically unknown to research until the closing years of the last century. When large-scale archaeological excavations were undertaken, the magnificent relics that had lain buried for centuries in the soil of the island, were brought to light and preserved in their place of origin. Today, very few examples of the Minoan civilization are to be seen in the Museums of Europe and America, and all the treasures of the ancient history of Crete, which constitutes the first brilliant chapter in Greek history, have found a permanent home in the Museum of Herakleion. In this part of the Hellenic world there appeared for the first time a great civilization with outstanding artistic manifestations, admirable social and state organization, and unprecedented economic development. Sole witness to these achievements are the carefully arranged and finely displayed archaeological finds in the Museum of Herakleion.

It should be noted that the archaeologist responsible for the display of material in the Museum, Professor N. Platon, a distinguished scholar in Cretan civilization, was fortunate in having at his disposal a new building with a rationally planned layout, specially designed for the antiquities it was to house. Professor Platon made the most of this opportunity. Later, in 1964, when a new wing of four galleries was added to the Museum, the present Curator, Dr. St. Alexiou, completed the exhibition in the same exemplary and scholarly fashion.

At this point we should also mention the names of J. Hazzidakis and St. Xanthoudidis, the pioneer Cretan archaeologists who founded both the first Museum (1904 - 1912) and the Greek Archaeological Service in Crete. Possibly attracted by the early finds of the Herakleiot antiquarian Minos Kalokairinos, who discovered the palace of Knossos in 1878 and attempted the earliest excavations on the site, J. Hazzidakis, then president of the local "Society for the Promotion of Education", started a collection of antiquities as early as 1883, long before Sir Arthur Evans began his great excavations in 1900. This Society, in collaboration with Professor F. Halbherr, excavated the well-known cave sites *Idaion Antron* on Mt. Ida and *Speos Eileithyias* at Amnisos, which yielded a great number of valuable votive offerings. The famous inscription of the laws of Gortyn, perhaps the most important epigraphic text of ancient Greece, was unearthed in that same year.

The Minoan Palaces

In the Museum of Herakleion the visitor may enjoy and the scholar may study all the relics of Minoan civilization, with the exception, of course, of the most significant antiquities — the buildings themselves. A tour of the ruins so far uncovered by excavations is recommended before a visit to the

Museum, as it will afford a better understanding of the splendid features of the Cretan world. Architecture is the highest and most complex expression of the character of every civilization, since it reflects its economic activity, political power, religious faith and artistic inspiration. In Crete, moreover, the culminating phase of the Minoan civilization (1700 - 1450 B.C.) was founded on the great palace centres: the magnificent palaces had been the cradle of every creation and activity which spread over the entire island, or at least over its central and eastern parts. The building of palaces seems to have marked both the cultural and political history of Minoan Crete most profoundly. The recently applied division of the Minoan civilization into three phases — The Pre-Palace period (2700 - 1900 B.C.), the Old Palace period (1900 - 1700 B.C.) and the New Palace period (1700 - 1450 B.C.) — is not a mere archaeological convention, but indicates actual divisions in that civilization.

Neolithic and Pre-Palace period

The earliest finds recovered from various Cretan sites have been assigned to the Neolithic period. However, the so-called Minoan civilization emerged with such intensity in the period following the Neolithic, that the earliest investigators regarded it as a "sudden miracle" and attributed it to the invasion of a new people from Asia Minor. We have now reached the conclusion that the change effected was partly due to the infiltration of these tribes, but that it was neither sudden nor ignorant of the achievements of the earlier Neolithic inhabitants, who had survived the invasion and welcomed the great discovery, i.e. bronze, which the invaders brought with them. Thus the beginnings of the great era of Cretan history are to be traced to this Pre-Palace period, when the inhabitants of settlements scattered throughout the island, and chiefly the central and eastern sections, initiated a rapid development of the arts and crafts. It is worth noticing that this early period produced fine examples of all the branches of art, which were to reach their height in the following periods: principally pottery, but also metal-work, gold-work, stone-carving, and particularly seal-engraving. The objects exhibited in the galleries of the Museum of Herakleion demonstrate with unbroken continuity the achievements of the Minoans in every field. Notwithstanding the remarkable development of Crete during this early phase, the island retained the character of a society based primarily on a fragmentary agricultural economy, and, to a lesser degree, on trade and some sort of industry. We must assume that this fragmentation also existed in public life, which cannot possibly have achieved advanced political systems, capable of leading to the creation of a strong state power.

Old Palace period

Archaeological finds, which mark the beginning of the Old Palace period, testify to the vital change that was to lead to a new social and political organization. In about 1900 B.C. palaces were built for the first time at key positions: at Knossos, Phaistos, Malia, and perhaps at two or three other places (Hania ?). This indicates the concentration of authority in the hands of strong leaders, able to rule over large areas and exercise control over trade and all produce, agricultural and industrial. The parallel development of the palace centres also signifies their peaceful coexistence and the absence of warlike antagonism. The contemporaneous creation of large towns bears witness to the social change that had taken place in these years, while the strongly religious character of many of the finds leads us to believe that the whole system had the same theocratic character as that encountered in other great Eastern nations, such as Egypt and Assyria. It is therefore not surprising that at this age the Cretans should discover and use the art of writing in its most ancient form, the hieroglyphic; it is also natural that there should be a rapid development in all the branches of art which had already borne fine fruit in the previous period.

New Palace period

Archaeologists have succeeded in proving that these "old" palaces were destroyed three times in the two hundred years of their existence. But while the two first destructions were not total, the third, which took place c. 1700 B.C., and seems to have been caused by an earthquake, had terrible results. It is however strange that the ruin of the palaces was not followed by a more general collapse of political activity. On the contrary, life on the island continued to flourish, and the New Palace period that follows (1700-1450 B.C.) is the most productive and creative phase of Minoan civilization. New palaces were raised on the site of the old, after the area had been levelled; and other palaces, such as that of Zakros, or rich villas were speedily built, and in considerable numbers. Everything testifies to the fact that the ancient tradition which elevated King Minos to the sphere of myth, and preserved the memory of his sea-power and his justice, was not a figment of fantasy. The excavations of Sir Arthur Evans at Knossos were needed before we could understand the myth of the labyrinth, or realize that even if Daidalos is a mythical name, his achievements were not mythical.

The architecture of the new palaces presents all the elements illustrative of Minoan society and civilization. The largest palace, that of Knossos, invites the visitor to complete it with his imagination. Round the vast central court rise many-storeyed buildings; open corridors, numerous staircases, and walls pierced with many doors, lofty light-wells, coloured surfaces and columns, and frescoes brightly coloured, form a whole where the masses lose their weight and seem to move in light and shade affording protection from the warm climate of this Mediterranean island and offering a visible picture of the active and cheerful world that lived in buildings like these.

The collections of the Museum

After a tour of the sites, a visit to the Museum of Herakleion, where all the finds of the Cretan excavations are housed, provides further knowledge of this civilization, its art and way of life. In the Museum galleries, therefore, one can follow the history of Minoan art in all its branches: pottery, first and foremost, then stone-carving, seal-engraving, metal-work, work in gold, and finally the great painting of the frescoes.

Pottery and vase-painting

Pottery was among the first arts of Neolithic man, and the earliest examples found in Crete are assigned to that age. But the first rich collections of vases displayed in the Museum belong to the Proto-Minoan or Pre-Palace period (2700-1900 B.C.). Already by this time the Cretan craftsmen knew the use of the potter's wheel and were thus able to give elegant and elaborate shapes to their pottery. The cases of the Museum contain a delightful large collection of ware from Eastern Crete, in the style called Vasiliki, from the site where the greatest number and the most typical examples were found: jugs with a high beak-shaped spout, and above all broad open vases with vertical handle and spout like the beak of an exotic bird. Their dark surface is brightened by a rich light-coloured decoration in which the curved line dominates, often in its most dynamic shape, the spiral. In the most evolved examples of this pottery the decoration has already achieved a polychromy, which is in keeping with its rich foliate patterns.

The Kamares ware

This charming polychrome decoration is again encountered in the finest examples of Minoan pottery which represent almost the entire Old Palace period (1900-1700 B.C.) and owe their name, *Kamares Ware* to the cave where they were first discovered (figs. 2 and 4). Their technical perfection is on a level with their high artistic value. The vibrant colours, the incredible variety of decorative themes with their flexible and spontaneous spreading over the surface of the vase, suggest that the society which created and used this ware must have lived an easy, festal, mediterranean life, rejoicing in the sunlight and worshipping nature. Yet, the decoration of the Kamares Ware does not include naturalistic forms. The golden, blue, yellow, red lines and surfaces, with their forceful and elastic curves, spread over the vase, following its shape and emphasizing the characteristic features of its structure. If the complexity of these curves should give the visitor the impression of an exotic picture and bring strange plants and animals to his mind, he should not allow himself to be deceived into thinking that this was part of the artist's intention. However, in the process of creation, the artist was beginning to distinguish some forms that were to develop later into well-known plant and animal themes. In the beginning, therefore, decoration was abstract and the designs, like many-coloured fireworks, radiated in every direction from a central nucleus. The visitor admiring these fine vases may wonder how this ancient feeling of baroque came into being, and how in time it gave way to the forceful Greek geometric style. Yet this art, which is in the grip of an unrestrained fantasy and moves towards the unsymmetrical, rarely forgets that its function is to adorn the fragile surface of a vase; it always respects this basic fact, and remains, as one might say, intelligently decorative.

Floral and Marine style

The creative ceramic tradition continues into the following period, that of the new palaces (1700-1450 B.C.). Among the rich decorative elements of the Kamares style there gradually appear plant and animal forms which take the place of abstract designs, while in time the colour relation between decoration and surface is reversed: there is now dark decoration on a light-coloured ground. Large elegant vases have a flexible floral decoration: a "gentle and airy naturalism", a delicate exploitation of form, design and decorative composition gives grace and charm to these vases. Two styles, named "floral" and "marine" prevail, and are now typical of Minoan pottery. Stirrup-jars and flasks are most skilfully decorated with the form of the octopus that spreads its twining feelers and covers the whole surface of the vase (fig. 3). Rhyta of severe shape are decorated with the wealth of the sea, including the nautilus, the murex, the starfish and coral. At the same time every sort of plant form — lilies, papyrus, crocus, iris, and foliage — seems to retain the freshness of the plant while giving the impression of a unique geometrical ornament (figs. 5-6).

Palace style

The infiltration of geometrical severity was accomplished in the last phase of the New Palace period. We cannot yet be certain whether this were the consequence of Mycenaean influence from the continent or the historical development of tendencies already existing in the previous two styles. The result, however, is striking, and the so-called "palace" style constitutes the remarkable last chapter to a long artistic chronicle. This last development was confined to Knossos: examples of this style were found only in the splendid palace of Knossos. The large vases with their severe construction and ornament, where wild plants and wild creatures of the sea begin to obey geometrical principles and architectural forms, have their own stately force. The lively Minoan impulse, the love of movement, the fascination of the curve are ever-present. These, however, are now subjected to a geometric stylization, and the acceptance of more rhythmical and rational principles indicates that a new spirit has breathed among them (fig. 7). Even if there had been no destruction by the forces of nature, Minoan art would have given place to another art, based on more nature powers.

Stone-carving

Stone-carving is an art that particularly flourished at every stage of Minoan civilization. Even if the Cycladeans and the Egyptians gave the first lessons in stone work to the Minoan craftsmen — and this seems very probable — we can say that not only did the Minoans perfectly assimilate this foreign instruction, but that they very quickly outstripped their masters. Already from the Pre-Palace period stone vessels, which are real works of art, were being made in Crete. The stone chosen offered a wealth of colour and endless possibilities for the exploitation of its veining: many-coloured marble, steatite, basalt, alabaster were chiselled with admirable skill. Many unusual shapes were created, some of the greatest elegance, with their small handles, ingenious spouts, turned bases and curved lips. The veining was particularly well employed, to emphasize the shape of the vase, to bring out its articulation or to make its functional features distinct.

In the Old Palace period the splendour of the Kamares Ware somewhat eclipses the stone work. Nevertheless the production of stone vases continues, and their quality remains at a high level. The technical experience and the artistic sensibility of the early stone-cutters was to bequeath a rich heritage to the following and most flourishing period of Minoan civilization.

By this time craftsmen have learned how to work with more ease in the harder stones, basalt, porphyry, rock-crystal etc., and succeed in creating elaborate and dynamic shapes whose perfection gives form to the most daring fantasy, while the exploitation of the coloured veins in the stone shows remarkable intelligence and sensibility (fig. 8). The stone vessels from the treasuries of the sanctuaries of the palaces of Knossos and Zakros are among the most valuable collections of the Museum of Herakleion.

Stone vases with representations in relief

Among the ceremonial stone vessels of the New Palace period there is a category which deserves a special place not only in the history of Minoan stone-carving, but in that of Minoan art as a whole. A series of rhyta in black steatite have relief representations on their surface. Their significance is manifold; for the first time we have anthropomorphic representations depicting scenes from Cretan life; these representations, which exhibit surprising skill in execution and composition, confirm that the palace frescoes were not the only works in which human figures predominate in the artist's repertoire.

Scenes with many figures, like the festal procession of harvesters with their lively movements, on the rhyton from Hagia Triada, (figs. 11-12), and scenes of athletic life, with the incredibly daring stance of the athletes, on the other rhyton from Hagia Triada, show the same skill in design, in composition and in the plastic rendering of the human body as do the simpler but striking figures of the young warriors on the Chieftain Cup (again from Hagia Triada, fig. 10), and they are not at all inferior to the charming agricultural-religious composition of the wild goats climbing the rocks of the peak sanctuary on the rhyton of Zakros.

These able craftsmen sometimes gave the form of an animal to a whole stone vase: rhyta have the shape of a bull's head, whether carved in black steatite (palace of Knossos, fig. 15), or green chlorite (palace of Zakros), and a marble rhyton is in the shape of a lioness's head. These exquisite specimens are evidence of the artist's skill and talent and denote his fondness not only of the work but also of the animal depicted.

Seal-engraving

In seal-engraving, a branch of art in which they were unique, the Minoan craftsmen showed their skill in impressing on hard stone, the most difficult of materials, the animal world in such a way as to exhibit both a perfect knowledge of that world and of the requirements of art. The making of seal-stones begins in the Pre-Palace period, at first in soft stone, and later in hard semi-precious stones. In the Old Palace period the seal-engravers worked in agate, sard, jasper, haematite, amethyst and other semi-precious stones, and with astonishing accuracy they succeeded in representing countless forms from the natural and animal world on the limited surfaces of the seals. But as in other branches of art, so also in seal-engraving, the New Palace period was the most creative. Not only is there a far greater quantity of seals, but their quality is incomparable; without exaggeration we may call them works of a great art. With the crystal purity of design, the cunning exploitation of space, and the admirably studied composition, the scenes represented on the small, bright-coloured surface of the stone give a unique aesthetic pleasure (fig.17): the life of nature, the violent conflicts between animals, religious scenes, bull-fights, birds and trees, men and monsters, all are living, and yet they are all subdued to the discipline demanded by this art of miniature, an art in which we find all the characteristics of Minoan civilization — the love for the artistic and the elegant, for liveliness and movement, for colour and light, but not for large dimensions and monumental effects.

Minor Sculpture

The Cretans always remained faithful to their character and to their forms of artistic self-expression, and never attempted to imitate their neighbours — e.g. the Egyptians — in the creation of huge works of sculpture. We shall search in vain for works of major sculpture for, despite the fact that Minoan art with its knowledge of the human body, early felt the need to give it plastic representation, it was always satisfied with figures of a small size, as the clay and bronze examples of the Old Palace period testify. In the New Palace period Minoan minor sculpture succeeded, by the use of precious and delicate material, in the production of unique masterpieces. The statuettes of the Snake Goddess in faience, with her rich and elegant Minoan robe, slender waist, characteristically protruding breasts and outstretched arms with the snakes, combine plastic feeling with love of colour, a permanent feature in Minoan art (figs. 1 and 21). Of an ivory composition that represented a bull-jumper on the horns of the bull, we have only the figure of the young athlete and even this is incomplete — the gold parts of the work are missing. This acrobat-athlete is shown at the moment when he has grasped the bull's horns with both his hands and with a vigorous motion of the feet backwards and upwards he is about to turn a somersault (fig. 13). The rendering of this unique moment, when all the limbs of the body have become tense as a spring, leaves us amazed at the artist's daring and at his almost incredible dexterity.

Work in gold

The Minoan goldsmiths also move with ease in this world of elegant miniature art. Since the Pre-Palace period they had already learned to make use of filigree and granulation. Bracelets and hair ornaments, necklaces and rings of delicate form, decorated with floral and animal motifs, are revealing of the wealth of Minoan society and its fondness of these elegant and charming objects (figs. 25-31). Throughout all the periods of Minoan civilization the creation of jewellery from gold and precious stones continued, with ever increasing artistic imagination and technical skill. It is enough to have seen the two wasps sipping a drop of honey from Chrysolakkos at Malia (fig. 30), to understand the perfect execution, the exquisite purity of the forms and the masterly combination of the parts that compose the whole. And even the zoomorphic beads representing lions, stags, wild goats etc., or others that represent miniature plants, flowers or fruits, not only exhibit the exterior form of the world of nature, but also its essence, in a rendering of it that, while subject to the principles of art, can preserve the vitality of living things.

Metal-work

In all creative periods art is not confined to the production of works, outside everyday life and its needs, but it permeates all human creations, even the most humble and useful. This can be observed in the Museum of Herakleion whose collections include household vessels and tools, as well as weapons and sacred axes. The metal-workers of the palaces, especially of the New Palace period, rivalled the other craftsmen both in their careful manufacture and in their handsome form and ornament. Some of the daggers and swords are true works of art: archaeologists doubt whether these had been actually used as weapons and believe that they merely formed part of the elegant ornaments worn by their noble and rich owners.

Wall-paintings

Having seen in a short general review all the creations of Minoan civilization, which enable us to imagine its wealth, artistic sensibility, and unique character, we may turn and admire one of the most striking examples of its art, the large paintings that covered the walls of great and small palaces, of rich villas and noble houses, bringing to life the places where men lived who rejoiced in this civilization (figs. 32-35). The surviving remains of these vast frescoes are scarce and their place in the whole composition is often uncertain; nevertheless there is enough to allow us to form an idea of the quality and essential characteristics of Minoan painting, which followed the same principles as the other arts and was the true expression of Minoan society. It did not adopt unassimilable loans from the other great contemporary civilizations, e.g. the Egyptian. In none of the Minoan frescoes do we find the representation of historical events or the apotheosis of kings, encountered in the monumental compositions of the great kingdoms of that time. In painting, as in the other arts, what dominates is the love of the natural world, and of social and religious life. However we do not find anywhere the "naturalism" which so many seem to have discerned. Forms and colours are subject to the laws of art, and subserve the decorative purpose of the frescoes. The artists are aware that the walls where they paint their conceptions are a solid element which they have no right to destroy; thus they create a kind of painting that expands in two dimensions, and never tries to attain an effect of depth. The same principles are behind the use of colour which spreads over the broad clear surfaces without aimless chromatic gradations and without any attempt at trompe l'oeil effects. Some historians who have studied Minoan art like to use the term "chromatic silhouette" as an accurate description of this deliberately flat painting that wisely ignores or denies the depth of the subject. The colour scale is exactly in keeping with this principle. Red and green, blue and yellow, beside black and white, the basic colours of the spectrum suffice, with a few touches of varied colour, to form a vivid and delightful harmony able to brighten the walls with mediterranean light, without making violent breaks in them. This chromatic tact is completed by the fine draftsmanship of the forms: their clear design, their forceful but always delicate curved out line, their harmonious composition — like a musical unity — where every element contributes its clear tone to complete the harmony of the whole. The plants and beasts which earn their place in this harmony, have acquired their colour and shape from the requirements of fresco-painting, not from their counterparts in nature. For this reason it is often difficult and sometimes impossible to determine the kinds of plants or animals depicted.

Wall-paintings in low relief

In an early phase, soon after 1600 B.C., the Minoan artists, possibly under the influence of Egyptian models, created a type of composition in fresco which combines painting with low relief. The figures modelled in plaster are given an almost imperceptible inflation, which is nevertheless hidden under the vivid colouring. Such compositions include the famous "Prince with the Lilies" (in fact the Priest-King) (fig. 34), the remarkable bull from the north entrance to the palace of Knossos, and various "Ladies" from Eastern Crete. The fact that this device was not farther pursued shows the fidelity of the Cretan craftsmen to the principles of their art.

The large frescoes

The large compositions with many-figured scenes have particular significance for our knowledge of Minoan painting. Here we see the human form play a predominant role beside forms from the plant and animal world — as we have seen in the works of minor sculpture. There are religious scenes in which charming priestesses or goddesses (such as the celebrated "Parisienne" fig. 32) receive offerings or watch priestly ceremonies; processions where slender youths carry solemnly and gracefully elegant vases to the queen or goddess; and social gatherings, which Evans called "garden parties", where hundreds of miniature female figures are represented making lively gesticulations — they are evidently watching dances or contests from verandahs. There are also scenes showing such contests, for example the "bull-jumping", where the fearful strength of the bull and the elastic agility of the acrobat-athlete make a wonderful combination (fig. 35).

The sarcophagus of Hagia Triada

The unique stone sarcophagus found at Hagia Triada (fig. 36) is valuable from many points of view. It is unique in its rich painted decoration which depicts scenes of offerings, libations to the dead, chariots etc. Difficult as it is to interpret its religious symbolism, it excites the special interest of both the archaeologist and the layman, and is a remarkable example of the last years of Minoan painting; nevertheless it can at once be perceived that although its religious and archaeological interest is of particular significance, the artistic quality of the painting does not correspond to its archaeological value.

Sub-Minoan phase

After the end of Minoan civilization, c. 1100 B.C., and before the appearance of what we call Geometric art, Crete, like the rest of Greece passed through a transitional period, here called the Sub-Minoan, insignificant from the point of view of civilization, since the once flourishing centres were ruined and only remote districts preserved agricultural settlements. The Minoans, however, retained their ancient beliefs, and thus the very ancient Minoan goddess with raised arms was worshipped in the sanctuaries of these settlements, as many idols in this form testify (figs. 37-38).

Archaic Greek art

The splendour of Minoan art gives the Museum its special character. In the historical age, however, there was one more creative period, which though brief in duration and limited in extension, made Crete worthy to be distinguished among other Greek provinces. In the last years of the 8th and throughout the 7th century B.C. art in Crete made a robust and rich appearance. First ceramic and metal-work and then major sculpture produced so significant and original works that curiosity is excited about the historical causes for this renaissance and its sudden and swift end. In a small wing of the Herakleion Museum the visitor may see some of the most remarkable works of early Greek art — that which we call Archaic — from its first stage, the orientalizing, until the mature period when better examples are found in other areas.

It is worthy of note that some archaeologists call this "orientalizing" Greek art "art of the Idaean style", because they believe that its most typical examples, those which show beyond doubt the sources of influence, are the finds from the Idaean cave in Crete which are the first impressive exhibits in this part of the Museum: bronze shields with reliefs of the Great Goddess, the "Lady of wild beasts", with hunting scenes or representations of lions and griffins, and the great bronze *tympanon* which depicts the God who overcomes wild beasts. These works are so obviously oriental in origin that the only doubt that archaeologists can entertain is whether to attribute them to foreign artists established in Crete, or to Cretan artists who had studied in the East (fig. 40). There can be no doubt that Cretan craftsmen made the three statuettes of Apollo, Leto and Artemis: those hammered bronze figures found in the Archaic temple of Dreros, are the earliest and almost unique examples of this technique. To Cretan artists also are due the bronze plates where a fine technique has rendered the human form so vividly.

Many have supported the hypothesis that Crete was the place where Greek major sculpture came into being, though all specialists have not been convinced of this. Nevertheless everyone agrees that the stone reliefs of Cretan work that belong to the second half of the 7th century B.C. testify to admirable technical accomplishment and unusual artistic vision (fig. 41). What survives in the Museum of Herakleion is only a small part of a rich and significant production, but it is sufficient to allow us to estimate accurately the contribution of this great island to the common endeavour of a most productive epoch, in which the strong foundations were laid of the whole superstructure that was to give glory to Greece in the following centuries. And it is a splendid prelude to the history of Greek art that we may follow in unbroken continuity in the other museums of modern Greece.

1. The smaller 'Snake Goddess'. Faience statuette found in the 'central sanctuary' crypt of the Palace of Knossos. 1600-1580 B.C.

2. *Fruit bowl from Phaistos in the Kamares style. Particularly admirable is the spiral design on the inside of the bowl. c. 1800 B.C.*

3. *Nine-handled vase. Decorated with octopuses beautifully twining their tentacles over the surface of the vase. A brilliant example of the Marine style. c. 1450 B.C.*

4. *Krater with sculptured decoration of flowers. A 'baroque' creation in the Kamares style from the Old Palace of Phaistos. c. 1800 B.C.*

5. *Beak-spouted jug, decorated with dense foliage which gives the impression of a geometric ornament. A characteristic example of the Floral style. c. 1530-1500 B.C.*

2

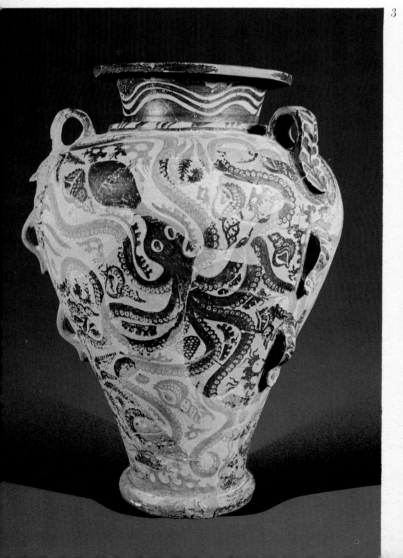

3

4

5

6. *Rhyton decorated with starfish and shells. A characteristic example of the Marine style. c. 1500 B.C.*

7. *Libation jug with beak-shaped spout and very delicate neck, exceptionally elaborate both in shape and decoration. An example of the last years of the New Palace period. c. 1400 B.C.*

8. *Beautiful ceremonial vase from the 'basin of purification' at Zakros. Unique in the skilful and clever use of coloured marble and in the astonishing sensitivity and boldness of its shape. c. 1450 B.C.*

6

7

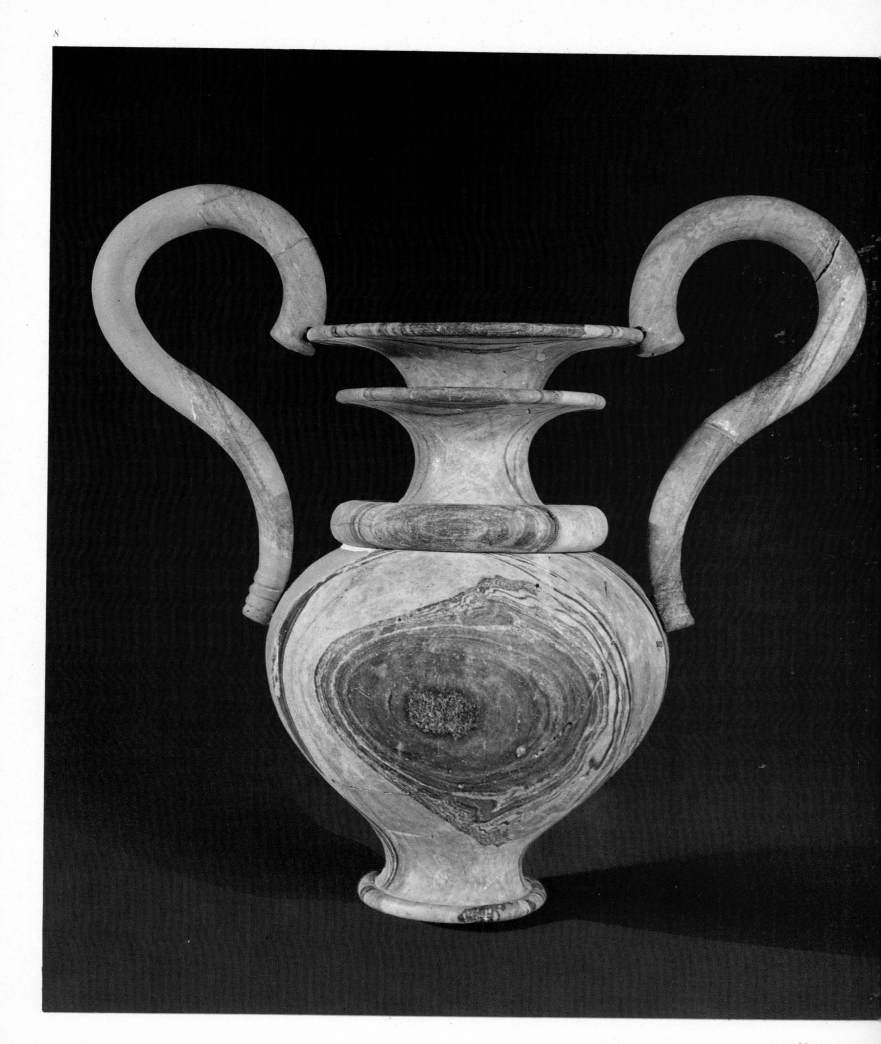

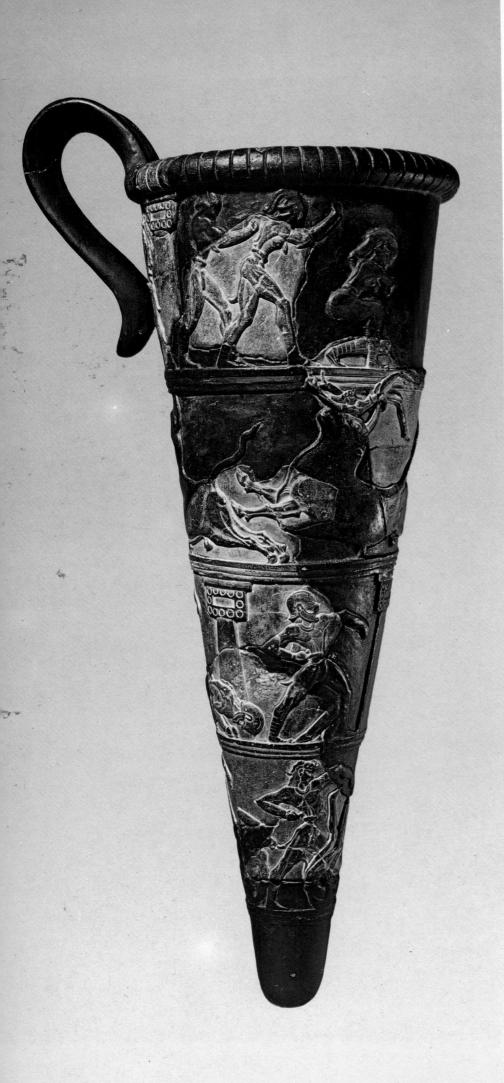

8

9. *Steatite rhyton with representations in relief divided into four zones: top zone, wrestling; second zone, bull-jumping; next, helmeted men boxing; and bottom zone, young men boxing. Found at Hagia Triada. 1550-1500 B.C.*

10. *Steatite vase with representations in relief, known as 'the Prince's Drinking-Cup'. An imposing figure, sceptre in hand, stands in front of a building; turned towards him, is a young man with helmet, sword and a tasseled wand; behind him are three men carrying the skins of large animals. Found at Hagia Triada. 1550-1500 B.C.*

11-12. *The famous 'Harvester Vase' from Hagia Triada, a masterpiece of Minoan stone-carving. The representation shows a group of men, returning from farm work carrying their tools on their shoulders; the procession is headed by singing musicians; the first musician carries a seistron. 1550-1500 B.C.*

9

10

11

12

13

13. The 'Bull-Jumper'. Ivory figure of an athlete at the moment of turning a somersault over the horns of the bull (which has not been preserved). c. 1550 B.C.

14. Head of a royal sceptre made of schist stone. The handle is in the shape of a leopard at one end and that of an axe at the other. Palace of Malia. c. 1650 B.C.

15. A superb steatite rhyton in the shape of a bull's head. The horns (now lost) were made of gilded wood, the eye of rock-crystal, and the white around the nostril of shell. Little Palace of Knossos. 1550-1500 B.C.

14

16. *An exquisite rock-crystal rhyton. The crystal ring at the neck is decorated with gilt faience; the beads on the handle were wound together with bronze wire. Palace of Zakros. c. 1450 B.C.*

17. *The seal-engraving art of the New Palace period in Minoan Crete created real masterpieces: the miniature figures engraved with great accuracy on hard semi-precious stones have both plastic completeness and incomparable expressive forcefulness.*
a) haematite seal-stone: lioness attacking a bull; b) sard seal-stone: fine representation of bulls; c) chalcedony seal-stone set in gold: lion and tamers; d) cyanos seal-stone set in gold: lion and male figure (god?); e) sardonyx seal-stone: goddess between winged griffins, the double axe over her head.

18

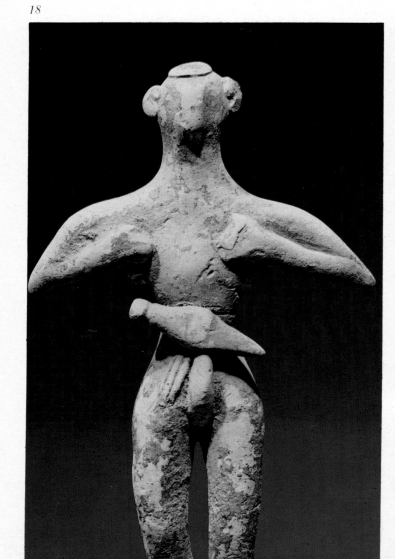

19

20

18. Clay statuette from the 'Peak sanctuary' of Petsofa. It represents a worshipper, as is indicated by the position of his hands on his breast; he wears a belt with a dagger. c. 1950 B.C.

19-20. Faience plaques found in the repositories of the Palace of Knossos. The first represents a wild goat nursing her young. The second, a cow with her calf. The perfect feeling for natural forms, which is a major element of Minoan art, finds its most forceful expression in works of this kind. c. 1600 B.C.

21. The larger 'Snake Goddess', a faience statuette. A snake curls around her outstretched arms and body, its head reaching her tall headdress; she wears a long robe and an apron and her two breasts, symbols of fertility, are bare and characteristically protruding. c. 1600 B.C.

22

23

24

22. *Faience plaques represent-*
ing Minoan houses; they may
have formed the decoration of
a wooden chest and they de-
picted a whole town. In spite
of their small size, they give
us a clear picture of the multi-
storied Minoan houses. 1700 -
1600 B.C.

23. *The famous 'Disk of Phai-*
stos'. Hieroglyphic symbols,
each an independent charac-
ter, are imprinted in the cir-
cular clay disk, on both sides.
Archaeologists have not suc-
ceeded in deciphering the
script, and its content remains
unknown. It is presumed to
be a hymn to a divinity. c.
1600 B.C.

24. *Bronze statuette from Ty-*
lissos. It represents a young
man wearing the Minoan loin-
cloth; he has a necklace and
bracelets on his wrists and
ankles. His right arm is lifted
to his forehead in the charac-
teristic position of salutation
or prayer to a divinity, while
his left arm is stretched out
and resting on his thigh. c.
1500 B.C.

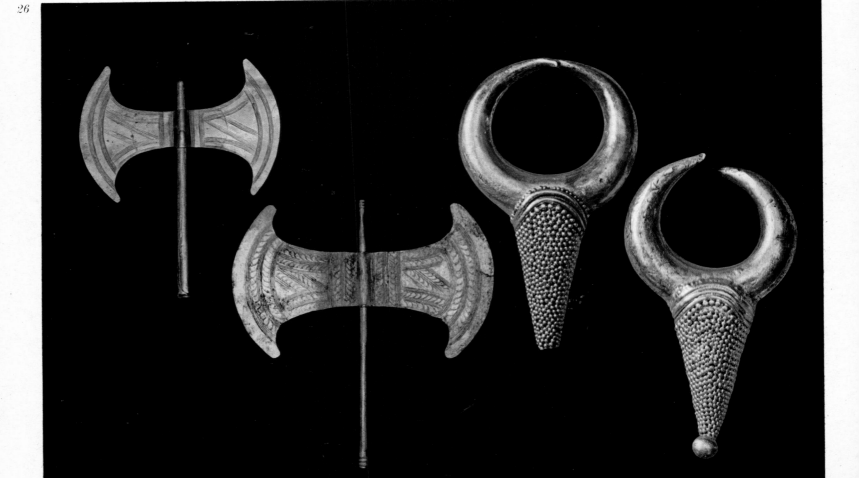

25. Gold jewellery from the region of Archanes. c. 1400 B.C.

26. Gold Minoan objects. The double axes come from the sanctuary in the cave of Arkalochori. Before 1600 B.C. The other two objects are earrings and come from Mavro Spelio near Knossos. c. 1450 B.C.

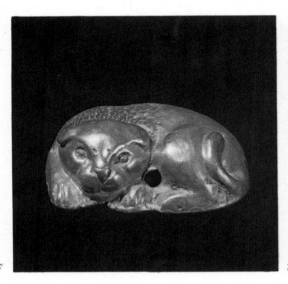

27. Gold necklace bead in the shape of a lion, from Hagia Triada. c. 1500 B.C.

28. Gold pendant in the shape of a bull's head, from Zakros. c. 1450 B.C.

29. Gold necklace bead in the shape of a duck, from the Palace of Knossos. c. 1500 B.C.

30. Gold ornament, accessory to a necklace, from Chryssolakkos at Malia. Two wasps are sipping a drop of honey. An exquisite example of Minoan gold-work. c. 1500 B.C.

31. Gold ring from a tomb at Isopata, decorated with a cult scene. Four female figures with long Minoan robes and bare breasts stand in a floral landscape. Many believe this scene to represent an 'epiphany' of the goddess. c. 1500 B.C.

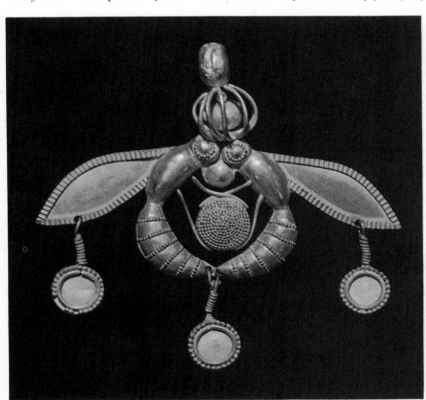

32. The celebrated 'Parisienne' of the Palace of Knossos. It is a fragment from the fresco of 'libation offerings', as it has been named by the archaeologists, who believe that this figure represents a priestess. c. 1500-1450 B.C.

33. Fragment from a larger fresco found in the 'House of frescoes' at Knossos. It represents a bird, named the 'Blue Bird' because of its colour. The rest of the fresco might have represented royal gardens with exotic birds. c. 1500 B.C.

34. Colour relief of the 'Prince with the Lilies' or the 'Priest-King', as he has been called by experts. The slender young figure is wearing the Minoan loin-cloth and a splendid crown of lilies and peacock feathers. With his left hand, he was probably holding and leading a sacred animal, a sphinx or a griffin. Palace of Knossos. c. 1500 B.C.

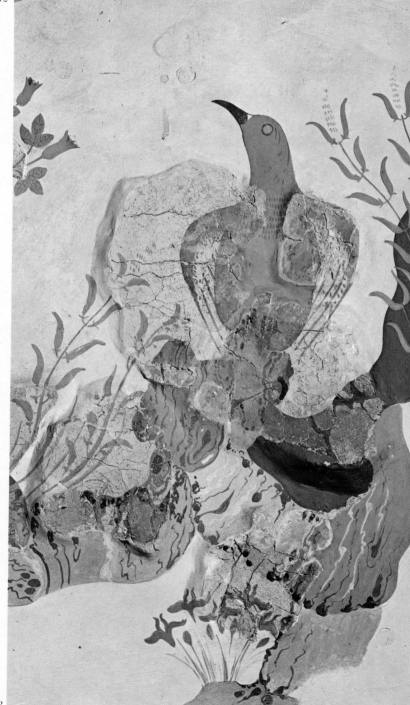

32

33

34

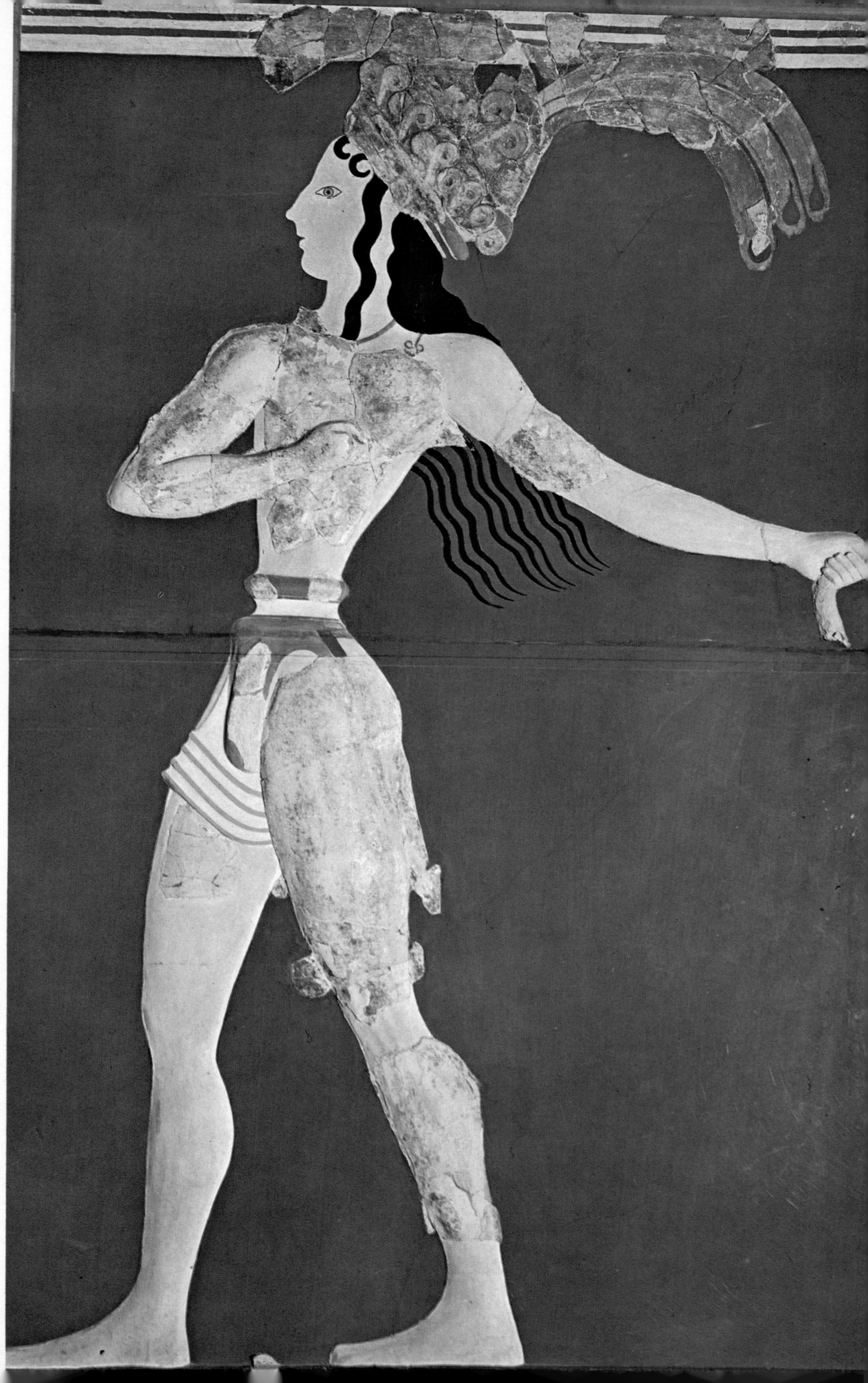

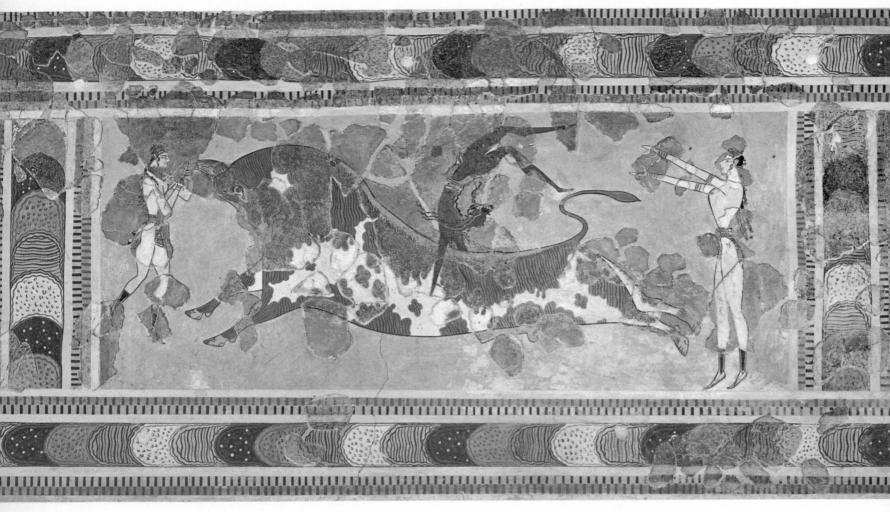

35

35. *Fresco of bull-jumping from the east wing of the Palace of Knossos. The bull is charging violently, while the acrobats are leaping with admirable suppleness over his horns to his back and to the ground. Both men and women (as is seen from the different shading of the bodies, the women being painted white) are taking part in this contest which demanded exceptional acrobatic skill and a great deal of training. This representation shows all phases of the contest, while in other Minoan representations we see only single moments from it. The painting of this dangerous but fascinating sport is beautifully executed: the artist conveys perfectly the contrast between the powerful animal and the supple athletes, with their elegant and calculated movements. The harmony of colours completes the artistic quality of the work. c. 1500 B.C.*

36. *One side of the unique stone sarcophagus of Hagia Triada, which is decorated with religious representations on all four sides. The interpretation of these representations is one of the most difficult problems for archaeologists; many solutions have been proposed so far. On the side shown here we find, on the right, a figure that seems to be rising from the ground, with a hide covering the entire body including the hands. It is usually interpreted as the body of the heroized dead for whom the ceremonies are being performed. Behind the figure is a sacred (?) building with a tree and stepped altar in front of it. Three men wearing animal skins are approaching the figure, the first one carrying a miniature ship, the other two carrying, animals, no doubt offerings to the dead person. On the left are two tall double axes with bird figures on top of them, and between them, a jar into which a female figure wearing an animal skin is pouring something from a vase. Behind her another, more imposing woman, wearing the long Minoan robe and a crown, holds a similar vase: next a man in a long feminine robe plays on the seven-string lyre. c. 1400 B.C.*

37

37. *Rare model of a small circular temple. Through the open door can be seen the figure of the goddess with arms raised; the door is a removable panel. There is an animal, probably a dog, on the conical roof, and two human figures are looking in through the skylight. 1100 - 1000 B.C.*

38. *Large clay statuette of the goddess with arms raised. The figure of the goddess emerges from a cylindrical base formed by her stylized robe. On her head are various symbols, birds, horns, etc. From the sanctuary of Gazi, near Herakleion. 13th century B.C.*

39. *This vase in the shape of a three-wheeled carriage pulled by three bulls is one of the last examples of Cretan ceramic ware. The old tradition of Minoan art with its love for natural forms is replaced in the Sub-Minoan period by a Geometric stylization. 11th century B.C.*

40. *Bronze tympanon found in the Idaean cave on Crete together with many other bronze shields. They are examples of the oldest 'Orientalizing' influences on Greek art of the late Geometric period. It depicts Zeus stepping on a bull and dismembering a lion; left and right are Kouretes in the shape of winged Assyrian daemons. 8th century B.C.*

41. *The frieze of Prinias. Found in the Archaic temple of Prinias (c. 650 B.C.), it represents horsemen with shields and spears on enormous horses. The Archaic artist has captured with clarity the impression created by the ceremonial procession of horsemen.*

41

PELLA MUSEUM

PELLA MUSEUM

The birth of the Macedonian kingdom

When the Hellenic tribes drew near the shores of the Mediterranean, a section of the "nation of the Dorians and the Macedni", as Herodotos called it, did not advance into the regions of southern Greece, but stayed behind and took root in the mountains and plains of Macedonia. Isolated from the large centres of Hellenism, this group retained the primeval institutions of kingship and of a strictly military and agricultural society, and thus had no part in the rapid evolution that marked the Archaic period. Kings bearing some of the most ancient Greek names, such as Aeropos, Alketas, Amyntas, succeeded in founding a powerful state; its capital, Aigai, was in the mountainous western region (where Edessa now stands), and dominated over the fertile Macedonian plain. As the years went by, however, the Macedonian kings realized that it was necessary to move the seat of the kingdom nearer to the sea, to that element which has so often and so decisively determined the destiny of Hellenism.

Pella, the new capital of the Macedonians

One of the most enlightened of the Macedonian kings, Archelaos (413-399 B.C.), finally took this important step. In the deepest recess of the Thermaic gulf (which penetrated much deeper inland than it does today), a little beyond the mouth of two great rivers, the Axios and the Aliakmon, there was a small township originally named Bounomos. At a distance of 22 kilometres from the coast, up the navigable river Loudias, and 50 kilometres from the old capital, lay the ideal spot for what Archelaos had in mind. And so it became the site of the new capital, Pella, the city which was destined to play a vital part in the history of Greece and the whole world throughout the 4th century B.C. It was only natural that Archelaos should have the ambition of entrusting the embellishment of his city to celebrated artists, as the rulers of other Greek cities had done. So he invited Zeuxes, the leading painter of his age, to come to Pella and decorate his palace with murals illustrating the myths that were the pride and joy of the Greeks. But beyond this, his cultural background and education caused him to seek out the noblest spiritual enjoyment known to the Greeks: tragic poetry. He therefore invited to Pella the most illustrious of the Athenian tragic poets; first and foremost, Euripides, to whom he offered permanent hospitality, so that he might draw inspiration from that unique landscape, which included the seat of the gods, Mount Olympos, and the abode of the Pierid Muses, the Pieria Mountains. We know very little about the tragedy that bore the king's name, *Archelaos,* because only a few fragments of it have survived. But the loss appears insignificant when we consider the powerful and stirring tragedy which Euripides wrote and presented in the Macedonian capital: the *Bacchai*. The last great tragedian of the ancient world had been considered a disciple of the Sophists, and accused of being a rationalist, a destroyer of the tragic myth; yet with the *Bacchai,* he went much further than simply bring to life a tragic figure: he immersed himself deeply into the primordial Dionysiac spirit and, "possessed by the god", he sang in the most authentic terms Dionysos' power which can transport man beyond this world into higher, divine spheres. It seems that the poet's inspiration in writing this play was largely derived from the spiritual climate that he found in Pella, to the vigorous, uncorrupted religious and historical traditions, which we can perceive in a tangible form in the Dionysiac scenes that adorn the krater of Derveni in the Museum of Thessalonike. This also explains the abundance and diversity of the poet's output during his brief stay in Macedonia. In addition to *Archelaos* and the *Bacchai*, he also produced there *Iphigeneia in Aulis* and *Alkmeon*.

The lack of written sources relating to the early history of Macedonia does not allow us to form as complete a picture as we would wish of this important part of the Hellenic world, at least not until after the impressive intervention of Philip in Panhellenic affairs. By that time, Pella had become the centre that succeeded Athens and Sparta and acquired primary historical importance; it reached even greater eminence as the city from which the legendary Alexander set out to change the face of the ancient world and spread Hellenism to the ends of the earth.

However, we may eventually find some compensation for the lack of written sources in the finds that will result from excavations, in particular on the site of the ancient Macedonian capital and a few other Macedonian cities, such as Dion, etc. Until the time when archaeologists will uncover the earlier layers of these ancient sites, we have to limit our knowledge to a few accidental early finds and to finds relating to more recent times.

The excavations of Pella

At the present stage of archaeological research in Macedonia, the excavation of Pella is of exceptional importance, and the study and publication of its results are most urgently called for in the interest of both archaeology and history. Now that archaeologists have completed the excavation of the unique palace of Vergina, an impressive example of Greek architecture in the early 3rd century B.C., the excavation of the ruins of Pella will enable us to form a clear and complete picture of Macedonian architecture in its most complex form: town-planning. Over and beyond architecture, however, it will offer us the various data needed to acquire some knowledge of the private and public life of the Macedonian capital in a period that marked the peak of its power and prosperity.

Before excavations were started, a remarkable funerary stele (tombstone), of the late 5th century B.C., representing a young warrior, was discovered at Pella; it has now been transferred to the Museum of Constantinople. The significance of this outstanding monument reaches beyond the limits of the history of art, because it provides irrefutable proof that in the 5th century B.C. Greek culture was not the privilege of the king alone, but extended to larger sections of the community, since this funeral monument did not adorn the tomb of a sovereign, but of an ordinary citizen.

The first excavations at Pella began immediately after the liberation of Macedonia. In 1914, G. Oikonomos undertook a brief, but fruitful investigation of the site, which resulted in the discovery of a section of a house and a number of fine bronze objects. War conditions, however, caused the excavation to be interrupted. Furthermore, the erroneous view prevailing in those days, that the layers of soil covering the ruins of Pella were of considerable depth, discouraged the archaeologists of Macedonia from resuming excavations, as they already had so many other urgent tasks on their hands. But in 1957, when the base of an Ionic column was revealed in the course of construction work, archaeologists proceeded to systematic excavations, and Northern Greece acquired its most important archaeological site, which was soon to yield unexpectedly fine and abundant treasures. Under a thin layer of soil, excavators discovered in rapid succession the foundations of imposing edifices, broad, straight roads and piping that betrayed the existence of an admirable water-supply system. It became immediately evident that Pella had been built according to the well-known "Hippodameian" plan, which consisted of regular, rectangular building blocks, and that the dwellings had all the characteristic features of the Greek house, i.e. a central peristyle court surrounded by open porticoes. The preservation of the architectural parts of the first building made it possible to restore the slender Ionic columns, so that we can see their white shapes standing out today against the background of the Macedonian plain. The innumerable roof tiles that littered the floors of the dwellings after they had been destroyed were stamped with a single word, in the beautiful lettering of the late 4th century B.C., which provides an answer to the visitor wishing to know the name of the place: PELLA. Other tiles bore the adjective BASILIKOS (ROYAL), and others various proper names: ALEXIMACHOS, ANTIGONOS, SOSIAS, LYSIMACHOS, etc.

Archaeologists were well aware that there was not much hope of finding the rich household objects of the Pella dwellings, not only because the protective layer of soil that covered them was very thin, but mainly because ancient sources state quite explicitly that the Romans who defeated the Macedonians had plundered the land in the most ruthless manner. The display of the valuable spoils which the Roman general Aemilius Paulus brought home to Rome from Pella lasted a whole day. Nevertheless, the ceramic and bronze objects unearthed among the ruins of excavated buildings are by no means insignificant.

The Museum

The small Museum of Pella, erected on the excavation site, houses all these finds and enables the visitor to complete the impressive picture provided by a walk amidst the ancient ruins. In the museum, the visitor may also read a number of inscriptions, mostly engraved on tombstones, originating from the area where the cemeteries were; they were first assembled in a small collection created by the community of the present town of Pella.

There are not many important works representing Greek sculpture among these exhibits. The most outstanding is a marble dog (fig. 7). It is squatting on its haunches, with its two front legs erect, both guardian and ornament to some tomb. The modelling is very sensitive and caused archaeologists to ascribe it to about the mid-5th century B.C., a date that will have to be drastically revised, in my opinion, as soon as a more thorough and systematic study of this work becomes possible.

A statuette of a youth and a mutilated statue of a horseman, dating from the Hellenistic period, cannot really sustain the visitor's interest for very long. He may, however, feel more impressed by two statuettes of Poseidon and Athena. The one of Poseidon (fig. 8) is a bronze "copy" of the late Hellenistic period and reproduces in smaller size a well-known work of Lysippos, the famous Sikyonian sculptor, who worked for a considerable time in Macedonia and was Alexander's favourite sculptor. Archaeologists have named this type of work a "Lateran Poseidon", because the better-known Roman copy is to be found in the papal Lateran collection.

The terracotta statuette of Athena immediately attracts the visitor's attention, just as it roused the interest of scholars on account of its unusual features, particularly the goddess' strange helmet, adorned with two horns (fig. 6). There can hardly be any doubt that this Hellenistic product of miniature art, of which three copies have survived, was modelled after some original larger statue of Athena. Most probably, the original was the cult statue that once stood in Athena's own temple. Ancient sources inform us that the goddess was worshipped in Pella as Athena Alkídemos; even though we are not familiar with the attribute of the goddess conveyed by the adjective *Alkidemos*, there is no difficulty in surmising that the attribute was very much akin to that of Pallas and Promachos; in other words, it expressed the concept of a martial goddess, as she was known to the Greeks when they first descended into mainland Greece; it was under this early guise that the Macedonians chose to preserve her, wholly intact from any subsequent associations which may have derived from the southern Greeks' contact with the pre-Hellenic pantheon of indigenous deities.

The late Hellenistic portrait of Alexander the Great (fig. 1) comes from the neighbouring area of Yannitsa. Although it is not one of the most important portraits of Alexander to have reached us, it does render quite vividly the heroic features with which Greek art has endowed him: the forceful gaze, the passionate expression, the undulating hair rising high above the forehead. In the museum of the Macedonian general's native land, his figure seems to be enhanced by a peculiar radiance which makes his presence keenly felt throughout the place.

The mosaics

However, all the exhibits we have mentioned so far occupy no more than secondary place in the small Museum of Pella. The great discovery of the excavation of Pella was the floor mosaics. Until then, Olynthos took first place in the history of Greek mosaics, and it still retains a chronological pre-eminence. But Pella has come to supersede Olynthos in the high artistic quality of its mosaics.

Seven mosaic compositions in all have been discovered at Pella: five decorated the floors of large chambers, and two the thresholds of rooms. These finds have not yet been subjected to systematic study, so we are unable to determine their exact date. There can be no doubt, however, that they are all almost contemporaneous and that to ascribe them to a date around 300 B.C., would probably be correct. The first composition we will mention is a mosaic representing Dionysos riding his favourite animal, a panther (fig. 2). The rather soft modelling of the god's naked body on the sinuous back of the great feline beast is reminiscent of the refined figures of the late 4th century B.C. On the other hand, the luminous composition standing out against the black background brings to mind the red-figured representations of the Classical age.

The second composition, found in the same building as the first, shows a lion-hunt (fig. 4); we notice that the drawing of the naked male bodies and the powerful beast is far more dynamic. The lion is in the centre of the picture, and there is definitely a sense of perspective in the way it is drawn; on either side two youthful figures are shown raising their weapons to strike at it. Some archaeologists have found this composition reminiscent of the statuary by the famous sculptor Leochares, which represented Alexander and his friend Krateros hunting a lion, and support the view that both works deal with the same subject. No matter how attractive we may find this idea, it cannot be accepted without considerable hesitation, because neither of the two youths in the mosaic have any of the distinguishing features which are to be found in the numerous representations of the great Macedonian.

The mosaic discovered in the second building represents a stag-hunt, (fig. 3) and there is far greater wealth here in the colouring and modelling, in the rendering of space and volumes, in the architectural composition of the figures, and finally in the illusion created by the whole picture, within its elaborate frame of undulating floral ornamentation. On the upper part of the mosaic, there is an inscription which reads:ΓΝΩΣΙΣ ΕΠΟΙΗΣΕΝ (GNOSIS MADE THIS), which informs us it is the work of the oldest mosaicist known to us until now.

A second mosaic composition, which represents an Amazonomachy, was found in the same building. Neither the design nor the execution can be compared to the stag-hunt mosaic. The craftsman who made it was not only conservative and academic, but worse still, clumsy and obviously unable to draw the human form correctly.

The discovery of these admirable works was certainly a singular stroke of luck, but good fortune seemed to stop short, for the largest and finest mosaic of Pella was found half-destroyed; at the moment of writing, it still has not been restored. However, a large section of it, in which the figures have survived practically intact, allows us to appreciate the powerful and noble composition of this mosaic. The subject is the abduction of Helen by Theseus, as shown by the names of the heroes which appear in the composition (fig. 5). The four-horse chariot with its charioteer has survived, but of the other figures — Theseus, Helen, and a friend of Helen's, named Dieaneira — only the last has been preserved to a certain extent. The artist probably modelled his work on some important original painting of the 4th century B.C., like the artist who gave us the well-known mosaic of Alexander and Darius. In spite of all the considerable differences between the two works, I would venture to say that the horses in the Pella mosaic belong to the same noble family as those appearing in the famous mosaic of Neapolis.

1. Head of Alexander the Great. Late Hellenistic period.

2. *Floor mosaic. Dionysos, naked, is shown riding his beloved panther, an animal sacred to him; in his left hand he is holding a beribboned thyrsos. The soft, tender flesh of the young god blends beautifully with the sinuous body of the feline beast. c. 300 B.C.*

3. *Floor mosaic. The principal composition is framed by an exceptionally beautiful floral border of stalks and tendrils flowing and unfolding in innumerable convolutions, interspersed with flowers. The scene in the middle depicts a stag-hunt. The sense of space, the sense of perspective in the rendering of the figures, the way the plasticity·of the bodies is conveyed by means of the skillfully calculated interplay of light and shade are all very characteristic. The inscription on the upper part of the composition: ΓΝΩΣΙΣ ΕΠΟΗΣΕΝ (Gnosis made this) records the name of the mosaicist; he is the oldest craftsman in this field that we know by name. c. 300 B.C.*

3

ΚΥΝΗΓΙΟΝ ΛΕΟΝΤΟ[Σ]
LION HUNTING SCEN[E]

4

4. *Floor mosaic. The subject here is a lion-hunt. The sense of perspective in the rendering of the lion and the brilliant colouring of its mane are particularly impressive. Some archaeologists believe that the artist used as a prototype the famous sculpture by Leochares immortalizing the lion-hunt of Alexander the Great and his friend Krateros. c. 300 B.C.*

261

5. *Floor mosaic. This is the largest composition to have been found so far in Pella. Inscriptions next to the various figures in the picture allow us to interpret the representation as the abduction of Helen by Theseus. In the section that has survived best, we see the four-horse chariot with its proud horses and charioteer (the inscription next to him tells us his name was Phorbas); he is about to welcome the hero and the abducted girl. This is one of the most powerful Hellenistic mosaics, probably based on some lost original painting. c. 300 B.C.*

6. *Terra-cotta statuette of Athena. Her unusual helmet, adorned with two horns, is particularly noteworthy; this is possibly a rendering of the cult statue of Athena Alkidemos who was worshipped at Pella. Late Hellenistic period.*

7. *Funerary dog that once adorned a tomb in Pella. The exceptional modelling of this piece has led archaeologists to ascribe it to the mid-5th century B.C. However, a dating after the mid-4th century B.C. seems more probable.*

5

6

7

263

8

8. Bronze statuette of Poseidon. It is modelled on a famous work, known as the 'Lateran Poseidon', by the great sculptor Lysippos. Late Hellenistic period.

THESSALONIKE MUSEUM

THESSALONIKE ARCHAEOLOGICAL MUSEUM

The Museum of Thessalonike might be described as the National Archaeological Museum of Northern Greece; like its Athens counterpart, it was the first museum to be built after the liberation of the region from Turkish rule in 1912. For many years, before the other Northern Greek cities acquired suitable museums of their own, the Museum of Thessalonike was the place where all the archaeological finds of Macedonia and Thrace were collected and exhibited.

Prehistoric times in Northern Greece

Northern Greece has a very long cultural history, beginning at the dawn of prehistory, while its more recent chapters were irradiated by "our glorious Byzantinism", to recall the words of the poet Cavafy. As mentioned in the introduction to this volume, the presence of the human species in Greece since remotest antiquity was confirmed by the discovery of a skull at Petralona, in the Chalkidike peninsula, 30 kms. from Thessalonike. Anthropologists identified this skull as belonging to Neanderthal man, who is believed to have lived on the European continent 75-50 thousand years ago. Moreover, man-made tools ascribed to the Palaeolithic age were found in Thrace. Northern Greece may thus be considered the cradle of human history as far as Greece is concerned. But in the second phase of prehistory as well, the one scientists have named "great revolution" because of the expansion of Neolithic civilization which occurred at that time, Macedonia may aspire to first place owing to the very early and important settlement of Nea Nikomedeia, near the town of Veroia; this is believed to be the most ancient Neolithic settlement in the whole of Greece. From that age onwards, an ever increasing number of finds over the whole expanse of Macedonia and Thrace has enabled us to follow all the successive stages of Neolithic civilization without interruption. Prehistoric settlements have been brought to light in quick succession from Servia in Western Macedonia to Paradimi in Thrace (near Komotini), and from Armenochori near Florina to the shores of the Chalkidike peninsula.

We must remember that when the earliest Hellenic tribes reached Greece, Macedonia was the first area they encountered; a section of these tribes, known as the "Macednon nation" and sometimes identified with the Dorians, remained in the north of Greece and took root there. I believe it is not in the least unlikely that these tribes remained in the north over a long period of time, before the main bulk proceeded south. This hypothesis may explain the vital significance of the great Macedonian mountain, Olympos —the seat of the gods— in Greek religion. Next to Olympos, another mountain-range known as the Pieria mountains, were thought by the Greeks to be the abode of the Muses, those mythical creatures who were the personification of culture.

From the Mycenaean age to the Archaic period

Like the inhabitants of several other Greek regions —Akarnania, for instance— the Macedonians lived for a great many number of years isolated from the great centres of Hellenism, but without quite losing contact with them. Although Mycenaean finds in Macedonia have so far been scanty, they provide evidence of some contact with the rest of the Hellenic world, a contact which was to grow in the centuries that followed. The Protogeometric style, which emerged in Athens in the 11th century B.C. and rapidly spread to nearly all the regions of Greece, eventually reached Macedonia as well, as we can ascertain from the existence of a local workshop, which was very probably influenced by similar workshops in Thessaly and the Cyclades. Examples of pottery of this period are cropping up in growing numbers as archaeological excavations in Macedonia have become more intensive in recent years and shed more and more light on the early phases of historic times. It is hoped that research might be equally rewarding with respect to the Geometric age, which is not very well represented at present in the museums of Northern Greece. This is due to chance and to the fact that very few excavations have been undertaken so far in the north, for, both at Karabournaki, in Thessalonike, and at Nea Anchialos, a few kilometres west of Thessalonike, where limited investigations have been conducted, a large number of sherds from Geometric vases were discovered, carrying on the Protogeometric tradition in an unbroken line.More abundant still were pieces of Corinthian pottery, which had conquered the markets of the Hellenic world, both east and west, in the 7th and early 6th centuries B.C., thanks to the commercial activity of Corinth at that time, but was displaced from the 6th century B.C. onward, by the products of the Attic workshop. Attic vases of every period have been found in Macedonia, and the Museum of Thessalonike contains many remarkable examples of this art, providing evidence of a direct and close contact between the northern Greek region and the great centre of ancient Greece.

The influence of Ionic art in Northern Greece

In the Archaic period, the wealthy Ionian cities in Asia Minor and on the large islands of the eastern Aegean occupied a very special place in the history of Greek civilization. We all know that Ionia was the cradle of Greek philosophy; to this day, the Ionian philosophers exert a particular fascination on the modern mind, owing to their surprisingly daring theories and the power and density of their thought. We can't help noting, however, that the artistic production of Ionia is not as well--known as it deserves to be, and the same can be said of the influence of the Ionian workshops on the rest of Greece. It is enough to mention that in the very heart of the Dorian world, in Sparta itself, the famous monument known as the "Amyklaian throne" was made by the Ionian Bathykles. This influence was particularly strong in all the areas north of Attica; from Boiotia to Thrace, sculptural works of the Archaic and even the early Classical period bear the vivid stamp of the Ionian spirit. But apart from the plastic arts, the influence of Ionic art in general on northern Greece is indubitable. On the island of Thasos, at Neapolis on the opposite coast (modern Kavala), at Therme (Thessalonike), Ionic buildings occupy first place among the architectural creations of the Archaic period. Furthermore, the presence of Greek art was not restricted to the coastal areas, nor did it vanish with the end of the Archaic world, as the visitor may ascertain when going through the various rooms of the Museum of Thessalonike. This is evidenced even more convincingly by the Archaic kouros discovered at Kilkis, another smaller kouros found in the region of Pieria, and above all, a fine marble metope of the Classical period discovered at Aedonochori, near the town of Serrai and exhibited at present in the Museum of Kavala. The metope is a splendid remnant of a Doric temple which must have been on a par with the temples of Southern Greece, judging from the exquisite modelling of the relief figures that adorn it.

The rise of the Macedonian kingdom and the foundation of Thessalonike

The growth and prosperity attained by Macedonia during the reigns of Philip and Alexander are well-known. In the introductory note to the museum of Pella, there has been mention of the fact that even before those two illustrious kings, another less-known king, Archelaos (413-399 B.C.) embellished his new capital, Pella, not only with works of art, but with the presence of the most famous intellectuals of Greece, not least among them Euripides, who wrote four of his great tragedies in Macedonia and ended his life there. At this point we should perhaps stress the significance of the foundation of Thessalonike by Kassandros in 316 B.C. Whereas Pella did provide a possible opening to the sea, the new historical conditions of the Hellenistic period demanded the creation of a coastal city with a safe harbour, allowing immediate communication by sea with all the other great ports of the eastern Mediterranean. The subsequent history of Thessalonike fully justifies Kassandros' choice

268

of the site. During both the Hellenistic and Roman periods, Thessalonike played a primary role in the political and cultural history of Macedonia, as attested by written sources and the monuments housed in the museum. Later still, when the Roman empire became confined to its eastern section, where it gradually grew into the vast Byzantine state, Thessalonike was known as the *symbasileuousa* (the co-reigning city), almost equal in importance to Constantinople. It is the only city in the Byzantine empire that has preserved an uninterrupted series of typical examples of Byzantine architecture, from the 5th to the 14th century A.D., which makes it the most vital and exciting museum of Byzantine art.

The fascination of Byzantine monuments and their admirable mosaics, beginning with the Rotunda, which dates from the 4th century A.D., and ending with the church of the Holy Apostles, which offers us late examples of mosaic art dated to the 14th century A.D., leave the traveller little time or inclination to complete his sight-seeing with a visit to the archaeological museum. Yet such a visit would not only give a full picture of the city's artistic life, but would also allow him to follow the historical and cultural evolution of Hellenism throughout Northern Greece.

The exhibits at the Museum of Thessalonike

To an experienced eye, this museum has never lacked interest; indeed, some of the collections housed in it are quite unique and of exceptional importance. Recent finds have added a particular attraction to it, rousing more than the purely scholarly interest of archaeologists, and appealing to everyone who appreciates beauty in art. Within the new museum, discreetly built in the centre of the city, all these finds are exhibited with expert knowledge and good taste, in a methodical way that enables the visitor to form a clear and accurate idea of their considerable value and of the museum's particular character.

Prehistoric exhibits

The first important group of exhibits consists of Prehistoric finds from Macedonia and Thrace; of special interest are the numerous Neolithic vases found at Paradimi, in Thrace (near Komotini), during the first excavation carried out by the Faculty of Philosophy of the University of Thessalonike, under the direction of Stratis Pelekidis and Stilpon Kyriakidis. Although these finds have not yet been subjected to systematic study, they can be ascribed with some confidence to the last phase of the Neolithic age. The fact that such a considerable number of vases (about 200 in all), quite often of large size have survived intact from such a remote period of antiquity, is in itself very significant. Their diversity and the functional conception of their shape speak of a civilization with remarkable development and of a society that was already well beyond the first stages of organization.

The second group of exhibits, consisting of the finds from the cemetery of Vergina, near Veroia, make up a unique collection of the early Iron Age (1000-700 B.C.), as the Prehistoric period corresponding to the Geometric times has been termed. Approximately five hundred vases, of over 50 different shapes, give a clear picture of the artistic skill of those ancient inhabitants of Macedonia, as well as their relations and contacts with other places; for instance, a large number of vases in the collection are Protogeometric in style, beautifully and simply decorated with concentric circles and semicircles; as is well-known, this style originated in Attica. Then there are two vases of Mycenaean shape, several ceramic pieces which are almost certainly related to the art of Central Europe, and finally a large vase decorated in three colours, indicating that it came from Cyprus. There are also several hundreds of bronze ornaments, found in women's tombs. Beautiful spectacle fibulae, multi-spiral bracelets, rings, hair-ornaments, a diadem, double axes and several *omphalia* from belt-clasps, are among the most typical examples. Finally, iron weapons, swords, knives, spear-heads, etc. provide the other side of the picture and complete our knowledge of the people, the social structure and the civilization of the Macedonian community during the early centuries of the 1st millennium B.C.

The finds at Olynthos

The collection of finds from Olynthos has a multiple importance. This well-known city of the Chalkidike peninsula, which acquired fame through the great speeches of Demosthenes, was built in 432 B.C. and destroyed in 348 B.C. by Philip of Macedonia. American excavations have uncovered a large section of the city revealing the best preserved Greek city of the Classical age. Built according to a well-defined plan, known as the "Hippodameian system", with broad rectilinear avenues intersected by narrower streets, with regular building blocks consisting of ten houses each, with an admirable water-supply and sewerage system, with bath-tubs, wash-basins and lavatories of a surprisingly modern form, Olynthos provides tangible proof of the high standard of living of the ancient Greeks, and permits a reconstruction of their private life on the basis of concrete data. Unfortunately, the most important finds of Olynthos, the floor mosaics that have survived in excellent condition are not accessible to archaeologists or antiquarians. These are the oldest mosaics in the history of Greek art. Several years ago a layer of soil was thrown over them in order to protect them, and they now await the time when they will once again emerge to the light of day and offer themselves to man's admiring gaze. The other finds of Olynthos, however, household utensils, vases, jewellery, weapons, tools, objects of domestic cult etc., are all exhibited in the Museum of Thessalonike.

Sculptures from the Archaic and Classical ages

This museum, like most other Greek museums, shelters within its walls characteristic works of art that are an integral part of the history of Greek art, but at the same time throw an unexpected light on the local history of the region. As already mentioned, Thessalonike was founded by Kassandros in 316-315 B.C., on the site of ancient Therme. During the Archaic period, Therme was an important city, with a clearly Greek character and culture; this has been ascertained in the most irrefutable manner by the splendid, impressive remains of a large Ionic temple that stood at the centre of the site presently occupied by the city of Thessalonike. Ionic capitals, marble door-frames, Ionic and Lesbian *cymatia* and a small relief fragment (fig. 2), dating from approximately 500 B.C., all these are examples of a robust Ionic architecture, comparable to the best of this kind produced in Ionia itself, or the Cyclades and corresponding to those found at Kavala.

Two Archaic statues —a clothed kouros and a kore— brought along by the refugees from Eastern Thrace, belong to the same period and the same Ionian world. From Western Thrace we have a fine funerary stele of the mid-5th century B.C., which is the product of some Cycladic workshop. Even in areas much nearer Thessalonike, archaeologists have discovered works testifying to the living presence of Greek art —Ionic in particular— and its extensive influence as far south as Boiotia. One of the finest and most recent acquisitions of the museum is a funerary stele from Nea Kallikrateia in the Chalkidike peninsula. It belongs to a series of outstanding Cycladic gravestones of the "severe style" and the early Classical period, representing young girls. The Thessalonike stele represents a young girl holding a dove, her head slightly inclined forward. The skill and sensitivity of the island artist have succeeded in making the marble undulate and pulsate with life.

Works of secondary quality are certainly at a disadvantage next to this masterpiece. However, two other gravestones, of which only fragments have survived, are good enough to complete the overall picture of Northern Greek sculpture as it took shape under the influence of Ionia. One of these (fig. 3) was found in the area of Dion, the sacred city of the Macedonians at the foot of Mount Olympos, and the other (fig. 4) at Kassandra in the Chalkidike peninsula. The first shows a young girl's head, and is contemporaneous to the stele from Nea Kallikrateia; the second depicts a youth's head and dates from the end of the 5th century B.C.

To this group we must also add three works originating from three different areas of Macedonia. There is a funerary stele of the early 4th century B.C. (*c.* 370 B.C.) showing a young lyre-player (fig. 6), which comes from the Chalkidike peninsula and still retains traces of Ionic influence. A second gravestone of the mid-4th century B.C. from Vergina, is inscribed with an epigram —which makes it one of the oldest written monuments of Macedonia— and denotes that Attic art had by then replaced Ionic art as an influence in Northern Greece. This is corroborated by the third stele, which comes from Pieria, but is much inferior in quality.

Roman copies of Classical works

Apart from these original creations, the museum includes some Roman copies of well-known Greek Classical works. There is a colossal head of Athena (fig. 5); this head and the right foot are the only remains from the copy of a famous statue of Athena by Pheidias. Two other heads, whose high polish indicate they were made in Roman times, are most probably copies of works by the same great artist. The most important copy is a headless statue of Aphrodite, known under the Roman name of *Genetrix*. It is not only the fine craftmanship of this copy that places it in an outstanding position among the fifty other copies of this work scattered in various museums across the world; the Thessalonike copy is of particular interest because it is the only one to have survived with its pedestal, thus enabling us to see it in its correct position. This simple fact is of fundamental relevance for a proper artistic appreciation of this work. On the basis of this copy, we have good reason to suggest that the opinion shared by most archaeologists, ascribing this work to Kallimachos, the famous sculptor of the 5th century B.C., must be revised.

The krater of Derveni

There is no need to point out that from Philip's reign onward, Macedonia assumed the leadership of the Hellenic world; it is equally unnecessary to stress the wealth accumulated in that part of Greece since Alexander's time. However, the unbroken continuation of human life in the same locality has deprived us of most relics from this many-sided flowering. Yet archaeological research or the buldozers of great modern construction projects sometimes reveal treasures we had not dared hope for. This is precisely what happened 12 years ago, at Derveni, 10 klm. outside Thessalonike, when tombs dating from the 4th century B.C. were discovered by chance in the course of opening up the national highway linking Thessalonike to Kavala. These finds were not only unexpected and unique of their kind, but also so numerous that they now occupy a whole room in the Museum of Thessalonike. The most important find has now become famous throughout the world, because it immediately took up an outstanding place in every history-book of Greek art. The object in question, which has no equal in the whole world, is a large bronze krater, 0.91 m. high, covered with sculptured ornaments (fig. 1). There is an inlaid inscription along its rim which reads: "ΑΣΤΕΙΟΥΝΙΟΣ ΑΝΑΞΑΓΟΡΑΙΟΙ ΕΣ ΛΑΡΙΣΑΣ". We are thus informed that the owner's name was Asteiounions, son of Anaxagoras, from Larisa. On the main body of the krater we see a group of Silenoi and Maenads gathering in Bacchic ecstasy around the sacred couple, Dionysos and Ariadne. On its shoulders, there are four sculptured figures belonging to the Dionysiac *thiasos* (company): Dionysos himself with a Maenad (fig. 7), on one side, and a Silenos with a Maenad on the other. Within the volutes there are four bearded figures (fig. 8); the neck of the krater is decorated with twelve inlaid animals (deer, griffins, panthers, lions, etc.). The krater's reliefs betray supreme artistry, retaining all the nobility and refinement of Praxitelian creations, with the addition of a passionate, almost ecstatical quality which the craftsmen of the 4th century B.C. acquired from the great Parian sculptor Skopas (fig. 9).

Apart from the krater of Derveni, the visitor can admire several other bronze vases (figs. 10-16) and weapons, gold ornaments and elegant glass vases *(alabastra)*. But the most distinctive among all these exhibits are undoubtedly a number of silver vases, both elegantly and audaciously shaped; the decoration is discreet and the workmanship of excellent quality (fig. 17). Finally, the tombs of Derveni have also yielded fragments of the only Greek papyrus scroll to have been found on Greek soil; if this is not the oldest surviving Greek papyrus, it cannot be very far apart, chronologically speaking, from the famous Timotheos papyrus, which is dated to the late 4th century B.C. The text of the papyrus consists of 18 verses from an Orphic poem with allegorical comments.

Before we proceed to the sculptures, which represent the largest and most characteristic group of exhibits in the museum, it is worth taking note of the finds from another tomb, dug up in the town quarter of Neapolis. These finds consist of fine gold jewellery (bracelets, a necklace, earrings, etc.), terracotta statuettes, a glass vase and a faience vase. Like the krater of Derveni, this last item, of a beautiful green colour, with low-relief representations of Artemis and various animals, is unique of its kind (fig. 18). It is a product of Egypt at the time of the Ptolemies and one of the most admirable examples of this type of vase. It has been ascribed to the mid-2nd century B.C., this date being confirmed by the terracotta statuettes that were found with it.

Roman sculptures　　But the most considerable contribution of the museum of Thessalonike is that it offers both the scholar and the layman an opportunity to admire one of the richest collections of Roman sculptures, dating from the 1st century B.C. to the end of antiquity. The numerous funerary and votive reliefs may not always be works of high quality, but the series of portraits can certainly claim first place in the art of portraiture, which thrived during that period. Among these portraits, we must single out a 1st century B.C. head, which marks the transition from the artistic climate of the late Hellenistic period to the age of the Roman republic (fig. 23). The statue of Augustus (fig. 25), among the innumerable statues of this kind which had been set up in the various territories conquered by the Romans, is remarkable for its sturdy structure, its sensuous modelling and the well-balanced combination of the intellectual and military aspects in a single human personality. There is another outstanding portrait made of bronze and quite rare of its kind, representing Alexander Severus (A.D. 222-235), the boy who became emperor at 14, who enjoyed reading Plato's *Republic* and was responsive to the new religious currents from the East (fig. 26). Next to this boyish figure, stands the portrait of a man in his maturity (fig. 24), which strikes us as rather coarse, weighed down by experience; he apparently lived during the terrible years that succeeded the dynasty of the Severi, the years of the Gordiani (A.D. 235-244). However, the most significant works, as regards the history of ancient sculpture, are three portraits belonging to the end of the ancient world. First, the statue of a venerable lady (fig. 28), who lived during the reign of Constantine the Great: this is one of the rare examples of sculpture of that late date. The spiritualized face, the introverted expression, the dreamy gaze reveal how radically, how irreversibly man's views had changed. The woman's body, enfolded in heavy draperies, has practically ceased to exist; it has become a shapeless stump, rather like a pillar, whose sole function is to support the head, which is where all the subject's expressiveness is now concentrated. There are two other busts portraying a man and a woman (fig. 29-30); both these works carry to extremes the tendencies noted in the previous portrait. Dating to the turn of the 4th century A.D., they are the last examples not only of the art of ancient portraiture, but of ancient sculpture in general. We cannot help admiring the artist's ability in eliminating completely the material, physical aspect of his subject and transforming it into a vehicle for elusive states of mind. This is particularly true of the male figure, with its uncertain, enigmatic gaze, the imperceptible contraction of the lips, the modelling of the cheekbones, the intricate arrangement of the hair, and above all the unworldly expression of the face, which make it one of the most powerful portraits of any period.

The collection of sarcophagi is of considerable importance. Apart from the various examples of sarcophagi decorated very simply with garlands, cupids, relief portraits of the dead, or representations of a religious character (for instance, there is a particularly interesting sarcophagus decorated with themes related to the cult of Isis), there are sarcophagi of the 2nd and 3rd centuries A.D., known as "Attic", elaborately decorated with mythological themes (fig. 27). These representations in relief are a continuation of the ancient tradition of Greek sculpture and indicate how familiar and popular was the world of myth even during the last centuries of antiquity. Orpheus among the wild beasts, the hunting of the Kalydonian boar, Amazonomachies, Centauromachies, sea-battles, Dionysiac scenes (thiasoi), etc. are the main subjects that inspired the artists who made these sarcophagi. There are instances when one can single out among the reliefs certain figures which originate from famous Classical prototypes, proving how deep and permanent was that great flowering of the Greek spirit.

Among hundreds of secondary works, mostly small funerary or votive reliefs of the Roman age, which offer abundant and rewarding material to the student of the religion of those times, one can single out some exhibits which are unquestionably the work of plain craftsmen, yet display unusual sensitivity, sound technical knowledge and a certain artistic power. First and foremost, we must mention a small female portrait in relief —part of a gravestone, no doubt— which immediately impresses the spectator with the simplicity of its features, the solidity of its modelling and the vigour of its expression. A second relief consists of the busts of a family group; the plastic modelling of the faces is quite remarkable: sharp edges, smooth simple planes, clear-cut geometric volumes, conveying a purely cubistic and modern impression. Finally, among the numerous relief sculptures picturing what has become known in the history of art and religion as a "Thracian horseman", there is a small figure, which for all its unsophisticated craftsmanship, shows how an age-old tradition in sculpture has been able to endow this ordinary, unimportant little object with nobility, confidence and ease. It may be worth while to make a systematic study of all such simple, unpretentious products of an art which one might describe as "popular", and to delineate the geographical boundaries within which the creations of these humble craftsmen maintained the old tradition of Greek sculptural skill, as opposed to some other areas of the Roman empire where the very same themes were rendered with all the coarseness and clumsiness resulting from the lack of such a historical heritage. A study of this kind would undoubtedly pinpoint those areas where Hellenism grew out of a deep and ancient tradition and was not the result of Hellenistic expansion or, to a much lesser degree, of Roman conquest. Anticipating such a study, we can already affirm that these areas extended in all directions, far beyond the frontiers of Greece as we know them today.

Glass vases

There is yet another collection in the Museum of Thessalonike which is sure to attract the attention of both scholar and layman: Roman glassware (figs. 21-22). Not all these exhibits are of a high quality, but they are typical and representative examples of ancient glasswork which set the foundations of the technique and eventually replaced both ceramic and faience products. Although nowadays our daily contact with glass objects has made us so familiar with this material that our aesthetic instinct does not always react as powerfully as it should at their sight, there are some ancient glass vases that immediately rouse our interest and exert a peculiar attraction. Those ancient glass-workers, full of the enthusiasm and vigour that came from discovering a new material, succeeded in giving their works daring new forms, alive and sensual. Terracotta prototypes did not hinder their inspiration; they supplied craftsmen with a starting-point, beyond which they could move forward, using their imagination and their responsiveness to the new material.

Mosaics

The last exhibits awaiting the visitor of the museum are the Roman floor mosaics discovered in Thessalonike. The largest and most important is a multi-figured composition from Dionysiac mythology; in the centre, we see Ariadne, reclining, and Dionysos approaching her; he is surrounded by various figures of the Dionysiac thiasos (company). Each separate figure, as well as the composition as a whole, display the mosaicist's remarkable skill, technique and experience; in those days, his craft had reached a high degree of development throughout the Roman empire, as evidenced by the innumerable mosaics discovered all over the then known world, from the British shores to the regions of the East. Such mosaics can be found everywhere in Greece, from Nikopolis in Epeiros to the Aegean islands. The most recent finds are the famous mosaics of Mytilene, illustrating the comedies of Menander and including the poet's portrait. In the Museum of Thessalonike there is also a series of mosaics representing busts of male and female figures related to the mythology of the sea, as shown by the various symbols in the compositions: anchors, claws from crustaceans, etc. (figs. 31-32). However, as we have already remarked at the beginning of this text, anybody interested in mosaics need only visit the numerous architectural monuments of Thessalonike in order to follow the evolution of this art from the 4th century A.D., beginning with the Rotunda, going on to the churches of Hosios David, Saint Demetrios, the Acheiropoietos, Saint Sophia, and ending up with the Holy Apostles, where the mosaics of the Palaiologean renaissance bring us back to the Hellenistic sources, which nurtured Greek Christian art over the course of many centuries.

2. *Archaic head in relief. It was part of the sculptural decoration of a fine Archaic temple that stood at the centre of the site now occupied by the city of Thessalonike. Several architectural members, Ionic in style, have come from the same temple. c. 500 B.C.*

3. *Relief figure of a young girl, from a funerary stele found at Dion in Pieria. The influence of Ionic art is quite marked. Mid-5th century B.C.*

4. *Relief figure of a youth, from a funerary stele found at Kassandra in the Chalkidike peninsula. Ionic influence is gradually giving way to the Attic style. Late 5th century B.C.*

5. *Roman copy of a 5th century B.C. statue of Athena by Pheidias.*

6. *Funerary stele of a young lyre-player, found in the area of Poteidaia, in the Chalkidike peninsula. The modelling still retains traces of the Ionic style. c. 370 B.C.*

5

6

7

8

7. *Figure of a Maenad, sculptured in the round, from the bronze krater of Derveni. c. 330 B.C.*

8. *Bearded figure, most probably Herakles, from the volutes of the bronze krater of Derveni. c. 330 B.C.*

9. *Embossed representation of a Silenos on the main body of the Derveni krater. c. 330 B.C.*

9

10. *Bronze amphora with lid, from Derveni. Late 4th century B.C.*

11. *Silver oinochoe with gilt ornamentation, from Derveni. Late 4th century B.C.*

12. *Bronze amphora from Derveni. Late 4th century B.C.*

13. *Bronze oinochoe from Derveni. Late 4th century B.C.*

14. *Bronze vessel from Derveni. Late 4th century B.C.*

15. *Bronze kylix from Derveni. Late 4th century B.C.*

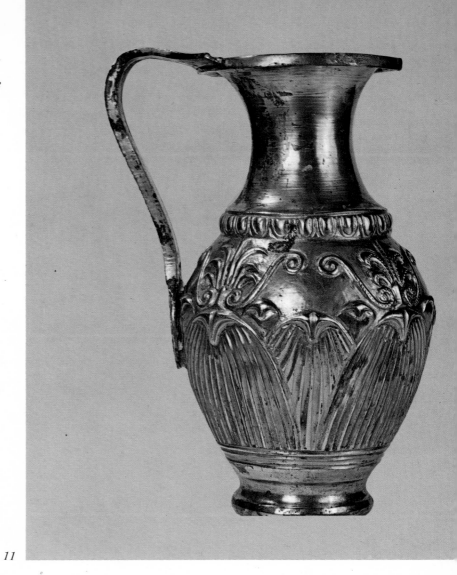

11

10

12

14

16

17

16. Bronze oinochoe from Derveni. Late 4th century B.C.

17. Silver ethmos (strainer) from Derveni. The craftsman has skillfully exploited the possibilities offered by the precious metal for the creation of elaborate figures. Late 4th century B.C.

18. A remarkable faience vase, unique in Greece; the decoration consists of low-relief representations; Artemis is shown standing in a forest. This piece came from Ptolemaic Egypt and was found in a 2nd century B.C. tomb in Thessalonike.

18

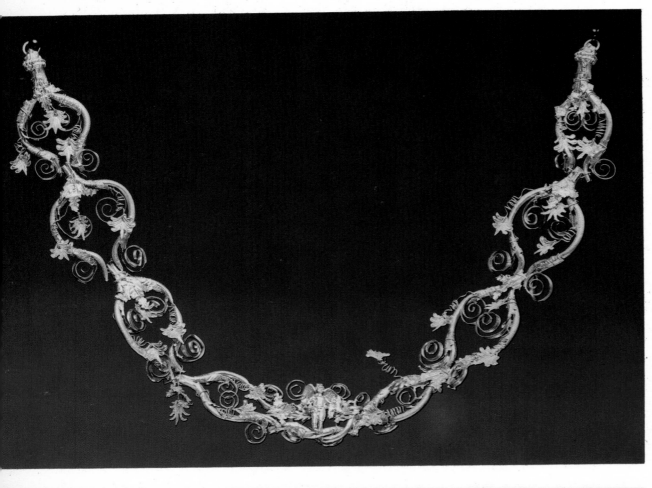

19

20

19. Gold necklace from a tomb at Sedes, near Thessalonike. Late 4th century B.C.

20. Gold medal portraying Olympias on one side and a Nereid on horseback on the other. It was probably minted around the middle of the 3rd century A.D. on the occasion of the Olympic games held in Macedonia.

21-22. Glass vases of the Roman age. This new material, with its subtle diversity of colour, gave artists fresh opportunities to create beautiful forms.

21

22

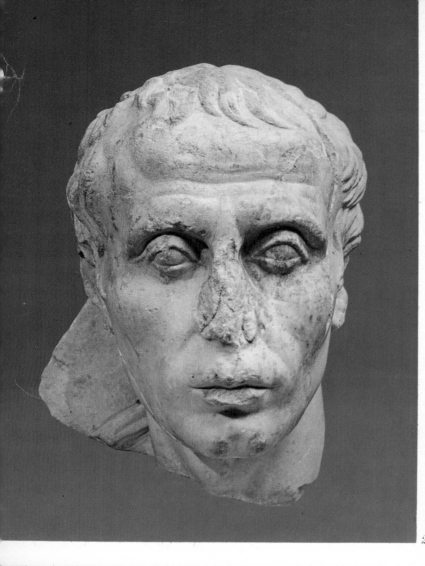

23

24

23. *Male portrait of the 1st century B.C. The vitality of Hellenistic tradition has been successfully grafted on to the plastic arts of the Roman republic.*

24. *Male portrait of the mid-3rd century A.D. The impressive realism of this work reflects the turbulence of this phase of the Roman age.*

25. *Portrait statue of emperor Augustus (27-14 B.C.). The features of the great Roman leader have retained the nobility and spirituality of earlier Greek portraits.*

26. *Bronze portrait of emperor Alexander Severus (A.D. 222-235). An excellent example of imperial portraiture.*

26

27. *A sarcophagus of the Roman imperial times, with representation of the Amazonomachy. The themes of Greek mythology, enriched by a variety of eschatological symbols, offered the craftsmen who fashioned these grave monuments the appropriate plastic elements required for their decoration.*

28. *Statue portraying a Roman lady in the reign of Constantine the Great. This rare example of the sculpture of late antiquity illustrates the radical transformation that took place in the plastic treatment of the human body.*

29. *Male bust of the late 4th century A.D. The fine modelling of the figure and the unworldly expression of the face are indicative of the spiritual and cultural trends of that crucial historic time, marking the end of the ancient world.*

30. *Female bust of the late 4th century A.D. Like the male bust of which it is a counterpart, it represents the last glow of the ancient world, while at the same time it announces the emergence of a new world.*

27

29

30

31. *Fragment of a floor mosaic of the Roman imperial times, with a female figure symbolizing the marine world.*

32. *Fragment of a floor mosaic of the Roman imperial times, with a male figure symbolizing the marine world.*

CYPRUS MUSEUM

**History
of the Museum**

As one of the countries in the Mediterranean, Cyprus has had one of the most complex civilizations and one of the most agitated histories. Eight millennia of life concentrated within the narrow limits of this island have bequeathed to it a legacy of some wonderful works of art. As the visitor to the Cyprus Museum moves from room to room, he can trace the development of Cypriot civilization from Neolithic times to the Early Christian period. The fact that its exhibits all come exclusively from Cyprus makes this museum of special interest to the scholar but also to the ordinary visitor. In the pottery and sculpture galleries, the exhibits have been arranged according to typological evolution so that one can easily observe artistic development at its various stages throughout the ages.

It has taken years for the Museum to assume its present form. Its history began in the previous century; and by the enactment of the first Antiquities Law in 1905, the Museum acquired a semi-official status. Since 1935 the Museum has been under the jurisdiction of the Government Department of Antiquities, which was created that year by a new law. The construction of the original building, which served as the nucleus of the present one, started in 1908 and was completed in 1924. It reached its current proportions after a number of extensions and additions, culminating in the inauguration of a large new hall in 1972.

The Cyprus Museum forms a vital part of the Antiquities Department, which acts as a center for all archaeological activity on the island. Even after the events of the summer of 1974 and the ensuing disorganization of life on the island, this Service carried on major excavations on four large sites along with some rescue operations all over the island. There were also as many as seventeen foreign archaeological expeditions digging in various regions of Cyprus. As the finds from all these excavations are collected and preserved in the Cyprus Museum, its treasures keep increasing all the time giving it the just reputation of being one of the richest in the world.

The entire history of Cyprus and the special character of its civilization unfold before the visitor's eyes, with the objects themselves acting as guides. Some of these objects are brilliant works of art, while others are just moving witnesses to the daily toil and aspirations of Man throughout the ages. A short historical retrospection will help place the finds in a historical context so as to enable the visitor to move along with greater ease.

**Cypriot
civilization
Neolithic period**

A great and important part of the Cypriot contribution to the history of civilization goes back to prehistoric times. An already developed phase of Neolithic culture, probably imported from the neighbouring countries of Asia, appeared in Cyprus around the beginning of the sixth millennium. More than thirty Neolithic settlements have been identified on the island. But most of our information about life in that period is derived from the settlement of Khirokitia, excavated between 1936 and 1939. The Neolithic inhabitants of this settlement, estimated at four to five thousand, lived in well-built circular huts with thatched roofs within well-organized social groups. They hunted, tilled the earth, had already domesticated wild animals, practiced weaving, and used soft stones — later clay — to make utensils and figurines. They had trade relations with Asia Minor and Northern Syria.

Bronze Age

The discovery of copper brought about a fundamental change in the cultural history of Cyprus, comparable to the industrial revolution of modern times. Beginning with the third millennium, the rich Cypriot copper mines changed the fabric of life on the island; tools, weapons, and vessels were now manufactured out of metal, and this precious mineral was also exported to neighbouring countries, turning the island into an important trading center. The great wealth that poured into the island as a result of this commercial activity had a direct effect on the artistic production of the Cypriots. New shapes appeared in pottery, and clay models of sanctuaries illustrate richer forms of worship.

During the Middle Bronze Age (1850-1600 B.C.), the northern coast of the island was abandoned as the southern and eastern shores around Kalopsidha began to grow more popular. New settlements, such as Enkomi and Kition, were founded, and these were to grow still more in subsequent centuries. From this new geographical position communication with the opposite coasts of Syria and Palestine was made easier, and there must have been trade relations with these regions, copper being the main export. It was only natural, therefore, that during this period the Cypriots would be exposed to cultural influences from the opposite shore.

Mycenaean period

The great development of Cyprus occurred under Mycenaean influence in the Late Bronze Age (1550-1050 B.C.). The first Mycenaean traders settled on the southeastern shores of Cyprus around 1400 B.C. which was the period of their trade expansion eastward. The towns of this area grew very prosperous, judiciously expanding on the basis of an excellent city-planning system, and, later, with walls erected around them. The most important and wealthiest settlement was Enkomi, and this has been amply demonstrated by the excavations there, which enriched the Museum collections with a great many Mycenaean vases, jewellery, sculptures and other objects. The Mycenaean traders and craftsmen who settled in Cyprus were succeeded around 1230 B.C. by the first Achaean settlers. Gradually these took over political power, introduced their own script and language, as well as their religion and culture, so that the 12th century found Cyprus Hellenized. This important change laid the foundations for the subsequent development of Cyprus in both the political and the cultural fields and decisively determined the course of her history to our own days.

At the end of the 2nd millennium a major earthquake destroyed all the Bronze Age towns, bringing the island's Mycenaean civilization to an end. Enkomi was abandoned in 1075 B.C., but on the coast further east its inhabitants founded Salamis, the other large town which was to play a leading role in the history of Cyprus until Early Christian times. Its founding is mythologically associated with the end of the Trojan war and the Homeric hero Teukros.

Historical period

The first millennium B.C. was characterized by a rapid expansion of Eastern peoples. Strongly aggressive, these peoples gradually spread throughout the Eastern Mediterranean, including Cyprus. In spite of strong influences from the East, however, the basically Hellenic character of Cypriot culture was never lost, its conservative character encouraging the Cypriots to cling tenaciously to Mycenaean customs and ancient forms of expression in religion, art, language, and script.

The Phoenicians were the first among Eastern peoples to settle on the island. They did so peacefully during the 9th century B.C. At Kition, they founded a Phoenician dynasty, which survived to the 4th century B.C. The Phoenician element, always careful to be on the side of the conquerors, facilitated the successive conquests of the island, between the end of the 8th and the end of the 4th century B.C., by the Assyrians (end of the 8th century B.C.), the Egyptians (6th century B.C.), and the Persians ((525 B.C. onwards). Despite its state of dependency, Cyprus did not fare badly under these suzerainties, but managed on the contrary to preserve both its kingdoms and a kind of autonomy. It was only around 500 B.C. that the Cypriots started their wars of independence against the Persians. In these wars they were joined by the Greeks of Ionia, but Cyprus was unable to free herself from the Persian yoke at this time. The animated efforts of the Greeks of the mainland, under Kimon's leadership, during the 5th century also failed to achieve the liberation of Cyprus, and once again were the Cypriots left to themselves to continue their struggle for freedom alone.

At the end of the 5th century B.C., a great figure appeared in Cypriot history in the person of King Euagoras I of Salamis, whose name is associated with the struggles of the Cypriots against the Persians. Even more important was his policy of establishing strong spiritual bonds between Cyprus and the rest of the Hellenic world, bonds that were to last for ever after. An ardent advocate of Isokrates' concept of panhellenic unity, he strengthened Hellenism on the island and saw Cyprus achieve another great period of wealth and progress under his reign (411-374 B.C.).

It was Alexander the Great who finally liberated Cyprus from the Persian yoke. Later, during the conflicts among the Diadochoi (Alexander's successors), Cyprus passed to the Ptolemies (318-58 B.C.). During Hellenistic times, Cyprus enjoyed a new period of prosperity, maintaining close cultural ties with the great Hellenic centres of Macedonia and Alexandria.

After the Roman conquest (58 B.C.), Cyprus slowly began to lose its special cultural identity until it finally became just one more province of the Roman Empire. Many stately public and private buildings of Roman times are preserved to this day. Cyprus was to recover its Hellenic character in a new form within the framework of Christianity.

An attempt will now be made to place the artistic contribution of ancient Cyprus, as reflected in the Cyprus Museum, within the context of this brief historical survey. It may be that the level of civilization which Cyprus has to display cannot equal that of Minoan Crete. But it does deserve credit for the steadiness and originality of its artistic production throughout the centuries of its long history. Variety of form and expression, together with constant change, have enabled it to maintain its vitality and a certain youthful quality.

Sculpture Neolithic figurines

In sculpture, Cyprus has no monumental works to show like those of the other Middle-Eastern countries, nor has it ever achieved the perfection of Greek mainland sculpture. The principal reason for this was perhaps the lack of marble or hard stone on the island; Cypriot limestone is hardly a suitable material for the creation of monumental sculpture. But, as early as the 6th millennium, an innate propensity to artistic creation led Neolithic man to attempt to carve the human form on stone. Using andesite, which abounds on river beds, he created figurines of an extremely simple form (fig. 3). The human body was rendered only schematically, but there was some emphasis on its most characteristic attribute — the face. Its shape varied, but its principal features — the eyes and the nose — were carved in relief (fig. 2). More rarely, Neolithic man made animal protomes, which were probably used to cap sceptres, while figurines imitating the human form must have served some ritual function. Out of the same material he made his first vessels, using tools made of stone. The simple lines and well-worked gray surface of these early specimens of primitive Cypriot art, heralding as they do styles of Cycladic sculpture, are aesthetically pleasing to the contemporary viewer who has learned to appreciate the simple forms of modern art.

At the beginning of the third millennium, a new material — steatite — opened up new horizons to sculpture. Its dense texture and smooth surfaces made it possible for the artist to reproduce the details of the human body and face, while the variety of shades in gray and green available in steatite gave his figurines a special charm. The head, supported on a long neck, now became smaller, acquiring its true proportions, and the figure as a whole took on the shape of a cross, with the arms outstretched and the legs close together (fig. 4). Moved by an impulse to create something different, the artist sometimes gave new forms to these cruciform figurines: two figures together, without arms, joined in the shape of a cross. One of the two figures has clearly noticeable breasts, and it may be assumed that this is related to fertility, a common theme in primitive art. It is not without significance that when, later, Neolithic man discovered clay and used it as the principal material in pottery and the plastic arts, the first form he created was the goddess of fertility with bare breasts and strongly marked female characteristics.

Clay-modelling

The use of clay played an important part in the history of Cypriot sculpture. Clay-modelling dominated nearly the whole of the Bronze Age. But even during subsequent centuries and up to Hellenistic times terracotta remained the favourite means of artistic expression among the Cypriots. A larger number of terracottas have in fact been found in Cyprus than in any other part of the ancient world.

The craftsmen of the Bronze Age used clay with skill and originality. Characteristic examples are two miniature models of open-air sanctuaries and a scene from daily life representing ploughing. The two models of sanctuaries, one from the necropolis of Vounous and the other from the necropolis of Kotchatis, date from the Early Bronze Age (2300-1850 B.C.) and, apart from their artistic value, provide a unique insight into the religion of the period around 2000 B.C. The grouping from Vounous (fig. 6) represents a circular open-air sanctuary surrounded by a high wall; within it, many figures appear to be participating in some sort of ritual ceremony. The sacred area, set apart from the rest of the space, is indicated by three figures *(xoana)* in relief against the wall of the sanctuary. The three figures wear bulls' masks and have snakes hanging from their joined hands. The model from Kotchatis has only the sacred area with the three *xoana* and no snakes; in the foreground, a figure is pouring a libation into a large vessel (fig. 5).

It must have been from such cult figures that the large plank-shaped clay figurine (fig. 7) was influenced. The details of the face and body are incised on the flat polished surface and, as on vases of that period, the incised motifs are filled with plaster. This creates a nice contrast between the light details and the dark background. Such flat plank-shaped figurines continued to be produced through-out the first half of the second millennium, but now a greater effort was made to render the various parts of the body more realistically by colouring the details.

Terracotta continued to be a favourite medium in the Late Bronze Age (1500-1050 B.C.) too, but the forms were now much more naturalistic and technically advanced. Influenced by animal-shaped vases, the ceramist fashioned hollow, rather than solid, figurines. The form of the fertility goddess, often holding an infant in her arms like a mother-goddess, continued to dominate the scene. The bird-like facial features, the large earrings, and the accentuated genitals are reminiscent of Eastern representations, which must have surely influenced the Cypriot craftsman (fig. 14).

Bronze statues

Toward the end of the Late Bronze Age the principal kind of sculpture was no longer terracotta but bronze. Under a new impetus given to metal-work by the early Achaean settlers, the first bronze statues made their appearance. The statue of the horned god from Enkomi, 55 cm. high, is the largest and finest work of sculpture found thus far from that period (fig. 20). The strength of the god is embodied in his athletic torso and robust limbs; the youthful and harmonious features of his face, expressing beauty and divine serenity, herald Greek Archaic sculpture. The figure of this god appears more severe in a smaller statue from Enkomi, of a somewhat later date; in it the god — bearded, with a horned helmet, and fully armed — stands on a base shaped like a copper ingot, as the protector of copper, which was the main source of Cypriot wealth. Numerous other bronze statuettes have been found, smaller in size and with no special artistic pretension. Among them are models of 'sacred vehicles' carrying bulls to sacrifice with an escort of human figures.

Archaic terracotta figurines

During the 7th and 6th centuries B.C. there was a revival of religious spirit, and rural sanctuaries, where the faithful dedicated clay idols, appeared in many places. Clay-modelling witnessed a new flowering, and figurines were abundantly produced in a great variety of size and form. The human figure predominated, although it no longer represented a god but man himself, who offered his image to the sanctuary so as to be under the god's protection. Hundreds of such votive figurines have been found in the Archaic sanctuary of Hagia Irini. Their size varies from 10 cm. to lifesize; the facial features in many of them are distinct enough to suggest portraits. From a strictly artistic point-of-view, these clay figurines may not be of very high quality, but as a group they are impressive, and for this reason they are exhibited in the Museum exactly as they were found. Besides the figurines and life-size statues of human beings, figures of animals and Centaurs have also been found. There are also such groups as bull and men, horses and riders, chariots and warriors, ships and crew, and scenes from daily life (figs. 29-32). It is interesting to note that, as the artist tried to render the human figure as realistically as possible, what he often really succeeded in doing was to give it and the groups a humorous touch. Since this tendency is also noticed in vase-painting, it may well be considered a more general characteristic of Archaic Cypriot art.

Monumental sculpture

It was during the Archaic period that the Cypriots first created monumental sculpture, that is, life-size or larger than life-size statues, fashioned out of the local limestone. The first impetus for monumental art came from the East as a result of the cultural influences to which Cyprus was exposed during the rule of the Assyrians, the Egyptians, and, later, the Persians. In the Early Archaic years, the influence of Egyptian art in sculpture, as in all areas of artistic endeavour, is quite evident. But toward the end of the 6th century, Cyprus re-established cultural contacts with the Aegean world and, during the entire 5th century, joined the common Greek political cause against Persia. The cultural influence of this contact with Greece lasted until the Roman period. The mingling of the characteristics of the Archaic sculpture of Greece, particularly of Ionia, with Cypriot elements led to the emergence in Cypriot sculpture of a mixed style, which could well be termed Cypro-Ionic. The Museum has many statues in this style, dated to the end of the 6th and the beginning of the 5th century B.C. One of the best and most representative specimens is the head of a Kore with Ionian facial features, but with ornaments on her head and around her neck that are of a purely Cypriot character (fig. 33). The Greek gods were a favourite subject of the Cypriot sculptor, who liked to portray them in his own original way. One such statue is that of Keraunios Zeus (Zeus of the Thunderbolt) from Kition; originally the god held a thunderbolt and an eagle; but the fact that he is represented wearing a long *chiton* and an *aegis* suggests that the artist was not much used to depicting the male body in the nude (fig. 27).

The Greek way of life and Hellenic ideas of the 5th century B.C. inspired many works of art, such as the handsome head of an athlete, from Potamia (fig. 1), and many gravestones, from Marion. This city, located on the northwestern coast of the island, had close trade relations with Athens, receiving from it strong and direct cultural influences. This is demonstrated by the marble stele of Stases (fig. 35) and by a limestone stele representing a seated woman holding a bird (fig. 36). The concentration in the eyes, the Attic dress, and the comfortable stance suggest Attic influence of the art of 420 B.C.

In a copper-producing land, it was only natural that there would be numerous bronze statues created by both Cypriots and sculptors from Greece proper. The bronze head of Apollo of Tamassos, known as the 'Chatsworth head', now in the British Museum, is an excellent example of the artistic creativity of the 5th century B.C. Bronze statuettes and groups, like the Satyr of Kourion, the group of lions and a bull, and the admirable cow from the temple of Athena in Vouni palace, are excellent examples of the sculptural production of Cyprus and its indubitably Hellenic character. From this period onwards, Cypriot sculpture pursued a course that was parallel to that of the sculpture of Greece. The Cyprus Museum has some admirable examples of Cypriot sculpture, dating from the 4th century to Hellenistic times. The marble head of Aphrodite, or Hygeia, from Salamis (fig. 38), with the delicate moulding of the facial features and the sensitive rendering of the hair, is reminiscent of Praxitelian creations and reflects the Greek atmosphere that was prevalent at the beginning of the 4th century at the court of King Euagoras. Many clay heads found in the cenotaph of Nikokreon, the last king of Salamis, date from 311 B.C. when that dynasty came to a dramatic end. (Nikokreon chose to put himself and his entire family to death rather than submit to the Ptolemies.) The heads of youths have an idealistic quality about them, obviously under the influence of the manner of Lysippos (fig. 39). Another fine head from the sanctuary of Aphrodite in Arsos suggests the climate of the art of Skopas at the beginning of the 3rd century B.C. (fig. 37). Hellenistic art is represented by a charming and delicate statue of Aphrodite who, according to legend, was born in Cyprus (fig. 40).

Sculpture also flourished during the Roman period, though it did not have any distinct Cypriot character any longer; every work of art now bore the stamp of the official imperial style. The gymnasium, the theatre, and the other public buildings recently excavated at Salamis have yielded a rich collection of marble statues belonging mainly to the Hadrianic School of sculpture of the 2nd century A.D. The most important specimen of Roman sculpture in the Cyprus Museum is the bronze statue of the Roman emperor Septimius Severus (2.08 m. high); its head is a magnificent example of Roman portraiture (fig. 41).

Neolithic pottery

But it is the evolution of pottery and vase-painting that can be studied in the Cyprus Museum to best advantage. During the second phase of the Neolithic Age (3500-3000 B.C.), there appeared an advanced type of pottery; large bowls with spouts and jugs with narrow necks and no handles are the most common shapes at this time; their surface is covered with a reddish slip. The distinguishing feature of Cypriot vases belonging to this period is 'combed' decoration. On the other hand, the Chalcolithic Period (3000-2300 B.C.) is characterized by variety as regards both shape and decoration. There are large jars, bowls of various sizes and shapes, jugs, and composite vases which herald the great flowering of ceramics in the Early Bronze Age. During the Chalcolithic Period vase decoration usually consisted of geometric and floral motifs, painted in red on the white surface of the vase. Intricate designs drawn with a firm hand and harmoniously arranged across the surface of the vase have produced an important art of vase-painting which has only recently begun to be better known.

Bronze Age pottery

The wealth of the Early Bronze Age (2300-1850 B.C.) is admirably reflected in its pottery. It is a pottery characterized by a forceful, dynamic quality. Apart from utensils made for daily use, the potter of that age, exuberant in imagination, created intricately shaped vases, which, however, did not lack elegance of form (fig. 8). Some of them he decorated with incised or relief ornamentation and often with figures in the round (fig. 10). Sometimes he fashioned them in the form of birds or animals; he also made miniature sanctuaries and imitated in clay objects made of other materials, such as swords and spindles. All these were intended to be offered as grave gifts to the dead. The red polished surface and incised decoration of the vases are suggestive of bronze vessels, which were surely produced during that period even if none has survived. The relief decoration usually consisted of birds and animals, bulls' heads and serpents. But such ornamentation is unsuitable for pottery; it is too heavy and disrupts the harmony of the shape.

In the Middle Bronze Age (1850-1550 B.C.), a new style of pottery began to evolve, rather akin in technique to the pottery of the Chalcolithic period. The decoration is either red or black painted on white ground (fig. 9). Motifs moulded in the round are often used for handles, or placed beside the handles, but their use is not inordinate as in the Early Bronze Age. In his desire to enliven his creations, the potter frequently endowed them with anthropomorphic features, such as eyes, ears, noses, breasts, and the like. The shapes of the vases grew more balanced; also more refined by being stripped of the over-elaborate ornamentation of the earlier composite vases. But some composite wine-jugs continued to be produced during this period, thus introducing some variety in the ceramic output.

Trade relations between Cyprus and the Middle Eastern countries brought the Cypriot potter into contact with Oriental ceramic art. Numerous specimens of this foreign pottery were imported into Cyprus, inevitably influencing the local craftsman. Many new styles made their appearance at this time. Some were simply a natural development of the Middle Bronze Age pottery as, for instance, vases decorated with geometric designs on white ground, or vases imitating metal forms, usually with a ring-shaped base. Other styles were imported from neighbouring countries; such were the wheel-made vases with a decoration in two colours and the long and slender red lustrous bottles.

Mycenaean vases

But the most important event in Cypriot ceramics of the Late Bronze Age (1550-1050 B.C.) is the appearance in large numbers of Mycenaean vases in Cyprus soon after 1400 B.C. Apart from the purely Mycenaean shapes, there were also shapes inspired from the Orient as, for instance, cups with a triangular, horizontal handle and flasks with a lentoid body. Most of the Mycenaean vases which have representations on them (of chariots, warriors, animals, birds, fish, etc.) have been found in Cyprus, and these are representative examples of a pictorial style of purely Aegean inspiration. However, the fact that this style appears much more frequently in Cyprus, coupled with the fact that certain Mycenaean vases imitate Cypriot shapes, has led a group of scholars to conclude that these vases were made in Cyprus by Mycenaean craftsmen who arrived with Mycenaean tradesmen and settled with them in the commercial centres along the southern and eastern coasts of the island. At present, this is the most prevalent theory. Other scholars believe that all these vases were made in the Peloponnesos with a view to being exported to Cyprus. Apart from their harmonious shapes, their textural excellence, and rich decoration, these vases in the pictorial style are also of special icono-graphic interest because some of their representations are believed to refer to scenes from Greek mythology. The representation on the famous amphoroid krater from Enkomi has been interpreted as picturing Zeus standing in front of chariots and holding the scales of the warriors' destiny before their departure for the battlefield — a scene which occurs frequently in Homer (fig. 11).

The first Achaean settlers brought with them the severe style in vogue in the Peloponnesos in about 1200 B.C. This style soon prevailed in Cyprus and gradually ousted the local one; it was also perpetuated throughout the 12th century when new waves of Achaean settlers arrived in the island. At the same time, this severe style was enriched, and new shapes and themes of Oriental inspiration, some of them in the pictorial style, were introduced. This style, which has only recently become the subject of systematic study, set the foundations for the evolution of Cypriot pottery and vase-painting in the Geometric period. Cretan influences of the sub-Minoan period are also evident. It appears that Cretan refugees driven out from their island by the Dorians settled in Cyprus around 1100 B.C.

Geometric and 'free-field' style

The geometric style in pottery covers the first three centuries of the first millennium. The shapes and decoration of the vases are inspired primarily from the last phase of Mycenaean pottery, but also enriched with Oriental and Cypriot elements. The new feature introduced by the geometric style is the use in the decoration of two colours — red and black — which softens somewhat the austerity of the geometric patterns. Cypriot craftsmen could never quite reconcile themselves to the severe style in art; that is why they soon began to break away from the restrictions imposed by geometric tradition. The first pictorial motifs to make a cautious appearance were mostly birds but also human and animal figures, and these accommodated themselves as best they could to the geometric requirements of the remaining decoration. A full-grown pictorial style, containing a great wealth of motifs and composi-tions, appeared toward the end of the Geometric period, around 750 B.C. The Hubbard amphora, named after its donor, carries on one side an intricate cult scene in honour of a dead person and, on the other side, a group of dancers with a lyre-player — a scene common enough in Greek geometric vase-painting (fig. 13). The figures have the typical vitality and primitive naïveté of Archaic terracotta statuettes.

During the 7th century B.C., under the influence of engraving, particularly of engraved metal vases, the pictorial style reached a high artistic level. Vase-painters now drew in the 'free-field' style, i.e. without framing the design within a border, but taking care to adapt the representation to the curved surface of the vase. There was a marked preference for jugs which, because of their shape and limited surface, lend themselves particularly well to the 'free-field' style, so typical of Archaic Cypriot vase-painting (figs. 24-25). The use of two colours gives an especially graceful quality to this admirable phase of vase decoration, which was developed mainly in eastern Cyprus. The western part of the island produced other, more austere, styles, the most important of which had a decoration in black on red ground.

In the 6th century, when relations with mainland Greece, Rhodes, and Ionia were revived, Greek vases made their large scale appearance on the Cypriot market, first as luxury items and later as ordinary ware for practical uses. Cypriot potters, especially those working in the Marion area, which was the centre of trade with Greece, perhaps in an effort to compete with the superior quality of imported ware, invented a new type of vase: the jug with a spout and the figure of a Kore in the round on its shoulder. Later, they began to imitate the decoration of Greek vases, copying meanders and palmettes. But this was an unequal competition and eventually brought about the end of the distinctive character of Cypriot pottery. Large-scale importation of Attic vases and the relatively hard times that followed in Cyprus as a result of the wars against the Persians were responsible for the gradual decline of the local art, which was thus restricted to the production of ordinary undecorated vessels for daily use. There was something of a flowering much later with the appearance of decorated jars during the Hellenistic period, but that could hardly be described as a distinctly Cypriot creation. As was to happen later, during the Roman period, artistic styles were by now shared in common almost everywhere throughout the Eastern Mediterranean.

Metal vases

Besides its clay vases, the Cyprus Museum has a remarkable collection of metal vessels, belonging mainly to the Late Bronze Age. One of these is quite unique: it is a silver cup of the 14th century B.C., found in a tomb at Enkomi, decorated with inlaid gold and niello (fig. 15). The decoration consists of lotus flowers and ox-heads in a harmonious composition enhanced by the multi-coloured materials. Fine silver and bronze bowls were made in Cyprus in the 7th century B.C. with engraved or embossed pictorial patterns in the Cypro-Phoenician style, but the Museum owns only a very few specimens.

Another unique specimen is the bronze cauldron, dated to about 700 B.C., which was found on the *dromos* of a royal tomb at Salamis (fig. 26). Decorated with eight griffin protomes and four bifacial 'Sirens' of an Oriental style, it stands upon an iron tripod. Until recently, this type was known from a number of specimens discovered in Etruria, Olympia, and Delphi. Since this is the first of its kind to have been found in the Orient, it confirms the conviction of archaeologists that this type is of Eastern origin. Other noteworthy exhibits are the Early Christian silver plates with embossed representations from the life of David (fig. 42). They come from the Treasure of Lambousa. The largest part of this Treasure is now at the Metropolitan Museum of Art in New York.

As has already been mentioned, during the Late Bronze Age, trade between Cyprus and Egypt and the Syro-Palestinian coast was lively with the result that numerous exotic works of art were imported into Cyprus from the East, although some of them, like the faience vases, may have even been made in Cyprus. The most important piece is the conical rhyton, from Kition, dated to the 13th century B.C. (fig. 19). Its blue enamel surface is decorated with painted and inlaid polychrome motifs in three registers, representing galloping animals, a bull-hunt, and vertical running spirals. This rhyton of mixed origin, combining elements from the Aegean and the East in both shape and decoration, is a characteristic specimen of Aegeo-Oriental art, which reached its peak in Cyprus in the Late Bronze Age.

Gold and silver jewellery

Gold and silver ornaments have captivated Cypriot womenfolk ever since the Early Bronze Age. The earliest hair-ornaments in gold, silver, and bronze have been found in women's graves. Before that, the primitive necklaces and amulets of Neolithic and Chalcolithic women were made of steatite and sea-shells. But the goldsmith's art reached a flourishing state in the Late Bronze Age, which was an age of great prosperity. Gold necklaces made of beads in the shape of pomegranates, figure-of-eight shields, or other motifs; head-bands or diadems with moulded floral, pictorial, and geometric patterns, rings, earrings and pendants have been found in large numbers among the grave gifts in tombs of the 14th and 13th centuries B.C. The figure-of-eight shields used in necklaces (fig. 16), the Mycenaean sphinxes used in diadems (fig. 23), and some other motifs testify to the influence of the Aegean world on Cypriot goldwork. Also to be noted are the rings with engraved representations, like the one shown on fig. 17, from Enkomi, on which the lion's figure is definitely of Mycenaean inspiration. However, there are also several purely Cypriot specimens, such as the earrings in the shape of a bull's head (fig. 18) and the pendants with granulated decoration in the shape of pomegranates.

Some remarkable works of art in gold and silver belong to the Archaic and the Classical periods. The Arsos necklace (fig. 34a), with its granulated beads and elaborate cylindrical agate pendant, must have been quite fashionable to judge by Archaic statues of Korai found in that same region. During the Classical period and under the influence of Persian goldwork, a beautiful type of bracelet was made which terminated in rams' or lions' heads (fig. 34b).

The minor arts

Ivory was among the exotic materials from the East which exerted a great attraction upon Mycenaean and Cypriot craftsmen, especially during the 12th century B.C. The smooth surface of ivory plaques was skillfully decorated with relief or engraved representations. Among the articles which Cypriot artists were particularly fond of fashioning in ivory were mirror handles. One such handle in the Cyprus Museum that comes from Palaipaphos is decorated with the relief representation of a hero — one might see in him an ancestor of the mythical Heracles — struggling with a lion (fig. 21). However, the most important and numerous ivories have been found in Royal Tomb 79 of Salamis. The magnificently decorated throne is exhibited in a separate room in the Museum (fig. 28). The masterfully executed decoration consists of ivory plaques in relief which represent a sphinx and a composite lotus flower. The surface of the ivory plaques is also decorated with inlaid polychrome faience and thin gold-leaf, a technique developed by the Phoenicians in Northern Syria. The elaborate decoration is reminiscent of the description of Penelope's throne in Homer.

The Cyprus Museum has numerous other collections of the minor arts. The cylinder seals in the Aegeo-Oriental style are particularly important; they must have been made in Cyprus under the influence of Aegean art. Also important is the numismatic collection. Of special interest are the coins of the period of the kings of Salamis, with the figures of familiar gods (Athena, Aphrodite, Apollo) but also with Oriental symbols, which by that time had been adopted all over Cyprus.

There are also glass and alabaster vases, oil-lamps, and other objects of appeal to the interested visitor. Here, only the most characteristic groups of exhibits have been presented along with those that illustrate the various stages and aspects of the cultural evolution of the island. Although the Classical collections and those of Graeco-Roman times are by no means insignificant, the section of the Museum which is bound to impress most for its originality is the one devoted to the more remote periods from the Neolithic to the Archaic. That is the time-span which corresponds to the birth of Cypriot civilization, its peak, and the long period of its struggles to survive as a separate entity among the great and powerful civilizations of the East.

1. Life-size head of a young athlete, made of limestone. Found in the Potamia sanctuary. Late 5th century B.C.

2

3

4

302

2. *Head from a small figurine, made of andesite. Found at the Neolithic settlement of Khirokitia. 5800-5250 B.C.*

3. *Figurine of a schematized human form, made of andesite. Found at Omodos. 5800-5250 B.C.*

4. *Cruciform figurine of the Chalcolithic period, made of steatite. The advanced type of this figurine can be discerned, despite the schematization, in the articulated limbs and the relief features of the face. From the Paphos district. 3000-2300 B.C.*

5. *Clay model of a sanctuary of the Early Bronze Age, from the necropolis of Kotchatis: it consists of three idols (xoana) with bulls' heads and a human figure, in front, pouring a libation into a large vessel. 2100-2000 B.C.*

6. *Clay model of a circular open-air sanctuary of the Early Bronze Age, from a grave in the Vounous area: it represents a mystical ritual being held in the sanctuary, centering around three idols wearing bulls' heads and holding serpents in their hands. 2100-2000 B.C.*

5

7. Plank-shaped figurine of the Early Bronze Age, with two heads growing out of a rectangular trunk and incised decoration on the red polished surface. Found in a grave at Dhenia. 2100-2000 B.C.

8. Red polished composite vase with engraved pattern, from the cemetery of Vounous: it is composed of seven small and large intercommunicating jugs with double or triple necks. Early Bronze Age. 2100-2000 B.C.

7

9. White painted oinochoe of the Middle Bronze Age with geometric decoration. Intricate protuberances on the neck and body of the jug. Found in the necropolis of Hagia Paraskevi on the south of Nicosia. 2000-1600 B.C.

10. Composite vessel of the Early Bronze Age from the cemetery of Vounous: it consists of four contiguous bowls with a single handle and a plank-shaped figurine representing a mother and infant. 2300-1850 B.C.

10

11. *Mycenaean amphoroid krater from a grave at Enkomi. The representation has been identified with a well-known scene from the Iliad: Zeus is holding the Scales of Destiny in front of the warriors' chariot before their departure to join the battle. Early 14th century B.C.*

12. *Mycenaean amphoroid krater: the octopus has been stylised into a decorative motif, symmetrically covering the whole surface of the vase with its tentacles. Early 14th century B.C.*

13. *The Hubbard amphora is one of the earliest and foremost examples of the pictorial style. On one side of it, there are female figures engaged in the sepulchral custom of sipping some liquid with a straw from a pitcher—a custom known from Oriental representations; the other side shows women dancing to the accompaniment of a lyre—a familiar theme in Greek late Geometric vase-painting. 8th century B.C.*

14. *Terracotta figurine of a mother-goddess of bird-like facial features and with two pairs of earrings hanging from enormous pierced ears. This type of figurine is of Eastern origin and believed to be a precursor of Astarte, the goddess of fertility. 1400-1200 B.C.*

11

14

13

15

16

308

19

15. *Silver cup from a grave at Enkomi, with inlaid decoration of gold and niello: bulls' heads, lotus flowers, and rosettes. Early 14th century B.C.*

16. *Necklace from Enkomi, with gold beads in the form of figure-of-eight shields and tubular spacers of gold wire. 13th century B.C.*

17. *Gold-plated bronze ring, from a grave at Enkomi. The bezel is decorated with an engraved lion in the Mycenaean style. 14th century B.C.*

18. *Gold earrings in the shape of bulls' heads. Found in a grave at Enkomi. 13th century B.C.*

19. *Conical faience rhyton with enamel coating. It is divided into* **three registers: the upper has galloping animals, the middle** *one shows a bull hunt, and the lower one is decorated with a vertical* **running spiral pattern. Found at Kition, 13th century B.C.**

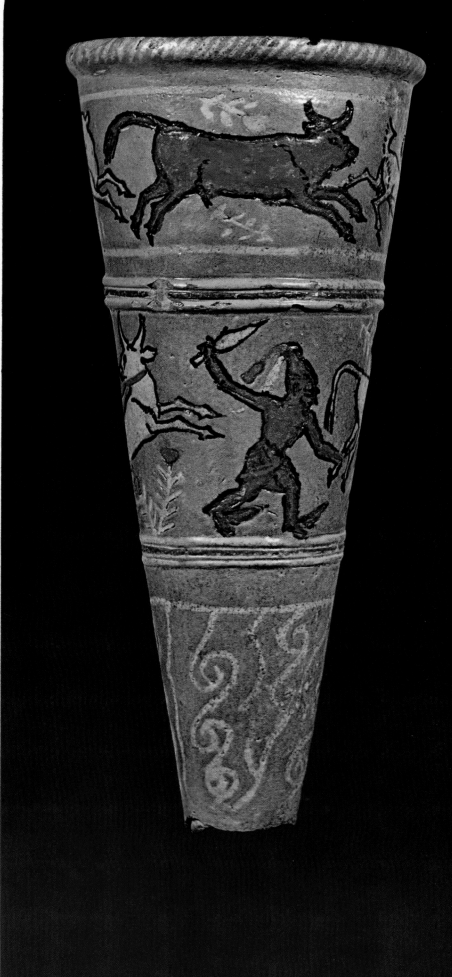

17

18

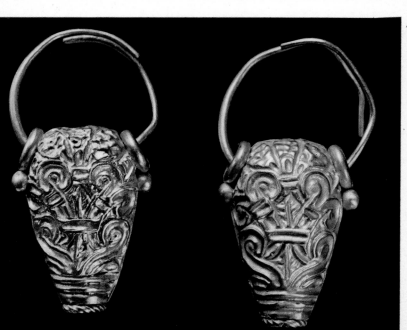

20. Bronze statue of a **horned** god from a sanctuary at Enkomi, possibly a representation of Apollo **Keraiates,** whose cult was brought to Cyprus by the first Achaean settlers. 12th century B.C.

21. Ivory mirror handle, from a grave at Palaepaphos: the upper section is decorated with a relief representation of a hero struggling with a lion. 13th century B.C.

22. Royal gold sceptre from a tomb at Kourion: the upper section, decorated with cloisonné enamel, consists of an orb supporting two vultures. 11th century B.C.

23. Gold diadem from a grave at Enkomi: embossed decoration of sphinxes in the Mycenaean style. 13th century B.C.

21

22

23

24. *Jug decorated in the 'free-field' style, from a grave at Arnadi, with a charming representation of a bull smelling a lotus flower. 7th century B.C.*

25. *Jug decorated in the 'free-field' style, with a stylized bird and fish in the bichrome technique. 7th century B.C.*

25

26

27

26. *Bronze cauldron supported on an iron tripod, decorated around the rim with eight stiffin protomes and four bifacial 'Sirens'. From the royal tomb 79 at Salamis. Late 8th century B.C.*

27. *Limestone statue of Zeus Keraunios (Zeus wielding the thunderbolt), clearly revealing Greek Archaic influence. The god is shown about to hurl the thunderbolt with his right hand; in his left hand he held an eagle. Found at Kition. c. 500 B.C.*

28. *Engraved ivory plaque with inlaid faience decoration, carved on both sides with the representation of a sphinx among lotus flowers. This was part of the decoration of a throne discovered in the royal tomb 79 at Salamis, together with several other valuable pieces of furniture. Late 8th century B.C.*

29. *Terracotta figurine of a horse and a rider, decorated in red and black paint. 6th century B.C.*

30. *Terracotta group of a bull in the center, flanked on either side by a human figure on a smaller scale. From a rural sanctuary dated to c. 500 B.C.*

31. *Polychrome terracotta figurine of a Centaur with a quiver. 6th century B.C.*

32. *Clay model of a war chariot, with two warriors and a groom leading the horses. 6th century B.C.*

29

31

28

30

32

33. Limestone head of a Kore, clearly influenced by Ionian sculpture of the early 5th century B.C. Found at Idalion.

34. a. Gold necklace consisting of beads with granulated decoration and an agate pendant. From the sanctuary of Aphrodite Golgia at Arsos. Early 6th century B.C. b. Two gold-plated bronze bracelets terminating in rams' heads. From Kourion. 5th century B.C.

33

35. Marble gravestone, from Marion: a youth standing in front of a stele bearing an inscription in the Cypriot syllabary: 'I am (the stele) of Stases, son of Stasioikos'. 5th century B.C.

36. Limestone gravestone, with vestiges of green paint: a seated woman holding a bird in her left hand. An engraved inscription in the Cypriot syllabary reveals her name; it reads: 'I am (the stele) of Aristila, from Salamis, daughter of Onasis'. Found at Marion. c. 420 B.C.

37. This head of a limestone statue of a woman is a magnificent specimen of Cypriot sculpture of the early 3rd century B.C. The self-concentration and a certain dramatic quality in the expression suggest the influence of Skopas. From the sanctuary of Aphrodite at Arsos.

35

36

37

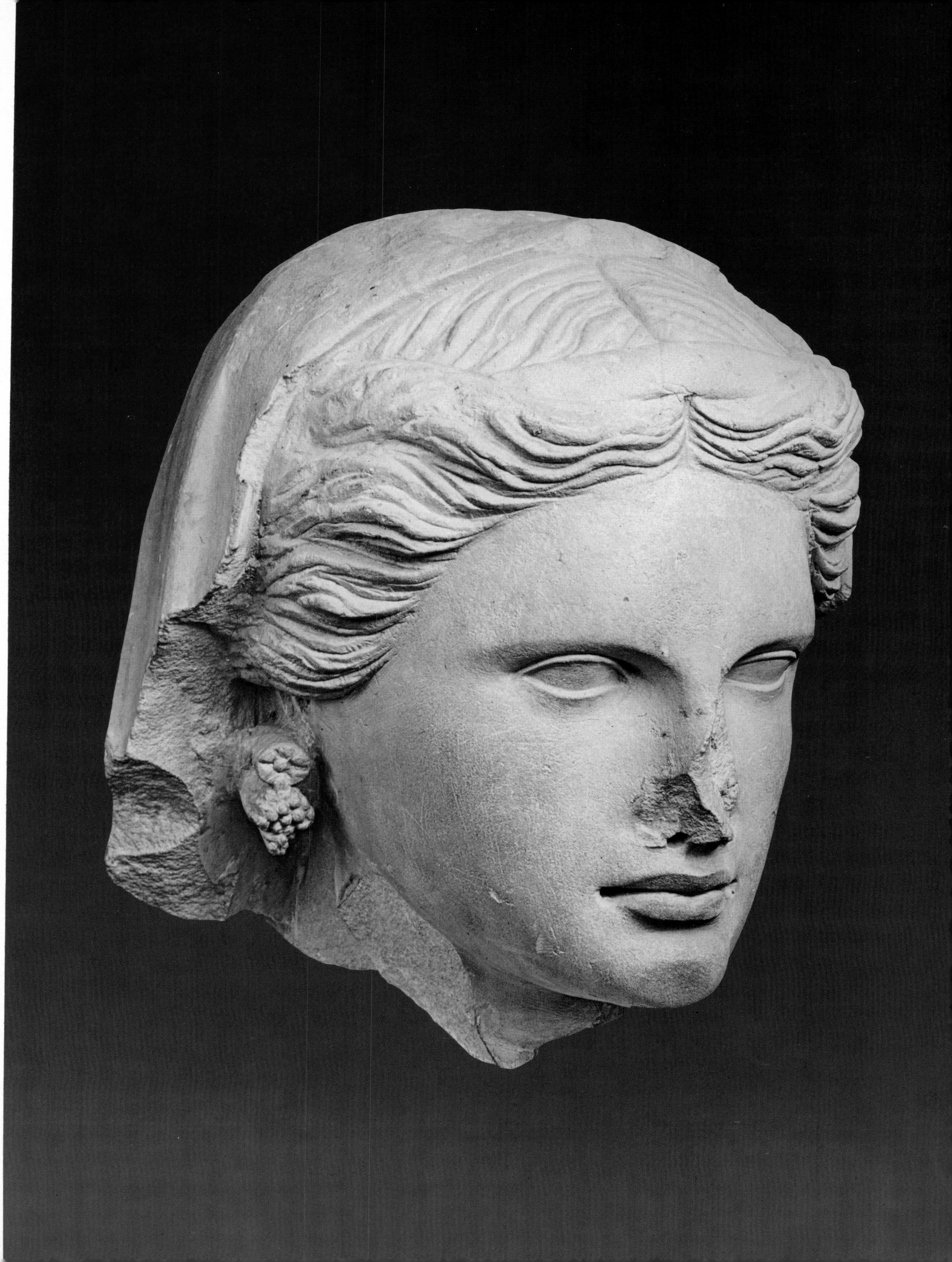

38

39

40

38. *Marble head of Aphrodite, by a Greek sculptor probably working in Cyprus. From the Gymnasium of Salamis. Early 4th century B.C.*

39. *Clay head of a young man with idealistic features in the manner of Lysippos. It comes from the funeral pyre of the cenotaph of King Nikokreon in the necropolis of Salamis. Late 4th century B.C.*

40. *Marble statue of Aphrodite, from Soloi. 1st century B.C.*

41. *Bronze over life-size statue of the Roman emperor Septimius Severus (A.D. 193-211). Found in the vicinity of the ancient city of Chytroi (Kythraia).*

41

42

42. *Silver plate from the famous Treasure of Lambousa: the inner surface of the plate is decorated with an embossed scene from the wedding of David. Early 7th century A.D.*

BYZANTINE MUSEUM

BYZANTINE MUSEUM

Introductory note

The Byzantine Museum is a unique one in so far as it is exclusively devoted to Byzantine art. To the visitor it may consequently prove to be an extremely useful introduction to the art of this great period in the history of Hellenism. It would not be inappropriate therefore to precede this study with a few essential informative observations regarding the basic characteristics of Byzantine art and the way in which this art developed throughout the course of its thousand-year-old existence and its aftermath to the end of the 18th century.

The Byzantine heritage

Byzantium is a conception which cannot be confined within the elastic geographical limits of an empire, as it has endured beyond the chronological span of the history of a state. Byzantium always remains alïve, not only in the historical memory, but also in the life of modern Hellenism. Among the various Orthodox peoples who inherited the prodigious legacy of civilization bequeathed by the Greek mediaeval empire — it extended over vast areas for over a thousand years — the Greeks have had the privilege to remain in direct contact and actually live, until now, with the still vital essential elements of which the Byzantine world was composed. The Greek language continues to evolve uninterruptedly from the Byzantine, both in the "demotic" and official tongues. The liturgy and other ecclesiastical functions, which are still associated with the most crucial moments in the life of a modern Greek — from the day of his birth to that of his death — are celebrated in the same ecclesiastical tongue, to the accompaniment of the same ecclesiastical chants. The same religious and social customs and habits remain alive; with them too are closely related the works of Byzantine and post-Byzantine art whose roots are deeply implanted in Greek soil. The Byzantine or Byzantine-style icon continues to be an indispensable and highly revered household object. The very existence of Hellenism under foreign domination, for century after century, played an important role in the preservation and survival of these mediaeval traditions.

But the modern way of life, which is constantly and ever more intensively undergoing a levelling process, is increasingly fraying the basic structure of that traditional way of life and alienating men from their origins. A conscious fear of the possible loss of something which is vital to the spiritual and moral nature of the nation has induced enlightened men — not only in Greece, but also in the West

— to concentrate their scholarship on further research into the history of Byzantium and to attempt to recover, conserve and assemble all the proven tokens of Byzantine civilization and its post-Byzantine aftermath. In doing so, they have given priority to the works of Byzantine art.

The expanse of Byzantine art

When we refer to Byzantine art, we mean the art which flourished, above all, in the areas constituting the Byzantine Empire during a long period which lasted from the foundation of its capital in A.D. 330 until its fall in 1453. The actual geographical limits within which Byzantine art spread are considerably wider, for within them must be included areas which were once Byzantine (but not so later), such as the provinces of Ravenna and Sicily, before being conquered by the Lombards and Normans in the 7th and 11th centuries respectively, and the Greek East prior to the Arab conquest in the 7th century. Other areas, such as Crete, Cyprus, the smaller islands of the Aegean and Ionian archipelagoes, remained noteworthy centres of Byzantine art even after their subjection to foreign rule (13th century).

Apart from these areas which were dependencies, in one way or another, of the Byzantine state at different times, one must also take into account the wide sphere of influence penetrated by Byzantine art, to a whole world over which the Orthodox Church held sway: in other words, to those lands of South-Eastern Europe, to Russia and Georgia, where Byzantine artists and authentic works of the official art of Constantinople sowed the seeds from which new shoots sprouted and enabled regional schools to be founded.

Finally, since Byzantine art was closely associated with the fortunes of the Empire, the leading role it played, and the place of honour accorded to it, in a world betwixt East and West, were the natural consequences of the ecumenical authority enjoyed by Byzantium.

Constantinople

Special significance is attached to the epithet "Byzantine" (even if only in a purely conventional sense), for it is of course associated with the name of "Byzantium", a Greek colony at the entrance to the Bosporos. This new city, New Rome, the oecumenic centre and largest city in the world during the Middle Ages, was Constantinople itself; and it was Constantinople that was destined to become the prime factor in the formation of the particular characteristics of Byzantine art. When the capital was transferred by Constantine the Great to the banks of the Bosporos (A.D. 330), the city had no artistic traditions whatsoever; but the entire imperial sphere over which New Rome was mistress already possessed a common artistic language developed in the large Hellenistic cities of the Eastern Mediterranean: Alexandria, Antioch, Ephesos: even Rome itself. Constantinople, at once capital of the Empire and head of the Orthodox Church, did not only absorb and assimilate this quasi-universal artistic language, with all its various nuances, but also formed, fashioned and elaborated it in conformity with the new philosophical views and aesthetic ideas which were in the process of being developed in the capital. These progressively evolving artistic forms, stamped with the authority of authenticity, spread to the periphery in various ways. Plans of churches, for instance, would be despatched by the Emperor to monasteries enjoying his favour, and the carved marbles of Prokonesos would be carried in ships to all the ports of the Mediterranean in order to decorate new churches. Then there were the mosaicists and the painters who were commissioned by the Arab caliphs to decorate their mosques; and the illuminated manuscripts — codices and scrolls — as well as the priceless works of the minor arts executed in the most effective techniques.

The regulating and creative role of a capital of a centralized and basically theocratic state was one of the principal factors which enabled Byzantine art to preserve its fundamental homogeneousness in all its various manifestations, despite the gradual though essential developments it underwent during the course of its life-span, whether in the capital itself or in those places beyond the frontiers of the state where the influence of Constantinople was still predominant. Furthermore, as Byzantine art acquired its unity and style in the Greek environment of Constantinople, it remained stamped, throughout its historical evolution, with the seal of its own origins.

The dual origins of Byzantine art

It is not easy to determine the precise moment of the birth of Byzantine art. Conventionally, it is dated to the time of the foundation of Constantinople — a further indirect recognition of the importance of the role played by the city in the development of Byzantine art. In effect, assimilation and transubstantiation of this universal artistic language, which was of Hellenistic origin, as we have already noted, must have been under way before the foundation of Constantinople. The evidence is not lacking. An iconographic cycle of scenes from the Old and New Testaments, as well as a symbolical medium of the Christian faith, had been formed at an earlier date: in the Catacombs, for instance. Even during the period of the great monarchical states, which preceded the Byzantine, representations of the cycle of imperial iconographies existed. These iconographies possessed a style, at once sober and official, imbued with the grandeur befitting them: a style that was destined to prevail in similar Byzantine representations and to proliferate in those of ecclesiastical iconography.

Besides the classical tradition, with its roots in ancient Greek art, certain anti-classical trends, which emerged in the form of a rough, robust and more popular art and developed in the peripheral provinces of Asia Minor, Syria and Mesopotamia, must also be taken into account. This expressionist art succeeded in becoming an official state art during the Tetrarchy (c. A.D. 300). Some scholars identify this art with a simplified misconception of classical models on the part of craftsmen lacking Greek culture: with, in fact, a so-called democratization of Greek art. Others see in it an artistic trend aiming at an aggressive revival of a somewhat indigenous character. Parallel manifestations may be observed in Sasanian art in Persia (3rd - 7th centuries). Generally speaking, this style is characterized by flat forms with bold outlines, by expressive attitudes and gestures, divorced of any feeling for nobility and elegance, by a preference for two-dimensional representation and an indifference for the real dimensions regulating the relations between human figures. This trend, taken in conjunction with similar expressionistic characteristics, which manifest themselves in varying degrees, reveal a conscious opposition to the classical tradition. The trend does not merely survive, it actually constitutes one of the main determining factors in the formation of a Byzantine Style.

The cyclical recurrence of traditions. Byzantine 'philanthropy'

These dual roots were constantly to influence Byzantine art: on the one hand, with the survival or revival of general subjects or special motifs as well as modes of artistic expression; on the other, with a prevailing general disposition in favour of one or another of the tendencies in question.

The classical tradition constitutes, more especially, a living heritage bequeathed by antiquity; it possesses an authentic ring of humanism which does not belong to the closed circles of Atticistic scholars, but is a value of wider significance which saturates Byzantine art and distinguishes it from that of both the West and the East. This humanistic conception of Byzantine art — of whatever period and of whatever trend — becomes intelligible when we comprehend its total devotion to the human form, to its proportions and to the organic relation between its various parts. This conception applies even when the claims of a compositional rhythm and transcendental representation, corresponding more closely to an idea of the intelligible world (which ought to become a tangible one), necessitate certain abstractions which ultimately lead the figurative art to a point beyond the mere imitation of the natural form. This Byzantine *philanthropy* humanized God through the power of sympathy and compassion and deified man by endowing him with a transcendental reality extending far beyond a mere momentary or subjective experience of the world. Even in architecture the dimensions are calculated to the measure of man; this is not only so in small churches; it also applies to those edifices which aim at the grandiose, such as St. Sophia. In the latter one does not feel overwhelmed, as in a Gothic cathedral, by the mass; on the contrary, one feels both surrounded and transported by the grandeur of the enclosed brightly illuminated space, which, in spite of its dimensions, does not diminish one's stature.

The classical revivals

From time to time, however, the triumph of anti-classical trends would, in its turn, bring about a conscious return to classical models. This kind of renascence — it has in fact been called a "renaissance", whereas the Byzantines themselves termed it a "revival" — often coincided with the accession to the throne of an emperor who may also be the founder of a new dynasty. The tradition followed by the Romans was Hellenistic in origin. In the Ist century A.D. Augustus favoured a return to Praxitelean models — idealized, full of serenity, charm and beauty — in contrast to the realistic-materialistic art of the period. Theodosios the Great (4th century A.D.) put an end to the predominance of provincial concepts which still found expression in the reliefs at the base of his honorific stele erected in Constantinople (known as the Obelisk of Theodosios), in which the figures, depicted frontally, are aligned in successive series. In the 6th century Justinian too, in his general policy aimed at the reestablishment of the Roman Empire, returned to Roman stylistic devices. A similar tendency is observed in the reign of Herakleios (7th century). The love shown by the members of the Macedonian dynasty (9th-10th centuries) for Hellenistic subjects and styles, which is apparent in the preference shown by the Macedonian emperors for carved ivories and illuminated manuscripts executed in the palace workshops, must also derive from the same tradition. There is a return, therefore, not only to unaltered mythological representations and to the medical and pharmaceutical subjects of, among others, Hippokrates and Dioskourides, but also to Byzantine imagery — particularly in the Psalters — rendered in the manner, and by the use of motifs, typical of mythological scenes or episodes from ancient drama. Similar manifestations are observed during the reign of the Komnenoi (11th-12th centuries), as represented by the mosaics at Daphni. Later, during the reign of the Palaiologoi (13th-15th centuries), the return to earlier iconographic and stylistic means of expression acquired a more universal character because it corresponded to a general disposition for emphasis on grace and picturesqueness or dramatic content and lively movement. This periodic revitalization of the classical tradition, even if it originated in aristocratic or exclusively court circles, served as an active incentive for the constant renewal of the wider Hellenistic trends which had never ceased to animate Byzantine art.

Islamic influences

From time to time, however, revivals of the other, the anti-classical, trend were apparent; sometimes in the form of a return to Sasanian decoration (9th-10th centuries) and frequently in a ready acceptance of the influence exercised by contemporary Islamic art, particularly in the field of decorative work and handicrafts. In textiles, in ceramics, in silverware and the goldsmith's craft, even in decorative sculpture, the contacts remained unbroken.

It must, however, be stressed that the dual origins in Byzantine art, which emerge as two parallel traditions, in reality co-exist in close union and frequently influence each other. It may therefore be claimed that they have lost the character attributed to their origins and simply constitute two different means of expression; they may also be apparent in the same work executed by the same artist — even in the same illuminated manuscript — for reasons which are not always easy to verify. This mutual infiltration, as much in the sphere of technique as in that of iconography and style, is an important factor in the maintenance of the basic morphological unity of Byzantine art of all periods; its function is parallel to that of numerous other factors, as well as the intricate structure of Byzantine life, whose unity secured an unbroken continuity and demanded the existence of a fully developed artistic language with a conservative character and a recurring pattern.

The historical framework of Byzantine art

The history of Byzantine art is closely linked with the fortunes of the Empire, and its division into periods, made in the interests of convenience, generally correspond to actual historical periods.

The Early Christian era begins either with the recognition of Christianity as the official religion of the State (313) or with the foundation of the capital (330) and closes with the end of the reign of Justinian (565) or, according to other scholars, whose contention I personally support, with the end of the reign of Herakleios (630). During this period the tradition of a grandiose imperial art of Roman character remained vigorous and unbroken; it therefore coincides with what archaeologists call Late Antiquity. During this period the basic architectural types were also formed, and a new monumental style emerged in painting. The beginning of the Iconoclast period (725-843) is one of extreme importance, for it witnessed the destruction of many works of art, and the development of representational art was arrested as a result of the official attitude regarding the proscription of icon-worship. Religious painting consequently acquired a purely secular or decorative character. This period corresponds with a great internal crisis in the state which is crystallized in the dispute over the significance of the icons.

With the end of Iconoclasm (843) and the rise of the Macedonian dynasty (861) begins the Middle Byzantine period which lasted until 1204. For the first time the great capital fell and remained in the hands of the Crusaders. In 1261 Michael Palaiologos, the self-styled "New Constantine", ushered in a new period; a painful one for the fortunes of the Empire, but an important one as regards the fortunes of an art which, with noteworthy achievements, made use of new forms of expression, always returning to, and making selections from, older models of a kind which suited its own particular character. Byzantine art did not come to an end with the fall of Constantinople in 1453. It remained alive in the Cretan school of painting and in woodcarving; it manifested itself in the grand architectural edifices of the monasteries raised on Mt. Athos and elsewhere, in metal-work and, in a general way, in numerous sophisticated works of the minor arts, whose creators, after the disappearance of the great melting-pot constituted by the capital, moved to the peripheral areas of the former Empire.

Architecture

It is now time to examine the various categories of Byzantine works of art.

In architecture there are the large edifices of the Graeco-Roman period, with the modifications effected by the demands of the new official religion both as regards its ideological presentation and the practice of the new faith. The main types of religious edifices — basilicas, centralized buildings, domed basilicas, octagonal and other constructions planned in such a way as to conform to their particular function (churches, martyria, baptisteries, etc) — were formulated in the Early Christian period. New architectural features, such as the transverse aisle of the basilica and the dome raised by means of different combinations of methods for supporting it, were created. The church was furthermore adorned with the Holy Table, with a *ciborium*, episcopal throne, *synthronon, ambon,* altar screen, closure panels, etc. All these architectural features were executed in carved polychrome marbles and decorated with lavish materials (sometimes with precious stones) or covered with silver, gold and enamel. The numerous columns — frequently taken from ancient temples — were crowned with elaborately worked capitals which supported the elegant arches. In poorer districts the floors of churches were paved with decorative mosaics, whereas more lavish constructions were adorned with huge plaques of matching marbles so that the veins formed decorative designs. The walls were covered with framed marbles, the barrel vaults, arches and domes with mosaics whose gold ground reflected the light which filled the church from numerous windows. The whole of the splendid illuminated interior, of whatever architectural type, corresponded to a microcosm, to a symbolic picture of the universe which must be provided by the church.

For historical reasons, Byzantine architecture after the 6th century never again possessed the majestic forms which distinguished it in the Early Christian era; it never again had the same wide variety of types nor did the abundance of solutions to architectural problems exist any longer.

The type subsequently destined to prevail was the cruciform church with dome. It developed slowly, with a constant attempt on the part of architects to preserve the unity of the large dome-covered central space which tended to break away from the four supports of the dome, whether pilasters or columns.

With the achievement of the solution of the constructional problem of supporting the dome with lighter buttresses, or even with their total removal in the octagonal type evolved in the 10th-11th centuries, and with the consequent elongation of the arms of the cross, the pattern of the cross itself and the organic structure of the building became far more apparent in the roof and exterior surfaces. The clarity of the design and the harmonious proportions now matched a classical conception of form. The interior surfaces were covered with precious materials, marbles, mosaics, wall-paintings. The exterior also became more elaborate, the surfaces being either plastically executed of consisting of perfectly wrought masonry, embellished with lavish brick decoration.

Sculpture

After the 6th century the carving of statues in the round ceased; sculptured reliefs, however, continued to be executed in abundance, especially as component parts of architectural features. Some sculptors were faithful to classical traditions; others borrowed examples from neighbouring Eastern countries. In the use of this two-dimensional technique sculptors frequently tried to imitate the technique of enamels by resorting to the use of coloured materials or even painting. In the smaller plaques of ivory and later of steatite (a cheaper material which replaced the more expensive ivory) a refined technique of low relief was evolved. The representations were greatly influenced by the classical tradition, irrespective of whether they possessed a secular or religious character.

Monumental painting
Mosaics
Wall-paintings

In monumental painting — whether mosaic or wall-painting — Byzantine artists endeavoured to fulfil the requirements of the new religion: namely, to glorify the triumph of the Church in pictorial symbols, to narrate the history of the Old and New Testaments to the ignorant and create representations with an authentic and orthodox dogmatic significance.

The two elaborate techniques involved in mosaic and wall-painting were inherited by Byzantine artists, together with corresponding artistic styles, from earlier periods.

A large number of mosaics of the Early Christian period, in which cycles of cosmological representations are often encountered, are preserved in pavements. To these are related the "mural" mosaics, which are superior in quality from an artistic standpoint, such as those in the Rotunda of St. George, Hosios David, St. Demetrios and the *Acheiropoietos* (all in Thessalonike), at Ravenna, in the remote Monastery of St. Catherine on Mt. Sinai and elsewhere. An official style, characterized by figures depicted frontally standing in front of buildings, with the emphasis on the portrait-like aspect, and by drapery resembling the flutings of columns prevails, in varying degrees, in these mosaics. Here one may trace the gradual transformation of Hellenistic portraiture and iconography into the transcendental icon, with the eventual disappearance of three-dimensional space, accompanied by a trend towards an inorganic articulation of the figures and a tendency for the face to be depicted with large eyes. This transformation took place between the 5th and 7th centuries. The same style is encountered in contemporary wall-paintings, many of which are in Rome — executed by craftsmen from the East — in the islands and elsewhere. It is important to stress the fact that indications of certain contemporary trends are also encountered in churches of the first importance, such as St. Sophia and the Holy Apostles in Constantinople, which possessed lavish but non-figurative decorations (crosses, etc.).

After the Iconoclast period (725-843) the chief trends in Byzantine painting, which had existed in diffused form at an earlier date, assumed a definite form; these trends were furthermore apparent in imperial circles, as one may observe in the decoration executed in St. Sophia during the 9th century and later. The entire mosaic decoration in churches, such as that in St. Sophia at Thessalonike, Hosios Loukas, Nea Moni on Chios, and Daphni, represents trends which are basically in opposition to each other: on the one hand, we have a return to classical models; on the other, the avoidance of any reference to antiquity. Features deriving from different trends, always of a high artistic quality and of outstanding technical perfection, coexist in a single strikingly dramatic art. The wall-paintings of the period, many examples of which are to be found in, among other places, Thessalonike, Kastoria, Achris, Cyprus and at Hosios Loukas, reveal the monumental character of these large compositions with imposing figures rendered in most impressive manner. By the end of the 12th century, however, this style was to lead the way to the adoption of a somewhat affected one, known as a linear mannerist style, in which the figures become extremely elongated and are clad in light clinging garments with elaborate draperies.

The 13th century was a critical period for monumental painting which now followed a new road. Works of art were executed in the smaller court centres of the dismembered Empire and neighbouring Balkan states. A reaction to the mannerist style of the 12th century is encountered in wide tranquil compositions in which the desire for the expression of a kind of epic grandeur reached its zenith at Sopoçani (1265) and in the mosaics in the *Paregoretissa* at Arta (1295), where the very free use of a painter's means are apparent. A style, full of liveliness, expressed in a highly dramatic manner, with the depiction of plethoric figures which often possess a definitely violent character, flourished around 1300. This style has been called "Macedonian", because some of the finest specimens are encountered on Mt. Athos and in the Macedonian areas. At the same time painting of high quality was being executed in Constantinople, as also elsewhere. Although somewhat academic in character, it did not lack elegance of design or distinction of colour. Despite certain variations, this style lasted until the end; it was accompanied by a tendency to diminish the monumental aspect and replace it with an episodic often charming narrative quality. After the fall of Constantinople the style continued to animate the works of the artists of the Cretan school during the 16th and 17th centuries, but it became more austere in character and the compositions tended to be more classical. Italian influences are also evident.

Portative icons

The portative icon is one of the purest Byzantine creations throughout all the periods, in the course of which it preserves the unmistakable mark of its origins in ancient portraiture. The earliest and best examples (6th century), executed in the old technique of encaustic painting, are in the Monastery of St. Catherine on Mt. Sinai. In the succeeding centuries, following the Iconoclast period, the meaning of the icon, which is itself an as it were active participant in the divine grace enjoyed by the saint whose portrait it represents, because of its likeness to him, is further established, in terms of neoplatonic theory.

As regards style, the painting in the portative icon follows the actual development of painting in general; it is, however, associated, according to its size, function and subject, with either monumental painting or the art of the miniature. The gradual development of the screen of the altar into a tall wide iconostasis, with its iconographic programme, which is gradually formed and stabilized after the 11th century, together with the frequent repetition of archetypes of famous miraculous icons, also contributed to the flowering of the portative icon.

Miniatures

The method adopted in the execution of the illuminated manuscript — whether in the form of a scroll or codex — is continued, in conformity with the ancient Greek conception, in the art of the miniature. The illustrations transfer the narrative to the sphere of the visual arts and thus become more explicit. The Old and New Testaments are consequently illustrated and the various elements of the miniature — the shapes, attitudes and gestures, the depiction of the garments — derive from the illustration of ancient texts, as well as from representations from Graeco-Judaic monuments.

During the Byzantine period the illustration of liturgical books underwent a great diffusion, particularly in the case of Books of Gospels; sometimes it is confined to depictions of the four Evangelists; sometimes too, it may include the Twelve Feasts of the liturgical calendar. The composition is more carefully studied, less descriptive, and the miniature often becomes a model for a representation of larger dimensions, for a portative icon or a work of monumental painting. The liturgical books also include Psalters, *Menologia* (accompanied by scenes from the lives and martyrdoms of the saints pertaining to each month) and, above all, the more rare liturgical scrolls. The miniatures develop on parallel lines with the portative icon, with which they are stylistically closely related.

It is also possible to study the survival and revival of the various traditions in the art of the miniature. Some lavish parchment codices have been preserved which were undoubtedly executed in the court *scriptoria;* in them one may detect, with absolute assurance, the source of each revivifying trend in the centres of high culture.

The Museum

The Byzantine Museum, one of the most important in the country, was not a feature of the Athenian scene until 1930. Its establishment is owed to the late George Sotiriou, who succeeded through his own efforts, favoured by the general political and cultural climate of the times, to have at his disposal an assembly of buildings, until then occupied by a military service of secondary importance. The original buildings had been commissioned by the Duchesse de Plaisance, a romantic and aristocratic French lady, in 1840. At the time, the site lay on the outskirts of the new capital, on the banks of the Ilisos, whose river-bed is now covered by a broad thoroughfare serving all that part of the city which has spread far beyond the Duchess' former country house. The place was called *Ilissia* (perhaps an allusion to the Parisian Elysées), the front entrance being, as it is today, on Vasilissis Sophias Avenue, but with the main view on the Ilisos and Hymettos.

The group of buildings was designed by Stamatios Kleanthis, one of the few oustanding Greek architects of the period, who provided the main edifice with the simple and elegant style of a Florentine Renaissance mansion.

It was not an easy task to convert a private residence into a museum of mainly religious art, with the emphasis on its didactic character. The contribution of another architect, Aristoteles Zachos, proved to be of considerable value in effecting a successful architectural arrangement of, above all, the ground floor which was intended to give the impression of a model of the three types of churches prevailing in the Greek world: the Early Christian basilica, the Byzantine cruciform church with dome and the post-Byzantine single-space religious building. Furthermore, the collections allocated to other parts of the museum had to be arranged in such a manner as to facilitate a logical classification of objects.

The museum was avowedly intended, in the words of George Sotiriou, "to provide a picture of the evolution of the art developed in the Greek world from the close of antiquity to the time of the deliverance of the Greek Nation from the Turkish yoke." The assembled collections intended for display in the new museum did in effect correspond to this wide scope; for the most part they consisted of works of mediaeval art in the Helladic area, although some of the objects cannot, in all cases, be said to the confined to these geographical limits.

The collections

One of the large basic collections consisted of numerous marble sculptrures found on the Acropolis and in various ruined or demolished churches in the Athens area and formerly assembled by the Archaeological Service in the "Theseion". A second collection included a few pieces of wall-paintings which had been removed at various times from demolished churches in Athens, Delphi and Atalante, as well as some impressive icons of the Palaiologan period and gold-thread embroideries from the Thessalonike area. A large collection of icons, manuscripts, liturgical objects, vestments, etc., came from the Christian Archaeological Society formed in 1884 by a number of distinguished amateurs, among whom the moving spirit was George Lambakis. An enthusiastic admirer of Christian art, he succeeded, over a period of several decades, in acquiring donations, in publishing a *Deltion* (bulletin) containing valuable information and in photographing the monuments he saw in his frequent travels to remote localities.

After the Asia Minor disaster of 1922 the uprooted refugees brought a further collection of valuable ecclesiastical relics from their homelands. A selection of fine liturgical objects was shared between the Byzantine and Benaki Museum. Of foreing provenance is a small collection of Coptic inscriptions and so-called Coptic textiles presented to the museum by Anthony Benaki with a view to giving visitors an opportunity to form an impression of this art.

When the Byzantine Museum was first founded in 1914 the collections were housed in the unsuitable and wholly inadequate accommodation provided by a basement in the megaron of the Academy. When transferred to the restored edifice by the Ilisos they were displayed in the halls of the three wings and in the large court which was transformed in such a way as to resemble a monastic one, with cypress trees and a *phiale*. Later a fountain was added and a plane tree planted.

New donations were made and new legacies inherited as a result of the prestige acquired by the museum after its establishment at the present site. The collection of portative icons was thus enriched with the acquisition of the private collections of Christianos Lampikis, Professor John Katsaras, George Makkas, Melissidis, etc. The museum also continued to be enriched with murals detached from the walls of churches, sculptures from the collection of various scattered antiquities, objects (particularly glassware and ceramics) uncovered in the course of excavations, icons from confiscated antiquities, as well as other objects obtained by means of purchases or from donations made by private individuals.

In order to house all these acquisitions, both old and new, and exhibit them properly it was found necessary in 1951 to build another spacious well-lit hall in the east wing.

The foundation of a Central Laboratory of Conservation (of wall-paintings, mosaics and icons) in 1963 was a landmark in the history of the museum. The members of the laboratory were responsible for the preservation of wall-paintings in hundreds of churches throughout Greece, for the restoration of mosaics on the walls and floors of churches. Many fragments of Byzantine wall-paintings had to be detached from walls and removed for restoration to the Byzantine Museum, where some of them are now exhibited. A special apartment was reserved for the laboratories in which the icons in the museum underwent the various processes required for conservation, and the activities of the Central Laboratory were extended to include the conservation of monuments as far afield as Cyprus and Palestine and of wall-paintings and icons in the Monastery of St. Catherine on Mt. Sinai.

Early Christian works (4th-7th century)

The Byzantine Museum is perhaps the only one exclusively devoted to works of Byzantine and post-Byzantine art. The museum owes its regional character to the fact that since its foundation, it has included representative works of art of the Byzantine era and the age of the Turkish rule as developed within the confines of the present Greek state. That is why the collections possess such a pronounced local character. This is a very pertinent point. For it should be recalled that Northern Greece with Thessalonike as its centre fell within the area subject to the immediate influence of the Capital, while the rest of Greece south of Mt. Olympos was a Byzantine province with somewhat independent historical fortunes determined by its position in the Mediterranean. Here, along the limitless shores, in the numerous islands of the Aegean and Ionian Seas, in the large and famous ancient cities — Corinth, Athens, Megara, Sparta, Argos, Boiotian Thebes, Phthiotic Thebes and Gortyna in Crete, among others — life followed its own course.

Judging from the great number of large ruined churches and from the high quality of their decoration uncovered in the course of excavations, one must conclude that the whole area now consisting of modern Greece must have been a prosperous one during the Early Christian period. The objects from Thessalonike, Asia Minor and elsewhere, exhibited in the ante-chamber of the ground floor of the museum, were fashioned in a superb technique, betraying the catholicity of their style. The next hall, which is in the form of a three-aisled basilica, gives the visitor an idea of the disposition of a church of this type, with the low screen of the sanctuary, the *synthronon* and throne, the Holy Table, *ambon* and closure panels. Early Christian sculptures — offering tables, closure panels from the Ilisos basilica and other churches — have been assembled in this hall. (Pieces from the mosaic floor of the Ilisos basilica are displayed in the west gallery of the court). The funerary group of Orpheus (fig. 2) strikes a different note. The seated figure of the harpist is surrounded by an arched frame consisting of beasts, birds and other animals (both real and fantastical) disposed in successive series so that the empty spaces between them and between the frame and the central figure create hollows which give the impression that the entire composition has been executed in the manner of open-work technique. In spite of the plastic modelling of each figure, the entire group conveys an impression, heightened by the deeply incised folds of drapery, of a flat representation. The modelling is a typical example of the period (*c.* A.D. 400), but the Christian character of the representation (possibly a symbolical figure of Christ?) remains doubtful.

To the same period of flourishing belongs the "Mytilene treasure" (figs. 27-29): a hoard of gold, silver and bronze objects, as well as gold coins, which was found in 1951 at the locality of Krategos, where they had been hidden by persons in fear of some Arab raid. The owners, it would appear, never had the opportunity of returning and recovering them. The gold objects consist of jewellery (fig. 27): three necklaces with open-work decoration, earrings, two belts, bracelets, buckles, rings. The technique, of Roman origin, is evolved, and the craftsmen were obviously aiming at the creation of precious objects that would convey an impression of considerable brilliance. It is not strange that the decoration occasionally bears obviously Christian traces, for the gold coins with which they were found are of the period of the Emperors Phokas (602-610) and Herakleios (613-629/30).

To the same period clearly belong the silver objects from the same treasure, all of which are *pentasphragista:* that is to say, stamped with the five official seals of the controller of the quality of silver. The dish is simply decorated with a cross surrounded by a tendril with ivy leaves (fig. 28). All the objects are decorated with niello, i.e. darkened silver. On the hollow object with a handle, called a *trulla,* a nude female figure and four youthful ones are incised on the wide handle and lip respectively (fig. 29). The decorative subject must derive from some revival of pagan worship in Late Antiquity; but the linear incisions reveal the various transformations that this kind of art had undergone by the 7th century.

Art of the Middle Byzantine period in Greece (8th-12th century)

From the mid-7th to mid-9th century pestilence, Arab raids on the coasts and hostile incursions from the north caused widespread devastation and the depopulation of the maritime areas. The country was only able to breathe again when Crete was liberated (961) and the Bulgar threat effectively removed. It must be stressed, however, that Greece's economic means were at a very much lower ebb than they had been during the Early Christian period. The collection of marble pieces of architectural decoration of the post-Iconoclast period in the museum is nevertheless a very rich one. The pieces include a large number of door-frames, lintels, closure panels and architraves of screens, as well as some rare large marble icons with the Virgin in an attitude of prayer carved in relief. Although possessing the general artistic characteristics of the period, all this material, carved in Pentelic marble, must represent the fruits of labour of workshops in the Attica-Boiotia area. Let us take a look at a closure panel representing the old Eastern theme of the Tree of Life in a symmetrical but dynamic composition with two lions rising to bite the tree, their hind-paws treading on its roots whence water gushes forth (fig. 4). The shallow relief, the stylized manes, the *horror vacui* shown by the sculptor would in themselves suffice to betray the Eastern provenance of the subject and style, were it not further verified by the pseudo-Cufic inscription on the two lateral sides of the frame. Other similar inscriptions in the form of decorative features, whose provenance cannot be disputed, are to be found on other pieces in the museum which, in many cases, formed part of buildings and reliefs of the 10th and 11th centuries in Southern Greece, and provide evidence of a temporary change in taste in favour of Islamic art of the Eastern Mediterranean. The same change is evident in another closure panel with the extremely ancient motif of a lion about to tear its prey to pieces (fig. 6). The execution is more rough, the rendering of the relief more flat, but the fact that the composition is equally dynamic in conception underlines the difference between the piece in question and the Eastern models. Sculptures with similar subjects decorate the walls of the Church of St. Eleutherios (otherwise known as the *Gorgoepekoos* or Little Metropolis). These were removed from earlier Athenian churches. Double knotted crosses decorate other closure panels, like the one with the metrical dedicatory inscription (fig. 5) from the demolished Athenian Church of St. John of Mangoutis. The manner in which the eagles are depicted within medallions, even though in heraldic attitudes and rendered with a certain academic plasticity, is an indication of the different origins of this kind of sculpture.

The sculptures we have examined so far are all of Athenian provenance. An interesting piece representing three Apostles, James Alphaius, Philip and Luke (fig. 3) comes from Thessalonike which remained in direct contact with Constantinople. The somewhat short standing figures, depicted frontally, are accompanied by vertical incised inscriptions with impeccably designed majuscules. An interesting technique, known as *champ-levé,* has been used. The outlines of the figures are drawn with the removal of interior surfaces, whereas the folds of the garments — this applies to all three figures — are indicated by fine projecting edges. The hollows are filled with mastic wax on which the draperies with the many folds, the faces and large hands are painted. It is clear that the technique used in the depiction of flat figures and the separately painted stains is, in this instance, an imitation of the *cloisonné* enamels and, in painting, of the one applied to portative icons. This valuable plaque, which should be dated to the 10th rather than the 11th century, must have formed part of the lavish decoration of a marble screen (of a length exceeding 4.50 metres) and constituted a section of the usual screen architrave of the period representing the Great *Deesis* (the three main figures with the twelve Apostles).

The Frankish occupation and the Palaiologan period (1204-1453)

The brilliant period of the 11th and 12th centuries, which is represented by monuments of such superior quality as Hosios Loukas and Daphni, together with other beautiful churches of the Helladic school, was followed by the Frankish occupation which began in 1204 and came to an end with the Turkish conquest in 1456. Churches continued to be raised during this period and their walls to be painted; but they were of smaller dimensions, built of cheaper materials and more scattered as a result of a decentralizing tendency which caused many people to dwell in private family domains. An idea of monumental painting in Attica and the islands during the 13th century can be obtained from pieces of wall-paintings detached from the walls of churches and exhibited in the museum.

The tall slender figure of a young deacon (fig. 8), St. Stephen (?), is painted on a narrow pilaster beside the hierarchs on the altar of a new ruined church at Oropos. The striking facial features, the heroic character, the firm outlines and the modelling rendered by means of the use of both warm and cool colour tones, relate this wall-painting to similar ones of the mid-13th century in Euboia and at Kranidi which we have reason to attribute to an Athenian school of painting. At Kranidi the paintings are signed by a certain John of Athens and dated 1244.

Paintings in the islands under Frankish domination underwent a different development. A conch of the apse of a church at Lathreno, Naxos, has been detached from the wall (fig. 7). Its poor state of preservation indicates that it might have suffered total destruction had it not been removed. The large central figure of Christ is out of proportion with the two flanking figures in the *Deesis*, those of the Virgin and St. John the Baptist, which are preserved intact. These wall-paintings provide evidence of the way in which the repercussions of new trends in Constantinople were felt in the occupied provinces, as well as the manner in which Western influences affected Byzantine taste.

The large mosaic icon of the Virgin and child, "*the Glykophilousa*" from Triglia in Bithynia, which is one of the outstanding relics brought by the refugees in 1922, should be assigned to a slightly later date: namely, the early 14th century (fig. 1). The size of the icon, as well as that of the tesserae, indicates that the work was still closely related to the kind of art whose origins lay in monumental mosaics, whereas other outstanding mosaic icons possess the dimensions of miniatures. Furthermore, as the icon bears the inscription Η ΕΠΙΣΚΕΨΙΣ, it must be a reproduction of some miraculous icon of the *Glykophilousa,* in which the Virgin holds the Child in her right arm (the subject was also rendered in the remarkable Virgin of Vladimir in the 12th century). In the Byzantine Museum icon the fleshy luminous faces and the bulky bodies, which are characteristic of a contemporary trend, have been rendered in a closed condensed composition with soft outlines. The bright colours with the abundant gold lights conceal certain weaknesses in the design.

Icons

Of all the exhibits in the Byzantine Museum the portative icons, with their wide range of geographical provenance, provide the most comprehensive picture of the different styles.

The Crucifixion (provenance: Northern Greece) is depicted on one side of a double-sided icon, whose history is best summarized in its lack of homogeneity (fig. 15). In the 13th century the principal figures were repainted over the early icon of the 9th century which possessed flat and linear features, such as the angles and the stars. Grief and suffering are expressed in a striking but restrained manner which matches the simplicity of the colour scheme and composition.

Another double-sided icon comes from the same area, namely Kastoria. St. George is depicted full-size, carved on the wood of the icon which is framed by little painted scenes from the saint's life and martyrdom (fig. 11). The wood relief, the stiff and awkward attitude of the figure, the nimbus executed in relief and the shape of the shield betray Frankish influences of Romanesque origin. The expressionist technique used in the small scenes of the frame recall miniatures painted at the time of the Frankish kingdoms of Jerusalem and Cyprus. The prolonged cohabitation of peoples in various areas of the Eastern Mediterranean resulting from the Frankish occupation raised the enduring problem of reciprocal exchange of influences which are not always easy to verify. The large icon of Christ (fig. 14), for instance, which may have come from St. Sophia in Thessalonike, is rendered distinctive by two features: by the broad and ugly face, which is in complete contrast to the usual type of idealized Christ, and by the affectedly realistic light and shade effects which give the nimbus an unusual plasticity, as in the relief of the nimbus of St. George (fig. 11). This ugliness — the words of the prophet, "and when we shall see him *there is* no beauty that we should desire him" (Isiah, 53, 2) are not inappropriate here — reflects a clearly anti-classical trend, although the execution is of high quality; moreover the Western-type nimbus may even suggest the origins of this anti-classical tendency. The icon of the Virgin holding the Child from Thessalonike is not alien to this tendency. The serious and aristocratic physiognomy of the Mother of God possesses strikingly individual features, while the figure of the Child, with the high forehead and expression of displeasure concentrated in the disproportionately plump face, as well as the oblique glance and the awkward attitude, does not seem to be in contact with the Mother. Peculiarities of this kind, already observed in the icon of Christ from Thessalonike, would have been inconceivable before 1300; they are typical of a spiritual and artistic movement of the early 14th century which did not possess a particularly regional quality.

The classical revival

The opposite trend, which remained faithful to the so-called classical tradition, is represented in several outstading icons from the important centres, including the well known one of the Archangel Michael "the *Megas Taxiarches*" (fig. 12). The fine youthful figure is well set up, with the "cast shadow" across the neck, the delicately elaborated drapery with the deep gold lights conveying an impression of something infinitely precious, and the black band, a symbol of authority. Crowned by a lavish arrangement of the hair, the noble face combines the gentle quality of a girl with the serious air of an ephebe; it thus reflects an idealized serene beauty which is full of warm humanity and high moral character. The exceptional artistic quality, taken in conjunction with certain specific features, indicate that the icon is of Constantinopolitan provenance and should be dated after the mid-14th century — or possibly slightly later.

The superb Crucifixion from Thessalonike belongs to about the same period and is in the same tradition (fig. 17). Lacking all narrative elements, the three-figured composition retains its monumental character. The three figures, each one concentrated and isolated within the space of the icon, are related to each other by the harmonious rhythm of attitudes and gestures expressing a grief shared in common. The figure on the Cross is just slightly relaxed, its curve being repeated in the sturdy body of St. John, whereas the Virgin, tall and slender, wrapped in a *maphorion,* stands erect as a column, her attitude and gestures serving as a counterpoise to those of St. John which originate from ancient funerary stelai. The exceptional height of the figures introduces a new element into the icon. Moreover, the figures are made to appear even taller by the low horizon of the houses of Jerusalem and the diffused light which just permits reflections to fall on the soft folds of drapery and on the nude body on the Cross. The simple colours graduate between a range of brown and gold on which a limpid blue casts a glow.

The nobility of the attitude of the young Daniel depicted in motion as he worships, with a large red cloak thrown elegantly over his shoulders, and the fine workmanship enable us to attribute the icon of the prophet in the den of lions to the same tradition (fig. 16). The prophet Habbakuk, depicted in small scale, is led by an archangel as he proceeds to offer nourishment to Daniel who is now in disgrace.

The large gold-thread *Epitaphios* from Thessalonike (fig. 38), one of the most striking examples of a series of gold-thread works of the Palaiologan era is also assigned to a period associated with a new flowering of the arts. It was designed by an outstanding artist of the early 14th century. Dogmatic ideas are dramatically expressed in three·scenes, whereas the perfection of the technical execution, together with a judicious feeling for detail rendered by the use of a variety of precious materials, indicate the high degree of skill attained by the needleworkers, who may well have been noble ladies.

The arts after the fall of Constantinople Cretan icons

After the fall of Constantinople icon painting continued to occupy the predominant place in the religious art of the Orthodox world, and Greek icons did not cease to be held up as examples of dogmatic orthodoxy and artistic faith in the great Byzantine tradition. The Hospitality of Abraham (fig. 21) is an outstanding example of the art which flourished in the large cities of Crete, the most important centre, where painting, with its attachment to the best Palaiologan models, continued to be of high quality. In this symbolic depiction of the Holy Trinity features of common everyday life, such as the three young people partaking of a repast, are blurred and the icon acquires the air of an other-worldly representation, as in the case of the Constantinopolitan model of the Palaiologan period in the Benaki Museum (fig. 23, p. 371). In the Byzantine Museum piece, however, the figures have grown larger and advanced into the foreground, filling the entire space, so that the buildings in the background have lost their importance. The entire composition is subjected to a geometric conception, the influence of which is observed in the disposition of the drapery: the soft and pliant folds have been succeeded by angular forms. An additional feature provided by the aristocratic nobility of the figures and their attitudes enables us to obtain an idea of the main characteristics of Cretan painting of the 15th-16th centuries.

Painters in the Byzantine tradition possessed a particular ability to render the venerable figures of the chief protagonists of the Christian faith in its most ascetic and idealized aspects. The figure of St. Anthony, a very popular with painters, was a subject that greatly attracted them in the exercise of this lofty artistic medium (fig. 20). The austere and tormented face, illuminated by only a few rays of light, the rhythmic folds of drapery which emphasize the extremely tall silhouette and register the movement of the legs, are an expression of the nobility of the ascetic ideal.

Another of the Byzantine icon painter's ideals finds expression in the depiction of female saints martyred in the first flush of their youth, like that wise young princess, St. Catherine (fig. 19). Indications of the ideal of feminine beauty most favoured during the different periods are observed in this kind of icon. An actual physiognomical type is apparent here, fairly common even at present in various parts of Greece. Other characteristics of Cretan painting of the 15th-16th centuries consist of bright colours, a faultless technique employed in the vigorous modelling and the accurate rendering of minor details in dress and ornament which betray Italian influences.

A feeling for maternal tenderness is shown by the Cretan painter Angelos (c. 1600) in a not unknown but nevertheless unusual type of the Virgin holding the Child, the *Brephokratousa* (fig. 18). The attitude of the Child, nestling in the Virgin's affectionate embrace, is awkward; but the fact that everything remains in a certain abstract atmosphere is a considerable achievement, which may be observed in other works too, on the part of the Cretan painter.

The icon decorates the large iconostasis of the church (fig. 26); but it can also be interpreted as an expression of individual worship, of personal gratitude, as in the case of the icon dedicated by Capetan Ardavanis to the Virgin of the Venetians who rescued him from a shipwreck (fig. 23). The dramatic scene, represented in the summary but lively manner of Cretan painters, is set on a seashore near the Kourtzoula islets where the battle of Lepanto (Naupaktos) was fought.

In other parts of Greece, outside Crete and the areas in which Cretan painting was diffused, icons and wall-paintings continued to be executed. Cretan artists were commissioned to carry out the painted decoration of the large monasteries on Mt. Athos, at Meteora and elsewhere; but native painters, generally peasants, continued to practise their hereditary and traditional art in smaller churches. Their works, rendered in their own simpler manner, are not uninfluenced by Cretan iconography. The triptych (fig. 22), which must come from Central Greece, represents the Transfiguration on the central panel, the Tree of Jesse and the Vine, two corresponding symbolical representations from the Old and New Testaments, on the left and right panels respectively. The whole work, with the decorative rendering of the symmetrical trees, the brightness of the colours, possess the quality of a handicraftsman's perfectionist work.

Popular painting in the 18th century

A similar but more authentically popular mode of expression is observed in the paintings detached from the walls of the church in the old village of Kastri which was demolished in order to enable the excavation of the ancient Gymnasium of Delphi to be carried out. One of the works, dated to 1751, represents an old monk in a boat, while large sea monsters — the "dragons of the sea" of the Psalter — emerge out of the turbulent waters and belch forth the members of the victims they have devoured on the Day of Judgement (fig. 10). The artist's indifference to the scale of the monsters in relation to reality is evident. Another wall-painting of the same period, detached from the wall of a ruined church at Atalante, represents St. James the Persian (fig. 9), whose exotic apparel displays an attractive colourfulness.

The *Galaktotrophousa* (The Virgin suckling the Child), which is distinguished by an individual kind of realism corresponding to contemporary fashion (fig. 24), is the subject chosen by the monkish painter Makarios from Galatista in the Chalcidike. The type of the Virgin suckling the Child is one of the oldest in Christian iconography, but, a certain prudery inhibited painters from repeating it frequently. The accuracy of a handicraftsman's skill is evident in the rendering of the adornments and nimbuses — an indication that painting has passed into the sphere of handicrafts.

Popular painting in the 19th century inherited the technique and basic principles of hagiography, which in itself had already become a popular art, as one may observe in the charming didactic picture of the blind Eros and the Sirens (fig. 25). The work dated 1825 is by a humble priest and hagiographer from the island of Siphnos.

Minor arts

The museum also contains lavish collections of vestments, *Epitaphioi* (gold-embroidered veils carried in procession on Good Friday) and other liturgical objects representative of the handicrafts, often executed in numerous varied techniques and possessing a high degree of perfection (figs. 30-39). In accordance with their provenance and the period in which they were executed these objects reflect Byzantine survivals, as well as Persian and Western influences. Of the many centres of handicrafts, the most important were in Epeiros, the islands, Asia Minor and Constantinople, as well as in numerous monasteries.

The technical skill and good taste shown by the artists of the Byzantine world, preserved in the unbroken tradition of the Hellenic diaspora, still survive in all their vigour and are constantly undergoing rejuvenation. This too constitutes a direct link with Byzantium.

1. Mosaic icon of the Virgin and Child, 'The Episkepsis'. Provenance: Bithynia. 14th century.

2. *Funerary stele. 4th-5th century. Orpheus, playing on his lyre, fascinates the animals (real and imaginary) which surround him. Relief depicting hunting scene on the base. The group must possess some symbolical meaning associated with immortality.*

3. *Plaque depicting three apostles. Provenance: Thessalonike. The work must have formed part of a marble screen of the 10th-11th century. Screens had developed into one of the most lavish features decorating the interior of contemporary churches.*

4,6. *Marble closure panels from a screen of the 9th-10th century, with the extremely ancient subjects of confronted animals (No. 4) and animals in combat (No. 6), which must have lost their symbolical meaning and were probably a survival from Iconoclast thematology.*

5. *The Victory cross, a Christian symbol of the 9th-10th century with an apotropaic meaning, was commonly carved on closure panels.*

3

4   5   6

7. *Wall-painting from apsidal conch with the Deesis theme. Provenance: Lathreno, Naxos. 13th century. Below: bishops conducting the liturgy.*

8. *Wall-painting detached from wall of ruined church at Oropos. Early 13th century. A tall slender young deacon is clad in a white 'sticharion'. In his left hand, covered by a red encheirion (cloth), he holds a tall gold incense box.*

9. *Wall-painting depicting St. James the Persian. The strange type of the Eastern saint, developed by 16th century Cretan painters, is repeated in the 18th century, but with simpler means. Provenance: demolished church at Atalante.*

10. *Wall-painting from a demolished church at Delphi (1751). A fantastical scene with a boat painted with realistic exactitude.*

7

9

10

343

11. Icon of St. George in painted relief (a somewhat rare technique in the Byzantine world). The little donor at the saint's feet is clothed in Frankish dress. 13th century. Provenance: Kastoria area.

12. The 14th century icon of the Archangel Michael must have formed part of a set of five or seven icons on the upper tier of an iconostasis including the Deesis, as indicated by the three letters on the globe.

12

Ο ΑΡ
ΟΜΕΓΑΣ

ΜΙΧΛ
ΤΑΡΑΧΗΣ

13. *Icon of the Virgin and Child. c. 1300. The personal features of the faces reveal a particular trend in Palaiologan painting.*

14. *Large icon of Christ, representative of a high quality anti-classical trend of the early 14th century. Provenance: Thessalonike.*

15. *The Crucifixion. The angels and stars are of a 9th century layer, whereas the main figures are typical of the 13th.*

16. *The prophet Daniel. The subject, rare in portative icons, is depicted here in the elegant manner of Palaiologan painting.*

17. *The Crucifixion. Outstanding work of Palaiologan painting, from Thessalonike.*

17

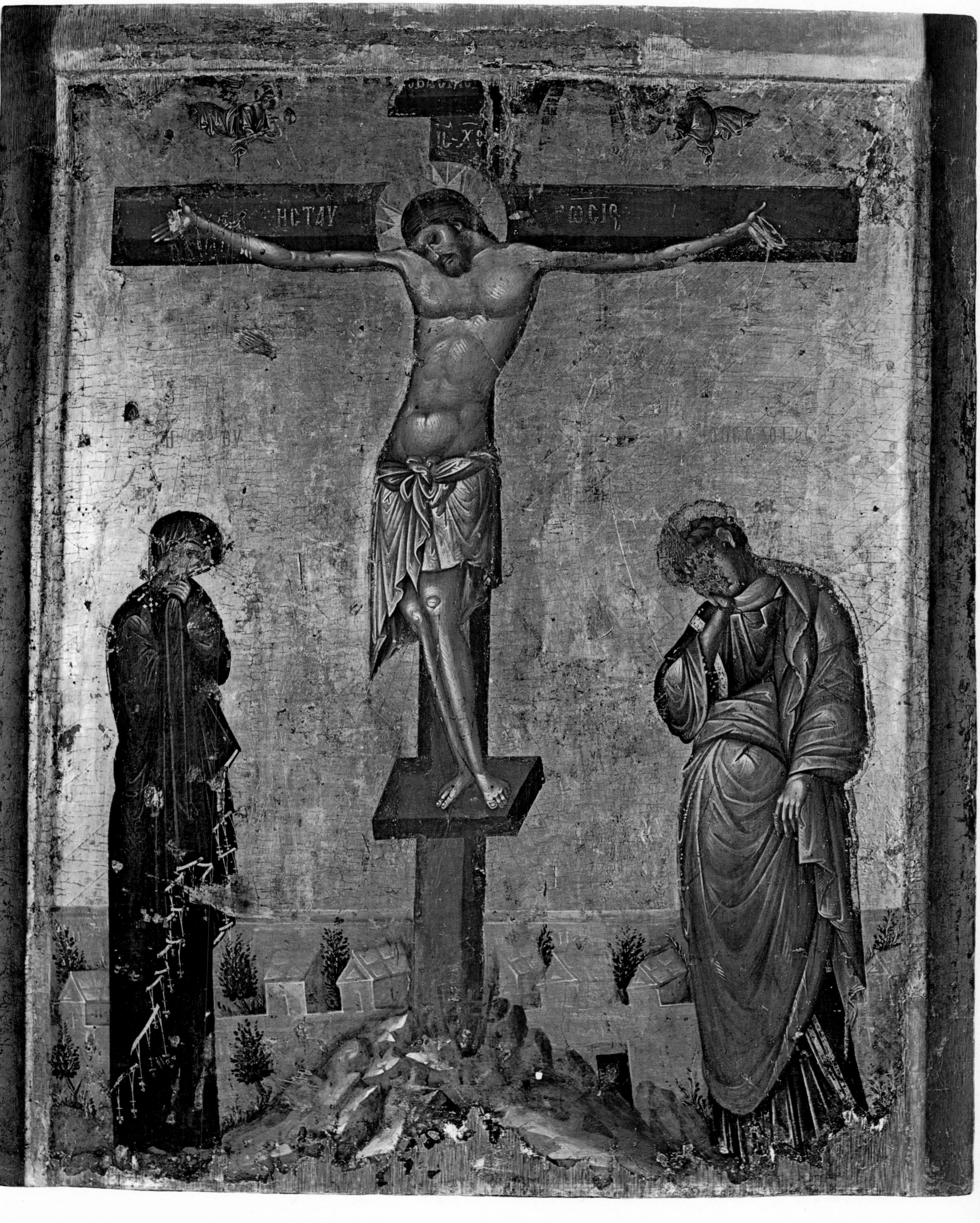

18

19

20

18. *Icon of the Virgin and* **Child**, *'The* **Kardiotissa**' : *a work of the Cretan painter Angelos. c. 1600. Probably a copy of a Cretan miraculous icon.*

19. *St. Catherine. Cretan icon. 15th-16th century. The princess is represented with her attributes : the martyr's cross and wheel.*

20. *St. Anthony depicted standing full-length in an iconostasis door. This Cretan work of the 15th-16th century preserves the technique of the preceding period, as well as the nobility of, and reverence felt for, the ascetic figure.*

21. **Icon** *of the Hospitality of Abraham symbolizing the Holy Trinity. With its serene and lofty air, its concentrated geometric composition and stiff drapery, it represents a classical phase in Cretan painting of the first half of the 16th century.*

22. *Triptych of the Transfiguration flanked by the Tree of Jesse and the Vine. The simplicity of the shape and the lack of finish of the frame are much in keeping with the popular art character of 17th century painting in Central Greece.*

23. *The Virgin and the rescue at sea of Sior Ardavani. 17th century. Provenance: Ionian Islands. The icon, which represents both the Virgin in the role of protectress and the maritime incident, belongs to a type with a Western votive character.*

24. *Icon of the Virgin and Child, 'The Galaktotrophousa' by the monk Makarios of Galatista (1784). Typically Athonite work, in which the exactitude associated with a handicraftsman's work is particularly evident.*

25. *A didactic icon of popular art (1825). Its representation of the blind Eros and the Sirens shows how non-religious themes were still interpreted in the manner of mediaeval painting at the time of the Greek War of Independence. The work is by one Agapios Manganaris of Siphnos.*

22

23

24

25

26. *The wooden iconostasis, as developed in the 16th and 17th centuries, continued to be a well-constructed feature with lavish carving. The icons of Christ and the Virgin, dated 1680, are by the Cretan Emmanuel Tzanes, the Italicizing closure panels by another Cretan artist, Elias Moskos, a contemporary of Tzanes, who worked in Zakynthos.*

27. *Jewellery from a treasure found in Mytilene, dated by means of gold coins to the early 7th century. Roman traditions prevail in the necklaces, whereas the buckles have a clearly Byzantine character.*

28. *Silver plate with incised cross and ivy tendrils. Provenance: Mytilene treasure.*

29. *'Trulla'. 7th century vessel with non-Christian incised representations. Provenance: Mytilene treasure.*

28

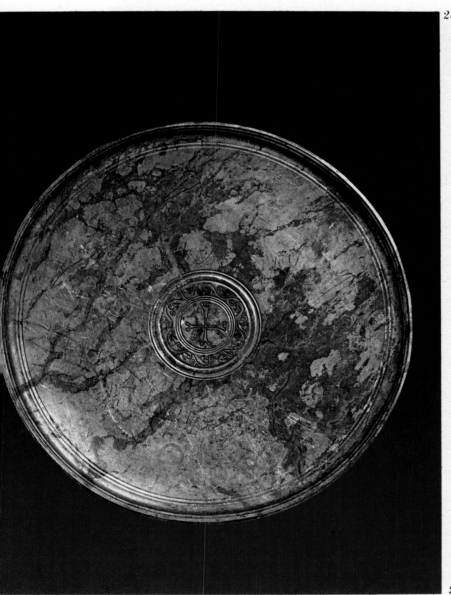

29

30

30. Gospel book cover from Trebizond with features associated with different periods. Three of the corner adornments, consisting of embossed medallions with arabesques, are of the 14th-15th century, the fourth (top right), which is less skillfully worked, of a later period. The central cross with the engraved representations is of the 16th-17th century. The correct position for the medallions would be Christ in the middle and the angel above, as appropriate in a Deesis representation.

31. Pastoral staff of Bishop Neophytos of Adrianople (1653-1658) decorated with precious stones, rubies and enamels. Work of fine quality. Provenance: possibly Constantinople. Painted enamels in the medallions: Christ, the Virgin, three hierarchs and St. John.

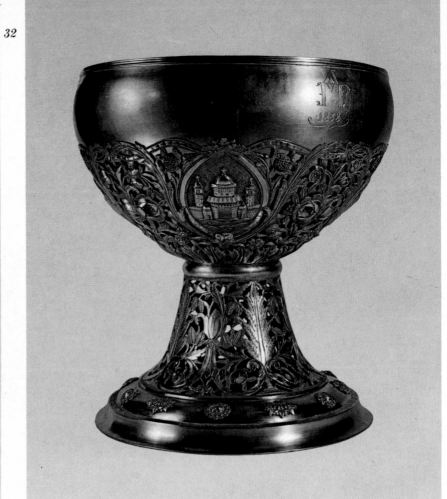

36

32. *19th century silver censer with lid and engraved and open-work decoration. Western influences are apparent. Provenance: Asia Minor relics.*

33. *Silver vessel for Holy Water from the Monastery of Prodromos, near Serrai. Date: 1838. Embossed representations of the monastery and other decoration in open-work.*

34. *17th century spherical crown of chandelier from Kythera. Collection of the Christian Archaeological Society. Elegant incised decoration with foliate themes.*

35. *Large pyx (artophorion) from the Metropolis, Adrianople. The rough and unskilled silver and gilt relief contrasts with the Homeric style metrical inscription finely wrought in enamel which commemorates the donor, Neophytos, Bishop of Adrianople (1669).*

36. *Large cross, dated 1654, with fine enamel decoration which does not wholly match the unskilled wood-carved representations of the Feasts.*

37. The Entry into Jerusalem. Detail from a silver-thread embroidered stole depicting the Twelve Feasts. Although lacking variety in technique, it preserves an artistic accuracy and a serene and well-balanced composition which is nevertheless entirely flat in its simple chromatic range.

38. Gold-thread 'Aer' from Thessalonike. Outstanding work of art of the early 14th century. This liturgical piece of cloth was destined to cover the chalice with the bread and wine; consequently, the representations of the Holy Community and Christ-Amnos (The Lamb) refer to the mystery of the Eucharist. Later, this kind of cloth, with the same central representation, served as an epitaphios during Holy Week. The embroidery has been executed so skillfully that the subjects are rendered in the manner of a painting, while fully exploiting the possibilities of expression provided by the special technique, with its use of costly materials, gold and silver wire, silks, and a variety of stitches with different reflections which create an effect of delicate constantly changing tones.

39. Gospel book cover, dated 1755, with adjoining moulded little plaques framed with filigree and coloured stones. The Despotic Feasts and saints are represented. Their order must have been altered when the book cover was repaired at some later date.

39

362

BENAKI MUSEUM

BENAKI MUSEUM

The Building

In the heart of Athens, across the street from the National Park, stands one of the few great residences that have survived in that section of Vasilissis Sophias Avenue. These elegant houses were built around 1900 for upper-class families of Athens in a pleasing traditional style. The neoclassical building across the Park, with its portico of Doric columns and marble balconies and jambs, was bought and enlarged by Emmanuel Benaki, a national benefactor from Alexandria, when he decided to settle in Athens. The house was the work of the architect Anastasios Metaxas. After completing the necessary alterations and additions, Emmanuel's son Anthony Benaki, used it in 1930 to house his personal art collections and to establish in it the Benaki Museum.

The Benaki collections and the founding of the museum.

Anthony Benaki (1873-1954) was an important cotton merchant in Egypt, and his wealth enabled him to acquire a considerable number of works of art. In 1927, upon settling in Athens, he devoted himself to a number of civic projects but mainly to the organization of this museum. When this young patrician lover of art and sport began buying precious Oriental weapons, he probably did not have in mind to found a fully-equipped museum. But thirty years spent in the methodical selection and purchase of works of art from Egypt, Greece, and the world market in Western Europe resulted in the accumulation of a vast number of valuable objects, which eventually came to form almost complete series of important works of art in diverse fields. With the contentment of a mature collector and the ambition to render an important public service, Anthony Benaki decided in 1927 to found a museum — a μουσεῖον in the best cultural sense of this ancient term — and to offer it to the Nation.

Anthony Benaki's personal contribution.

His donation was not limited to the signing of a formal contract with the State, but included his own services as well — the personal labour of a highly experienced collector of cultivated taste who also possessed the will and the power to substantiate the dream begotten by his enthousiastic imagination.

It took him three years of incessant work to extend and convert his father's house into a museum. Emmanuel Benaki's other heirs all gladly offered their share of the inheritance for this purpose. It was also necessary to design hundreds of show-cases, frames, and stands and to study the problems of lighting and of the protection of the exhibits from exposure. The most perfect devices known at the time were used throughout. Every single item, from the extension and conversion of the building down to the last detail, was decided by him personally.

Owing to the great diversity of the collections, the disposition of the rooms in the museum presented difficulties, and there were also practical problems arising from the transformation of a building designed for family life into a museum. This task required not only sound knowledge and a fine sense of the materials involved and of the chromatic and tactile quality of each exhibit, but also considerable inventiveness in finding practical solutions. Anthony Benaki combined these qualities to an astonishing degree. He set up his museum almost single-handed. Thousands of objects, whether works of fine art or pieces of native handicraft, all chosen through a lifetime of judicious collecting, were arranged by him and exhibited in 270 show-cases and on the walls of 24 rooms. This purely personal offering was perhaps even more valuable than the huge amounts of money spent on purchasing the collections and on installing and endowing the museum.

Benaki did not consider his mission completed with the foundation and endowment of the museum. After its inauguration and incorporation as an autonomous foundation in 1931, he continued to enrich it with admirable new acquisitions; he also supervised and financed the training of specialized personnel, the compilation of catalogues by Greek and foreign scholars of world repute, and the publication of a large two-volume album containing coloured illustrations of Greek national costumes. Until 1942, all these expenses were met by Benaki himself; it was only during the dark years of the enemy occupation of Greece that he was compelled to ask the Government to grant the museum some financial assistance, mainly in order to enable the staff of the Museum to survive in those difficult times. This assistance has continued since then in the form of a State subsidy.

When World War II was declared in 1939, Benaki began to pack the museum exhibits in special cases with his own hands, working many hours every day for several months. It was with the same untiring devotion that he set up the museum once again after the liberation of Greece, adding new show-cases and planning additional improvements.

A perfect identification of the creator with his creation, touchingly expressed in Benaki's testament by the wish to have his heart walled in the museum, was the essential factor that bound together diverse collections in a unified whole. This personal touch, guided as it was by good taste rather than by any rigid prescriptions for chronological or geographical classification, is nevertheless impressively convincing, generating an atmosphere of warm intimacy in a museum whose rooms have retained the aspect of a private residence. The arrangement of the exhibits has also retained the character of a personal collection, and this is what distinguishes the Benaki Museum from museums of a strictly specialized nature.

The spirit of an age

At about this time, Greek intellectuals were turning their attention to the art of medieval and modern Greece. It is no coincidence that the first Byzantine museum in Greece was founded at about this time, or that Photis Kontoglou, a painter and writer working in the Byzantine manner, emerged on the scene with a school of followers. There was also a marked trend toward folk art, which soon became the object of intensive study and at times even of emulation. The work of Angelike Chatzimichali, A. Zachos, and others in this field, the Delphic festivals organized by Angelos and Eve Sikelianos, and the multitude of societies and exhibitions devoted to these new concerns were also parts of this trend. Anthony Benaki enthusiastically helped all these manifestations with financial contributions and his personal prestige. Yet it was his museum that gave the movement a permanently tangible expression. Thus seen, it stands as testimony to the intellectual and aesthetic aspirations of a generation in an era which may have been fraught with difficulties but which was also culturally flourishing.

The donors

The high educational mission with which Benaki wished to invest his museum from its very inception and the scrupulous care taken in the presentation, annotation, and preservation of the exhibits quickly raised the Benaki Museum to a position of great prestige. From the very beginning, various organizations and individuals entrusted the museum with the valuable relics and works of art in their possession. The Exchange of Populations Foundation donated some of the religious treasures which had been brought to Greece by refugees from Asia Minor, the Pontos, and Eastern Thrace in 1923; the Eleutherios Venizelos Foundation presented it with that great statesman's files and a series of memorabilia which had belonged to him; more recently, the St. Dekozis - Vouros Foundation offered to finance the construction of a two-story wing to house lecture halls and exhibition rooms.

As regards individual donors, G. Eumorphopoulos gave the museum his collection of Chinese pottery, complete with appropriate show-cases. Damianos Kyriazis donated his large collections of embroideries; pottery; drawings, water-colours and lithographs on Greek themes; a considerable number of rare books; and massive historical records. The room that bears his name was built also at his own expense. After several sporadic donations, Mrs. Helen Antoniou Stathatos offered the wood-carved panelling of a drawing-room from an 18th century upper-class residence in Kozani. This donation was accompanied by icons, embroideries, lithographs, jewellery, and miscellaneous other items. Through a State grant a special room was added to shelter the panelling and her other donations. Other donors were Marina Lappa-Diomedous, Christian Lampikis, and Mr. Loukas Benakis, to mention only some of the major donors. With the exception of the Chinese pottery collection donated by Eumorphopoulos, all these donations came to complete the original collections of Anthony Benaki.

This role of the museum as a repository in which private collections of varying sizes, and personal records of special interest may be preserved for posterity is yet another, no less important, function of the Benaki Museum.

The exhibits

To grasp the underlying unity that pervades the various collections, it might be useful to think of the exhibits as belonging to a pattern of three intersecting circles. The first circle consists of Greek works of art, from prehistoric times to the modern age. The emphasis here is on ancient Greek goldsmith's work and Byzantine and post-Byzantine art, including painting and miniature work. The second circle, which overlaps with the first, is devoted to modern Greek themes. These exhibits occupy most of the rooms of the museum. They represent Greek folk art in all its aspects together with similar specimens from the folk art of other countries; modern Greek historical relics; an important section of the Historical Archives; a large collection of drawings, water-colours, and lithographs picturing landscapes, scenes from everyday life, and various characters of modern Greece — all of them by foreign artists of the Romantic period; and also important informative material, whether in the form of documents or of art works related to Western philhellenism. The third circle consists of collections of minor arts and handicraft from the Eastern Mediterranean, both the coastal areas and the hinterland. This circle overlaps with both the preceding ones; for instance, the large collection of weapons includes Islamic and European masterpieces as well as Greek historical relics.

These three closely interdependant circles and the manner in which the collections are exhibited offer an eloquent picture of the unity of Greek tradition through the ages, not only in Greece proper, but across the whole area which received the impact of Hellenism in the course of centuries. In the field of folk art they also point to the existence of an essential affinity between neighbouring civilizations. Here are a few examples: the gold objects, which make up a separate collection, show a surprising continuity in certain techniques from the Mycenaean age to our own day. The Fayyum portraits of Greek art from Egypt (3rd and 4th centuries A.D.) refer us directly to the sources of Byzantine hagiographic portraiture. Works of religious minor art in metal, bone, wood, or gold reveal an unbroken continuity of this exquisite and costly type of craftsmanship from the early Byzantine years to the liberation of Greece in 1821. Here again, post-Byzantine minor art forms the connecting link between Byzantine art and the folk art of modern Greece. Classicizing Egyptian fabrics from the 4th to the 7th centuries A.D., of which there are many beautiful specimens in the museum, are clearly seen to lead to the museum's fine collection of Muslim fabrics of a later date, one of the largest in the world. To the discerning spectator, the relation between these fabrics and more recent Greek handwoven materials is quite evident. Finally, Byzantine ceramics, hardly distinguishable in some cases from contemporaneous Muslim ones, find their natural continuation in the ceramic works of modern Greek folk art. It is obvious that the projection of Greek art, in all its ramifications, contacts, and influences throughout the centuries, had been the collector's unwavering air.

Gold jewellery: ancient

This collection is one of the most interesting in the Benaki Museum. It includes some quite unique specimens as, for instance, the two gold cups of the third millennium B.C., which have apparently come from Northern Euboia (fig. 2). Their clearcut shapes have their counterparts in silver and ceramic ware, and so has their decoration of impressed parallel lines. Recent research in this field ascribe these cups to the transitional period between the Neolithic and the Bronze ages in Greece — the period known as Chalcolithic (3,000 B.C.). The funerary band from Kos, decorated with miniature sphinxes and rosettes, densely clustered together, is a rare example of the goldsmith's skill, worthy of Daedalic art (fig. 5a). The technique is still intensely Orientalizing, as in the jewels from Kameiros in Rhodes dating from the same period.

The fine Late Hellenistic specimens in the museum originally belonged to the so-called "Thessalian treasure", the larger part of which was donated by Mrs. H.A. Stathatos to the National Archaeological Museum (see National Archaeological Museum, figs. 99-101 and 105-106). The jewellery with its variety of techniques in filigree, granulation, and enamel, and the way in which motifs are selected and arranged, betrays a long tradition of technical skill and wisdom, and must be ascribed to the region of Macedonia. The goldsmiths living in the vicinity of Mount Pangaion where there were gold mines, were renowned for their skill throughout the centuries. The great diadem (fig. 5b) is one of the most opulent specimens both as regards the materials used and the variety of techniques involved; it is also one of the most elegant pieces of jewellery of its kind. The necklace with three rows of miniature amphorae testifies to the same high craftsmanship, albeit with a tendency to excessive elaboration, as regards the number and rows of pendants, which is typical of the 3rd century B.C. (fig. 6b). The "knot of Herakles" too was fashionable mainly during the 3rd century B.C.

Because most of the antique jewels that have come down to us were found in tombs, their subjects always have some religious significance, even when their obvious purpose is the achievement of elegance and the display of skill. On a charming earring (fig. 6a), a Muse is playing the lyre in the midst of luxuriant vegetation. On the head of a pin, of a kneeling Aphrodite — a theme common in Hellenistic art — on top of a capital is surrounded by four small Cupids (fig. 3). On a pair of earrings, hanging Cupids — those small winged infants of no particular significance — are shown wearing the garments of an Oriental god, who is a sort of a combination of Adonis and Attis (fig. 4).

Gold jewellery: Byzantine

Byzantine goldsmiths carried on the Roman technique of polychrome stones and gold leaf rather than solid gold, and also developed the enamel technique. With the help of small gold plates which outlined the design and encased the coloured enamel, it became possible to produce complete, detailed representations. This technique is known as "gold cloisonné enamel" (fig. 7d). A fairly large number of 6th and 7th century jewels, which have reached us as part of the caches or "treasures" that had been hidden away by their owners to safeguard them from invasions and raids (see Byzantine Museum, figs. 27-29 p. 334), shows that pagan elements progressively disappear, giving way to Christian symbols, such as crosses, ivy leaves, peacocks, and monograms until the main Byzantine era, when the dominant figures are finally those of Christ and various Christian saints (figs. 7d and 9).

Gold jewellery: post-Byzantine

Religious worship demanded a certain opulence in the materials used for liturgical books and sacred vessels in order to enhance their importance. Besides, the principal objects used during the Liturgy, such as the Gospel, the chalice, the incense-burners, the incense-boats, the cloth used for covering the chalice, and all the other ceremonial articles, are displayed to the congregation during the offertory procession and must therefore present an imposing appearance. This is the reason why even during Turkish rule, when money was scarce, craftsmen working in metal — mainly silver — continued to enrich the enamel used with precious stones. The same costly techniques were used for secular articles intended for the Christian and non-Christian nobility, and to this end flourishing handicraft industries existed in certain large cities. It is known that there were many fine Greek goldsmiths in Constantinople, whose work must have been of the same high quality as that of the buckle with the many inlaid stones in the elegant Persian style (fig. 8). A similar technique was used for the jewellery which was made in Constantinople in 1692 for the mother of Peter the Great of Russia and which in inventories of that period is described as "Greek handiwork". Enamel was not much used in works of this kind; as painted enamel, it was used much more extensively for the decoration of the one side of episcopal pendants, their other side being usually decorated with precious stones, such as sapphires, emeralds and diamonds, set in the characteristic style of Constantinople. A good example is the pendant of Bishop Parthenios of Caesarea, dating from 1738 (fig. 11). The same workshops are probably responsible for Parthenios' crosier, decorated with enamel and stones, and made in the same year (fig. 29).

Enamel was put to a different use on the Greek islands, where jewellery was usually made in the form of graceful ships. In marriage-contracts dating from that time, these miniature ships are referred to as "Venetika" (Venetians), which seems to point to the possibility that they may have been made in Venice by Greek goldsmiths in the 17th and 18th centuries. There is sufficient evidence supporting this possibility, for many ornaments and jewels did come from Venice during that period, and there were many Greek goldsmiths living in Venice at that time. The earrings with three-mast caravels in the museum confirm this assumption: one side of the ship's flag pictures the Lion of St. Mark, while the other bears the name of the donor: ΙΩ(άννης) ΜΠ(άος) (fig. 48). Larger enamel ships in the form of pendants, in a similar style and of the same origin, are to be found among the votive offerings in the monastery of Patmos (fig. 1).

Silverware

To return to religious ornaments, among the oldest and finest post-Byzantine works is an incense-boat of 1613 from Macedonia (fig. 27) which carries on the Byzantine tradition of using architectural forms in minor arts. In skylights, this tradition skillfully combines gold-plated silver with polychrome enamel. A similar tendency to incorporate various less distinct architectural forms may be attributed to the infuence of some incense-burners from the Northern Balkans mostly from Rumania and Transylvania, which imitate Gothic turret-shaped buildings, as in the incense-burner with a handle (fig. 28).

The covers of liturgical books are usually made of silver with embossed representations referring to the contents of the particular book (fig. 21). The degree of skill displayed in these book-covers depends very much on the region in which they were made and on how prosperous the region happened to be. Workshops in Asia Minor usually produced less refined specimens, whereas those in Western Greece betray Italian influence; in Moldovlachia, on the other hand, the over-elaborate ornamentation is often due to the influence of folk art.

Later silverwork preserved forms and types of liturgical articles which were in use in the early

Church. The Orthodox liturgy, which has remained practically unchanged through the ages, and the unbroken technical and artistic traditions of Orthodoxy have kept these forms alive in all their fundamental elements, although they each bear the distinctive marks of their time and place of origin. Thus the metal flabella   which participate in litanies and precede the offertory procession in the Great Entry during the liturgy have kept the form, even to the perforated ornamentation and decorative motifs, of their early prototypes. The finely-worked circular flabellum of 1690 (fig. 31), in addition to the usual conventional features, also includes a perforated centerpiece incised in the Persian style of the 17th century, while the technique of using gold-plated embossed motifs on a flat silver background is at least as old as classicizing Byzantine silverwork of the 6th and 7th centuries. Even the silver cross shown on fig. 32, dating as late as the 19th century, represents a continuation of the ancient tradition of large silver or bronze crosses intended for processional litanies, though it is adapted in form to the large wooden cross which usually crowns the iconostasis in post-Byzantine churches.

Sacerdotal vestments also betray a survival of old forms, not necessarily stemming from religious tradition. The bishop's mitre, though it came into general use only as late as the 16th century, retains the shape and decoration of the imperial head-dresses of the Byzantine age. A rather rare silver mitre in the museum (fig. 30) is a good example: under a series of arches, there are embossed gold-plated representations, with incised details, of the Deesis and various scenes from the Gospels. This mitre comes from the community of Argyroupolis in the Pontos, and the workmanship has that same rough quality as we find in silverware of the same period (17th century) in Georgia and the Caucasus.

Christian Egypt

The Early Christian collections from Egypt, especially of textiles and bone objects, are among the finest and largest, although there are also impressive collections of objects in bronze, wood, pottery, and other materials. Only a few pieces are shown in this volume, but they are sufficient to indicate a strong classical tradition in the Graeco-Roman and Hellenized cities of Egypt. Roman rule, which succeeded the Greeks in Egypt, encouraged the admixture of heterogeneous elements. This was an inevitable consequence of the long years of contact between the ruling Graeco-Roman world and the local religious and artistic traditions that still lived on among the upper classes of the Egyptian people. There was also some contact with African elements in the regions of the Sudan and Aswan. At times, this relationship lent a particular tone to artistic manifestations in Egypt in the early centuries of the Christian era, although on the whole, these manifestations never did move very far from the common artistic language prevailing at the time across the whole eastern basin of the Mediterranean. The funerary portraits found in considerable numbers, particularly in the Fayyum area, are typical examples. They reflect beliefs specifically related to Egyptian religion: the immortal soul, the "kâ", upon returning to the mummified body, must be able to recognize it without difficulty. But the techniques used in these innumerable portraits are the same as those used in cities as far apart as Pompei and Palmyra; in other words, these techniques followed a pattern of traditions which had influenced each other in the course of their evolution within that extensive area of the world. In the better examples, the effort is to render the human face realistically and to depict the psychological make-up and racial traits of the deceased individual. As a result, these portraits present a picture of Middle-Eastern humanity which corresponds quite closely to that of today.

The two portraits in encaustic wax technique represent two different trends. The male portrait (fig. 12) depicts with striking simplicity a complete human being: with a bit of brilliantly white cloth next to the purple face against a grey background. The face seems to project out of its narrow frame; the modelling is emphatic, and the eyes seem to gaze as if lost in memories. The hair-arrangement and various other features place it in the mid-3rd century A.D. In the second portrait, belonging to the 4th or 5th century A.D. (fig. 13), the modelling of the woman's face is more linear and the expression more extrovert; the subject was perhaps depicted full-size, which explains why her priestly gestures acquire a special significance. The hieratic Egyptian cross — the "ankh" — in her left hand may indicate that she was a Christian, for this type of cross had a double significance.

The impact of paintings in the Greek style upon decorative crafts, particularly heavy woollen handwoven materials used as wall-hangings or curtains, is shown in a piece of material representing a youthful figure in contours only; the great eyes retain, even as late as the 5th or 6th century A.D., vestiges from the painted portraits of Fayyum. The figure may have been meant to personify one of the four seasons (fig. 14).

The great thematic repertory of Egyptian textiles, that have survived in large numbers thanks to the dry soil in which they were found, often includes themes from Sassanid Persia as, for instance, the finely drawn and brilliantly coloured winged Pegasus of the 5th or 6th century A.D. (fig. 15).

Among the most characteristic products of Egyptian minor arts of Christian era, often erroneously referred to as "Coptic", are objects of carved bone. The figures which decorate these bone objects, often only in a fragmentary manner, are survivals of Greek mythology: Nereids, Silenoi, Dionysoi,

369

etc. The Benaki Museum collection, enriched by the Loukas Benakis donation, is one of the finest of its kind; but, here, a comb is singled out from the initial collection; it is carved on both sides and probably served some official function (fig. 17, top, right). The representation on each side is the personification of a city — probably Constantinople and Alexandria — in the form of an enthroned queen wearing the typical crown made of city ramparts known as a "polos". In these rather schematic seated figures, devoid of elegance, yet emanating a certain majesty, one can discern the transformation which the robust and imposing figures of Rome underwent in the course of time.

This should not be taken as a clumsy imitation of a classical prototype, but as the expression of a new aesthetic ideal, which was to characterize the art of the Middle Ages.

Small Byzantine sculptures

On the small carved plaques which were made in Constantinople during the reign of the Macedonian dynasty in the 9th and 10th centuries, the classicizing tastes of the aristocracy expressed themselves over a fairly considerable length of time in a revival of subjects and techniques from the Hellenistic and Roman traditions. The martial Saint George on an ivory plaque (fig. 17 left) is but an anaemic echo of this trend.

The small relief plaques of steatite —a soft, non-porous stone with soapy surfaces— are much more Byzantine in character. Since steatite was a much cheaper material than ivory, it became widely used during less prosperous periods, such as the 12th and 13th centuries. This stone, coming in shades of greenish grey, was covered with gold and various colours, a technique also applied to carved marble iconostases. The plaque picturing the Annunciation (fig. 17 bottom, right) retains easily visible traces of gold, red, and black paint, which seems to explain why the carving was rather carelessly done. The plaque depicting the Presentation at the Temple (fig. 18) is much more elaborate. The symmetrical composition is conventional enough, but the distinctive feature here is the triangular arrangement, emphasized by the tall arched baldachin and the slender, elegant figures, reminiscent of those produced during the late Komnenian period. The carved draperies, however, serene and rhythmical, hark back to classicizing prototypes.

Miniature painting

The two miniature paintings that decorate either side of a sheet of parchment (figs. 19-20), once belonging to a Mount Athos codex now at Dumbarton Oaks, also belong to the classicizing tradition. The codex, written and painted in 1084, contains the Psalter and the New Testament, illustrated with numerous miniature paintings taking up most of each page. It belongs to a type of Psalter known as "aristocratic", because the richness and skill of the miniature paintings and illuminated capitals, as well as the written text itself, reflect various trends of this fine art in Constantinople during the second half of the 11th century. The fine, almost weightless figures, the near-transparent draperies, the landscape with highlighted cliff-tops, are the main distinctive features in both works. Yet, in one of these, Jonah emerges from the whale, accompanied by a personification of the Deep, and the subtle gradation of colour in the landscape suggests a sense of atmospheric perspective, whereas in the second painting, picturing the Three Children in the Fiery Furnace, the composition unfolds on two parallel levels. Although both these works are by the same painter, they seem to follow different prototypes.

Icons

The revival of this classicizing tradition can best be observed in the portable icons of the Palaiologan dynasty. One that is among the better-known icons of that period represents the Hospitality of Abraham; it must have decorated the entrance to the Prothesis in the iconostasis, which explains its elongated, rectangular shape (fig. 23). The composition, a symbolic representation of the Holy Trinity, this supreme Christian doctrine, is perfectly adapted to this shape. The peaceful scene, with its gentle, ethereal, angelic figures and abstracted faces, represents a peak in the idealistic movement at the end of the 14th century. Space becomes meaningless; one can only just tell apart the plane of the angels from that of the buildings; the emphasis is on the decorative elements: the vertical and horizontal features of the conventional architectural forms enclose as in a frame the ellipsoid group of figures, and the dabs of colour dance about with a pleasing rhythm as if across a sparkling surface. (See Byzantine Museum, fig. 21, p. 337).

The 15th century triptych, representing themes from Mount Athos, such as the miraculous Virgin Portaetissa from the Iviron Monastery, Saint Paul of the Xeropotamos Monastery, and Saint Eleutherios (fig. 22), continues a trend of the Palaiologan style of painting which was in direct contrast to the classicizing tradition mentioned above. In this trend, there is a concern in giving more life to the face, without avoiding either grimacing or ugliness; this is well in keeping with the emphatic modelling and the broad, highlighted surfaces in the paintings. We have here a continuation of the anti-classical trend which we have already seen in the Christ of the Byzantine Museum (see Byzantine Museum, fig. 14, p. 366).

The tall, slender, airy figure of Saint Demetrios, with its rather sickly, expressionless, and faintly-lit face and the spindly legs, is the work of a Cretan painter of about 1500 (fig. 24). During this period, when the post-Byzantine Cretan school of painting first began to take shape, the themes and techniques appeared as a continuation of the Late Palaiologan period, quite frequently without any trace of Italian influences. However, Cretan painters were also capable of painting in the Italian style. An example of this kind of painting is the Adoration of the Magi, signed Domenikos (fig. 25). There is no reason why this painting in the Venetian manner, reminiscent of Bassano, should not be the work of the famous Cretan painter Domenico Theotocopuli, otherwise known as El Greco, painted when he was still a simple hagiographer in Crete in 1565 or thereabouts. His later apprenticeship under the great Venetian masters brought out the latent artistic potentialities which finally led him to produce works ranking among the highest in European painting.

Cretan painting, profoundly religious in content, reached its peak during the 17th century, producing a number of well-known artists. The Benaki collection of Cretan paintings includes outstanding works by both well-known and anonymous painters of the Cretan school. The icon shown on fig. 26 is the work of Theodore Poulakis, one of the most industrious Cretan painters, who divided his time between Venice and Corfu. When he wished to be up-to-date, he used as his models copper-plate engravings by the Flemish engraver Sadeler, and when he wished to be conservative, he used as models the better-known Cretan painters of the 16th century with a marked preference for George Klotzas. In this large complex icon entitled Hymn to the Virgin Mary, he was certainly inspired by a well-known icon by George Klotzas which was quite original for its time and which presented a certain narrative loquacity in its details. But, in the bottom part of the composition, Poulakis enriched his subject with additional scenes from the Second Coming, and, here, his rather baroque temperament betrays a fondness for dramatic scenes which are hardly at all Byzantine.

Asia Minor ceramics

This relatively small collection includes some of the finest products of this art from Asia Minor; the so-called Rhodian pottery, although it comes from Nicaea and Kütahya, both cities in Asia Minor, where it flourished between the 16th and 18th centuries. Here are a few typical specimens made for the Greek islands, where multicoloured ceramics were in great demand and, together with embroideries, formed the main ornaments of island homes: a plate picturing a three-mast ship with all its sails unfurled (fig. 33); an elegantly-shaped flask picturing fast-sailing boats (fig. 38); and a small jug picturing young he-goats arranged heraldically (fig. 37). All of these must certainly reflect Greek artistic tastes. The plate with the picture of a lion and a Greek religious inscription of 1666 (fig. 34) belongs to a different category. Dishes of this kind were made to be inserted into the outer walls of churches as a decorative feature. The egg-shaped objects (fig. 35-36) were also intended for churches; they were hung from chandeliers, having replaced the more common ostrich eggs. These eggs, as well as other ceramic objects for church use, of no great value, were still being made in Kütahya in the 18th century.

Embroideries

These ceramic plates introduced into the Greek home a taste of the Orient, featuring smooth flat colouring and Persian floral patterns.

The embroideries now to be discussed are the result of this acquaintance with Oriental decorative styles although they are the work of Greek women living in the islands or elsewhere in Greece. The Benaki collection of embroideries is extremely rich and contains specimens from every part of Greece; there is an enormous variety as regards geographical distribution, local tradition, and contact with other lands.

In the Skyros embroideries, the more common motifs are ships, flowers, imaginary woodcocks, young warriors brandishing swords, on foot or on horseback, and other enchanting subjects (figs. 40,43,44). All these have their own native quality, in both the strictly local and the wider Greek sense, regardless of their original ancestry. The Skyros embroideries differ considerably from those of other islands as, for instance, those of Crete, which may be polychrome or monochrome, but almost invariably contain certain steadily recurring motifs, like Gorgons and two-headed eagles amidst dense vegetation with clearly Western reverberations (figs. 41, 45). In contrast, the Jannina embroideries show a preference for Oriental floral patterns inspired from textiles, which makes them more akin to the Skyros specimens. In the wedding processions embroidered on nuptial pillow-cases, which feature richly attired horsemen, bridegrooms, brides, and attendants, the costumes are ostentatiously opulent; the prototypes in this case are to be found in the West or in Moldovlachia (fig. 42).

There is also great variety in the national costumes of Greece, whether those worn on special occasions or those intended for daily use; each region, not to say each village, had its own costume.

The Benaki Museum collection, not all of which is on show, is the most complete and important of its kind, and thus affords a good opportunity for a thorough study of the subject of Greek folk costume in all its variety. We shall only note here the unerring taste and high technical skill in the execution of the costumes as regards both the main lines, the tailoring, cutting, and sewing of each part, and the embroidered ornamentation in gold or coloured threads. These skills would indicate that the making of costumes was a professional occupation. Jannina was a famous centre of costume manufacturing, covering even export requirements for remote regions (fig. 46).

Wood-carving.   During the centuries of Turkish rule, wood-carving retained a consistently high quality, because painted and gilt wooden iconostases and other church furnishings made of wood, had replaced the marble screen of earlier periods. During the 18th century, Western Macedonia became an important wood-carving centre, serving Northern Greece and the neighbouring Balkan countries. Perhaps as a result of Western influence, it was the custom for the wealthier houses in that region to have rooms covered with finely carved wood-panelling. A reception-room of this kind from a residence in Kozani has been offered the Museum by Mrs. H.A. Stathatos (fig. 50). During that period, a certain degree of prosperity resulting from trade relations with Western Europe led to the construction of handsome large houses in the cities of Macedonia, combining in their decoration western styles with Oriental or purely local motifs. The skilled wood-carvers of Macedonia knew how to harmonize the flourishing local tradition with the cultured tastes of travelled Greeks. In this way the arts underwent a continuous process of renewal under the foreign rule that dominated the Hellenic world.

1. Pendant from Patmos, in the shape of a caravel, with gold, enamel, and pearls. Probably Venetian, 18th century.

2. *One of a pair of gold cups decorated with systems of lines. Found in Northern Euboia and probably dated to the Chalcolithic period (3000 B.C.), these cups are unique as specimens of craftsmanship in gold in that remote period between the Neolithic and the Bronze ages in Greece.*

3. *Head of a pin in the shape of a capital, upon which a miniature kneeling Aphrodite is surrounded by four small Cupids. Hellenistic, 3rd century B.C.*

4. *Earrings with pearls, inlaid stones, and small hanging Cupids wearing the attire of the Oriental god Attis. 1st century B.C.*

5. *a. Funerary band from the island of Kos, decorated with a procession of sphinxes interspersed with finely wrought rosettes. Archaic Daedalic work of admirable precision in its elaborate Orientalizing ornamentation. Mid-7th century B.C. b. Diadem featuring the 'knot of Herakles' with garnets and some enamel. From the 'Thessalian Treasure', 3rd century B.C.*

6. *a. Earrings with rosette and a hanging basket, in which a Muse, seated on a bed of foliage, is playing the lyre. Hellenistic, 4th or 3rd century B.C. b. Necklace in the form of a plaited band and small hanging amphorae in three rows; at each end, on a background of green enamel, the granulated inscription: ΖΩΙΛΑC. From the 'Thessalian Treasure', 3rd century B.C.*

2

4

a

b

c

d

7. a. Crescent-shaped earring with open work design: a monogram between two confronted peacocks; beads and small pearls. 6th-7th century A.D. b. Wide bracelet with disk of open work decoration and circular design with the 'horn of Amaltheia' (the horn of abundance) theme. Probably Syrian, 6th century A.D. c. Pair of crescent-shaped earrings with open work design: a disk with two confronted birds in a nest between two palmettes. 6th-7th century A.D. d. Ring with an enamelled representation of Christ Pantocrator in a square setting and the four beasts of the Apocalypse in small projecting disks. 12th or 13th century.

8. Belt buckle with inlaid stones in the Persian style and with the pomegranate, symbol of fertility and abundance as its motif. Greek work from Constantinople, 18th century A.D.

9. Pendant of rock crystal with Christ Pantocrator in relief. 12th or 13th century. The setting in gold and precious stones is of the 18th century.

10. Pendant in the shape of a one-masted caravel with enamel and hanging pearls. Spanish style, 16th century.

11. Bifacial pendant belonging to Metropolitan Parthenios of Caesarea, with sapphires and emeralds on the one side, and miniature painted enamel disks and inscriptions on the other. Greek specimen from Constantinople, 1738.

9

10

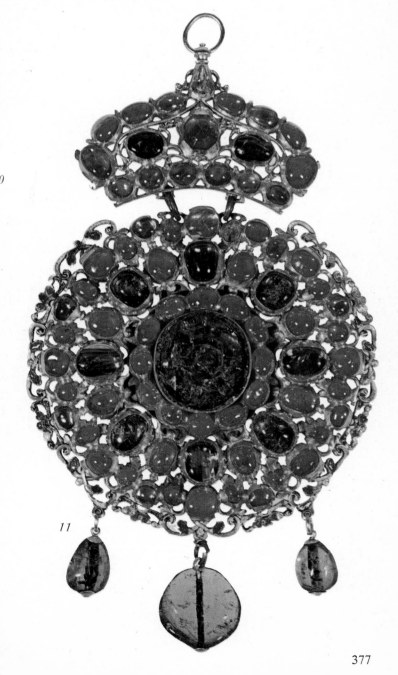

11

12. *Fayyum portrait of a young man. The portraits, which, for religious reasons, were buried with mummies in Egypt, make up the richest surviving collection of portraits of late antiquity. There are about 800 of them. The dark young man of this portrait, painted on linen in 'encaustic' technique, is one of the finest specimens of its kind. Mid– 3rd century A.D.*

13. *Fayyum portrait of a young woman. The flattened picture and the rather abstracted expression are well-suited to the frontal position and the formal apotropaic gesture. In her left hand the woman is holding the Egyptian cross, the 'ankh'. Female martyrs in Byzantine and post-Byzantine icons are shown in exactly the same posture.*

13

14

15

14. Representation of a female head—possibly the personification of one of the four seasons—clearly influenced by the painting of the Fayyum portraits, on a 'Coptic' woollen fabric. 5th or 6th century A.D.

15. 'Coptic' fabric from Egypt, with the Pegasus theme in the Persian-Sassanid manner under evident Greek influence. 5th or 6th century A.D.

16. Gold-embroidered fabric, the 'aer' used for covering the chalice and paten in the Eucharist, with a symbolic representation of the communion of the Apostles: Christ, under a baldachin, is shown holding a chalice; on his left and right, two Cherubim; a liturgical inscription on the border. 14th century.

16

17. Left: Small ivory plaque with representation in relief of St. George, standing. 10th century. Top, right: Bifacial comb made of bone: on one side, a female figure, seated on a throne with ciborium, is holding an orb and a spear; on the other side, a similar figure, less well preserved, is holding a horn of abundance and a palm-frond; she wears a 'polos' on her head. This type of figure was used for the personification of cities; the technique is of the imperial tradition. 5th or 6th century A.D. Bottom, right: Small steatite plaque, representing the Annunciation under a double arch. In the upper section, fragment of a figure; traces of gold and various colours. 12th-13th century.

18. Small steatite plaque with a peacefully symmetrical representation of the Presentation at the Temple; incised draperies worn by the tall figures. Last quarter of the 12th century.

19-20. Two pages from a Psalter. One page pictures Jonah's Ode: the Prophet, attended by a personification of the Deep, is shown emerging from the whale and praying in an idyllic landscape; in the background, a half-hidden villa amidst the delicately graded shades of the mountains. In contrast to this classicizing representation, the picture of the Three Children in the Fiery Furnace on the reverse is paratactically arranged in two dimensions. 11th century.

21. Gospel with silver cover from Saranda Ekklisies in Thrace. Gilt filigree decoration with characteristic enamels from that region. Crucifixion, Resurrection, the Twelve Feasts and the four beasts of the Apocalypse. Late 18th century.

22

23

24

22. *Triptych with the Virgin Mary the 'Portaetissa' from the Iviron Monastery, Saint Paul from the Xeropotamos Monastery and Saint Eleutherios. The blood on Mary's cheek refers to a miracle when the icon was struck by a Saracen on Mount Athos. 15th century.*

23. *The Hospitality of Abraham on an icon of the Palaeologan period: the gentle grace of the angelic figures and the luminous colours alternating with a few darker shades add a poetic touch to this symbolic scene. Late 14th century.*

24. *Saint Demetrios, full-size, holding a lance and shield. The cross was added at a later date. The tall, slender figure of the young warrior, painted around 1500, is in the tradition of the thin, elongated warrior saints of the 14th-15th century.*

25. The Adoration of the Magi. This is a work in the Venetian style, with the usual motif of ruins, the Magi and their retinue on horseback. The signature: *ΧΕΙΡ ΔΟΜΗΝΙΚΟΥ* (by the hand of Domenikos) may well belong to the famous Cretan painter Domenico Theotocopuli, better known as El Greco (1541-1614), who was still living in Crete in the year 1565. Many Cretan painters painted in both the Byzantine and the Italian styles at that time.

26. This complex icon by the Cretan painter Theodore Poulakis comprises scenes from the Genesis, the life of the Virgin Mary, the Dodecaorton (Twelve Feasts), the Second Judgement, etc., arranged in concentric circles. The signature reads: 'Being the result of the labour and art of Theodore Poulakis from Kydonia in the celebrated island of Crete'. 17th century.

25

26

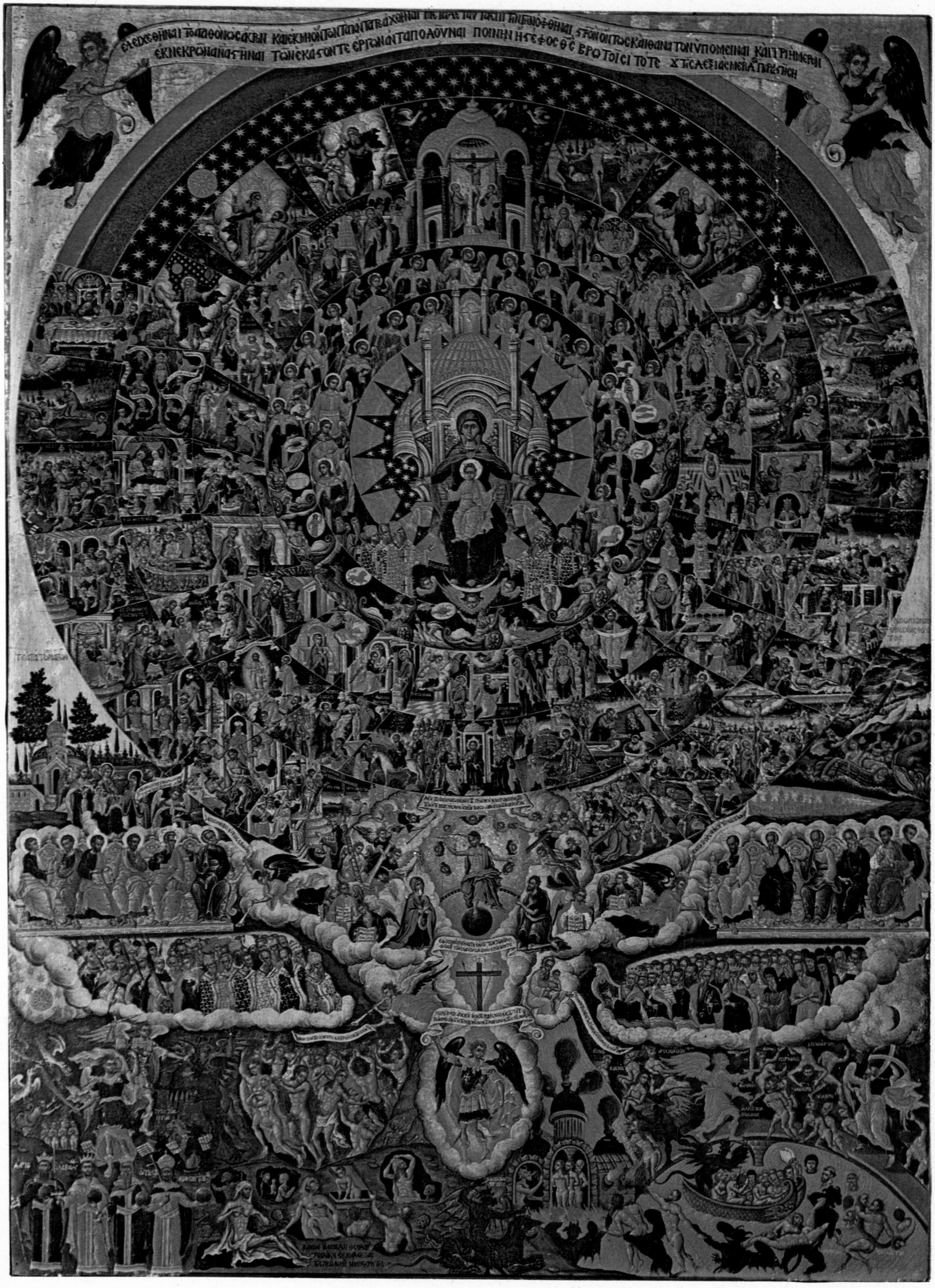

27. *Incense-boat of gold-plated silver and enamel in the shape of a small domed chapel. From the Monastery of St. John the Baptist at Serres, 1613.*

28. *Censer with handle, with embossed representations on the handle and architectural elements on the domed lid. From the collection of relics from Asia Minor, 18th century.*

29. *Pastoral staff with rubies and enamel from Constantinople, belonging to Metropolitan Parthenios of Caesarea. From the collection of relics from Asia Minor, 1738.*

30. *Silver mitre with gilt representations of an Invocation and various saints, probably dating from the 17th century, but restored in 1791. From Argyroupolis, the see of Chaldia in the Pontos.*

31. *Silver litany flabellum with gilt representations and an open work background. From the relics of Asia Minor, 1690.*

32. *19th century cross, from the collection of relics from Asia Minor.*

29

30

31

32

33. Plate from Nicaea in Asia Minor, with a three-mast schooner, all sails unfurled, and designs on the border copied from Chinese plates. 16th or 17th century.

34. Plate, of the kind made for use in churches, decorated with a lion and Oriental flowers. The Greek inscription on the border reads: 'Sun of justice, Christ of our thoughts, our God. 25th May 1666'.

35-36. Ceramic eggs from a church chandelier, picturing a two-headed eagle and Seraphim. From Kütahya in Asia Minor, 18th century.

37. Jug with painted confronted he-goats and Oriental flowers. Asia Minor pottery from Nicaea, 16th century.

38. Flask with painted ships. Asia Minor pottery from Nicaea, 16th century.

33

34

39

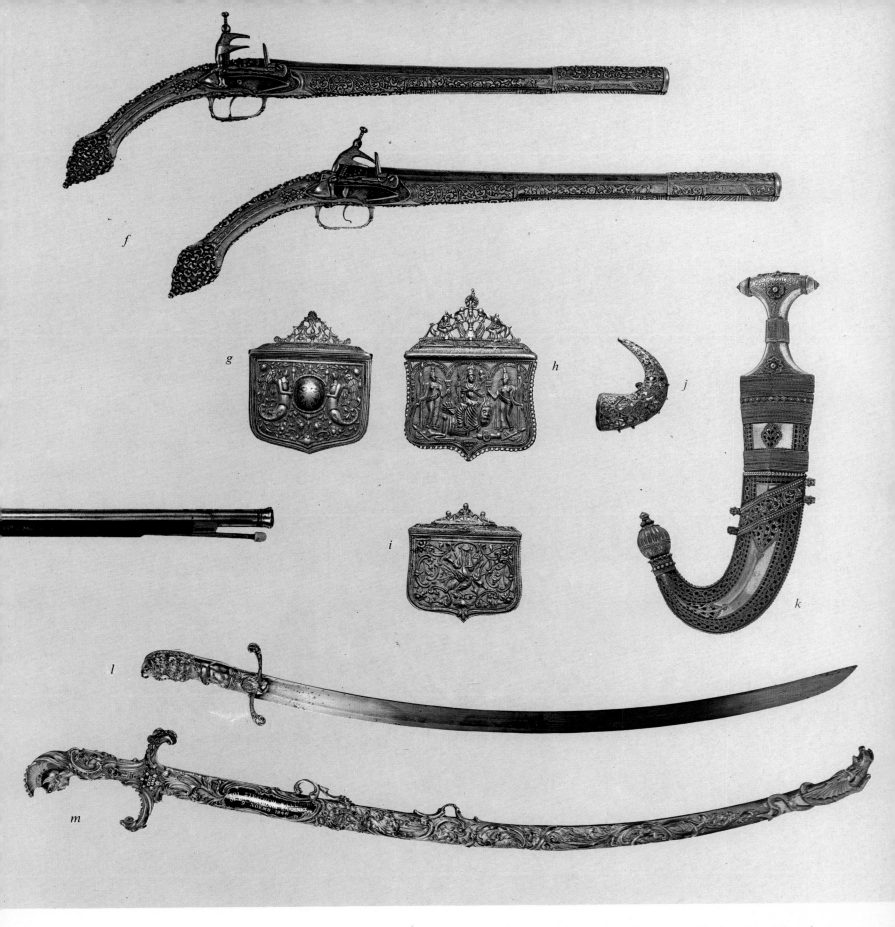

39 a-m. Gun, swords, pistols, and cartridge-cases from the Greek War of Independence and the reign of King Otto. (Several of the arms belonging to the fighters of the War of Independence were spoils of war). a. Sword belonging to Nikolas Petimezas. b. Yataghan belonging to Admiral Yakoumis Tombazis. c. Yataghan with decorated silver scabbard, belonging to the Suliot Photis Tzavellas. d. Muzzle-loader belonging to Nikolas Petimezas; the butt-end is decorated with inlaid mother-of-pearls. e. Pair of pistols decorated with coral. f. Pair of pistols, with embossed silver ornamentation, belonging to Petrobey Mavromichalis. g. Cartridge-case with embossed Gorgon motif, 19th c. h. Cartridge-case, with a representation of Athena between two personifications, belonging to Petrobey Mavromichalis. i. Cartridge-case with embossed decoration. j. Oriental gunpowder-case. k. Dagger with curved blade. l. Sword belonging to General Demetrios Kallergis, with a lion's head in the Classical style decorating the hilt. m. Sword offered to General Demetrios Kallergis by the Greeks of London in 1846 in appreciation of his part in the revolution of 3rd September, 1843.

40

42

41

43

44

45

46

40. *Bedspread from Skyros picturing a horseman who wears 'Frankish' clothes and holds two swords. On the bottom part, a pot of flowers forming a border. 18th-19th century.*

41. *Cushion from Crete. The motif of a Gorgon holding her forked tail dates from ancient Greece, whereas the two-headed eagle is Byzantine. 18th-19th century.*

42. *Nuptial cushion-cover from Jannina: in the centre, the bride and her parents; on the left and right of the group, the bridegroom is shown arriving on horseback; costumes in the Moldovlachian fashion; Oriental flowers in the background, 18th century.*

43. *Cushion from Skyros: a three-mast war schooner embroidered in silk: birds, small human figures, and other motifs in the background. 18th-19th century.*

44. *Detail from a Skyros bedspread: woodcocks in a row within a fanciful setting created by the juxtaposition of flowers and animals in the decoration. 18th-19th century.*

45. *Embroidered border from a Cretan bedspread: two-headed eagles among pots of flowers and other birds. The decoration reflects Western influences. 18th-19th century.*

46. *Sleeveless overcoat from Epeiros with gold embroidery on red felt. 19th century.*

47. *Top: Belt buckle from Epeiros in gold-plated silver filigree. 19th c. Bottom: Belt buckle, from Saframpolis in Asia Minor, of gold-plated silver with semi-precious stones and pieces of coral. 19th century.*
48. *Top left: Earrings in the shape of three-mast caravels hanging from bows. The elegant design and the fine workmanship in gold and enamel reflect Western rococo tendencies. From Siphnos, early 18th c. Bottom left: Earrings with bow and filigree pendants decorated with enamel. From an Aegean island. 18th century? Right: Long earrings, meant to frame the face like the Byzantine imperial 'perpendulia'. Filigree technique with mobile pendent elements. From the island of Kos, 18th century.*

47

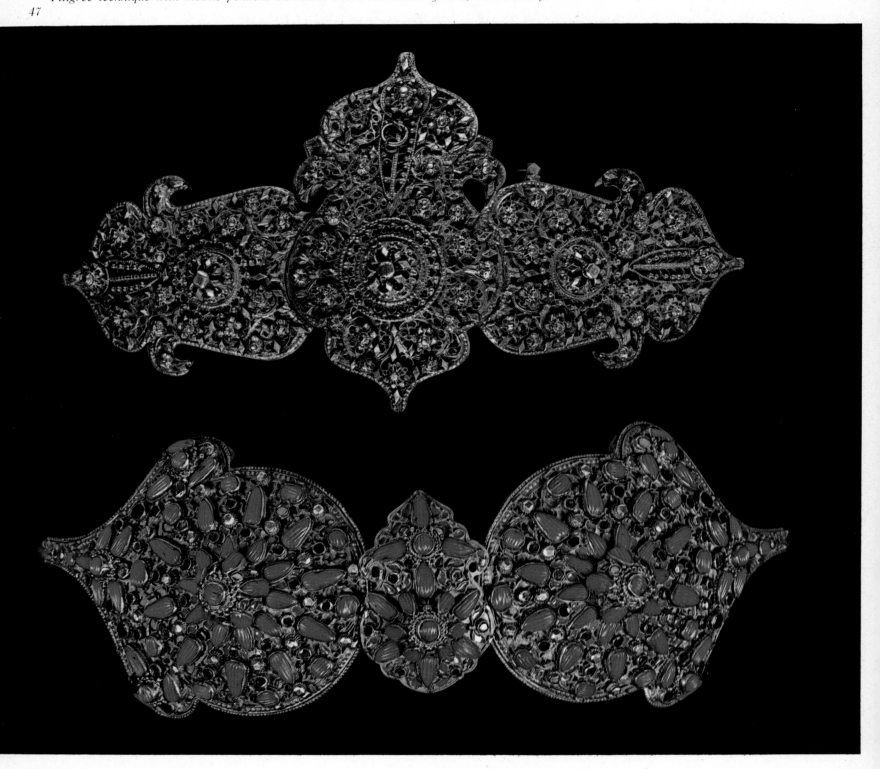

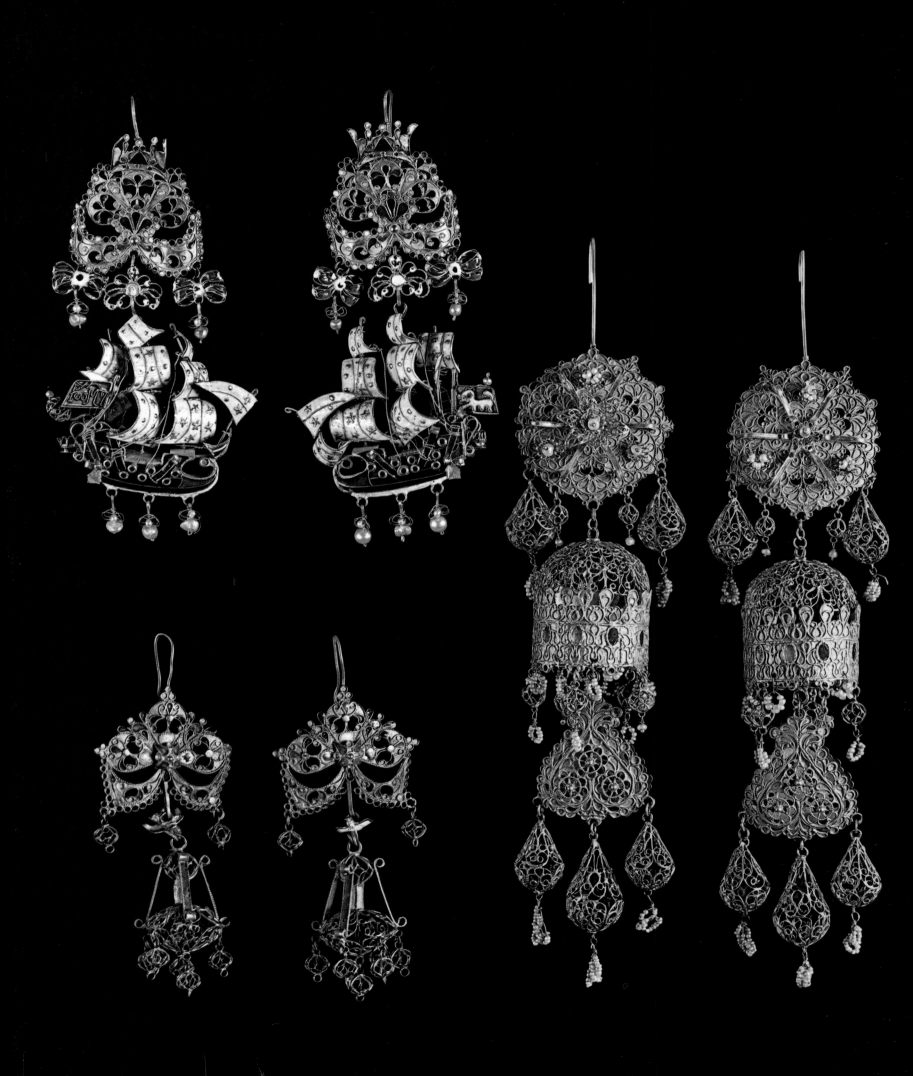

49. *Open work distaff with a representation of Saint George and the inscription: 'Memento 1920'.*

50. *Carved wood-panelling from a reception-room in an upper-class Kozani house, indicative both of the prosperity of that region at the end of the 18th century and of the fine work of Macedonian wood-carvers whose main occupation was the carving of iconostases for churches throughout the Balkans.*

49

51. Chest from Skyros, painted in gold and various colours, used for the transportation of bottles containing precious fluids. 18th-19th century.

51

TABLE OF CONTENTS

Publisher's Preface   7

Introduction . . . .   9 - 16

The Museums of Greece, 9. The Stone Age, 10. The Bronze Age, 10. The
first appearance of the Hellenes, 11. Minoan civilization reaches
its peak, 11. Mycenaean civilization, 11. The end of Mycenae and the
emergence of geometric art, 12. Eastern influences, 12. The Archaic
period, 12. Classical art, 13. The Hellenistic period, 14. Byzantine art,
14. The survival of Greek civilization, 15.

National Archaeological Museum . . . .   17 - 106

History of the Museum, 19. The Neolithic and Helladic civilizations, 20.
Cycladic civilization, 20. The Thera frescoes, 21. Mycenaean civilization,
22. The treasures of the royal shaft graves, 23. The Vapheio cups, 23.
The gravestones, 23. Frescoes, vase-painting and sculpture, 23 - 24.
The end of the Mycenaean era. Geometric art, 24. Assimilation of
Oriental influences, 24. Black-figure vases, 26. Red-figure vase-
painting, 27. White-ground vases. White-ground lekythoi, 28. Sculpture.
The different kinds of Greek sculpture, 29. The earliest Greek
sculpture, 30. Archaic Kouroi, 30. The Piraeus Apollo, 31. The Poseidon
of Artemision, 32. 4th century B.C. bronze statues, 32. Sculptured
female figures, 33. Reliefs, 34. Pedimental sculptures, 34. Attic
gravestones of the Archaic period, 35. Gravestones from other parts
of Greece, 36. Attic funerary reliefs of the Classical period, 36.
Votive reliefs, 37. Portraiture, 38. Hellenistic sculpture, 39. Metal
works. The minor arts, 39. Jewellery, 40. The Numismatic collection, 40.
Figures (1 - 120) pp. 43 - 106.

Acropolis Museum . . . .   107 - 148

History, 109. Archaic period, 109. The Periklean plan,
110. The Parthenon, 110. The Propylaia, 111. The temple of
Athena Nike, 112. The Erechtheion, 112. The Museum, 113.
Archaic pedimental sculptures, 113. Early Archaic votive offerings,

114. The Archaic Korai, 114. The pediment of the temple of the Peisistratidai, 115. From Archaic to Classical art, 115. The Parthenon sculptures, 116. The sculptures from the parapet of the temple of Athena Nike, 116.
Figures (1 - 40) pp. 117 - 148.

Delphi Museum . . . .   149 - 182

Delphic myths, 151. The site, 151. The history of Delphi, 152. The Hellenistic period, 152. The growing fame of the Delphic Oracle, 153. The Sanctuary of Athena Pronaia, 154. The Sanctuary of Apollo, 154. The excavations, 155. The Museum. Kleobis and Biton, 155. The metopes of the Treasury of the Sikyonians, 156. The Siphnian treasury, 156. Pedimental sculptures, 156. The frieze, 156. The treasury of the Athenians, 157. The Charioteer, 157. The votive offering of Daochos, 158. The "dancers", 158. Hellenistic and Roman votive offerings, 158.
Figures (1 - 32) pp. 159 - 182.

Olympia Museum . . . .   183 - 216

The ancient cult and myths of Olympia, 185. The Olympic games, 186. The significance of the games in Greek history, 186. Architectural arrangement of the sanctuary, 187. Excavations and research, 187. The Museum. The pediments of the temple of Zeus, 187. The metopes of the temple of Zeus, 188. Archaic sculptures, 189. Clay sculpture in the severe style, 189. The Nike of Paionios, 189. The Hermes of Praxiteles, 190. The bronze statuettes, 190. Bronze sheets, 190. Bronze weapons, 191. Breast-plates, 191. Greaves and helmets, 191. Shield devices, 192. Architectural bronzes, 192. Tripods, 192.
Figures (1 - 36) pp. 193 - 216.

Herakleion Museum . . . .   217 - 250

A brief history of the Museum, 219. The Minoan Palaces, 219. Neolithic and Pre-Palace period, 220. Old Palace period, 220. New Palace period, 220. The collections of the Museum, 221. Pottery and vase-painting, 221. The Kamares Ware, 221. Floral and Marine style, 221. Palace style, 222. Stone-carving, 222. Stone vases with representations in relief, 222. Seal-engraving, 222. Minor sculpture, 223. Work in gold, 223. Metal-work, 223. Wall-paintings, 223. Wall painting in low relief, 224. The large frescoes, 224. The sarcophagus of Hagia Triada, 224. Sub-Minoan phase, 224. Archaic Greek art, 225.
Figures (1 - 41) pp. 227 - 250.

Pella Museum . . . .   251 - 264

The birth of the Macedonian kingdom, 253. Pella, the new capital of the Macedonians, 253. The excavations of Pella, 254. The Museum, 255. The mosaics, 255.
Figures (1 - 8) pp. 257 - 264.

Archaeological Museum of Thessalonike .... 265 - 290

Prehistoric times in Northern Greece, 267. From the Mycenaean age to the Archaic period, 268. The influence of Ionic art in Northern Greece, 268. The rise of the Macedonian kingdom and the foundation of Thessalonike, 268. The exhibits at the Museum of Thessalonike, 269. Prehistoric exhibits, 269. The finds at Olynthos, 269. Sculptures from the Archaic and Classical ages, 270. Roman copies of Classical works, 270. The krater of Derveni and other finds discovered in tobms, 270. Roman sculptures, 271. Glass vases, 272. Mosaics, 272.
Figures (1 - 32) pp. 275 - 290.

Cyprus Museum .... 291 - 324

History of the Museum, 293. Cypriot civilization, 293. Neolithic period, 293. Bronze Age, 294. Mycenaean period, 294. Historical period, 294. Sculpture, 295. Neolithic figurines, 295. Clay-modelling, 295. Bronze statues, 296. Archaic terracotta figurines, 296. Monumental sculpture, 296. Neolithic pottery, 297. Bronze Age pottery, 297. Mycenaean vases, 298. Geometric and 'free-field' style, 298. Metal vases, 299. Gold and silver jewellery, 299. The minor arts, 300.
Figures (1 - 42) pp. 301 - 324.

Byzantine Museum .... 325 - 362

Introductory note, 327. The Byzantine heritage, 327. The expanse of Byzantine art, 328. Constantinople, 328. The dual origins of Byzantine art, 328. The cyclical recurrence of traditions. Byzantine 'philanthropy', 329. The classical revivals, 329. Islamic influences, 330. The historical framework of Byzantine art, 330. Architecture, 330. Sculpture, 331. Monumental painting. Mosaics. Wall-paintings, 331. Portative icons, 332. Miniatures, 332. The Museum, 333. The collections, 333. Early Christian works (4th - 7th century), 334. Art of the Middle Byzantine period in Greece (8th - 12th century), 334. The Frankish occupation and the Palaiologan period (1204 - 1453), 335. Icons, 336. The classical revival, 336. The arts after the fall of Constantinople. Cretan icons, 337. Popular painting in the 18th century, 338. Minor arts, 338.
Figures (1 - 39) pp. 339 - 362.

Benaki Museum .... 363 - 404

The Building, 365. The Benaki collections and the founding of the museum, 365. Anthony Benaki's personal contribution, 365. The spirit of an age, 366. The donors, 366. The exhibits, 367. Gold jewellery : ancient, 367. Gold jewellery : Byzantine, 368. Gold jewellery : post-Byzantine, 368. Silverware, 369. Christian Egypt, 369. Small Byzantine sculptures, 370. Miniature painting, 370. Icons, 370. Asia Minor ceramics, 371. Embroideries, 371. Wood-carving, 372.
Figures (1 - 51) pp. 373 - 404.

LIST OF ILLUSTRATIONS

The upright numerals refer to pages of illustrations and the numerals in italic to pages of the text.

NATIONAL MUSEUM

1. Head of the Poseidon of Artemision, 43, *32*.
2. Clay idol of a seated male figure; from Thessaly (h. 50 cm.), 44, *20*.
3. Neolithic vase from Dimeni (h. 25.5 cm.), 44, *20*.
4. Neolithic vase from Lianokladi (h. 14.4 cm.), 44, *20*.
5. Stone idol of a female corpulent figure (h. 15 cm.), 45, *20*.
6. Marble idol of a harpist from Keros (h. 22.5 cm.), 46, *21*.
7. Marble idol of a flute-player from Keros (h. 20 cm.), 46, *21*.
8. Large marble statue of a female figure from Amorgos (h. 1.52 m.), 47, *21*.
9. Clay object in the shape of a frying-pan from Syros (h. 30 cm.), 47, *21*.
10. Stone utensil with lid from Naxos (h. 7.2 cm.), 47.
11. The fresco of the Boxing Children from Thera, 48, *22*.
12. The fresco of the Fisherman from Thera, 49, *22*.
13. Fresco of the Antelopes from Thera, 50, *22*.
14. The 'lady', fresco from the House of the Ladies at Thera, 51.
15. The fresco of the Spring from Thera, 51, *21*.
16 - 17. The fresco of the Naval Campaign from Thera (preserved length 6 m.), 52 - 53, *22*.
18. Gold rhomboidal sheet (l. 65 cm.) and 7 lance-shaped laminae from Mycenae, 54, *23*.
19. Hexagonal wooden pyxis covered with plates of gold from Mycenae (8 × 8.5 cm.), 54.
20. Gold funerary mask from Mycenae (h. 26 cm.), 55, *23*.
21, 22. The two gold cups from Vapheio in Lakonia (h. 8 cm.), 56, *23*.
23. Silver rhyton in the shape of a bull's head (h. 15. 5 cm. without horns), 57, *23*.
24. Gold sword-handle from Staphylos in Skopelos (l. 24 cm.), 58, *23*.
25. Bronze dagger with elaborate gold handle (l. 11.5 cm.), 58, *23*.
26. Bronze dagger with inlaid gold spirals (l. 24.3 cm.), 59, *23*.
27. Bronze dagger with inlaid gold lions (l. 21.4 cm.), 59, *23*.
28. Bronze dagger with gold handle from Pylos (l. 32 cm.), 59, *23*.
29. Bronze dagger with inlaid gold marine nautili from Pylos (l. 25 cm.), 59, *23*.
30. Bronze dagger with inlaid panthers and birds (preserved l. 16.3 cm.), 59, *23*.
31. Bronze dagger with inlaid hunting scene in gold (l. 23.8 cm.), 59, *23*.
32. Gold rhyton in the shape of a lion's head (h. 20 cm.), 60, *23*.
33. Gold signet-ring from Tiryns (w. 5.6 cm.), 61.
34. Gold seal-stone from Mycenae (2.2 × 1.5 cm.), 61.
35. Gold head of a silver pin from Mycenae (h. 6.7 cm.), 61.
36. Rock-crystal vessel in the shape of a duck (l. 13.2 cm.), 61.
37. Ivory head of a warrior carved in relief (h. 8.3 cm.), 62, *24*.
38. Ivory group : 'The Ladies and Boy from Mycenae' (h. 7.8 cm.), 62, *24*.
39. Limestone head of a sphinx (?) (h. 16.8 cm.), 63, *24*.
40. The Warrior Vase from Mycenae (h. 41 cm.), 64, *24*.
41. The Mycenaean Woman, fresco from Mycenae, 65, *24*.
42. Geometric amphora from the Dipylon Gate, Kerameikos (h. 1.55 m.), 66, *25*.
43. Geometric krater from the Dipylon Gate, Kerameikos (h. 1.23 m.), 66, *25*.
44. 'Melian' amphora (h. 95 cm.), 67, *26*.
45. The Nessos amphora from Dipylon Gate, Kerameikos (h. 1.22 m.), 68, *26*.
46, 47, 48. Sculptured vases in the shape of human heads (h. 12 - 13 cm.), 69.
49. Painted wooden tablet from the cave of Pitsa, near Corinth (15 × 30 cm.), 69, *38*.
50. Red-figure *pelike* (h. 37 cm.), 70, *28*.
51. Red-figure calyx-krater (h. 44 cm.), 70.
52. Red-figure *stamnos* (h. 43 cm.), 71.
53. Panathenaic amphora (h. 73 cm.), 71, *27*.
54. The *epinetron* of Eretria (l. 29 cm.), 71, *28*.
55. White-ground *lekythos*. Young spearman in front of gravestone (h. 49 cm.), 72, *28*.
56. White-ground *lekythos*. The dead man is depicted sitting on the base of the stele (h. 49 cm.), 73, *29*.
57. White-ground *lekythos*. Charon in his boat and Hermes (h. 36 cm.), 73.
58. The Dipylon Head (h. 42 cm.), 74, *30*.
59. The Kouros of Volomandra (h. 1.79 m.), 74, *30*.
60. 'Kroisos', Archaic Kouros from Anavyssos (h. 1.94 m.), 75, *31*.
61. 'Aristodikos', Archaic Kouros from Anavyssos (h. 1.98 m.), 75, *31*.
62. The Diskophoros Head, part of an Archaic gravestone (h. 34 cm.), 76, *35*.
63. Stele of the Running Hoplite (h. 1 m.), 76, *35*.
64. The stele of Aristion (h. 2.40 m.), 76, *36*.
65. The Piraeus Apollo, bronze statue (h. 1.92 m.), 77, *31*.
66. Statue base with carved representations of young athletes (w. 79, h. 29 cm.), 78.
67. Statue base with procession of chariots and hoplites in relief (w. 60, h. 28 cm.), 78.
68. The Poseidon of Artemision, bronze statue (h. 2.09 m.), 79, *32*.
69. The great Eleusinian votive relief (h. 2.20, w. 1.52 m.), 80, *37*.
70. A youth crowning himself, votive stele (h. 48, w. 49.5 cm.), 81, *37*.
71. Gravestone of a youth from Salamis (h. 104, w. 81 cm.), 81, *37*.
72. Gravestone of Hegeso (h. 1.49 m.), 82, *37*.
73. The stele of Ilisos (h. 1.68 m.), 82, *37*.
74. The funerary temple-shaped edifice of Aristonautes (total h. 2.91, w. 1.55, h. of figure 2 m.), 83, *37*.
75. Nereid on horseback, *akroterion* from the temple of Asklepios at Epidauros (h. 78 cm.), 84, *35*.
76. Votive relief. The hero Echelos on his four-horse chariot abducting the heroine Basile (h. 75, w. 88 cm.), 84, *38*.
77. The head of Hygeia from Tegea (h. 28.5 cm.), 85, *33*.
78. The Ephebe of Antikythera, bronze statue (h. 1.94 m.), 86, *33*.
79. Bronze statue of Athena found at Piraeus 1959 (h. 2.35 m.), 87, *33*.
80. Bronze statue of Artemis found at Piraeus 1959 (h. 1.50 m.), 87, *34*.
81 - 82. The Boy of Marathon, bronze statue and detail (h. 1.24 m.), 88 - 89, *33*.
83. Bronze head of a boxer from Olympia (h. 28 cm.), 90, *38*.
84. Bronze head of a philosopher found in the sea at Antikythera (h. 29 cm.), 90, *38*.
85. Bronze head of a man found in the palaistra at Delos (h. 32.5 cm.), 91, *38*.
86. Marble statue of the goddess Themis, found in the temple at Rhamnous (h. 2.22 m.), 92, *34*.
87. The Poseidon of Melos (h. 2.45 m.), 92, *39*.

88. Group including Aphrodite and Pan, found at Delos (h. 1.32 m.), 93, *39*.
89. Large relief of a horse and a little black groom (h. 2m.), 94, *39*.
90. Bronze horse and jockey boy of Artemision (h. of horse 2.05 m., 1. without tail 2.50 m., h. of boy 84 cm.), 95, *39*.
91. Bronze figurine of a horse with its base (h. 14 cm.), 96, *40*.
92. Bronze bust of a griffin from Olympia (h. 26 cm.), 96, *40*.
93. Bronze statuette of Zeus from Dodone (h. 11.5 cm.), 96, *40*.
94. Bronze rider from Dodone (h. of the horse 11, of the rider 9.5 cm.), 96, *40*.
95. Bronze idol of Athena in the Promachos type, from the Acropolis (h. 30 cm.), 97, *40*.
96. Bronze head of Zeus from Olympia (h. 17 cm.), 98, *40*.
97. Bronze head of a youth from the Acropolis (h. 13 cm.), 98, *40*.
98. Cheek-piece of bronze helmet from Dodone; representation of two warriors (h. 17 cm.), 99.
99. Gold object in the form of a little temple; high relief representation of Dionysos and Satyr (14.5×9 cm.), 100, *40*.
100. Gold bracelet terminating in bulls' heads (w. 12.5 cm.), 101, *40*, *368*.
101 a - b. Two gold bracelets in the form of a snake (diam. : left 7.5, right 6 cm.), 101, *40*, *368*.
102. Gold earrings with precious stones (h. 7.5 and 6.8 cm.), 102, *40*.
103. Gold Byzantine earring with precious stones (h. 2.5 cm.), 102, *40*.
104. Two small gold clasps (l. 4.8 cm.), 102, *40*.
105. Gold diadem from Thessaly (circumference 50 cm.), 102, *40*.
106. Gold medallion with bust of Artemis (diam. 11.5 cm.), 103, *40*.
107. Gold necklace with bulls' heads and acorns (l. 39 cm.), 103, *40*.
108. Tetradrachm, Athens, 104, *40*.
109. Tetradrachm, Mende, 104, *40*.
110. Tetradrachm, Rhodes, 104, *40*.
111. Gold stater, Pantikapaion, 104, *40*.
112. Tetradrachm of Philip II, 104, *40*.
113. Stater of Amphiktyonic League, 104, *40*.
114. Tetradrachm of Lysimachos, 105, *40*.
115. Gold stater with the head of Titus Quinctus Flamininus, 105, *40*.
116. Tetradrachm of Perseus, 105, *40*.
117. Tetradrachm, Smyrna, 105, *40*.
118 - 119. Gold octadrachm of Ptolemy V, 105, *40*.
120. Cameo of sardonyx probably representing Alexander the Great (19×23 mm.), 106, *40*.

ACROPOLIS MUSEUM

1. The Karyatids of Erechtheion, 117, *113*.
2. The Parthenon, NW view, 118 - 119, *110*.
3. The temple of Athena Nike, 120, *112*.
4 - 12. The western side of the Parthenon frieze. Slabs and details (h. of frieze 1.06 m.), 121 - 129, *111*.
13. Poros pediment; Herakles overcoming the Lernaian Hydra (0.80×5.32 m.), 130 - 131, *114*.
14. Large poros pediment; Herakles and Triton, the 'Three-headed Demon' (preserved lengths 3.53 and 3.40 m.), 130 - 131, *113*.
15. Marble votive relief with 4 horses, 130.
16. Archaic marble Sphinx (h. 73 cm.), 131.
17. The 'Calf-Bearer', archaic marble statue (h. 1.65 m.), 132, *114*.
18. The 'Rampin Horseman' (h. 1.105 m.), 133, *144*.
19. Marble statue of a hound (1. 1.25 m.), 133, *144*.
20. The 'Kore of Antenor' (h. 2 m.), 134, *114*.
21. Athena from the pediment of the temple of the Peisistratidai (detail), 135, *115*.
22. The 'Peplos Kore' (h. 1.20 m.), 136, *114*.
23. Archaic Kore (h. 1.225 m.), 136.
24. Kore called 'Maiden of Chios' (h. 55 cm.), 137.
25. Small head of Kore no. 643 (h. 14.5 cm.), 137, *114*.
26. Kore, wholly preserved (h. 1.15 m.), 138.
27. Archaic Kore no. 674, 'the Kore with the almond eyes', (h. 92 cm.), 138, *115*.
28. The 'Euthydikos Kore' (h. of the upper half 58 cm.), 139, *115*.
29. Votive relief with dance representation (h. 39.5 cm.), 140.
30. Head of the Kore no. 674, 141, *145*.
31. Statue of a horse, the fore part (h. 1.13 m.), 142, *115*.
32 - 33. Head of 'the Blond Youth' (h. 24.5 cm.), 142 - 143, *116*.
34. The 'Kritios Boy' (h. 86 cm.), 143, *115*.
35. Relief of the 'Mourning Athena' (h. 54 cm.), 144.
36. Slab from the north side of the Parthenon frieze; three youths lead two oxen (h. 1.06 m.), 145, *111*.
37. Slab from the north side of the Parthenon frieze; six men carry olive-branches (h. 1.06 m.), 145, *111*.
38. Slab from the eastern side of the Parthenon frieze; Poseidon, Apollo, Artemis (h. 1.06 m.), 146, *111*, *116*.
39. Slab from the north side of the Parthenon frieze; three 'hydria-bearers' (h. 1.06 m.), 147, *111*.
40. 'Nike unlacing her sandal', from the parapet of the Nike Temple (h. 1.06 m.), 148, *112*, *116*.

DELPHI MUSEUM

1. The Delphic *omphalos* (navel-stone) (h. 98 cm.), 159, *151*.
2. Kleobis and Biton, two Argive Kouroi (h. 2.16 m.), 160, *155*.
3. Metope from the Sikyonian Treasury; Polydeukes, Kastor and Idas leading oxen (h. 58, original w. 87 cm.), 161, *156*.
4. Flying Victory, *akroterion* of the Archaic temple of Apollo (h. 1.135 m.), 162.
5. 'Karyatid' from the Siphnian Treasury (h. 1.65 m.), 162, *156*.
6. The Sphinx of the Naxians (h. 2.22 m.), 163, *156*.
7. The east pediment of the Siphnian Treasury; dispute between Herakles and Apollo over the Delphic tripod (h. 0.74, l. 5.83 m.), 164 - 165, *156*.
8. Assembly of gods, from the eastern frieze of the Siphnian Treasury (h. 64 cm.), 164 - 165, *156*.
9. Battle between Greeks and Trojans, from the eastern frieze of the Siphnian Treasury (h. 64 cm.), 166, *156*.
10. Gigantomachy, from the north frieze of the Siphnian Treasury (h. 64 cm.), 167, *156*, *157*.
11 - 12. Gigantomachy, from the north frieze of the Siphnian Treasury (h. 64 cm.), 166 - 167, *156*, *157*.
13 - 15. Details from the north frieze of the Siphnian Treasury 168 - 170, *157*.
16. Four-horse chariot, from the south frieze of the Siphnian Treasury (h. 64 cm.), 171.
17. Theseus and Antiope, metope from the south side of the Athenian Treasury (67×63 cm.), 172, *157*.
18. Herakles and Kyknos, metope from the north side of the Athenian Treasury (67×63 cm.), 172 - 173, *157*.
19. Herakles overcoming the Kerynitian stag, metope from the north side of the Athenian Treasury (67×63 cm.), 173, *157*.
20 - 21. The Charioteer of Delphi, bronze statue and detail (h. 1.80 m.), 174 - 175, *157*.

22. Column with three girls dancing (total h. 13 m.), 176, *158*.
23. Statue of Agias dedicated by Daochos (h. 1.97 m.), 177, *158*.
24. Statue of a philosopher (h. 2.17 m.), 177, *158*.
25. Portrait, perhaps of the Roman general Flamininus (h. 27 cm.), 178, *158*.
26. The statue of Antinoos (h. 1.80 m.), 179, *158*.
27. Bronze head of a griffin (h. 21 cm.), 180.
28. Bronze idol representing Odysseus (?) under a ram (l. 9.1 cm.), 180.
29. Bronze statuette of a 'daedalic' Kouros (h. 20 cm.), 180.
30. Bronze figurine of Apollo (h. 41 cm.), 180.
31. Bronze censer with *peplos*-clad female figure (h. 26 cm.), 181.
32. Apollo pouring libations. Interior of a white ground cup, 182.

OLYMPIA MUSEUM

1. Detail of Apollo from the west pediment of the temple of Zeus, 193, *188*.
2. Colossal head of Hera (h. 52 cm.), 194, *189*.
3. Clay head of Athena (h. 22.4 cm.), 194, *189*.
4. Zeus and Ganymedes, clay group (h. 1.09 m.), 195, *189*.
5. East pediment of the temple of Zeus, with representation of chariot-race between Oinomaos and Pelops (l. 26.4, h. 3.3 m.), 196 - 197, *188*.
6. West pediment of the temple of Zeus, with representation of a Centauromachy (l. 26.4, h. 3.3 m.), 196 - 197, *188*.
7. Oinomaos and Sterope from the east pediment, 198, *188*.
8. Figure of an old diviner from the east pediment, 199, *188*.
9. Deidameia and the Centaur Eurytion from the west pediment, 200, *188*.
10. Apollo, from the west pediment, 201, *188*.
11. Group of Lapith and Centaur, from the west pediment, 202, *188*.
12. A Lapith woman and a Centaur from the west pediment, 203, *188*.
13. 'The Golden Apples of the Hesperides', a metope from the east side of the temple of Zeus (h. of the slab 1.60 m.), 204, *188*.
14. 'The Augean stables', a metope from the east side of the temple of Zeus (h. of the slab 1.60 m.), 204 - 205, *188*.
15. 'The Stymphalian Birds', metope from the west side of the temple of Zeus (h. of the slab 1.60 m.), 205, *188*.
16. The Nike (Victory) of Paionios (h. 2.16 m.), 206, *189*.
17. The Hermes of Praxiteles (h. 2.13 m.), 207, *190*.
18. A one-winged figure of hammered bronze (h. 54 cm., diameter with the wing 59 cm.), 208, *190*.
19. Bronze statuette of a warrior carrying a sword (h. 14.3 cm.), 209, *190*.
20. Bronze statuette of a young runner (h. 10.2 cm.), 209, *190*.
21. Bronze horse of a votive offering representing a four-horse chariot (h. 22.8 cm.), 209, *190*.
22. Bronze sheet with an embossed representation of Centaurs and hero Kaineus (h. 22.5 cm.), 210, *191*.
23. Bronze sheet with an embossed representation of the departure of a warrior (22×33 cm.), 210, *191*.
24. Bronze sheet with embossed representation of Orestes killing his mother Klytaimnestra (32×16 cm.), 211, *191*.
25. Gorgoneion encircled by three revolving wings, shield device (largest diameter 78.5 cm.), 212, *192*.
26. Bronze helmet of the Illyrian type with applied silver figures (h. 26.5 cm.), 212, *192*.
27. Persian helmet, spoil from the battle of Marathon (h. 23.1 cm.), 213, *192*.
28. The helmet of Miltiades (h. 18.7 cm.), 213, *192*.

29. Two bronze greaves (h. 42 and 43 cm.), 212, *191*.
30. Bronze breast-plate (h. 43.5 cm.), 213, *191*.
31. Bronze breast-plate with engraved representations, 213, *191*.
32. A shield device with representation of winged Gorgo with dragon's tail and lion's legs (h. 56 cm.), 214, *192*.
33. Bronze tripod (h. 65 cm.), 215, *192*.
34. Two heraldic sphinxes from a large bronze vessel, 215, *192*.
35. Bronze head of a griffin (h. 25 cm.), 215, *192*.
36. Bronze sheet with a female griffin nursing her young (h. 79 cm.), 216, *192*.

HERAKLEION MUSEUM

1. The smaller 'Snake Goddess', faience statuette (h. 29.5 cm.), 227, *223*.
2. Fruit bowl in the Kamares style from Phaistos (diam. 54 cm.), 228, *221*.
3. Nine-handled pithos of the Marine style (h. 52 cm.), 228, *221*.
4. Krater with sculptured decoration of flowers (h. 45.5 cm.), 228, *221*.
5. Beak-spouted jug of the Floral style (h. 29 cm.), 229, *221*.
6. Rhyton of the Marine style (h. 33 cm.), 230, *221*.
7. Libation jug with beak-shaped spout (h. 45.5 cm.), 230, *222*.
8. Marble ceremonial vase from Zakro (h. 38 cm.), 231, *222*.
9. Steatite rhyton with relief representations (h. 49.5 cm.), 232, *223*.
10. 'The Cup of the Report', steatite vase with representations in relief (h. 10 cm.), 232, *222*.
11 - 12. 'The Harvester Vase' from Hagia Triada (largest diameter 11.5 cm.), 233, *222*.
13. The 'Bull-jumper', ivory figure (l. 29.5 cm.), 234, *223*.
14. Head of a royal sceptre in the shape of a leopard from the Malia Palace (l. 14.8 cm.), 234.
15. A steatite rhyton in the shape of a bull's head with gold horns (h. 20.6 cm.), 235, *222*.
16. A rock-crystal rhyton with beaded handle from the Zakros Palace (h. 20 cm., without handle 16.5 cm.), 236.
17 a - e. Seal-stones of the New Palace period, 237, *223*.
18. Clay statuette from the 'Peak sanctuary' of Petsofa (h. 17.5 cm.), 238.
19 - 20. Faience plaques with representation of a wild goat and a cow with her calf (l. 19 cm.), 238.
21. The larger 'Snake Goddess', a faience statuette (h.34.2 cm.), 239, *223*.
22. Faience plaques representing Minoan houses (3 to 5 cm.), 240.
23. The 'Disk of Phaistos' with hieroglyphic symbols (diam. 16 cm.), 240.
24. Bronze statuette of a young man from Tylissos (h. 15.2 cm.), 241.
25. Gold jewellery from Archanes, 242, *223*.
26. Gold double axes from the sanctuary in the cave of Arkalochori (l. 8.6 cm.), and gold earrings from Mavro Spelio of Knossos, 242, *223*.
27. Gold bead in the shape of a lion, from Hagia Triada (l. 2.5 cm.), 243, *223*.
28. Gold pendant in the shape of a bull's head from Zakro, (h. 5 cm.), 243, *223*.
29. Gold bead in the shape of a duck from Knossos (l. 2 cm.), 243, *223*.
30. Gold accessory of a necklace with two wasps from the Chryssolakkos at Malia (diam. 4.7 cm.), 243, *223*, *224*.
31. Gold ring with a cult scene from a tomb at Isopata (l. 2.6 cm.), 243, *223*.
32. The 'Parisienne', fragment of a fresco from the Palace of Knossos, 244, *223*, *224*.

33. 'The blue bird', fragment of a fresco from Knossos, 244, *223*.
34. The 'Prince with the Lilies', coloured relief from the Palace of Knossos (h. 2.25 m.), 245, *223, 224*.
35. Fresco of bull-jumping from the Palace of Knossos, 246, *223*.
36. The sarcophagus of Hagia Triada with religious representations (l. 1.375 m.), 247, *224*.
37. Clay model of a small circular temple (h. 22 cm.), 248, *225*.
38. Clay statuette of the goddess with raised arms (h. 52 cm.), 249, *225*.
39. Vase in the shape of a three wheeled carriage with three bulls (h. 50 cm.), 249.
40. Bronze tympanon from the Idaean cave (diam. 55 cm.), 250, *225*.
41. Frieze from the Archaic temple of Prinias with representation of horsemen with shields and spears (h. 84 cm.), 250, *225*.

PELLA MUSEUM

1. Head of Alexander the Great (h. 31 cm.), 257, *255*.
2. Floor mosaic with representation of Dionysos riding a panther (2.70 × 2.00 m.), 258, *255*.
3. Floor mosaic with representation of stag-hunt (full size 3.10 × 3.10 m.), 259, *255*.
4. Floor mosaic, lion-hunt scene (4.90 × 3.20 m.), 260 - 261, *255*.
5. Floor mosaic, the abduction of Helen by Theseus (8.36 × 2.80 m.), 262 - 263, *256*.
6. Terracotta statuette of Athena (h. 41 cm.), 263, *255*.
7. Funerary marble dog (h. 79 cm.), 263, *255*.
8. Bronze statuette of Poseidon (h. with the stone base 51 cm.), 264, *255*.

THESSALONIKE MUSEUM

1. The bronze krater of Derveni (h. 91 cm.), 275, *271*.
2. Head in relief from the Archaic temple of Thessalonike (h. 11.5 cm.), 276, *270*.
3. Relief figure of a young girl, from a funerary stele (h. 38 cm.), 276, *270*.
4. Relief figure of a youth, from a funerary stele (detail), 276, *270*.
5. Head of Athena, Roman copy (h. 69.5 cm.), 277, *270*.
6. Funerary stele of a young lyre-player, from the area of Poteidaia (h. 1.36 m.), 277, *270*.
7. Detail from the bronze krater of Derveni, 278, *271*.
8. Detail from the bronze krater of Derveni, 278, *271*.
9. Detail from the bronze krater of Derveni, 279, *271*.
10. Bronze amphora with lid, from Derveni (h. 37.5 cm.), 280, *271*.
11. Silver oinochoe with gilt ornaments from Derveni (h. 14 cm.), 280, *271*.
12. Bronze amphora from Derveni (h. 21.5 cm.), 280, *271*.
13. Bronze oinochoe from Derveni (h. 25.5 cm.), 281, *271*.
14. Bronze vessel from Derveni (h. 21 cm., with handles 28 cm.), 281, *271*.
15. Bronze *kylix* from Derveni (h. 8.6 cm.), 281, *271*.
16. Bronze oinochoe from Derveni (h. 26.5 cm.), 282, *271*.
17. Silver strainer from Derveni (diam. 22 cm.), 282, *271*.
18. Faience vase, with representation of Artemis in a forest (h. 13 cm.), 283, *271*.
19. Gold necklace from a tomb at Sedes (l. 50 cm.), 284.
20. Gold medal portraying Olympias on one side and a Nereid on the other (diam. 5.7 cm.), 284.
21 - 22. Glass vases of the Roman age (h. 8 - 17 cm.), 285, *272*.

23. Male Roman portrait (h. 31 cm.), 286, *271*.
24. Male portrait of the 3rd century A.D. (h. 25 cm.), 286, *271*.
25. Statue of the emperor Augustus (h. 2.03 m.), 286, *271*.
26. Bronze portrait of emperor Alexander Severus (h. 38.5 cm.), 287, *271*.
27. Sarcophagus with representation of the Amazonomachy (l. 2.12 m.), 288, *272*.
28. Statue portraying a Roman lady (h. 2 m.), 289, *271*.
29. Male bust of the late 4th century A.D. (h. without the base 57 cm.), 289, *271*.
30. Female bust of the late 4th century A.D. (h. without the base 59 cm.), 289, *271*.
31. Fragment of a floor mosaic with a female figure (63 × 62 cm.), 290, *272*.
32. Fragment of a floor mosaic with a male figure (110 × 77 cm.), 290, *272*.

CYPRUS MUSEUM

1. Head of an athlete, limestone (h. 30 cm.), 301, *297*.
2. Head of a figurine, made of andesite, 302, *295*.
3. Figurine made of andesite (h. 13.5 cm.), 302, *295*.
4. Cruciform figurine made of steatite (h. 13.5 cm.), 302, *295*.
5. Clay model of a sanctuary, from the necropolis of Kotchatis (h. 19 cm.), 303, *296*.
6. Clay model of a circular open-air sanctuary from the Vounous area (diam. 37, h. 8 cm.), 303, *295*.
7. Plank-shaped figurine from a grave at Dhenia (h. 30 cm.), 304, *296*.
8. Composite vase from the cemetery of Vounous (h. 83 cm.), 304, *297*.
9. Oinochoe with geometric decoration from the necropolis of Hagia Paraskevi (h. 24 cm.), 305, *298*.
10. Composite vessel with plank-shaped figurine handle, from the necropolis of Vounous (h. 46 cm.), 305, *297*.
11. Mycenaean amphoroid krater from a grave at Enkomi, (h. 43.5 cm.), 306, *298*.
12. Mycenaean amphoroid krater with an octopus pattern (h. 34 cm.), 306.
13. The Hubbard amphora from Platani of Famagusta (h. 68 cm.), 307, *298*.
14. Terracotta figurine of a nude mother-goddess with infant (h. 18.5 cm.), 307, *296*.
15. Silver cup with inlaid decoration of gold and niello from a grave at Enkomi (diam. 15.7, h. 6 cm.), 308, *299*.
16. Gold necklace with beads from Enkomi (l. 31.7 cm.), 308, *299*.
17. Ring with representation of a lion, from Enkomi (diam. 2.6 cm.), 309, *299*.
18. Gold earrings in the shape of bulls' heads, from Enkomi (h. 3 cm.), 309, *300*.
19. Conical faience rhyton with enamel coating (h. 27 cm.), 309, *299*.
20. Bronze statue of a horned god from a sanctuary at Enkomi (h. 55 cm.), 310, *296*.
21. Ivory mirror handle with relief motifs (h. 21.5 cm.), 311, *300*.
22. Two vultures on a royal gold sceptre from Kourion (h. 16.5 cm.), 311.
23. Gold diadem with embossed decoration of sphinxes from Enkomi (l. 14.9 cm.), 311, *299*.
24. Jug decorated in the 'free-field' style with a bull (h. 28 cm.), 312, *299*.
25. Jug decorated in the 'free-field' style with stylized bird and fish (h. 29 cm.), 313, *299*.
26. Bronze cauldron supported on an iron tripod, from tomb 79 at Salamis (h. of the cauldron 55 cm., h. of the tripod 70 cm.), 314, *299*.

27. Limestone statue of Zeus Keraunios (h. 56 cm.), 315, *297*.
28. Engraved ivory plaque from a throne descovered in the royal tomb 79 at Salamis (h. 16 cm.), 316, *300*.
29. Terracotta figurine of a horse and a rider (h. 21 cm.), 317, *296*.
30. Terracotta group of a bull and male figures (h. 28.5 cm.), 317, *296*.
31. Polychrome terracotta figurine of a Centaur (h. 16.5 cm.), 317, *296*.
32. Clay model of a war chariot with two warriors (h. 14.2 cm.), 317, *296*.
33. Limestone head of a Kore (h. 34 cm.), 318, *296*.
34. a) Gold necklace with pendant from Arsos, 319, *300*.
    b) Two gold-plated bracelets terminating in rams' heads, from Kourion (diam. 7 cm.), 319, *300*.
35. Marble grave stele of Stases, from Marion (h. 93.5 cm.), 320, *297*.
36. Limestone grave stele of Aristila, from Marion (h. 92 cm.), 320, *297*.
37. Limestone head of a female statue (h. 27 cm.), 321, *297*.
38. Marble head of Aphrodite from the Gymnasium of Salamis (h. 31.2 cm.), 322, *297*.
39. Clay male head from the funeral pyre of the cenotaph of king Nikokreon (h. 28 cm.), 322, *297*.
40. Marble statue of Aphrodite from Soloi (h. 81 cm.), 322, *297*.
41. Bronze statue of Septimius Severus (h. 2.08 m.), 323, *297*.
42. Early Christian silver plate with representation of the wedding of David (diam. 26.5 cm.), 324, *299*.

BYZANTINE MUSEUM

1. Mosaic icon. The Virgin and Child (107×73.5 cm.), 339, *336*.
2. Funerary stele. Orpheus playing the lyre (110×50 cm.), 340, *334*.
3. Marble plaque with three Apostles (47×93 cm.), 341, *335*.
4. Marble closure panel; two confronted lions (109×90 cm.), 341, *335*.
5. Marble closure panel; the Victory cross with inscription (73×82 cm.), 341, *335*.
6. Marble closure panel; lion in combat (100×71 cm.), 341, *335*.
7. Wall-painting from apsidal conch from Lathreno, Naxos, 342, *335*.
8. Wall-painting from a church at Oropos. A young deacon, full length (1.97×0.58 m.), 343, *335*.
9. Wall-painting; St. James the Persian (80×63 cm.), 343, *338*.
10. Wall-painting; a monk in a boat (41×60 cm.), 343, *338*.
11. Icon of St. George in painted relief (107×72 cm.), 344, *336*.
12. Icon of the Archangel Michael (110×82 cm.), 345, *336*.
13. Icon of the Virgin and Child (87×65 cm.), 346.
14. Large icon of Christ (1.54×1 m.), 346, *366*.
15. Icon with the Crucifixion (background with stars) (105×65 cm.), 346, *336*.
16. Icon of the prophet Daniel (28×33 cm.), 346, *337*.
17. The Crucifixion; portative icon from Thessalonike (103×85 cm.), 347, *336*.
18. 'The Kardiotissa'; icon of the Virgin and Child made by the Cretan painter Angelos (121×97 cm.), 348, *337*.
19. St. Catherine; Cretan icon (124×83 cm.), 348, *337*.
20. St. Anthony, full length; from an iconostasis door (207×56 cm.), 348, *337*.
21. Icon of the Hospitality of Abraham symbolizing the Holy Trinity (97×72 cm.), 349, *337*, *371*.
22. Triptych of the Transfiguration (54×33 cm., open 62 cm.), 350, *338*.

23. The Virgin and a scene from a ship wreck; a votive icon (45×33 cm.), 351, *337*.
24. 'The Galaktotrophousa', icon of the Virgin feeding the Baby (104×70 cm.), 351, *338*.
25. A popular art icon representing Eros and the Sirens (50.5×66.5 cm.), 351, *338*.
26. Wooden carved iconostasis (h. 2.60, w. 4.10 m.), 352 - 353, *337*.
27. Jewellery and coins from the Mytilene treasure. (Necklaces: left 49.8 cm., above 104.5 cm., below 95 cm. Bracelet, diam 5.7 cm. Amulet with cross, diam. 2 cm. Left buckle, l. 7.4 cm. Right buckle, l. 5.4 cm.), 354, *334*.
28. Silver plate with incised cross, from the Mytilene treasure (diam. 25.6 cm.), 355, *334*.
29. 'Trulla' with incised representations, from the Mytilene treasure (diam. 16.5 cm.), 355, *334*.
30. Gospel book cover from Trebizond (22×17.5 cm.), 356, *338*.
31. Pastoral staff decorated with precious stones, rubies and enamels (total h. 1.60 m.), 357, *338*.
32. Silver censer with lid (h. 28 cm.), 358, *338*.
33. Silver vessel for Holy Water; Monastery of Prodromos, Serres (h. 28.5, diam. 23 cm.), 358, *338*.
34. Spherical crown of chandelier from Kythera (diam. 10 cm.), 358, *338*.
35. Large pyx from the Metropolis, Adrianople (h. 70 cm.), 358, *338*.
36. Large cross with enamel decoration (two birds) (48×22 cm.), 359, *338*.
37. The Entry into Jerusalem. Detail from a silver-thread stole, 361, *338*.
38. Gold-thread 'Aer' from Thessalonike (0.70×2 m.), 360-361, *336*, *338*.
39. Gospel book cover (35×26 cm.), 362, *338*.

BENAKI MUSEUM

1. Pendant in the shape of a caravel, from Patmos. Donated by Mrs. Helen Stathatos (13.8×9.5 cm.), 373, *368*.
2. Prehistoric gold cup, found in Northern Euboia (h. 9.5 cm.), 374, *367*.
3. Gold head of a pin with representation of Aphrodite (h. of pin 16 cm.), 374, *368*.
4. Gold earrings with hanging Cupids (h. 4.35 cm.), 374, *368*.
5. a) Funerary band from Kos (l. 17, w. 1.6 cm.), 375, 368.
   b) Diadem, featuring the 'knot of Herakles' (l. 51, l. without the band 7.4 and w. 4.5 cm.), 375, *368*.
6. a) Earrings with rosette and a hanging basket (l. 6 cm.), 375, *368*.
   b) Necklace with small hanging amphorae (l. 35 cm.), 375, *368*.
7. a) Crescent-shaped earring with a monogram (h. 1.8 cm.), 376, *368*.
   b) Wide bracelet with disk (diam. 8 cm., diam. of the disk 3 cm.), 376, *368*.
   c) Pair of crescent-shaped earrings with open work design (h. 4.4 cm.), 376, *368*.
   d) Ring with an enamelled representation of Christ Pantocrator (diam. 2.2 cm.), 376, *368*.
8. Belt buckle with inlaid stones (h. 7, l. 24.5 cm.), 376, *368*.
9. Pendant of rock-crystal fastened with gold and stones (h. 6.1, w. 6 cm.), 377, *368*.
10. Pendant in the shape of a one-masted caravel (h. 4.5 cm.), 377.
11. Pendant with precious stones from Asia Minor (h. 17.5 cm.), 377, *368*.
12. Fayyum portrait of a youth (50×30 cm.), 378, *369*.
13. Fayyum portrait of a young girl (65×38.5 cm.), 379, *369*.

14. 'Coptic' woollen fabric representing a female head (20× 19 cm.), 380, *370*.
15. 'Coptic' fabric with the Pegasus (28×32.5 cm.), 380, *370*.
16. 'Aer', gold-embroidered fabric (52×65 cm.), 381.
17. Left : Small ivory plaque with St. George in relief (14.5× 3.5 cm.), 382.
    Top, right : Bifacial comb made of bone (14.5×8.5 cm.), 382.
    Bottom, right : Small steatite plaque representing the Annunciation (10×9.5 cm.), 382, *370*.
18. Small steatite plaque with the Presentation in the temple (10.7×8.8 cm.), 383, *370*.
19 - 20. Two pages from a Psalter (11×16 cm.), 384, *370*.
21. Gospel with silver cover (23.5×33 cm.), 385, *371*.
22. Triptych with the Virgin Mary the 'Portaetissa' from the Iviron Monastery (28.5×43.2 cm., open), 386, *371*.
23. The Hospitality of Abraham on an icon (33×60 cm.), 386, *370*.
24. Icon of St. Demetrios, full-size (66.5×36.5 cm.), 387, *371*.
25. The Adoration of the Magi, by El Greco (40×45 cm.), 388, *371*.
26. Complex icon by the Cretan painter Theodore Poulakis (91×64 cm.), 389, *371*.
27. Incense-boat of gold-plated silver and enamel in the shape of a small domed chapel (h. 21.9 cm.), 390, *368*.
28. Censer with handle (h. 26 cm.), 390, *368*.
29. Pastoral staff with rubies and enamel (head, w. 15.5 cm.), 391, *369*.
30. Silver mitre with gilt representations (h. 25.2 cm.), 391, *369*.
31. Silver litany flabellum with gilt representations (diam. 32 cm.), 391, *369*.
32. Cross from the collection of relics from Asia Minor (35×24 cm.), 391, *369*.
33. Plate with a three-mast schooner (diam. 29.5 cm.), 392, *371*.
34. Plate decorated with a lion and inscription (diam. 25.8 cm.), 392, *371*.
35 - 36. Ceramic eggs from a church chandelier (7.8×7.5 cm. and 7.9×7.6 cm.), 393, *371*.
37. Jug with painted confronted he-goats (h. 15 cm.), 393, *371*.
38. Flask with painted ships (h. 34 cm.), 393, *371*.
39 a - m. Arms of the Greek War of Independence, 394 - 395.
    a) Sword belonging to Nikolas Petimezas, donated by Mr. Herakles Petimezas (1. 94 cm.).
    b) Yataghan belonging to Admiral Yakoumis Tombazis, donated by D. Tombazis-Mavrokordatos (1. 77 cm.).
    c) Yataghan belonging to Photis Tzavellas, donated by Prince George (1. 69 cm.).
    d) Muzzle-loader belonging to Nikolas Petimezas, donated by Mr. Herakles Petimezas (1. 130 cm.).
    e) Pair of pistols decorated with coral (1. 55 cm.).
    f) Pair of pistols belonging to Petrobey Mavromichalis, donated by P. Mavromichalis (1. 52.5 cm.).
    g) Cartridge-case with embossed Gorgon motif (15×12.5 cm.).
    h) Cartridge-case belonging to Petrobey Mavromichalis, donated by P. Mavromichalis (15.5×11.5 cm.).
    i) Cartridge-case, donated by Chr. Lambikis (11×10 cm.).
    j) Oriental gunpowder-case (1. 9 cm.).
    k) Dagger with curved blade (1. 30.5 cm.).
    l) Sword belonging to General Demetrios Kallergis (1.87 cm.).
    m) Sword offered to general Demetrios Kallergis, with inscription (1. 98.5 cm.).
40. Bed-spread from Skyros, embroidery with representation of a horseman, donated by Dam. Kyriazis (42×58 cm.), 396, *371*.
41. Cushion from Crete with main motif of a Gorgon (39× 54 cm.), 397, *372*.
42. Nuptial cushion-cover from Jannina, donated by Mrs. Helen Stathatos (38×88 cm.), 396 - 397, *372*.
43. Cushion from Skyros embroidered with a three-mast schooner (46×43 cm.), 398, *371*.
44. Detail from a Skyros bed-spread embroidered with woodcocks (motif 36×39.5 cm.), 398, *372*.
45. Embroidered border from a Cretan bed-spread, detail (h. of the motifs 27 cm.), 398, *372*.
46. Sleeveless overcoat with gold embroidery from Epeiros, 399, *372*.
47. Top : Belt buckle from Epeiros (25×14 cm.), 400.
    Bottom : Belt buckle from Saframpolis in Asia Minor (31.5×12 cm.), 400.
48. Top, left : Earrings in the shape of three-mast caravels, donated by Mrs. Helen Stathatos (12.5×5.9 cm.), 401.
    Bottom, left : Earrings with pendants decorated with enamel (h. 8 cm.), 401.
    Right : Long earrings, like the Byzantine 'perpendulia' from Kos (h. 20.5 cm.), 401.
49. Open work distaff with a representation of Saint George (1. 80 cm.), 402, *369*.
50. Carved wood-panelling from a reception-room in a Kozani house, donated by Mrs. Helen Stathatos, 402 - 403, *372*.
51. Wood - carved chest from Skyros (52×85 cm.), 404.

BIBLIOGRAPHY

ANCIENT GREEK ART

GENERAL WORKS

ANDRONICOS, M. : History of the Hellenic World (in Greek). *The Archaic Period*, pp. 182 - 195 and pp. 366 - 411. Athens 1971. *The Classical Era* (part II), pp. 270 - 327. Athens 1972.

CHARBONNEAUX, J.,
MARTIN, R.,
VILLARD, FR. : *Grèce archaïque*. Paris 1968.
— : *Grèce classique*. Paris 1969.

CHARBONNEAUX, J.,
ROLAND, M.,
VILLARD, FR. : *Grèce hellénistique*. Paris 1970.

HOMANN -
WEDEKING, E. : *Das archaische Griechenland*. Kunst der Welt. Baden - Baden 1966.

MATZ, FR. : *Geschichte der griechischen Kunst*, vol. I. Frankfurt 1950.

BAKALAKIS, G. : History of the Hellenic World (in Greek). *The Hellenistic Period*, pp. 424 - 452 and 458 - 468. Athens 1974.

SCHEFOLD, K. : *Klassisches Griechenland*. Kunst der Welt. Baden - Baden 1965.
— : *Die Griechen und ihre Nachbarn*. Propyläen Kunstgeschichte, vol. I. Berlin 1967.

SCHWEITZER, B. : *Die geometrische Kunst Griechenlands*. Kolon 1969.

PREHISTORIC ART

BLEGEN, C. : *The Mycenaean Age*. Cincinnati 1952.

BLEGEN, C.,
RAWSON, M. : *The Palace of Nestor at Pylos in Western Messenia* (vol. I). *The Buildings and their Contents*. Princeton 1966.

DEMARGNE, P. : *La naissance de l'art Grec*. Paris 1964.

EVANS, A. : *The Palace of Minos* (vol. I - IV and Index). London 1921 - 1936.

KARO, G. : *Schachtgräber von Mykenae*. Munich 1930 - 1933.

KENNA, V. : *Cretan Seals*. Oxford 1960.

LANG, M. : *The Palace of Nestor at Pylos in Western Messenia* (vol. II). *The Frescoes*. Princeton 1969.

MARINATOS, S.,
HIRMER, M. : *Crete and Mycenae*. New York 1960.

MATZ, FR. : *Kreta, Mykenae, Troja*. Stuttgart 1956.
— : *Kreta und frühes Griechenland*. Baden - Baden 1962.

MYLONAS, G. : *Ancient Mycenae, the Capital City of Agamemnon*. London 1957.
— : *Grave Circle B of Mycenae*. Studies in Medit. Archaeol., VII. Lund 1964.
— : *Mycenae and the Mycenaean Age*. Princeton 1966.
— : *Mycenae; A Guide to its Ruins and its History*. Athens 1967.

PLATON, N. : *Crète*. Archaeologia Mundi. Geneva 1965.

SAKELLARIOU, A. : Μυκηναϊκὴ σφραγιδογλυφία. Athens 1966.

TSOUNTAS, CH. : Μυκῆναι καὶ μυκηναῖος πολιτισμός. Athens 1893.
— : Κυκλαδικά. Ἀρχαιολογικὴ Ἐφημερὶς 1898, pp. 136 - 211 and 1899, pp. 74 - 134.

WACE, A.J.B. : *Mycenae; An Archaeological History and Guide*. Princeton 1949.

ZERVOS, CHR. : *L'art de la Crète néolithique et minoenne*. Paris 1956.
— : *L'art des Cyclades*. Paris 1957.

SCULPTURE

ALSCHER, L. : *Griechische Plastik*. Berlin 1954 sqq.

ASHMOLE, B. : *The Classical Ideal in Greek Sculpture*. Cincinnati 1964.
— : Some Nameless Sculptors of the Fifth Century B.C. *Proc. of the British Academy* 48 (1964), pp. 211 - 233.
— : *Architect and Sculptor in Classical Greece*. London 1972.

BECATTI, G. : *Problemi Fidiaci*. Milan 1951.

BIEBER, M. : *The Sculpture of the Hellenistic Age*. New York 1961 2.

BUSCHOR, E. : *Das hellenistische Bildnis*. Munich 1949.
— : *Frühgriechische Jünglinge*. Munich 1950.

DESPINIS, G.J., Συμβολὴ στὴ μελέτη τοῦ ἔργου τοῦ Ἀγορακρίτου. Athens 1971.

DOHRN, T. : *Attische Plastik vom Tode des Phidias bis zum Wirken der grossen Meister des IV. Jahrhunderts v. Chr.* Krefeld 1957.
FUCHS, W. : *Die Skulptur der Griechen.* Munich 1969.
HAFNER, G. : *Späthellenistische Bildnisplastik.* Berlin 1954.
HIMMELMANN -
WILDSCHÜTZ, N. : *Bemerkungen zur geometrischen Plastik.* Berlin 1964.
JOHANSEN, K.F. : *The Attic Grave - Reliefs of the Classical Period.* Copenhagen 1951.
LIPPOLD, G. : *Die griechische Plastik.* Handbuch der Altertumswissenschaft VI, 3, 1. Munich 1950.
LULLIES, R.,
HIRMER, M. : *Greek Sculpture.* London 1960 [2].
MÖBIUS, H. : *Die Ornamente der griechischen Grabstelen klassischer und nachklassischer Zeit.* Munich 1968 [2].
PICARD, CH. : *Manuel d'Archéologie grecque. La sculpture : I - IV.* Paris 1935 sqq.
RICHTER, G.M.A. : *Kouroi; A Study of the Development of the Kouros Type in Greek Sculpture.* London 1960 [2].
— *Korai; A Study of the Development of the Kore Type in Greek Sculpture.* London 1968.
— *The Archaic Gravestones of Attica.* London 1961.
ROMAIOS, K.A. : *Κέραμοι τῆς Καλυδῶνος.* Athens 1951.
SCHLÖRB, B. : *Untersuchungen zur Bildhauergeneration nach Phidias.* Waldsassen 1964.
SCHUCHHARDT, W.H. : *Die Epochen der griechischen Plastik.* Baden - Baden 1959.
SÜSSEROTT, K. : *Griechische Plastik des 4. Jahrhunderts v. Chr. Untersuchungen zur Zeitbestimmung.* Frankfurt 1938.

VASE - PAINTING

ARIAS, P.E.,
HIRMER, M. : *A History of Greek Vase - Painting* (transl. B. B. Shefton). London 1962.
BEAZLEY, J.D. : *Attic Red - Figure Vases in American Museums.* Cambridge 1918.
— *Attic White Lekythoi.* London 1938.
— *Potter and Painter in Ancient Athens.* London 1949 [3].
— *Attic Black - Figure Vase - Painters.* Oxford 1956.
— *Attic Red - Figure Vase - Painters,* vols. I - III. Oxford 1963 [3].
— *The Development of Attic Black - Figure.* Berkeley 1964 [2].
— *Paralipomena.* Oxford 1971.
BUSCHOR, E. : *Attische Lekythen der Parthenonzeit.* Munich 1925.
— *Griechische Vasen.* Munich 1969 [2].
COOK, R.M. : *Greek Painted Pottery.* London 1960.
DESBOROUGH, V.R.d'A. : *Protogeometric Pottery.* Oxford 1952.
KAROUZOU, SEMNI : *Τὰ ἀγγεῖα τοῦ 'Αναγυροῦντος.* Athens 1963.
NOBLE, J.V. : *The Technique of Attic Pottery.* New York 1965.
PAPASPYRIDI, SEM. : ῾Ο «τεχνίτης τῶν καλάμων» τῶν λευκῶν ληκύθων. *'Αρχαιολογικὸν Δελτίον* 8 (1923), pp. 117 - 146.
PAYNE, H.G.G. : *Necrocorinthia.* Oxford 1931.
PHILIPPAKI, BARB. : *The Attic Stamnos.* Oxford 1967.
RICHTER, G.M.A. : *Attic Red - Figured Vases.* New Haven 1958 [2].
RICHTER, G.M.A.,
MILNE, M.J. : *Shapes and Names of Athenian Vases.* New York 1935.
RUMPF, A. : *Malerei und Zeichnung.* Handbuch der Altertumswissenschaft VI, 4, 1. Munich 1953.
WEBSTER, T.B.L. : *Potter and Patron in Classical Athens.* London 1972.

THE MINOR ARTS — COINS

BECCATI, G. : *Orificerie antiche, dalle Minoiche alle Barbariche.* Rome 1955.
CHARBONNEAUX, J. : *Les bronzes grecs.* Paris 1958.
COCHE DE LA
FERTÉ, É. : *Les bijoux antiques.* Paris 1956.
HIGGINS, R. : *Greek and Roman Jewellery.* London 1961.
JENKINS, G.K. : *Monnaies Grecques.* Fribourg (Switzerland) 1972.
KUNZE, E. : *Kretische Bronzereliefs.* Stuttgart 1931.
— *Archaische Schildbänder.* Olympische Forschungen II. Berlin 1950.
LAMB, W. : *Greek and Roman Bronzes.* London 1929.
REGLING, K. : *Die antike Münze als Kunstwerk.* Berlin 1924.
SELTMAN, CH. : *Greek Coins.* London 1965 [2].

BYZANTINE ART
GENERAL WORKS

BYZANZ , Propyläen Kunstgeschichte, vol. III, 1969.
BYZANTINE ART , AN EUROPEAN ART, 9th Exhibition of the Council of Europe. Catalogue. Athens 1964 (also in Greek and French).

KRAUTHEIMER, R. :   *Early Christian and Byzantine Architecture*. Penguin Books 1965.
LAZAREV, V. :   *Storia della Pittura Bizantina*. Turin 1967.
ORLANDOS, A.K. :   *Ἀρχεῖον Βυζαντινῶν Μνημείων Ἑλλάδος*, vols. 1 - 12. Athens 1935 - 73.
WEITZMANN, K. :   *Greek Mythology in Byzantine Art*. Princeton 1951.

MOSAICS, FRESCOES

CHATZIDAKIS, M. :   *Studies on Byzantine Art and Archaeology*. London 1972.
DEMUS, O. :   *Byzantine Decoration*. London 1958.
GRABAR, A. :   *La peinture byzantine*. Geneva 1953.
GRABAR, A. ,
CHATZIDAKIS, M. :   *Greece, Mosaics*. UNESCO 1959.

ICONS

WEITZMANN, K.,
CHATZIDAKIS, M.,
MIATEV, K.,
RADOJCIC, SV. :   *Icons from Eastern Europe and Sinai*. London 1968.
WULFF, O.,
ALPATOR, M. :   *Denkmäler der Ikonenmalerei*. Hellerau bei Dresden 1925.

HANDICRAFTS — POPULAR ART

CHATZIMICHALI, A. :   *L'art populaire grec*. Athens 1937.
—   *La sculpture sur bois*. Athens 1950.
—   *Σκύρος*. Athens 1925.
—   *Τὰ χρυσοκλαβαρικά, συρματέινα, συρμακέσικα κεντήματα*. Athens 1952.
NATIONAL BANK OF
GREECE,   *Νεοελληνικὴ χειροτεχνία*. Athens 1969.

SPECIAL WORKS — GUIDES

National Museum

AMANDRY, P. :   *Collection Hélène Stathatos. Les bijoux antiques*. Strasbourg 1953.
KAVADIAS, P. :   *Γλυπτὰ τοῦ Ἐθνικοῦ Μουσείου. Κατάλογος περιγραφικός*. Athens 1890 - 1892.
KALLIPOLITIS, V.,
TOULOUPA, EVI :   *Τὰ χαλκὰ τοῦ Ἐθνικοῦ Μουσείου*. Athens 1972.
KAROUZOS, CH. :   *Ὁ Ποσειδῶν τοῦ Ἀρτεμισίου. Ἀρχαιολογικὸν Δελτίον* 13 (1930/31), pp. 41 - 104.
—   An Early Classical Disc Relief from Melos. *Journal of Hellenic Studies* 71 (1951), pp. 96   ff.
—   *Ἀριστόδικος*. Athens 1961.
—   *Τηλαυγὲς μνῆμα*. Χαριστήριον εἰς Α.Κ. Ὀρλάνδον, vol. 3, pp. 253 - 280. Athens 1966.
KAROUZOU, SEMNI :   *National Archaeological Museum : Collection of Sculpture* (transl. Helen Wace). Athens 1968.
KASTRIOTIS, P. :   *Γλυπτὰ τοῦ Ἐθνικοῦ Μουσείου. Κατάλογος περιγραφικός*. Athens 1908.
PAPASPIRIDI, SEMNI :   *Guide du Musée National*. Athens 1927.
SAKELLARIOU, A.,
PAPATHANASOPOU-
LOS, G. :   *National Archaeological Museum. I. Prehistoric Collections. A Brief Guide*. Athens 1964.
SVORONOS, J.N. :   *Das Athener Nationalmuseum I - III*. Athens 1908, 1911, 1937.
STAÏS, V. :   *Marbres et bronzes du Musée National*. Athens 1910 ².
PHILIPPAKI, BARB. :   *Ἀγγεῖα τοῦ Ἐθνικοῦ Ἀρχαιολογικοῦ Μουσείου Ἀθηνῶν*. Athens 1973

Acropolis Museum

BUSCHOR, E. :   *Phidias der Mensch*. Munich 1948.
BROMMER, F. :   *Die Skulpturen der Parthenon - Giebel. Katalog und Untersuchung*. Mainz 1963.
—   *Die Metopen des Parthenon. Katalog und Untersuchung*, vols. I - II. Mainz 1967.
CARPENTER, R. :   *The Sculpture of the Nike Temple Parapet*. Cambridge, Mass. 1929.
CORBETT, P.E. :   *The Sculpture of the Parthenon*. Penguin Books 1959.
DICKINS, G.,
CASSON, S. :   *Catalogue of the Acropolis Museum*, vols. I - II. Cambridge 1921.
MILIADIS, G. :   *A Concise Guide to the Acropolis Museum*. Athens 1965.
PAYNE, H.,
YOUNG, G.M. :   *Archaic Marble Sculpture from the Acropolis*. London/New York 1950 ².
SCHRADER, H.,
LANGLOTZ, E.,
SCHUCHHARDT, W.H. :   *Die archaischen Marmorbildwerke der Akropolis*. Frankfurt 1969 ².

WALTER, O. : *Beschreibung der Reliefs im kleinen Akropolismuseum in Athen.* Vienna 1923.
YALOURIS, N. : *La Grèce classique. Les sculptures du Parthénon.* Paris 1960.

Delphi Museum

CHAMOUX, F. : *L'Aurige.* Fouilles de Delphes, vol. IV. Monuments figurés : Sculpture, fasc. 5. Paris 1955.
DAUX, G. : *Pausanias à Delphes.* Paris 1936.
DELACOSTE -
MESSELIÈRE, P. : *Au Musée de Delphes.* Paris 1936.
DELACOSTE -
MESSELIÈRE, P.,
MIRÉ, G. : *Delphes.* 1943.
DOHRN, T. : *Die Marmor - Standbilder des Daochos - Weihgeschenks in Delphi.* Antike Plastik VIII, 1968, pp. 33 - 53, Plates 10 - 37.
KAHLER, H. : *Der Fries von Reiterdenkmal des Aemilius Paulus in Delphi.* Berlin 1965.
KAROUZOS, CH. : *Δελφοί.* Athens 1974.
KERAMOPOULLOS, A. : Ὁδηγὸς τῶν Δελφῶν. Athens 1935 [2].
MILIADIS, G. : *Δελφοί. Ἱστορία, ἐρείπια, ἔργα τέχνης.* Athens 1930.
PAPACHATZIS, N. : Παυσανίου Ἑλλάδος περιήγησις. Φωκικά. 1969.
ROUX, G. : *Delphi, Orakel und Kultstätten.* Munich 1971.

Olympia Museum

ASHMOLE, B.,
YALOURIS, N. : *Olympia; The Sculptures of the Temple of Zeus.* London 1967.
BUSCHOR, E.,
HAMANN, R. : *Die Skulpturen des Zeustempels zu Olympia,* vols. I - II. Marburg Lahn 1924.
DÉONNA, W. : *La Nikè de Paionios de Mendè et le triangle sacré des monuments figurés.* Brussels 1968.
DREES, L. : *Olympia. Götter, Künstler und Athleten.* Stuttgart 1967.
ECKSTEIN, F. : Ἀναθήματα. *Studien zu den Weihgeschenken strengen Stils im Heiligtum von Olympia.* Berlin 1969.
GARDINER, E.N. : *Olympia; Its History and Remains.* Oxford 1925.
HERRMANN, H.V. : *Olympia : Heiligtum und Wettkampfstätte.* Munich 1972.
KONTIS, J. : Τὸ ἱερὸν τῆς Ὀλυμπίας κατὰ τὸν Δ΄ π.Χ. αἰ. Athens 1958.
KUNZE, E. : *Neue Meisterwerke aus Olympia.* Munich 1948.
LEONARDOS, V. : Ἡ Ὀλυμπία. Athens 1901.
MALLWITZ, A. : *Olympia und seine Bauten.* Munich 1972.
PAPACHATZIS, N. : Παυσανίου Ἑλλάδος περιήγησις. Ἠλιακά. 1965.

Herakleion Museum

ALEXIOU, ST. : Μινωικὸς πολιτισμὸς μετὰ ὁδηγοῦ τῶν ἀνακτόρων Κνωσοῦ, Φαιστοῦ καὶ Μαλίων. Herakleion 1964.
PLATON, N. : *A Guide to the Archaeological Museum of Heraclion.* Athens 1964.
PLATON, N.,
ALEXIOU, ST. : *A Guide to the Archaeological Museum of Heraclion.* Athens 1968.

Pella Museum

ANDRONICOS, M. : Ancient Greek Paintings and Mosaics in Macedonia. *Balcan Studies* 5 (1964), pp. 287 - 302.
MAKARONAS, CH. J. : Ψηφιδωτὰ τῆς Πέλλας. Ἡμερολόγιον Ἰονικῆς καὶ Λαϊκῆς Τραπέζης 1963.
PAPAKONSTANTINOU -
DIAMANTOUROU, D. : Πέλλα. Ἱστορικὴ ἐπισκόπησις καὶ μαρτυρίαι. Athens 1971.
PETSAS, PH. : *Mosaics from Pella.* La Mosaique gréco-romaine. Paris 29 August - 3 September 1963. Paris 1963.
— Pella. *Studies in Med. Archaeology* 14. Lund 1964.
— Ten Years at Pella. *Archaeology* 17 (1964)
ROBERTSON, L.M. : Greek Mosaics. *Journal of Hellenic Studies* 85 (1965), p. 73 ff.

Thessalonike Museum

ANDRONICOS, M. : Stèles funéraires de Vergina. *Bulletin de Correspondence Hellénique* 79 (1955), pp. 87 - 101.
— Ἐπιτυμβία στήλη ἐκ Θράκης. Ἀρχαιολογικὴ Ἐφημερίς 1956, pp. 199 - 215.
— Portrait de l'ère republicaine au Musée de Thessalonique. *Monuments Piot* 51 (1959), pp. 38 - 52.
— Stèle funéraire de Kassandra. *Bulletin de Correspondence Hellénique* 86 (1962), pp. 261 - 267.
BAKALAKIS, G. : Satyros an einer Quelle gelagert. *Antike Kunst* 1966, pp. 21 - 28.
— Therme - Thessaloniki. *Antike Kunst,* Beiheft 1, 1963, pp. 30 - 34.
DESPINIS, G. : Ἡ ἐπανέκθεσις τῶν γλυπτῶν εἰς τὸ Μουσεῖον Θεσσαλονίκης. Ἀρχαιολογικὰ Ἀνάλεκτα ἐξ Ἀθηνῶν 1969, pp. 173 - 177.
PANTERMALIS, D. : *Capita Transformata.* Κέρνος (Thessalonike 1972), pp. 111 - 118.
— Ein Bildnis des Severus Alexander in Thessaloniki. *Archaeologischer Anzeiger* 1972, pp. 128 - 145.
PELEKANIDIS, S. : Ἄγαλμα γυναίκας τῆς ὕστερης ἀρχαιότητας. *Bulletin de Correspondence Hellénique* 73 (1949), pp. 294 - 305.

PELEKIDIS, S. :   Ὁ τύπος τῆς Ἀθηνᾶς τῶν Μεδίκων. Ἀρχαιολογικὸν Δελτίον 9 (1924/5), pp. 121 - 144.
RÜSCH, A. :   Das kaiserzeitliche Porträt in Makedonien. *Jahrbuch des deutschen Instituts* 84 (1969), pp. 59- 196.

Cyprus Museum

CASSON, S. :   *Ancient Cyprus.* London 1937.
CATLING, H.W. :   *Cyprus in the Neolithic and Bronze Age Periods.* Cambridge Ancient History, revised ed. vols. I - I
Cambridge 1966.
DIKAIOS, P. :   *Khirokitia.* Oxford 1953.
—   *Enkomi (Excavations* 1948 - 1958), vols. I - III. Mainz 1969 - 1971.
—   *A Guide to the Cyprus Museum.* Nicosia 1961 [3].
KARAGEORGHIS, V. :   *Treasures in the Cyprus Museum.* Nicosia 1962.
—   *Cyprus.* Archaeologia Mundi. Geneva 1968.
—   *Mycenaean Art from Cyprus.* Nicosia 1968.
—   *Salamis in Cyprus. Homeric, Hellenistic and Roman.* London 1969.
—   *Altägäis und Altkypros.* Tübingen 1972.
—   History of the Hellenic World. *Prehistory and Protohistory,* pp. 346 - 358. Athens - London 1974.
—   *The Archaic Period* (in Greek), pp. 358 - 365. Athens 1971.
—   Κύπρος. Μουσεῖα καὶ μνημεῖα τῆς Ἑλλάδος. Athens 1973.
SPYRIDAKIS, K. :   History of the Hellenic World (in Greek). *The Classical* Era (part II), pp. 169 - 173. Athens 1972.
—   Κύπριοι βασιλεῖς τοῦ 4ου αἰ. π.Χ. (411 - 311/10 π.Χ.). Nicosia 1963.

Byzantine Museum

CHATZIDAKIS, M. :   *Athens, Byzantine Museum, The Icons.* Athens 1970.
SOTIRIOU, G. :   *A Guide to the Byzantine Museum of Athens.* Athens 1962.
—   Ὁδηγὸς τοῦ Βυζαντινοῦ Μουσείου Ἀθηνῶν. Athens 1931.

Benaki Museum

VEÏ-CHATZIDAKI, E. :   Ἐκκλησιαστικὰ κεντήματα. Athens 1953.
BENAKI MUSEUM,   *A brief Guide.* Athens 1969 [3] (also in Greek, French and German).
BENAKI, A. :   (ed.) : *Album of National Greek Costumes,* 2 vols. Athens 1948 and 1954. Text by Ang. Chatzimichali.
XYNGOPOULOS, A. :   Κατάλογος τῶν εἰκόνων. Athens 1937.
SEGALL, B. :   *Katalog der Goldschmiede - Arbeiten.* Athens 1938.
CHATZIDAKI, E. :   Χριστιανικαὶ ἐπιγραφαὶ Μ. Ἀσίας καὶ Πόντου. Athens 1959.
CHATZIDAKIS, M. :   Κεραμουργήματα Μ. Ἀσίας μὲ ἑλληνικὲς ἐπιγραφές. Ζυγὸς 16 (1958), pp. 6 - 7.
—   Τὰ νεανικὰ τοῦ Θεοτοκόπουλου. Ἐποχὲς 4 (1963), pp. 33 - 37.

PHOTOGRAPHY

Spyros Tsavdaroglou
National Museum, figs. : 9, 19, 23, 31, 32, 35, 38, 40, 44 - 48, 51 - 64, 70, 71, 73, 75 - 77, 79 - 87, 89, 90, 92 - 94,
96, 97, 99 - 107, 114, 115, 117 - 120.
Acropolis Museum, figs. : 1, 3, 13 - 40.
Delphi Museum, figs. : 2 - 32.
Olympia Museum, figs. : 1 - 36.
Herakleion Museum, figs. : 2 - 14, 25, 28, 32, 34 - 37, 40, 41.
Pella Museum, figs. : 1 - 4, 6 - 8.
Thessalonike Museum, figs. : 1 - 32.
Cyprus Museum, figs. : 1 - 42.
Byzantine Museum, figs. : 1 - 39.

Makis Skiadaresis
National Museum, figs. : 4, 5, 11 - 17, 33, 34, 50, 66, 67, 72, 74, 78, 91, 95, 98, 108 - 113.
Herakleion Museum, figs. : 1, 15 - 24, 26, 27, 29 - 31, 33, 38, 39.
Benaki Museum, figs. : 1 - 51.

Nikos Kontos
National Museum, figs. : 2, 3, 6 - 8, 10, 18, 20 - 22, 24 - 30, 36, 37, 39, 41 - 43, 49, 65, 69, 116.
Delphi Museum, fig. 1.

Mauro Pucciarelli
National Museum, figs. : 1, 68, 88.
Acropolis Museum, figs. : 2, 4 - 12.
Manolis Vernardos
Pella Museum, fig. 5.

ACKNOWLEDGEMENTS

The publishers of this book are deeply indebted to the Directors of the Greek Museums for their courtesy in assisting our photographers. Furthermore, the German Archaeological Institute (Athens) must be thanked for furnishing assistance of great value in the selection and photography of subjects from the excavations at Olympia.
We are specially grateful to Dr. Giannis Miliadis, honorary director of the Acropolis Museum, for permission to publish, for the first time, the statue of Athena from the pediment of the Gigantomachy as well as to the members of the Academy of Athens, Professors Sp. Marinatos and G.E. Mylonas for permission to publish the frescoes of Thera and Mycenae.